The Method Works

Joseph F. Eska • Olav Hackstein
Ronald I. Kim • Jean-François Mondon
Editors

The Method Works

Studies on Language Change in Honor of Don Ringe

palgrave
macmillan

Editors
Joseph F. Eska
Department of English
Virginia Tech
Blacksburg, VA, USA

Ronald I. Kim
Faculty of English
Adam Mickiewicz University
Poznań, Poland

Olav Hackstein
Ludwig-Maximilians-Universität München
Munich, Germany

Jean-François Mondon
Global Studies
Muskingum University
New Concord, OH, USA

ISBN 978-3-031-48958-7 ISBN 978-3-031-48959-4 (eBook)
https://doi.org/10.1007/978-3-031-48959-4

This Palgrave Macmillan imprint is published by the registered company Springer Nature Switzerland AG.
The registered company address is: Gewerbestrasse 11, 6330 Cham, Switzerland

Paper in this product is recyclable.

Foreword

Over the past several decades, Indo-Europeanists have felt increasingly compelled to justify their 'old-fashioned' line of work to colleagues in theoretical, computational, and other 'modern' branches of linguistics. Unfortunately, as more than one scholar has bemoaned, it is a daunting task for any one person to master the methods of Indo-European historical and comparative linguistics along with the requisite philologies, while also keeping up with contemporary phonological, syntactic, and semantic theory. It is, therefore, hardly surprising that most researchers have shied away from this dilemma, preferring either to concentrate on traditional problems and methods or to abandon their focus on ancient and medieval languages for more general issues of language acquisition and change.

Our honorand, by contrast, has confronted this challenge from the very beginning of his career and, thereby, carved out a name as one of very few Indo-Europeanists in the late twentieth and early twenty-first centuries to make an impact on multiple subfields of linguistics. After receiving training in classical languages and Indo-European linguistics from some of the foremost names in the field such as Anna Morpurgo Davies at the University of Oxford and Warren Cowgill at Yale University, Don taught classics at Bard College for two years; and then, in 1985 he joined the faculty of the Department of Linguistics at the University of

Pennsylvania, where he has remained ever since. He quickly made a name for himself with publications on Ancient Greek dialect grammar, the topic of his dissertation, as well as pioneering studies of Tocharian historical phonology and morphology, culminating in his 1996 monograph on the relative chronology of sound changes from proto-Indo-European to proto-Tocharian. At the same time, Don did not hesitate to respond to the overblown claims of long-range comparison and linguistic macrofamilies that were then being hyped in the popular press, always taking care to explain the principles and mathematics behind the Comparative Method and the demonstration of genetic relationships among languages.

Don's career in the twenty-first century has been marked, above all, by two trends: his enormous contributions to English and Germanic historical linguistics; and his increasingly fruitful collaboration with computer scientists in developing models to test phylogenetic hypotheses of the relationships among the Indo-European languages. It is no exaggeration to say that the appearance of *From proto-Indo-European to proto-Germanic* (2006; ^{2}2017) caused a sensation in Indo-European and Germanic linguistics, and the follow-up volume *The development of Old English* (2014, with Ann Taylor) is, without doubt, the most thorough historical grammar in existence of Old English and its many dialects up to ca. 900 CE. He also put in print many of his views on language change in general, particularly in *Historical linguistics. Toward a twenty-first century reintegration* (2013, with Joseph F. Eska), and composed a series of pedagogically oriented guides such as *An introduction to grammar for language learners* (2018) and *A historical morphology of English* (2021). At the same time, he continued to investigate problems of linguistic classification and phylogenetic relationships from a mathematical and computational perspective. His work with Tandy Warnow and her associates, which stretches back to the 1990s, yielded a stream of publications in leading journals that have captured global attention and, in no small part, furthered the current upsurge of research in computational phylogenetics.

Throughout his career, Don has been inspired by a fervent belief that historical linguistics, and, for that matter, linguistics as a whole, is a science guided by scientific methods and principles. His statements to that effect and responses to disbelieving audiences not infrequently come across as pointed, even polemic; but all who have witnessed him in the lecture hall can testify to his genuine passion for the intellectual enterprise of studying language change. Whether the tried-and-true Comparative Method or the newly emerging computational methods for investigating language relationship, Don teaches that 'the method works' (on precisely controlled data, that is) and that the results are not only to be taken seriously even when they contradict expectations, but are themselves of intrinsic interest above and beyond what they can reveal about human prehistory. To a bored undergraduate's in-class query 'Why should we bother reconstructing dead languages?', only Don could respond with enthusiastic gestures of both arms and the honest retort: 'Because we can!'

We are proud to present this volume of original studies by 18 of Don's colleagues and former students as a small token of our admiration for his numerous achievements. In addition to the contributors themselves, we would like to thank Michael Weiss and especially Amy Forsyth for invaluable assistance in preparing the bibliography of Don's publications; Alisha George of the *Penn almanac* for furnishing the photo of Don; and Cathy Scott of Palgrave Macmillan for her help at every stage of the process, from proposal to publication. Please join us in congratulating Don on reaching this milestone in his life and career and wishing him many more productive years to come!

Blacksburg, VA, USA	Joseph F. Eska
Poznań, Poland	Ronald I. Kim
Munich, Germany	Olav Hackstein
New Concord, OH, USA	Jean-François Mondon
March 2024	

Bibliography of the Publications of Don Ringe[1]

Monographs

1984

1. *The perfect tenses in Greek inscriptions*. Ph.D. dissertation, Yale University.

1992

2. *On calculating the factor of chance in language comparison*. Philadelphia: American Philosophical Society.

1996

3. *On the chronology of sound changes in Tocharian* i, *From proto-Indo-European to proto-Tocharian*. New Haven: American Oriental Society.

2006

4. *A linguistic history of English* i, *From proto-Indo-European to proto-Germanic*. Oxford: Oxford University Press.

[1] N.B. that our honorand has published variously as Donald A. Ringe, Jr., D. A. Ringe, Jr., Don Ringe, Jr., and Don Ringe.

2013

5. *A new introduction to Old English*. MS, University of Pennsylvania.
6. Ringe, Don, & and Joseph F. Eska. *Historical linguistics. Toward a twenty-first century reintegration*. Cambridge: Cambridge University Press.

2014

7. Ringe, Don, & Ann Taylor. *A linguistic history of English* ii, *The development of Old English*. Oxford: Oxford University Press.

2017

8. *A linguistic history of English* i, *From proto-Indo-European to proto-Germanic*^{2}. Oxford: Oxford University Press.

2018

9. *An introduction to grammar for language learners*. Cambridge: Cambridge University Press.

2021

10. *A historical morphology of English*. Edinburgh: Edinburgh University Press.

Articles

1977

11. The accent of adverbs in -θεν: a historical analysis. *Glotta* 55: 64–79.

1981

12. Tzotzil affect verbs. *Journal of Mayan linguistics* 3: 61–86.

1984

13. Ionic ὀνονημένα. *Glotta* 62: 45–56.
14. Germanic '$\bar{e}_2$' and **r*. *Die Sprache* 30: 138–155.
15. Εἴληφα and the aspirated perfect. *Glotta* 62: 125–141.

1987

16. A closer look at Tocharian *e* and *o* and the Indo-European mediopassive. *Tocharian and Indo-European studies* 1: 98–138.
17. On the prehistory of Tocharian B accent. In *Studies in memory of Warren Cowgill (1929–1985). Papers from the Fourth East Coast Indo-European Conference, Cornell University, June 6–9, 1985*, ed. Calvert Watkins, 254–269. Berlin: De Gruyter.

1988

18. Laryngeal isoglosses in the western Indo-European languages. In *Die Laryngaltheorie und die Rekonstruktion des indogermanischen Laut- und Formensystems*, ed. Alfred Bammesberger, 415–441. Heidelberg: Winter.
19. Two notes on Greek epigraphical perfects. *Glotta* 66: 80–87.

1988/1990

20. Evidence for the position of Tocharian in the Indo-European family? *Die Sprache* 34: 59–123.

1989

21. Doric ἴσαντι. *Münchener Studien zur Sprachwissenschaft* 50: 123–157.
22. Tocharian B *ausu, auṣu, aultsu*. *Tocharian and Indo-European studies* 3: 35–50.
23. The imperative prefix /pə-/ in the Tocharian B dialects. *Tocharian and Indo-European studies* 3: 51–63.

1990

24. The Tocharian active *s*-preterite. A classical sigmatic aorist. *Münchener Studien zur Sprachwissenschaft* 51: 183–242.

1991

25. Laryngeals and Sievers' Law in Tocharian. *Münchener Studien zur Sprachwissenschaft* 52: 137–168.

1993

26. A reply to Professor Greenberg. *Proceedings of the American Philosophical Society* 137: 91–109.

1995

27. New directions for IE linguistics. Report on Mathematical Modelling Workshop. *Friends and alumni of UCLA Indo-European Studies newsletter* 5/1: 3–4.
28. Nominative-accusative syncretism and syntactic case. *University of Pennsylvania working papers in linguistics* 2/1: 45–81.
29. 'Nostratic' and the factor of chance. *Diachronica* 12: 55–74.
30. The 'Mana' languages and the three-language problem. *Oceanic linguistics* 34: 99–122.
31. Tocharians in Xinjiang. The linguistic evidence. *Journal of Indo-European studies* 23: 439–444.

1996

32. The mathematics of 'Amerind'. *Diachronica* 13: 135–154.
33. Warnow, Tandy, Don Ringe, & Ann Taylor. Reconstructing the evolutionary history of natural languages. In *Proceedings of the 7th Annual ACM-SIAM Symposium on Discrete Algorithms, SODA 1996*, 314–322. New York: Association for Computing Machinery / Philadelphia: Society for Industrial and Applied Mathematics.

1997

34. On the origin of 3pl. imperative -ντον. In *Festschrift for Eric P. Hamp*, ed. Douglas Q. Adams, ii 129–143. Washington, DC: Institute for the Study of Man.

1998

35. Probabilistic evidence for Indo-Uralic. In *Nostratic. Sifting the evidence*, ed. Joseph C. Salmons & Brian D. Joseph, 153–197. Amsterdam: John Benjamins.
36. Schwa-rounding and the chronology of sound changes in Tocharian. In *Mír curad. Studies in honor of Calvert Watkins*, ed. Jay Jasanoff, H. Craig Melchert, & Lisi Olivier, 611–618. Innsbruck: Institut für Sprachwissenschaft der Universität Innsbruck.
37. Some consequences of a new proposal for subgrouping the IE family. In *Proceedings of the Twenty-Fourth Annual Meeting of the Berkeley Linguistics Society, February 14–16, 1998. Special session: Indo-European subgrouping and internal relations*, ed. Benjamin K. Bergen, Madelaine C. Plauché, & Ashlee C. Bailey, 32–46. Berkeley: Berkeley Linguistics Society.
38. Ringe, Don, Tandy Warnow, Ann Taylor, Alexander Michailov, & Libby Levison. Computational cladistics and the position of Tocharian. In *The Bronze Age and early Iron Age peoples of eastern Central Asia*, ed. Victor Mair, 391–414. Washington, DC: Institute for the Study of Man.

1999

39. How hard is it to match CVC-roots? *Transactions of the Philological Society* 97: 213–244.
40. Language classification. Scientific and unscientific methods. In *The human inheritance. Genes, language, and evolution*, ed. Bryan Sykes, 45–73. Oxford: Oxford University Press.

2000

41. Some relevant facts about historical linguistics. In *America past, America present. Genes and languages in the Americas and beyond*, ed. Colin Renfrew, 139–162. Cambridge: The McDonald Institute for Archaeological Research.
42. Tocharian class II presents and subjunctives and the reconstruction of the proto-Indo-European verb. *Tocharian and Indo-European studies* 9: 121–141.
43. Kroch, Anthony, Ann Taylor, & Don Ringe. The Middle English verb-second constraint. A case study in language contact and language change. In *Textual parameters in older languages*, ed. Susan C. Herring, Peter van Reenen, & Lene Schøsler, 353–391. Amsterdam: John Benjamins.
44. Taylor, Ann, Tandy Warnow, & Don Ringe. Character-based reconstruction of a linguistic cladogram. In *Historical linguistics 1995. Selected papers from the 12th International Conference on Historical Linguistics, Manchester, August 1995* i, *General issues and non-Germanic languages*, ed. John Charles Smith & Delia Bentley, 393–408. Amsterdam: John Benjamins.

2002

45. Syncopated present indicative forms in Old English. In *Verba et litterae. Explorations in Germanic languages and German literature*, ed. Alfred R. Wedel & Hans-Jörg Busch, 125–156. Newark, DE: Linguatext.
46. *Tocharian B ṣp* 'and'. In *Indo-European perspectives*, ed. Mark R. V. Southern, 265–266. Washington, DC: Institute for the Study of Man.
47. Ringe, Don, Tandy Warnow, & Ann Taylor. Indo-European and computational cladistics. *Transactions of the Philological Society* 100: 59–129.

2003

48. An early rule of syncope in Tocharian. In *Language in time and space. A festschrift for Werner Winter on the occasion of his 80th birthday*, ed. Brigitte L. M. Bauer & Georges-Jean Pinault, 359–362. Berlin: De Gruyter.
49. Internal reconstruction. In *The Blackwell handbook of historical linguistics*, ed. Brian D. Joseph & Richard D. Janda, 244–261. Malden, MA: Blackwell.
50. Erdem, Esra, Vladimir Lifschitz, Luay Nakhleh, & Donald Ringe. Reconstructing the evolutionary history of Indo-European languages using answer set programming. In *Practical aspects of declarative languages. 5th international symposium, PADL 2003, New Orleans, LA, USA, January 2003*, ed. Veronica Dahl & Philip Wadler, 160–176. New York: Springer.
51. Historical linguistics. Methods. Computational methods. In *International encyclopedia of linguistics*², ed. William J. Frawley, ii, 169–171. Oxford: Oxford University Press.

2004

52. Old English *maþelian, mæþlan, mǣlan*. In *Indo-European perspectives. Studies in honour of Anna Morpurgo Davies*, ed. J. H. W. Penney, 417–435. Oxford: Oxford University Press.
53. Reconstructed ancient languages. In *The Cambridge encyclopedia of the world's ancient languages*, ed. Roger D. Woodard, 1112–1128. Cambridge: Cambridge University Press.
54. Some problematic consonant clusters in Tocharian. In *Per aspera ad asteriscos. Studia indogermanica in honorem Jens Elmegård Rasmussen sexagenarii idibus martiis anno MMIV*, ed. Adam Hyllested, Anders Richardt Jørgensen, Jenny Helena Larsson, & Thomas Olander, 469–473. Innsbruck: Institut für Sprachen und Literaturen der Universität Innsbruck.
55. Eska, Joseph F., & Don Ringe. Recent work in computational linguistic phylogeny. *Language* 80: 569–582.

2005

56. Brooks, Daniel R., Esra Erdem, James W. Minett, & Donald Ringe. Character-based cladistics and answer set programming. In *Practical aspects of declarative languages. 7th international symposium, PADL 2005, Long Beach, CA, USA, January 10–11, 2005*, ed. by Manuel Hermenegildo & Daniel Cabeza, 37–51. Berlin & Heidelberg: Springer.
57. Nakhleh, Luay, Don Ringe, & Tandy Warnow. Perfect phylogenetic networks. A new methodology for reconstructing the evolutionary history of natural languages. *Language* 81: 382–420.
58. Nakhleh, Luay, Tandy Warnow, Don Ringe, & Steven N. Evans. A comparison of phylogenetic reconstruction methods on an Indo-European dataset. *Transactions of the Philological Society* 103: 171–192.

2006

59. A sociolinguistically informed solution to an old historical problem. The Gothic genitive plural. *Transactions of the Philological Society* 104: 167–206.
60. Erdem, Esra, Vladimir Lifschitz, & Don Ringe. Temporal phylogenetic networks and logic programming. *Theory and practice of logic programming* 6: 539–558.
61. Evans, Steven N., Don Ringe, & Tandy Warnow. Inference of divergence times as a statistical inverse problem. In *Phylogenetic methods and the prehistory of languages*, ed. Peter Forster & Colin Renfrew, 119–129. Cambridge: The McDonald Institute for Archaeological Research.
62. Warnow, Tandy, Steven N. Evans, Don Ringe, & Luay Nakhleh. A stochastic model of language evolution that incorporates homoplasy and borrowing. In *Phylogenetic methods and the prehistory of languages*, ed. Peter Forster & Colin Renfrew, 75–90. Cambridge: The McDonald Institute for Archaeological Research.

2007

63. Old Latin *-minō* and 'analogy'. In *Verba docenti. Studies in historical and Indo-European linguistics presented to Jay H. Jasanoff by students, colleagues, and friends*, ed. Alan J. Nussbaum, 301–306. Ann Arbor: Beech Stave Press.
64. Brooks, Daniel R., Esra Erdem, Selim T. Erdoğan, James W. Minett, & Don Ringe. Inferring phylogenetic trees using answer set programming. *Journal of automated reasoning* 39: 471–511.

2008

65. Ringe, Don, & Tandy Warnow. Linguistic history and computational cladistics. In *Origin and evolution of languages. Approaches, models, paradigms*, ed. Bernard Laks, 257–271. London: Equinox.

2010

66. 'Thorn' clusters and Indo-European subgrouping. In *Ex Anatolia lux. Anatolian and Indo-European studies in honor of H. Craig Melchert on the occasion of his sixty-fifth birthday*, ed. Ronald Kim, Norbert Oettinger, Elisabeth Rieken, & Michael Weiss, 330–338. Ann Arbor: Beech Stave Press.

2011

67. A pilot study for an investigation into Atkinson's hypothesis. *Linguistic typology* 15: 223–231.

2012

68. An early 'Ingvaeonic' innovation. In *Multi nominis grammaticus. Studies in classical and Indo-European linguistics in honor of Alan J. Nussbaum on the occasion of his sixty-fifth birthday*, ed. Adam I. Cooper, Jeremy Rau, & Michael Weiss, 285–288. Ann Arbor: Beech Stave Press.
69. Cladistic principles and linguistic reality. The case of West Germanic. In *Laws and rules in Indo-European*, ed. Philomen Probert & Andreas Willi, 33–41. Oxford: Oxford University Press.

70. The *hi*-conjugation as a PIE subjunctive. In *Linguistic developments along the Silk Road. Archaism and innovation in Tocharian*, ed. Olav Hackstein & Ronald I. Kim, 121–140. Wien: Österreichische Akademie der Wissenschaften.

2013

71. The linguistic diversity of aboriginal Europe. In *Grammatica et verba / Glamor and verve. A festschrift for Hans Henrich Hock*, ed. Shu-Fen Chen & Benjamin Slade, 202–212. Ann Arbor: Beech Stave Press.
72. What is Old English? *NOWELE* 66: 127–140.
73. Barbançon, François, Steven N. Evans, Luay Nakhleh, Don Ringe, & Tandy Warnow. An experimental study comparing linguistic phylogenetic reconstruction methods. *Diachronica* 30: 143–170.

2015

74. Levelling and rule restructuring in Old English adjectives. *Indo-European linguistics* 3: 73–83.
75. Response to Kassian et al. 'Proto-Indo-European-Uralic comparison from the probabilistic point of view.' *Journal of Indo-European studies* 43: 348–356.
76. Anthony, David W., & Don Ringe. The Indo-European homeland from linguistic and archaeological perspectives. *Annual review of linguistics* 1: 199–219.

2016

77. Phonological rules and dialect geography in Ancient Greek. In *Sahasram ati srajas. Indo-Iranian and Indo-European studies in honor of Stephanie W. Jamison*, ed. Dieter Gunkel, Joshua T. Katz, Brent Vine, & Michael Weiss, 378–384. Ann Arbor: Beech Stave Press.
78. The nature of the South Greek dialect group. In *Tavet tat satyam. Studies in honor of Jared Klein on the occasion of his seventieth birthday*, ed. Andrew Miles Byrd, Jessica DeLisi, & Mark Wenthe, 278–283. Ann Arbor: Beech Stave Press.

2017

79. Indo-European dialectology. In *Handbook of comparative and historical Indo-European linguistics*, ed. Jared Klein, Brian Joseph, & Matthias Fritz, i 62–75. Berlin: De Gruyter Mouton.

2018

80. Indicative-subjunctive syncretism in West Germanic. In *Vina diem celebrent. Studies in linguistics and philology in honor of Brent Vine*, ed. Dieter Gunkel, Stephanie W. Jamison, Angelo O. Mercado, & Kazuhiko Yoshida, 390–396. Ann Arbor: Beech Stave Press.

2020

81. Legate, Julie Anne, Faruk Akkuş, Milena Šereikaitė, & Don Ringe. 2020. On passives of passives. *Language* 96: 771–818.

2022

82. Stative perfects. In शब्दानुगमः. *Indian linguistic studies in honor of George Cardona* ii, *Historical linguistics, Vedic, etc.*, ed. Peter M. Scharf, 85–98. Providence: The Sanskrit Library.
83. What we can (and can't) learn from computational cladistics. In *The Indo-European language family. A phylogenetic perspective*, ed. Thomas Olander, 52–62. Cambridge: Cambridge University Press.
84. Ringe, Don, & Charles Yang. 2022. The threshold of productivity and the 'irregularization' of verbs in Early Modern English. In *English historical linguistics. Change in structure and meaning. Papers from the XXth ICEHL*, ed. Bettelou Los, Claire Cowie, Patrick Honeybone, & Graeme Trousdale, 91–111. Amsterdam: John Benjamins.

Forthcoming

85. A new argument from old principles: Tocharian A *cmol* and its implications.

Technical Report

1995

86. Warnow, Tandy, Don Ringe, & Ann Taylor. 1995. *Reconstructing the evolutionary history of natural languages.* IRCS Report 95-16. Philadelphia: Institute for Research in Cognitive Science, University of Pennsylvania.

Reviews

1986

87. N. E. Collinge, *The laws of Indo-European.* Amsterdam: John Benjamins, 1985. *Diachronica* 3: 107–113.

1988

88. Alan J. Nussbaum, *Head and horn in Indo-European.* Berlin: De Gruyter, 1986. *Journal of the American Oriental Society* 108: 186–187.

1990

89. Douglas Q. Adams, *Tocharian historical phonology and morphology.* New Haven: American Oriental Society, 1988. *Language* 66: 400–408.
90. Sydney M. Lamb & E. Douglas Mitchell (eds), *Sprung from some common source. Investigations into the prehistory of languages.* Stanford: Stanford University Press, 1991. *Anthropological linguistics* 32: 376–380.

1993

91. Peter Schrijver, *The reflexes of the Proto-Indo-European laryngeals in Latin.* Amsterdam: Rodopi, 1991. *Diachronica* 10: 285–289.

2001

92. Helmut Rix et al., *Lexikon der indogermanischen Verben*. Wiesbaden: Reichert, 1998. *Diachronica* 18: 184–187.

2002

93. Joseph Greenberg, *Indo-European and its closest relatives. The Eurasiatic language family* i, *Grammar*. Stanford: Stanford University Press, 2000. *Journal of linguistics* 38: 415–420.
94. April McMahon, *Change, chance, and optimality*. Oxford: Oxford University Press, 2000. *General linguistics* 39: 156–159.

2015

95. *The Routledge handbook of historical linguistics*, ed. Claire Bowern & Bethwyn Evans. London: Routledge, 2015. *Language* 91: 488–491.
96. *Classification and evolution in biology, linguistics, and the history of science*, ed. Heiner Fangerau, Hans Geisler, Thorsten Halling, & William Hartin. Stuttgart: Franz Steiner, 2013. *Historische Sprachforschung* 128: 316–320.

Contents

Part I Subgrouping and Phylogeny 1

1 **The Continental Celtic Dialect Continuum** 3
Joseph F. Eska

2 **On the Phylogenetic Status of East Germanic** 21
Ronald I. Kim

3 **Progress on Constructing Phylogenetic Networks for Languages** 45
Tandy Warnow, Steven N. Evans, and Luay Nakhleh

Part II Linguistic Reconstruction 63

4 **Rethinking Stang's Law, with a Note on Gk. πότνια** 65
Jay H. Jasanoff

5 **The Sources of the *-*ono*- 'god' Suffix** 79
Lionel S. Joseph

6 **The Final Glottal Stop of the Kuṛux Verb Bases** 99
Masato Kobayashi

7 **Very Old Latin** 113
Michael Weiss

Part III Theoretical Approaches to Language Change 141

8 **Iceberg Phenomena and Synchronic Rules** 143
Olav Hackstein

9 **Forced to FORCE? Remarks on the Architecture of the Left Periphery of Early Irish and Absolute/Conjunct Morphology** 179
Jean-François Mondon and Joseph F. Eska

10 **On the Functional Superstructure of the Noun Phrase in Indo-European** 195
Augustin Speyer

11 **Understanding Translation Effects: Lessons from the Old English Heptateuch** 217
Ann Taylor

12 **Phonological Regularity and Breakdown. An Account of Vowel Length Leveling in Middle English** 237
Charles Yang

Part IV Indo-European Philology and Etymology 261

13 **Guests. Welcome or not** 263
Sara Kimball

14 **Asyndetic Verbal Pairs in the Classical Armenian Gospels and Their Treatment in the Other Five First Millennium CE Indo-European Versions** 279
Jared S. Klein

15 **Celt. *meh_2-ró- 'large, great' versus Gmc. *meh_1-ró- 'made known, spoken of'** 297
H. Craig Melchert

16 **'Between uneducated and educated, or hot and cold, or bitter and sweet ... there's a middle point': Varro and the Middle Accent** 307
Philomen Probert

17 **Obscured figurae etymologicae and Word Origins. Two Examples Involving Gothic** 327
Patrick Stiles

18 **South Oscan κλοπουστ (with an Appendix on [Osco-?]Lat. BVRVS)** 351
Brent Vine

Index 369

Notes on Contributors

Joseph F. Eska is Professor of Language Sciences at Virginia Polytechnic Institute and State University. His work focuses on the diachronic linguistics of the Celtic languages. He is the editor of the *North American Journal of Celtic Studies* and co-editor of *Indo-European Linguistics*, as well as co-editor of the forthcoming *Palgrave Handbook of Celtic Languages and Linguistics*.

Steven N. Evans was born in rural Australia. He received his undergraduate education (B.Sc., Hons. I & Medal) at the University of Sydney and Ph.D. at the University of Cambridge. After a brief stint as a banker in Australia and a postdoc at the University of Virginia, he joined the University of California at Berkeley, where he is a member of the Departments of Statistics and Mathematics with interests in probability and stochastic processes. He has been a Presidential Young Investigator and a Sloan Fellow, and he is a member of the National Academy of Sciences.

Olav Hackstein (visiting lecturer University of Pennsylvania 1989, Dr. phil. Albert-Ludwigs-Universität Freiburg 1993; Habilitation Martin-Luther-Universität Halle 1999) is a professor and Chair of Historical and Indo-European Linguistics at the Ludwig-Maximilians-Universität München. His research interests focus on the historical phonology, morphology, and syntax of the ancient Indo-European languages, including Germanic dialectology, Latin, Greek, Albanian, and Tocharian.

Jay H. Jasanoff is a historical linguist and Indo-Europeanist best known for his work on the proto-Indo-European verbal system. He holds a Ph.D. in Linguistics from Harvard (1968) and has held long-term teaching appointments at Harvard University and Cornell University. Along with numerous articles on problems around the Indo-European family, he is the author of *Stative and Middle in Indo-European* (1978), *Hittite and the Indo-European Verb* (2003), and *The Prehistory of the Balto-Slavic Accent* (2017).

Lionel S. Joseph, PhD, PsyD studied with Calvert Watkins, Jochem Schindler, and Jay Jasanoff at Harvard University, where he earned his first doctorate in 1980. He then had a second career as a clinical psychologist. Since his retirement, he has enthusiastically returned to Celtic and Indo-European studies.

Ronald I. Kim is an associate professor in the Department of Older Germanic Languages of the Faculty of English at Adam Mickiewicz University in Poznań, Poland. He holds a Ph.D. in Linguistics from the University of Pennsylvania (2002) and has also taught at Swarthmore College and Charles University in Prague. He is the author of the monograph *The Dual in Tocharian* and over 75 articles and co-editor of *Indo-European Linguistics* (Brill). His research focuses on the historical grammar of Indo-European languages, especially Tocharian, Iranian, Germanic, and Balto-Slavic, as well as language contact and morphology.

Sara Kimball A transplanted Yankee, Sara Kimball taught in the Department of English at the University of Texas at Austin for 29 years. Most of her research has been in Anatolian and Greek.

Jared S. Klein is Distinguished Research Professor of Linguistics, Classics, and Germanic and Slavic Languages at the University of Georgia, where he teaches courses on comparative and historical Indo-European linguistics. His publications include books, articles, and reviews on Vedic Sanskrit, Old Persian, Homeric Greek, Gothic, Classical Armenian, Old Church Slavic, and Latin. Most of his work deals with aspects of discourse structure, including conjunction, anaphora, deixis, and stylistic repetition.

Masato Kobayashi is Professor of Linguistics at the University of Tokyo. He earned his M.A. in Sanskrit from Kyoto University and his Ph.D. in Linguistics from the University of Pennsylvania in 2000 under the guidance of Dr. George Cardona. He has worked on Sanskrit, Pāṇinian grammar, and Dravidian tribal languages. His publications include *Historical Phonology of Old Indo-Aryan Consonants* (2004), *Texts and Grammar of Malto* (2012), and *The Kurux Language* (2017, co-authored with Bablu Tirkey).

H. Craig Melchert is Distinguished Professor of Linguistics and A. Richard Diebold Professor of Indo-European Studies Emeritus, University of California, Los Angeles. He previously taught at the University of North Carolina, Chapel Hill, for 29 years. His research centers on historical linguistics, with special emphasis on the Anatolian sub-family of Indo-European. His interests include the modeling of language change, reconstruction of the culture and society of the proto-Indo-European speech community, and application of modern formal linguistic theories to ancient Indo-European languages and their prehistory.

Jean-François Mondon is Associate Professor of Global Studies at Muskingum University. He primarily researches quagmires in Celtic languages, offering synchronic solutions couched in Distributed Morphology. He also actively writes pedagogical materials for various Indo-European languages.

Luay Nakhleh is the William and Stephanie Sick Dean of the George R. Brown School of Engineering at Rice University. He holds three degrees in computer science: Bachelor of Science from the Technion (Israel), Master of Computer Science from Texas A&M University, and Ph.D. from the University of Texas at Austin. His research interests include computational phylogenetics in biology and historical linguistics. He is a fellow of the International Society for Computational Biology and a recipient of Sloan and Guggenheim Fellowships among other honors.

Philomen Probert is Professor of Classical Philology and Linguistics at the University of Oxford and a fellow of Wolfson College. She has written *A New Short Guide to the Accentuation of Ancient Greek* (2003); *Ancient Greek Accentuation. Synchronic Patterns, Frequency Effects, and Prehistory* (2006); *Early Greek Relative Clauses* (2015); *Latin Grammarians on the Latin Accent. The Transformation of Greek Grammatical Thought* (2019); and together with Stephanie Roussou, *Ancient and Medieval Thought on Greek Enclitics* (2023). She is also the co-editor, with Andreas Willi, of *Laws and Rules in Indo-European* (2012).

Augustin Speyer studied Classics and German Language and Literature at the University of Tübingen and University of Oxford and afterward Linguistics (with a focus on Comparative Philology) at the University of Pennsylvania. He holds two Ph.D.s in Classics (Tübingen 2002) and Linguistics (UPenn 2008). After having held various positions in Saarbrücken, Tübingen, Frankfurt, Marburg, and Göttingen (Full Professor 2012), he was appointed Full Professor for German Linguistics at the University of Saarland in 2013. His main research areas are historical and synchronic syntax of German, information structure and information theory, and aspects of formal Indo-European syntax.

Patrick Stiles studied English at Oxford University and, after a spell at the University of Oslo, filled posts at the Universities of Manchester and Edinburgh. He then became a journalist for the *Financial Times*, while holding an honorary research position at University College London. His main field of activity is Old Germanic linguistics, with occasional forays elsewhere in Indo-European.

Ann Taylor has research focuses on variation and change in the history of English with a primary focus on syntax. She works within a framework that applies quantitative methodology first developed within variationist sociolinguistics to the structural analysis of historical data and combines formal syntactic analysis, statistical methods, and techniques of corpus linguistics. She is co-creator of three parsed corpora of historical English, the PPCME2, YCOE, and PCEEC, and continues to be interested in the creation and exploitation of annotated corpora for linguistic analysis.

Brent Vine is Distinguished Research Professor Emeritus, Department of Classics and Program in Indo-European Studies, at the University of California, Los Angeles. His research is mainly devoted to phonological, morphological, and etymological problems in Classical and Indo-European linguistics, with attention also to metrics, stylistics, and Latin literature and with occasional forays into English literature. Some work in progress includes studies of Latin accent and etymology, a textual problem in Petronius, prose rhythm in Apuleius, and a linguistic/stylistic analysis of Herman Melville's punctuation in his manuscript of *Billy Budd.*

Tandy Warnow (Ph.D. Mathematics, University of California Berkeley 1991) is the Grainger Distinguished Chair in Engineering in the Department of Computer Science at the University of Illinois at Urbana-Champaign. Tandy's research focuses on reconstructing complex and large-scale evolutionary histories, both for languages and for biological species and genes. She was awarded the David and Lucile Packard Foundation Award (1996), a Radcliffe Institute Fellowship (2003), and the John Simon Guggenheim Foundation Fellowship (2011). She was elected a fellow of the Association for Computing Machinery in 2015, of the International Society for Computational Biology in 2017, and of the American Association for the Advancement of Science in 2021.

Michael Weiss is Professor in the Department of Linguistics at Cornell University. He is the author of *Language and Ritual in Sabellic Italy* (2010), *Outline of the Historical and Comparative Grammar of Latin* (2nd ed. 2020), *Kuśiññe Kantwo. Elementary Lessons in Tocharian B* (2022), and articles on various topics in Indo-European linguistics.

Charles Yang works on mathematical models of child language acquisition which, at least at the University of Pennsylvania and according to Don Ringe, qualifies him as a historical linguist.

List of Figures

Fig. 3.1 Panel (a) shows a genetic tree with leafset *{A, B, C, D, E, F}*. Panel (b) shows the tree-based phylogenetic network formed by adding two contact edges to the genetic tree. Panel (c) shows an unrooted version of the rooted network in (b). Panel (d) shows all four rooted trees contained inside the rooted network from (b), with the first being the genetic tree from (a). Panel (e) shows the unrooted versions of the rooted trees in (d). Panel (f) shows three quartet trees; q_1 is displayed in T_1 and T_2, but not in T_3 or T_4; q_2 is displayed in T_3 and T_4, but not in trees T_1 or T_2; and q_3 is not displayed in any of these trees. Because q_1 and q_2 are each displayed by at least one tree in the network, the set $Q(N_r)$ of all quartet trees displayed by trees in the network N will contain both q_1 and q_2, but will not contain q_3 49

Fig. 3.2 Character evolution on a rooted tree. Panel (a) shows evolution without any homoplasy, panel (b) shows homoplasy due to parallel evolution (i.e., two 0→1 transitions), and panel (c) shows homoplasy due to back-mutation (note the 1→0 transition, where 0 is the ancestral state) 50

List of Tables

Table 7.1	Pre-rhotacism forms in the literary tradition: Non-names	120
Table 7.2	Pre-rhotacism forms in the literary tradition: Names	121
Table 8.1	Modern English {ing}: [ɪn] ~ [-ɪŋ]	146
Table 8.2	Verbal root {need}, [pres., 3, sg.] ↔ -[z]/-[Ø] as inheritance -[z] (a)–(c) and innovative 'modal 3sg. termination' -[Ø] (d)	151
Table 8.3	German adverbs in *-maßen*, diachronic lexical continuation	156
Table 8.4	Diachronic lexical continuation of adverbs in Ital., Span. *-mente* and Fren. *-ment*	159
Table 8.5	Lexicalization and semantic specialization of *mente* adverbs in French	160
Table 8.6	Shared gradience of Germ. *dünn*, Engl. *thin*, Germ. *äußerer*, Engl. *utter*, Germ. *weg*, Engl. *away*	162
Table 8.7	Overview of anomalies of predicative Germ. *voller* 'full of, fraught with'	166
Table 10.1	Combinations of noun and adjective/demonstrative: Cicero, epistulae ad Atticum	213
Table 10.2	Combinations of noun and adjective/demonstrative: Egeria	213
Table 11.1	Percentage of OE object pronouns with a Latin source: Ælfric versus the AT	228

Table 11.2 Percentage of OE object pronouns with a Latin source: Ælfric Genesis (ÆGen) separated from Ælfric's other books (ÆOther) 228
Table 11.3 Percentage of OE PPs with a Latin source: ÆGen and ÆOther separated 229
Table 11.4 Overall percentage of V-OP order 230
Table 11.5 Overall percentage of P-PRO order 230
Table 11.6 Percentage of OE V-OP order with and without a Latin source in comparison to non-translated Ælfric texts (ÆNonTrans) 231
Table 11.7 Percentage of OE P-PRO order with and without a Latin source in comparison to non-translated Ælfric texts (ÆNonTrans) 232
Table 12.1 Expected effects of Open Syllable Lengthening (OSL) and Trisyllabic Shorting (TSS) in Middle English (from Lahiri & Dresher, 1999, p. 680) 239
Table 12.2 Expected effects of OSL and TSS in Middle English on the vowel length of Old English nouns 240
Table 12.3 Four groups of nouns classified by their inflectional ending in Old English (OE), their expected length alternation, and their vowel length in Modern English (Modern) 248
Table 14.1 Initial verbs involved in asyndetic verbal constructions in the Classical Armenian Gospels 284
Table 14.2 Renditions by language of instances where Classical Armenian shows asyndetic verbal pairs 292

Part I

Subgrouping and Phylogeny

1

The Continental Celtic Dialect Continuum

Joseph F. Eska

§0. I am grateful to have had Don Ringe as a mentor during a post-doctoral year at the University of Pennsylvania in 1992–1993. I learnt much about methodological rigour that year, which I have tried to employ in the time since. A few years later, Don and I joined efforts to apply his phylogenetic methods to the early history of the Celtic language clade, a difficult endeavour given the somewhat sparse and recalcitrant data available. This contribution returns to this problem in a novel way. I dedicate it to Don with fond wishes.

J. F. Eska (✉)
Virginia Polytechnic Institute & State University, Blacksburg, VA, USA
e-mail: eska@vt.edu

J. F. Eska et al. (eds.), *The Method Works*,
https://doi.org/10.1007/978-3-031-48959-4_1

1 Prelude[1]

§1. Among the Continental Celtic languages, it appears that the Hispano-Celtic linguistic complex was the first departure from the (proto-)Celtic speech continuum (see, e.gg., Eska, 2010, pp. 23–24, 2017, pp. 1266–1267). This is upon the basis of Hispano-Celtic not sharing in changes that took place in the remainder of Celtic, e.gg.:[2]

(1) a. Proto-Celt. */st^{h}/ became the tau Gallicum[3] phoneme in Nuclear Celtic, e.gg., Cisalp. Celt. pron. **iśos** (LexLep VA·6) < */ist^{h}o/- and Transalpine Celtic Latinised dat. sg. theonym ḌỊṚỌṆẠ[E] (CIL xiii 3662) < *h_2*ster-* 'star', but was preserved in Celtiberian, e.g., in **PousTom** 'cow stable' (MLH K.1.1 A4 = Hesp. Z.09.01) < proto-Celt. **bou̯st^{h}o-* < proto-IE **g^{w}ou̯-sth$_2$-o-*.[4]

b. The proto-Indo-European stressed and fully inflected relative pronoun, at least in the available evidence, became an uninflected clitic in Nuclear Celtic, e.g., in Transalp. Celt. DVGIIONTI=IO 'who serve' (RIG L–13 = RIIG CDO-01-19) and elsewhere, but was preserved in Celtiberian, e.gg., masc. nom. sg. **ios**, masc./neut. acc. sg. **iom**, masc./neut. dat. sg. **iomui**, fem. acc. pl. **ias** (all MLH K.1.1 = Hesp. Z.09.01), and fem. nom. sg. **ia** (MLH K.1.3 = Hesp. Z.09.03).

[1] I should like to thank David Goldstein, Jean-François Mondon, Ronald Kim, Paul Russell, Corinna Salomon, and Michael Weiss for helpful commentary on earlier versions of this paper. All usual disclaimers apply.

[2] Epigraphic abbreviations: Square brackets [ ] indicate characters which are restored or can no longer be read; the underdot ̣ indicates characters which are damaged or no longer clearly legible; the pipe | indicates line breaks.

[3] The precise articulation of the tau Gallicum phoneme is uncertain. For some discussion, see Eska (1998a).

[4] In view of Iosad (2023), I reconstruct proto-Celtic forms as evincing a contrast between the plosive series via an overspecified system, the proto-Indo-European voiceless plosives being continued via the feature [spread glottis], the proto-Indo-European voiced plosives being continued via the feature [voice], i.e., */p^{h} t^{h} k^{h}/ vs. */b d g/. I posit that this contrast shifted to one of [spread glottis], i.e., /p^{h} t^{h} k^{h}/ vs. /p t k/, in Cisalpine Celtic after some of its distinctive innovations took place, but before its earliest attestations (Eska, forthcoming b). This may well obtain for Hispano-Celtic and Transalpine Celtic, as well, but further scrutiny is required.

We cannot know whether these changes took place while the post-proto-Celtic speech continuum was still intact,[5] but did not reach that part of the continuum which was to become the Hispano-Celtic linguistic complex, or took place after the Hispano-Celtic linguistic complex left the post-proto-Celtic speech continuum.

§2. The Hispano-Celtic linguistic complex, at least in Celtiberian, also evinces innovations not known elsewhere in Celtic, though these, of course, are not diagnostic of an early departure from the post-proto-Celtic speech continuum, for they might not have spread far from their respective focal points while the proto-Celtic speech continuum was still intact or been lost elsewhere in Celtic, e.gg.:[6]

(2) a. The development of a thematic genitive singular in **-o**, e.g., **aualo** (MLH K.0.2 = Hesp. Z.00.01) to nom. sg. **aualos** (MLH K.1.3 i 55 = Hesp. Z.09.03).
b. The extension of proto-IE abl. sg. **-d* from the thematic flexion to all stem classes, e.gg., *ā*-stem **areKoraTađ** (MLH A.52.1–2 & 5–6 = Hesp. Mon.52) and *i*-stem **PilPiliđ** (MLH A.73.1–3 & 5 = Hesp. Mon.73).[7]
c. The development of a feminine paradigm in nom. sg. **-i**, gen. sg. **-inos**, e.g., nom. sg. **Kari** (MLH K.1.3 iii 59 = Hesp. Z.09.03), gen. sg. **elKinos** (MLH K.1.3 iii 28 = Hesp. Z.09.03) after the well attested masculine paradigm in nom. sg. **-u**, gen. sg. **-unos** (Untermann, 1997, p. 404).

§3. There is little consensus about the topology of the remainder of the Continental Celtic portion of the family tree.[8]

[5] For this term, see §11.

[6] Forms that are not glossed are onomastic forms.

[7] Another possibility is that this feature is a retention from proto-Italo-Celtic lost in the rest of Celtic, as Michael Weiss points out to me.

[8] I presume that the Insular Celtic languages are unified under an Insular Celtic node on the family tree, the dual flexional system of the verb being so robust and unusual an innovation that it can validate the Insular Celtic node by itself (Eska, 2017, pp. 1269–1270). They formed the northwest periphery of the Celtic dialect continuum until this innovation was established. Cf. the common view that the shared accentual innovations of Baltic and Slavonic largely validate a Balto-Slavonic subgroup on their own, e.g.: 'The shared accentual innovations of the two branches are among the most telling proofs of their special relationship' (Jasanoff, 2017, p. 1[2]).

(3) a. Eska (2010, 2017) argues that Cisalpine Celtic—combining so-called 'Lepontic' and so-called 'Cisalpine Gaulish' together—and Transalpine Celtic are separate branches of the Celtic language clade.
b. Stifter (2020a, p. 336) regards 'Lepontic' and 'Cisalpine Gaulish' as separate languages, the latter essentially being 'Transalpine Gaulish' transplanted into northern Italy as the result of migrations, hence 'Cisalpine Gaulish' and 'Lepontic' are 'two separate, but probably closely related languages'; so also Stifter (2020b, pp. 4–6).
c. Previously, McCone (1996, pp. 68–69) was inclined to view 'Lepontic' as early 'Gaulish'.

Also bearing upon the matter is Eska's (2013a) conclusion that Galatian of Asia Minor (also with the Celtic linguistic remains of eastern Europe) was not significantly differentiated from Transalpine Celtic.

§4. A very different approach is adopted by Garrett (1999, passim) (cf. Garrett, 2006 for the approach). Owing to the variation that exists in some features in the Continental Celtic linguistic record, particularly those which are considered to be diagnostic of Celtic, he proposes that proto-Celtic—as well as proto-Italic and proto-Greek—was not a phylogenetic unit descended from proto-Indo-European, but developed via the convergence of various neighbouring languages/dialects. Under this view, proto-Celtic, if we are to speak of it at all, is the result of Sprachbund phenomena. In Garrett's model, '[w]hat is crucial … is that at some early date—say, at the beginning of the second millennium BCE—the dialects that were to become Celtic … shared no properties that distinguished them uniquely from the other dialects. The point is not simply that innovations could spread from one Indo-European branch to another: this is well known. The point is that while there was linguistic differentiation, the differentiation among dialects that were to become Celtic … was no more or less than between any pair of dialects. At this time, there was no such thing as Celtic …' In other words, as some of these dialects converged, they became what we call Celtic, but while they converged sufficiently to allow scholars to reconstruct what they call proto-Celtic—perhaps better quasi-proto-Celtic—, they did not converge entirely.

§5. A view somewhat in the same spirit has been advocated by some Celtic scholars in dealing with the question of whether there existed an Insular Celtic node vs. a Continental Celtic node or a Goidelic node vs. a Gallo-Brittonic node in the Celtic family tree. Koch (1992), Isaac (2005), and Sims-Williams (2007) do not go so far as to propose that proto-Celtic was not a phylogenetic unit, but look at various aspects of the structure of the Celtic cladistic tree as the result of language/dialect contact.

2 Dialect Continua and Dialect Areas

§6. Though there are, of course, convergence effects in the histories of languages, in this chapter I propose that the variation that exists in the Continental Celtic linguistic record is not due to incomplete convergence,[9] but to the fact that dialect areas—not areas created by convergence, but areas in which innovations occur, but do not spread far into the neighbouring parts of the speech continuum; or, conversely, relic areas which innovations do not reach—can be shown to exist within dialect continua.

§7. An important paper that underlies this approach is Heeringa & Nerbonne (2001). They examine 27 dialect sites in the Netherlands along a straight line from Scheemda in the northeast to Bellegem in the southwest and investigate the pronunciation of 125 words that are representative of the sounds in all dialects. Were one to presume a perfect continuum, the difference in pronunciation between dialects should correlate with geographic distance between dialects. One would expect that as a traveller moved from one end of the continuum to the other, changes in phonological distances would be cumulative, with only minor changes between neighbouring villages. But this is not what Heeringa & Nerbonne

[9] One must wonder how common the complete—or nearly complete—convergence of multiple languages/dialects into a mostly uniform language is. In contemporary languages in which there has been heavy contact (see Thomason, 1997 for examples) or which have been classified as mixed languages (see Bakker & Mous, 1994 for examples), it is not difficult to distinguish the contribution of the different dialects. An example of multiple dialects of the same language converging completely to become a new dialect, a phenomenon known as dialect leveling, is New Zealand English, on which see Gordon et al. (2004). If such is the case for proto-Celtic, would we not be obliged to regard the dialects that converged as dialects of proto-Celtic?

find. Sometimes the phonological distance between points on the dialect continuum is considerably more than the geographic distance predicts. In such circumstances, they determine that a dialect area can exist within a dialect continuum: '[W]e see that phonological distances can mostly be explained by geographic distance. This justifies the continuum perspective. In those cases where a dialect distance between successive points is significantly higher than would be expected on the basis of geographic distances, we may encounter a dialect border. This justifies the area perspective' (387). They then 'conclude that both the areal view and the continuum view are useful for gaining insight in the nature of the dialect landscape, which may be described as a continuum with varying slope or, alternatively, as a continuum with unsharp borders between dialect areas' (399).

3 Dialect Continua and Dialect Areas in Diachronic Perspective

§8. A good example of a dialect continuum of comparable size as the Celtic dialect continuum within which one finds dialect areas is the Cree-Montagnais-Naskapi (Algonquian) dialect continuum, which stretches from Alberta in the west of Canada to Labrador in the east and is the result of a rapid eastward expansion (cf. Goddard, 1994).[10]

The treatment of proto-Algonq. */r/ variously as /l r ð n j/ across the continuum is well known, the other major isogloss being the palatalisation, beginning in the seventeenth century, of */k/ > /ʧ/ before front vowels in the Province of Quebec (aside from in Atikamekw in the southwest of the province) and Labrador.

§9. MacKenzie (1980) demonstrates that the majority of innovatory sound changes that validate Cree-Montagnais-Naskapi occur across the continuum, including the neutralisation of proto-Algonq. */t θ/ as /t/, palatalisation of /t/, neutralisation of */e i/ as /i/, proto-Algonquian nasals > /h/ before /p t k ʧ/, and the loss of proto-Algonquian final short

[10] A useful map is provided by Campbell (1997, p. 361).

vowels.[11] Upon this basis, she concludes that Cree-Montagnais-Naskapi is a 'classical' dialect continuum.

§10. Only later do velar palatalisation, short vowel syncope, and depalatalisation occur in the Province of Quebec, which, thus, forms a dialect area within the dialect continuum. MacKenzie & Clarke (1981) extend the dialect area analysis to variation in the inflexional morphology of the verbal system.

4 The Continental Celtic Dialect Continuum

§11. Prior to discussing what I will call the Continental Celtic dialect continuum, it is important to address the methodological question of what we mean when we use a term such as 'proto-Celtic'. Clearly, the proto-Celtic period ceases when it disperses to the extent that we can speak of at least two different Celtic languages. In fact, strictly speaking, were an innovation X to spread incompletely through the speech continuum, only to be followed by an innovation Y that did spread throughout the continuum, we would need to say that the proto-Celtic period ceased when innovation X occurred and that innovation Y occurred in what we may call 'post-proto-Celtic'. Thus, it is also clear that we have to recognise that, leading up to this point, there had to have been considerable variation across the post-proto-Celtic speech continuum. From another perspective, we can ask at what point we can speak of proto-Celtic having come into existence? Do all of what we consider to be the diagnostic features of proto-Celtic have to have come into existence already? Of course, a certain number do, but I would say not all, and that a proto-language—as well as a post-proto-language—, like all languages, should be considered as in fieri. From the perspective of contemporary dialectology, it would hardly be expected that we should come to the conclusion that proto-Celtic came into being when all of its diagnostic features were present and that all subsequent changes necessarily led to

[11] For variation in the western and eastern parts of the continuum, respectively, see Rhodes & Todd (1981, pp. 55–56). In the west, the primary isogloss is that proto-Algonq. */s/ and */ʃ/ merge as /s/ in Plains Cree, Woods Cree, and Western Swampy Cree, whereas they remain distinct in Eastern Swampy Cree, Moose Cree, and Atikamekw.

the differentiation into distinct languages. Thus, Sims-Williams (2007, p. 309) states that 'Common Celtic [= my "proto-Celtic"] is thus an abstraction or working model relating to some period before *c.* 600 BC, a common denominator for the post-proto-Indo-European developments found in all attested Celtic languages'. He goes on to note the possibility that while the earliest innovations might be classified as proto-Celtic, others, labelled as pan-Celtic, might have started at some point within proto-Celtic and then spread throughout the clade (310). He also suggests that distinguishing proto-Celtic innovations from pan-Celtic innovations would be impossible. On this point, I would say that he is incorrect, for we find that some innovations did not spread through the entire proto-Celtic speech continuum, but that some subsequently did so. Thus, we can—sometimes—distinguish diagnostic features of proto-Celtic from subsequent post-proto-Celtic [= Sims-Williams' pan-Celtic] innovations. Three such cases are discussed in §§16–21.

§12. This essay proposes that, although some linguistic innovations are attested only in the Celtic of northern Italy and Switzerland, some only in Transalpine Celtic, and one only in Galatian and Eastern Celtic, all of Continental Celtic to the exclusion of the Hispano-Celtic linguistic complex should be modelled as a single dialect continuum, but one in which linguistic areas are embedded.

§13. The principal relevant features from the Celtic of northern Italy and Switzerland are the following:

(4) a. Regular effacement of nasals before voiceless plosives, e.gg., dat. sg. **PiuoTialui** (LexLep TI·36.2) < proto-Celt. *_biu̯-ont^h-_ < western proto-IE *_g^{w}iu̯-ont-_ and nom. sg. **KoPenaTis** (LexLep BG·41.5) < proto-Celt. *_k^{h}om-p^{h}enno-_.[12]

b. Regular effacement of nasals before voiced plosives at a morpheme boundary and assimilation of intramorphemic nasal + voiced plosives to geminate nasals, both illustrated in nom. sg. **anoKoPoKios** (LexLep NO·21.1) < proto-Celt. *_ando-k^{h}om-bog-_.

[12] In western Celtiberia, nasal effacement is attested before both inherited voiceless and voiced plosives both at morpheme boundaries and intra-morphemically.

c. Employment of **-alo-** as a patronymic suffix, e.gg., dat. sg. **Klanalui** (LexLep TI·44) and dat. sg. **Terialui** (LexLep TI·27.1) (only in the 'Lepontic' area).
d. Employment of 3. sg. pret. < perf. **-e** in the innovative *t*-preterite, e.g., **KariTe** prob. 'put up' (LexLep VA·6)[13] (only in the 'Lepontic' area).

§14. The principal relevant features from the Celtic of Transalpine Gaul are the following:

(5) a. Incorporation of some inherited *ī*-stem desinences into the *ā*-stem paradigm, e.gg., nom. sg. *adiega* (RIG L–98 1ª14) : gen. sg. *adiegias* (RIG L–98 1ª11), nom. sg. *seuera* (RIG L–98 1ª12) : acc. sg. *seuerim* (RIG L–98 1ᵇ8), nom./acc. pl. *brictas* 'magic' (RIG L–98 1ᵇ7) : instr. sg. *brixtja* (RIG L–100) (also attested in Goidelic).
b. Spread of athematic instr. sg. *-bis* to the thematic flexion and its subsequent syncretism with the dative plural, e.g., *mesamobi* 'worst' (RIG L–66) (also attested in Goidelic).
c. Employment of 3. sg. pret. < perf. **-u** in the innovative *t*-preterite, e.g., ΚΑΡΝΙΤΟΥ[?] 'inter' (RIG G–151 = RIIG VAU-11-01).[14]

§15. The one relevant feature from Galatian and Eastern Celtic is the following:[15]

(6) Loss of */w/ after /r/ (attested only in a single etymon), e.gg., Galat. ΒΡΟΓΙΤΑ|ΡΟΝ (OGIS 349) and ΔΕΙΟΤΑΡΙ|ΑΝΟΝ (IGRom. iii 472) and ECelt. DEIOTARVS (CIL iii 8065[29]) < proto-Celt. *t^h*aru̯o-* 'bull'; cf. Celtib. **Taruo-** (MLH K.23.2 = Hesp. SO.06.02), Transalp. Celt. TARVOS (RIG L–14b = RIIG PAR-01-01), OIr. *tarb*, OSWBrit. *taruu*, MW *tarw*.

[13] For potential etymological analyses of the form, see Eska & Mercado (2005, pp. 164–165).

[14] This form may be a 3. plural preterite whose final -Σ is lost, but it would imply a 3. sg. pret. in -ΟΥ. I take **KarniTu** (RIG E–5A = LexLep PG·1.4) and [**Kar**]**ṇiTu** (RIG E–5L = LexLep PG·1.2) to have come to the Italian Peninsula via migration from Transalpine Gaul.

[15] I note that, aside from the one dialectal innovation unique to Galatian and Eastern Celtic, all other innovations for which they provide evidence are also found in Transalpine Celtic.

5 Three examples

§16. *The loss of proto-IE */p/ in initial and intervocalic position.*[16] The loss of proto-IE */p/ > proto-Celt. */p^{h}/ in initial and intervocalic position is probably the most frequently cited diagnostic feature of proto-Celtic. However, in my view (Eska, 1998b, 2013b), it survives as /ɸ/ = ⟨**v**⟩ in Cisalp. Celt. **uvamoKozis** < proto-Celt. */uɸamo/- 'highest' < proto-IE **upm̥mo-* and **uvlTiauioPos** (both LexLep CO·48), which I take to be an error for ***liTauio-** 'pertaining to the earth' (following Stifter, 2002/2003: 239[1])[17]—cf. the theonyms Skt. *Pr̥thivī́* and Transalp. Celt. LITAVI (dat. sg.)[18] < proto-IE **pl̥th$_2$-u̯-ih$_2$* 'earth'—with prefix */uɸo/- 'under', thus proto-Celt. */uɸoɸlit^{h}awijo/- > Cisalp. Celt. /uɸlit^{h}awijo/- 'underworld' via haplology (Eska forthcoming a). Others view ⟨**uv**⟩ as a digraph for /w/ (most recently Dupraz, 2015)—note, however, that /w/ is represented by ⟨**u**⟩ medially in **uvlTiauioPos**—but such a view is antithetical to the fact that reforms to the Alphabet of Lugano always reduced the number of characters, and /wlt/- is in no way a permissible syllabic onset within Celtic.

Thus, in my view, loss of proto-Indo-European initial and intervocalic */p/ is not only not of proto-Celtic date, but one also cannot classify it as pan-Celtic—and certainly not as post-proto-Celtic—until after the engraving of these forms in the middle of the fifth century BCE, and then it certainly was the result of homoplasy rather than diffusion.

§17. *The thematic genitive plural desinence.* In Eska (2006), I argue that Celtib. gen. pl. **-um** -/uːm/, e.g., **uPoKum** (MLH K.1.1 A11 = Hesp. Z.09.01), vs. Transalp. Celt. *-on* -/on/, e.gg., *neđđamon* 'neighbour' (RIG L–50), and late Cisalp. Celt. **Teuoχ|Tonion** 'god and man' (RIG E–2 = LexLep VC·1.2) is to be accounted for as a matter of dialect geography, the shortening of long vowels before final nasals not having reached the portion of the proto-Celtic speech continuum which was to

---

[16] Proto-IE */p/ is not lost, but changes to [β] / V_L, [w] / V$_{[back]}$_n, and [x] / _{s t}; see Eska (2018, p. 325, 2018/2019, pp. 18–19) for the phonetic processes that led to these changes.

[17] The transposition of characters is a well attested epigraphical error; see Kent (1926) and Buonocore (2019) for discussion and examples.

[18] Either regularly continuing */ɸlitawijaːj/ 'pertaining to the earth' or exactly cognate with *Pr̥thivī́*, but remade as an *i*-stem.

become the Hispano-Celtic linguistic complex, while the raising of */oː/ > /uː/ / _C_0# later did. This provides evidence that */oː/ > /uː/ / _C_0# is a post-proto-Celtic change (or nearly so; see §20–21), since it occurred only after Vː > V / _$C_{[nasal]}$# propagated from its focal point, but did not reach the part of the (proto-)Celtic speech continuum that was to become the Hispano-Celtic linguistic complex.

§18. We may now note that the 'Lepontic' acephalous form]**eTiun** (LexLep BG·41.19) in a string of onomastic forms very likely is a genitive plural,[19] either displaying loss of the feature [bilabial] in the final nasal or representing an epigraphic error whereby 𐌍 = ⟨**n**⟩ was engraved for 𐌌 = ⟨**m**⟩.[20]

§19. Thus, it seems that the shortening of long vowels before final nasals had its focal point in the portion of the Celtic speech continuum that was to become Transalpine Celtic, but ceased to propagate not only before it reached the portion of the Celtic speech continuum that was to become the Hispano-Celtic linguistic complex, but also before it reached the portion that was to become 'Lepontic'. They are, thus, relic areas regarding this innovation, which, then, can only have occurred in post-proto-Celtic.

Under this view, Cisalp. Celt. gen. pl. **Teuoχ|Tonion** contains a form of the genitive plural desinence that came to Cisalpine Gaul with the population movements from Transalpine Gaul.

§20. *The thematic dative singular desinence.* While the thematic dative singular desinence appears in Transalpine Celtic at first as -ΟΥΙ -/uːj/, e.g., ΑΔΓΕΝ|ΝΟΥΙ (RIG G–208 = RIIG GAR-10-06)—cf. Celtib. **ueiđui** '?witness?' (MLH K.6.1 = Hesp. GU.01.01), Cisalp. Celt. **PelKui** (LexLep VA·6)—then later, with the loss of -/j/, as *-u*/-V, e.gg., *papu* 'each' (RIG L–66) and ALISANV (RIG L–133), it may be noted that there are some forms that differ, viz.:

(7) a. ΒΕΛΕΙΝΟ (RIG G–28 = RIIG BDR-10-01).
b. ΑΔΡΕΤ̣ΙΟ̣ (RIG G–216 = RIIG GAR-13-01).
c. ΑΒΡω̣ (RIG G–219 = RIIG GAR-15-01).

[19] In my view, it could hardly be any other category.

[20] The omission of a stroke in a character is a common epigraphical error; see Kent (1926) and Buonocore (2019) for discussion and many examples.

In the Swiss Alps, we may also add:

d. ΔΟΒΝΟΡΗΔΟ and ΓΟΒΑΝΟ (RIG L–106).
e. **Poenino** (LexLep VS·2).[21]

ΔΟΒΝΟΡΗΔΟ, ΓΟΒΑΝΟ, and **Poenino** are attested in locations and at times in which we expect the existence of a Latin milieu, so their desinences could, therefore, be borrowings from Latin. A borrowing from Greek is possible—though not very likely—with ΑΒΡΩ̣, as well, but not with ΒΕΛΕΙΝΟ or ΑΔΡϵΤ̣ΙΟ̣, for the Greek inscriptions of southern Gaul always employ omega in the thematic dative singular.[22]

§21. Thematic dative singular *-u*/-ν in later Transalpine Gaul is the result of the syncretism of dat. -/uː/, instr. -/uː/ < *-oh_1, and abl. -/uː/ < *-*ōd*. But ΒΕΛΕΙΝΟ and ΑΔΡϵΤ̣ΙΟ̣, at least, suggest that the dative singular forms in -ο represent a relic area in which proto-Celt.

*-/oː/ was not raised or was shortened before it could be raised.

6 Summing Up

§22. Rather than posit that the variation that is attested in the Continental Celtic linguistic record points towards the incomplete convergence of separate languages/dialects to form an uneven, variegated quasi-proto-Celtic, evidence from modern dialectal research points in the opposite direction. Once innovations occurred that did not spread across the entirety of the proto-Celtic speech continuum, we need to conclude that the proto-Celtic period had come to its conclusion. This does not imply that the Celtic speech continuum was no longer contiguous, so innovations could still spread across the entirety of the post-proto-Celtic speech continuum.

[21] See Eska & Eska (2022, pp. 168–171) for recent, more detailed discussion of the desinence of this form.

[22] I should like to thank Torsten Meißner for confirming this fact for me.

As a linguistic continuum spreads, dialect areas may form within that continuum. An innovation may begin at a focal area and spread throughout the continuum, or it may cease to propagate, sometimes for geographical reasons, with the result that dialect areas are formed.

§23. Thus, the nasal assimilation and nasal effacement attested in Cisalpine Celtic do not appear to have spread far, but the latter also emerged in western Celtiberia and did not spread to eastern Celtiberia.

The use of the inherited suffix **-alo-** as a patronymic exponent in the 'Lepontic' region probably was initially steered by the external guidance of Etruscan (and/or Raetic) gen. sg. **-al** under conditions of prestige and bilingualism (Falileyev forthcoming). However, this usage did not spread beyond Cisalpine Celtic, probably because the Etruscan factor was absent.

§24. A number of innovations found in Transalpine Celtic, e.gg., the incorporation of some *ī*-stem desinences into the *ā*-stem paradigm and the syncretism of the dative and instrumental plural desinences, are also found in Insular Celtic, which suggest that they, at least to some extent, cohered as a dialect area for some period.

§25. The best tree that we can draw for the Celtic language family, then, is approximately:

(8)

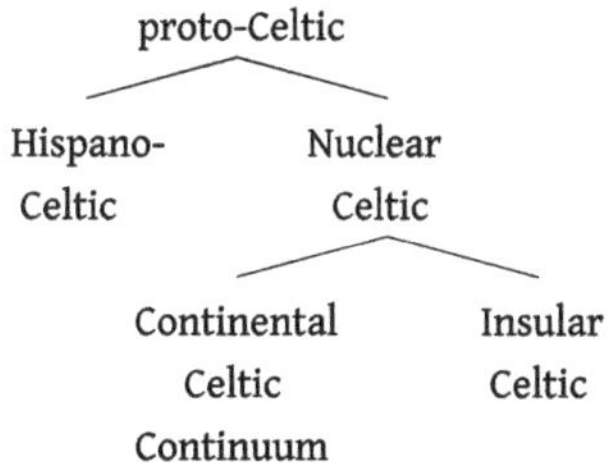

§26. But we need to recognise the dynamism of innovations arising at focal points around the continuum, which may have spread far or not so far, and which led to unevenness and variation and the creation of dialect areas, but with much mutual comprehension nonetheless, as we find in modern dialect continua. To extend Heeringa & Narbonne's slope metaphor, we would do well to think of the Continental Celtic dialect continuum much like a gentle ski slope laced with a number of moguls.

Terms such as Transalpine Celtic, Cisalpine Celtic, Lepontic, Eastern Celtic, and Galatian, thus, do not represent discrete languages, but designate areas within the Continental Celtic dialect continuum, much as Texan English, Southern English, Appalachian English, Brooklyn English, and New England English do for American English.

References

Bakker, P., & Mous, M. (Eds.). (1994). *Mixed languages. 15 case studies in language intertwining*. IFOTT.

Buonocore, M. (2019). *Cuiusve hominis est errare*. Tipologie di errore epigrafico nella trasmissione testuale antica e moderna. In A. Sartori & F. Gallo (Eds.), *L'errore in epigrafia* (pp. 17–39). Centro Ambrosiano.

Campbell, L. (1997). *American Indian languages. The historical linguistics of Native America*. Oxford University Press.

CIL = Mommsen, Theodor, et al. (1853). *Corpus inscriptionum Latinarum*. Georg Reimer.

Decourt, J.-C. (2004). *Inscriptions grecques de la France (IGF)*. Maison de l'Orient et de la Méditerranée—Jean Pouilloux.

Dupraz, E. (2015). Nochmals zum lepontischen Digraphen **uv-**. *Münchener Studien zur Sprachwissenschaft, 69*, 33–50.

Eska, J. F. (1998a). *Tau Gallicum*. *Studia Celtica, 32*, 115–127.

Eska, J. F. (1998b). PIE **p* ≯ Ø in proto-Celtic. *Münchener Studien zur Sprachwissenschaft, 58*, 63–80.

Eska, J. F. (2006). The genitive plural desinence in Celtic and dialect geography. *Die Sprache, 46*, 229–235.

Eska, J. F. (2010). The emergence of the Celtic languages. In M. J. Ball & N. Müller (Eds.), *The Celtic languages*[2] (pp. 22–27). Routledge.

Eska, J. F. (2013a). A salvage grammar of Galatian. *Zeitschrift für celtische Philologie, 60*, 51–63.

Eska, J. F. (2013b). In defense of Celtic /ɸ/. In A. I. Cooper, J. Rau, & M. Weiss (Eds.), *Multi nominis grammaticus. Studies in Classical and Indo-European linguistics in honor of Alan J. Nussbaum on the occasion of his sixty-fifth birthday* (pp. 32–43). Beech Stave Press.

Eska, J. F. (2017). The dialectology of Celtic. In J. Klein, B. Joseph, M. Fritz, & M. Wenthe (Eds.), *Handbook of comparative and historical Indo-European linguistics* (Vol. ii, pp. 1264–1274). De Gruyter Mouton.

Eska, J. F. (2018). Laryngeal Realism and the prehistory of Celtic. *Transactions of the Philological Society, 116*, 320–331.

Eska, J. F. (2018/2019). Grounding Celtic diachronic phonology I. *Die Sprache*, 53: 17–32.

Eska, J. F. (forthcoming a). Digamma and Prestino and related matters.

Eska, J. F. (forthcoming b). Script transfer and Laryngeal Realism, and script reform. On plosive phonology in ancient Celtic northern Italy.

Eska, J. F., & Eska, C. M. (2022). Epigraphic and linguistic observations on the inscription at the so-called *Mur d'Hannibal* (Liddes, Valais). *Zeitschrift für celtische Philologie, 69*, 159–182.

Eska, J. F., & Mercado, A. O. (2005). Observations on verbal art in ancient Vergiate. *Historische Sprachforschung, 118*, 160–184.

Falileyev, A. (forthcoming). The Cisalpine Celtic (patronymic) suffix *-al-*, revisited. In D. Stifter & C. Salomon (Eds.), *Cisalpine Celtic literacy*. Department of Early Irish.

Garrett, A. (2006). Convergence in the formation of Indo-European subgroups. Phylogeny and chronology. In P. Forster & C. Renfrew (Eds.), *Phylogentic methods and the prehistory of languages* (pp. 139–151). McDonald Institute for Archaeological Research.

Garrett, A. (1999). A new model of Indo-European subgrouping and dispersal. *Proceedings of the Annual Meeting of the Berkeley Linguistics Society, 25*, 146–156.

Goddard, I. (1994). The west-to-east cline in Algonquian dialectology. In W. Cowan (Ed.), *Actes du vingt-cinquième congrès des algonquinistes* (pp. 187–211). Carleton University.

Gordon, E., Campbell, L., Hay, J., Maclagan, M., Sudbury, A., & Trudgill, P. (2004). *New Zealand English. Its origins and evolution.* Cambridge University Press.

Heeringa, W., & Nerbonne, J. (2001). Dialect areas and dialect continua. *Language variation and change, 13*, 375–400.

Hesp. = *Hesperia. Banco de datos de lenguas paleohispánicas* http://hesperia.ucm.es/, ed. J. de Hoz, J. Gorrochategui, E. Orduña, et al. (1997–).

IGRom = Cagnat, René (with Jules Toutain, Pierre Jouguet, & Georges Lafaye). (1911–1927). *Inscriptiones Graecae ad res Romanas pertinentes*. Leroux.

Iosad, P. (2023). *Laryngeal ultra-Realism and early Celtic obstruents.* Paper presented to the Foundational Approaches to Celtic Linguistics series.

Isaac, G. R. (2005). Insular Celtic vs. Gallo-Brittonic. An empirical and methodological question. In W. Gillies & D. W. Harding (Eds.), *Celtic connections ii, Archaeology, numismatics, historical linguistics* (pp. 190–202). University of Edinburgh.

Jasanoff, J. (2017). *The prehistory of the Balto-Slavic accent*. Brill.

Kent, R. (1926). *The textual criticism of inscriptions*. Linguistic Society of America.

Koch, J. T. (1992). 'Gallo-Brittonic vs. Insular Celtic'. The inter-relationships of the Celtic languages reconsidered. In G. Le Menn (Ed.), *Bretagne et pays celtiques. Langues, histoire, civilisation. Mélanges offerts à la mémoire de Léon Fleuriot* (pp. 471–495). Presses Universitaires Rennes.

LexLep = *Lexicon Leponticum. A digital edition and etymological dictionary of Cisalpine Celtic* https://lexlep.univie.ac.at/wiki/Main_Page, ed. D. Stifter, M. Braun, C. Salomon, M. Vignoli, et al. (2009–).

MacKenzie, M. E. (1980). *Towards a dialectology of Cree-Montagnais-Naskapi*. PhD dissertation, University of Toronto.

MacKenzie, M. E., & Clarke, S. (1981). Dialect relations in Cree/Montagnais/Naskapi. Verb paradigms. *Recherches linguistiques à Montréal / Montréal working papers in linguistics, 16*, 135–191.

McCone, K. (1996). *Towards a relative chronology of ancient and medieval Celtic sound change*. Department of Old and Middle Irish, St. Patrick's College, Maynooth.

MLH A = Untermann, Jürgen. (1975). *Monumenta linguarum Hispanicarum i, Die Münzlegenden*. Dr. Ludwig Reichert.

MLH K = Untermann, Jürgen. (1997). *Monumenta linguarum Hispanicarum iv, Die tartessischen, keltiberischen und lusitanischen Inschriften* (pp. 349–722). Dr. Ludwig Reichert.

OGIS = Dittenberger, Wilhelm. (1903–1905). *Orientis Graeci inscriptiones selectae*. S. Hirzel.

Rhodes, R. A., & Todd, E. M. (1981). Subarctic Algonquian languages. In J. Helm (Ed.), *Handbook of North American Indians vi, Subarctic* (pp. 52–66). Smithsonian Institution.

RIG E = Lejeune, Michel. (1988). *Recueil des inscriptions gauloises ii/1, Textes gallo-étrusques. Textes gallo-latins sur pierre* (pp. 1–54). Centre National de la Recherche Scientifique.

RIG G = Lejeune, Michel. (1985). *Recueil des inscriptions gauloises i, Textes gallo-grecs*. Centre National de la Recherche Scientifique.

RIG L = Lejeune, Michel. (1988). *Recueil des inscriptions gauloises ii/1, Textes gallo-étrusques. Textes gallo-latins sur pierre* (pp. 55–194). Centre National de la Recherche Scientifique.

RIIG = *Recueil informatisé des inscriptions gauloises* https://riig.huma-num.fr/, ed. C. R. Darasse et al. (2022–).

Sims-Williams, P. (2007). Common Celtic, Gallo-Brittonic and Insular Celtic. In *Gaulois et celtique continental*, ed. Pierre-Yves Lambert & Georges-Jean Pinault, 309–354. Genève: Librarie Droz. [Reprinted in Sims-Williams, Patrick. 2007. *Studies on Celtic languages before the year 1000*, 1–42. Aberystwyth: CMCS.]

Stifter, D. (2002/2003). Review of Helmut Birkhan, *Kelten. Bilder ihrer Kulture / Celts. Images of their culture.* Wien: Österreichische Akademie der Wissenschaften, 1999. *Die Sprache, 43*, 237–243.

Stifter, D. (2020a). Cisalpine Celtic. *Palaeohispanica, 20*, 335–365.

Stifter, D. (2020b). *Cisalpine Celtic. Language. Writing. Epigraphy.* Universidad de Zaragoza.

Thomason, S. (Ed.). (1997). *Contact languages. A wider perspective.* John Benjamins.

2

On the Phylogenetic Status of East Germanic

Ronald I. Kim

Despite significant contributions to the historical grammar of Greek and Tocharian, our honorand is probably best known for his scholarship on Germanic, above all the first two volumes of *A linguistic history of English* (Ringe, 2017; Ringe & Taylor, 2014), as well as on linguistic phylogeny and long-distance relationships. Throughout his career, Don has insisted on methodological rigor and the formulation of precise hypotheses and arguments, in the belief that linguistics is indeed a true science. It is my pleasure to present this study as a token of my gratitude for his mentorship over three decades.[1]

[1] This essay has benefited greatly from the comments of Joe Eska, Olav Hackstein, and Craig Melchert. Thanks also to Frederik Hartmann for making available an advance copy of his 2023 monograph.

R. I. Kim (✉)
Faculty of English, Adam Mickiewicz University, Poznań, Poland

J. F. Eska et al. (eds.), *The Method Works*,
https://doi.org/10.1007/978-3-031-48959-4_2

1 Introduction: Germanic and East Germanic

The subgrouping of Germanic has been debated since the nineteenth century, and publications on the topic could easily fill a bookshelf.[2] Over the past two generations, the consensus has emerged that the Germanic languages may be classified into three subgroups, conventionally named East, North, and West Germanic; the latter two belong to a higher-order grouping, Northwest Germanic, characterized by a small, but robust, set of changes such as PGmc. **ē* > **ā*, word-final PGmc. **-ō* > **-u*, unstressed **a* > **u* before **m*, and replacement of **-aiz-* by **-ez-* in strong adjective endings (Stiles, 2013, pp. 8–9; Ringe & Taylor, 2014, pp. 10–24). Both North and West Germanic, in turn, are defined by a significant list of isoglosses; for West Germanic, see Stiles (2013, pp. 15–17) and Ringe & Taylor (2014, pp. 41–81).

In contrast to North and West Germanic, East Germanic is usually defined in terms of its archaisms, e.g., absence of umlaut, rhotacism of PGmc. **z*, or lowering of **ē* > **ā* and retention of reduplicated strong preterites and fientive weak verbs. Yet the sole form of East Germanic known from connected texts is the Gothic attested in surviving portions of Wulfila's fourth-century Bible translation, along with the *Skeireins* and several minor sources. This raises two questions: to what extent does it make sense to speak of a subgroup encompassing only one language; and what light can the meager remains of other languages shed on the status of East Germanic?

I argue that none of the features traditionally regarded as diagnostic of East Germanic constitutes support for a subgroup in the phylogenetic sense. It thus agrees with the conclusions of Hartmann (2020, 2023, pp. 178–192) and Hartmann & Riegger (2022), but revises them in several points by taking into account Crimean Gothic and carefully distinguishing among shared innovations, parallel changes, and retentions.

[2] For useful surveys, see Nielsen (1989, pp. 67–107), Grønvik (1998, pp. 67–82), Stiles (2013, pp. 5–15), and Rübekeil (2017).

2 Methodological Concerns

According to a principle established by Leskien (1876), only shared innovations, not retentions, are probative for determining the subgrouping of related languages. These innovations should moreover be sufficiently marked, unlikely to have taken place more than once independently.[3] Because most sound changes have some degree of phonetic 'naturalness', phonological innovations are of value for subgrouping only if (i) they are typologically unusual and/or (ii) they can be ordered in a relative chronology and it can be shown that two or more languages have undergone them in the same sequence.[4] In practice, then, it is morphological innovations that carry the greatest weight in determining subgrouping, as long as one can be reasonably certain in which direction the change has taken place.[5]

These considerations are central to evaluating arguments for the subgrouping of Germanic and existence of an East Germanic clade. To take one example, the treatment of proto-Germanic diphthongs is of little value given their manifold reflexes in the older Germanic languages. Just as no one today would seriously question the validity of West Germanic on the grounds of the divergent reflexes of PGmc. **ai* (OHG *ei* ~ *ē*, OS *ē*, OFris. *ē*, *ā*, OE *ā*), so it is unjustified to assign any importance to the preservation vs. monophthongization of **ai*, **au* in supposedly East Germanic languages (see below, §§4–6). Only if part of a relative chronology involving multiple changes can such developments be considered significant for dialect geography.[6] Thus the occlusion of *[ð] > [d], of limited worth by itself, is a West Germanic isogloss because it followed assimilation of *[ðw], *[zw] > *[ww] in PGmc. **feđwōr* 'four' > **feuwar* > OE *fēower*, OS *fiuwar* and PGmc. dat. pl. **izwiz* 'you' > **iuw(i)* > OE

[3] See Hoenigswald (1960, pp. 151–158, 1966) and Campbell (2021, p. 231).

[4] See Hoenigswald (1960, p. 154) and Ringe & Eska (2013, pp. 259–261).

[5] See Ringe et al. (2002, pp. 65–70), Nakhleh et al. (2005, pp. 395–396), and Ringe & Eska (2013, pp. 256–263). Clackson (2007, p. 6) goes so far as to state that 'only through morphological changes' can subgroups be confidently established.

[6] A famous example from American English dialectology is the monophthongization of /ai/ to [ɑː] in the U. S. South, the first step in a chain shift with implications for the entire vowel system (ANAE 242–254).

īow, OS, OHG *iu* (Stiles, 1985, pp. 89–94; Ringe & Taylor, 2014, pp. 41–43).[7] The establishment of such relative chronologies has revealed that changes specific to particular dialect areas could be followed by others that spread throughout Northwest Germanic or West Germanic, i.e., these languages made up a gradually diversifying dialect continuum in the early centuries AD.[8]

It is true that even 'trivial' sound changes, like lexical shifts, can shine a light on patterns of dialect differentiation, particularly where the data allow identification of focal areas, from which an innovation originated, and relic areas, which remained unaffected. The Romance languages offer numerous examples, e.g., monophthongization of Vulg. Lat. AU in the central varieties vs. retention in the periphery.[9] However, even if we had more substantial records of the languages spoken by the Visigoths, Vandals, Burgundians, and other peoples traditionally considered 'East Germanic', it is far from certain that they would lend themselves to such results. Not only were these communities continuously on the move during the *Völkerwanderung* period—sometimes over impressive distances, as with the Vandals, whose migrations took them from Eastern Europe to Gaul, Iberia, and North Africa—but the internal variation within them must have been complex, as groups of speakers came into contact, dispersed, and reassembled into new configurations.[10] As a result, what Roberge (2020, p. 332) calls 'Mediterranean Germanic' must have been made up of 'conglomerations of dialects with varying degrees of koineization and mutual intelligibility'.

---

[7] It is only for this reason that the raising of **e* in unstressed position and before **i* can be securely assigned to proto-Germanic despite the obliteration of the contrast between **e* and **i* in Bible Gothic, since raising was followed by loss of intervocalic **j* in PIE **tréi̯es* 'three' > **þrejiz* > **þrijiz* > PGmc. **þrīz* > BGoth. *þreis** (acc. *þrins*), ON *þrír*, OHG *drī* (Ringe, 2017, pp. 147–153 pace Fulk, 2018, p. 61). On possible evidence for raising in Vandalic and Burgundian, see §5 no. 3, §6 no. 5.

[8] See Ringe (2012), Stiles (2013, pp. 21–33), and Ringe & Taylor (2014, pp. 24–40 and 82–103). On the consequences of such gradual dialect divisions for the *Stammbaum* model, see Hoenigswald (1960, pp. 155–157) and Ringe & Eska (2013, pp. 262–263).

[9] Cf. Romanian *aur*, Romansh (Sursilvan) *aur*, Portuguese *ouro* vs. Italian, Spanish *oro*, French *or* < VL AURUM.

[10] See Heather (1996, pp. 3–7) on the ethnically composite nature of 'tribal' groupings during the period of migrations.

3 What Is East Germanic?

The curious fact about the East Germanic clade is that it is based exclusively on the testimony of a single language, namely Bible Gothic. As a result, the diagnostic features of East Germanic are regularly projected backwards from Bible Gothic, a practice justified by the quotation from Procopius (*Gothic wars* III.2.2–5) that 'the Goths, Vandals, Visigoths, and Gepids … have one language called Gothic'.[11] Though understandable, this methodology is illegitimate and has led to erroneous analyses, e.g., that the Germanic language of Crimea recorded in Oghier Ghislain de Busbecq's fourth Turkish letter of 1562 must be West Germanic because it retains the contrast of PGmc. **e* and **i* (vs. their merger in Bible Gothic) or shows ⟨o⟩ for PGmc. **u* followed by **a* ('*a*-umlaut'), supposedly a Northwest Germanic innovation.[12] Proponents of this view are then forced into special pleading to account for those features of Crimean Gothic which are not shared with West Germanic, as well as those shared with Bible Gothic, which must reflect later contact.[13]

Of course, comparison of Crimean Gothic or any other Germanic language with Bible Gothic is useful as a measurement of synchronic similarity or test of lineal descent. Thus Crimean Gothic cannot descend directly from Bible Gothic because it does not share in distinctively Bible Gothic changes, e.g., those affecting PGmc. **e* and **i* (see below, §4). This is, however, of little import for the investigation of phylogenetic

[11] To take two recent examples, '[o]stgermanische Morphologie ist eigentlich gotische Morphologie weil, mit Ausnahme des Gotischen, die Sprachen der Ostgermanen nur wenig bekannt sind' (Snædal, 2009a, p. 147); and 'EGmc has to be defined on the basis of Gothic', so that '"EGmc characteristics" are therefore essentially identical with Gothic characteristics' (Rübekeil, 2017, pp. 994 and 998). See also Penzl (1972, p. 143) and Stearns (1978, p. 119, 1989, p. 184). Marchand (1970, p. 121) concludes that it is 'falsch … von Ostgermanisch zu reden'. For Grønvik (1983, pp. 66–67), 'niemand weiß, was unter der Bezeichnung Ostgermanisch genau zu verstehen ist', so that East Germanic remains 'undefiniert … und wohl auch … undefinierbar'. Hartmann (2020, p. 116) observes that East Germanic is '[i]n some respects … a clade that was proposed in contrast to Northwest Germanic'.

[12] This view goes back to Loewe (1896); see Grønvik (1983, pp. 57–61 & passim), and cf. Stiles (2017, p. 903): 'so-called Crimean Gothic perhaps is to be classed as a North-West-Germanic dialect'.

[13] See the critical remarks in Nielsen (1986, pp. 67–68). Miller (2019, p. 6) notes that Grønvik's hypothesis 'would entail a very large number of direct borrowings from Gothic'.

relationships, which once again depends on identification of significant shared innovations, along with a relative chronology to the extent that this can be determined (§2). If there was, in fact, an East Germanic subgroup, it is fully expected that Bible Gothic would have undergone innovations of its own, which can only be determined through comparison with other languages of the subgroup.[14]

The status of East Germanic, thus, rests on an examination of the limited data from other Germanic-speaking peoples associated with the *Völkerwanderung*, under the working hypothesis that they too are East Germanic, to determine what if any innovations are shared exclusively by these varieties and Bible Gothic. Although the comparative basis has been expanded by recent publications on the almost entirely onomastic Vandalic and Burgundian corpora, our point of departure is Crimean Gothic, which has enjoyed a richer tradition of scholarship and received a widely praised analysis by Stearns (1978).

4 First Comparison. Bible Gothic and Crimean Gothic

The phonological systems of Bible Gothic and Crimean Gothic have been compared by Nielsen (2017), who like most scholars today takes the latter to be East Germanic.[15] From a diachronic perspective, we may group the distinctive features of Crimean Gothic as follows:

a. Archaisms:

   1. Retention of PGmc. **z*
      Cf. *Ies* 'he', *VVintch* (for **VVintsch*) /wints/ 'wind' < PGmc. **is* ~ **es*, **windaz* (BGoth. *is*, *winds*), *Schuos* (for **Schnos*) 'fiancée' < PGmc. **snuzō* (OE *snoru* 'daughter-in-law').

[14] See Stearns (1978, p. 119, 1989, p. 184) and Hartmann & Riegger (2022, pp. 64–65).

[15] I restrict myself to the Crimean Gothic word list proper, leaving aside the ingenious, but highly uncertain, interpretations of the *cantilena* by Grønvik (1983, pp. 71–105) and others.

2. Retention of PGmc. *[ðw]
   The only example in Crimean Gothic is *fyder* 'four' < PGmc. **feđwōr* ~ **feđur-* (BGoth. *fidwōr*).[16]

b. Typologically common changes shared with other Germanic languages:

3. Devoicing of word-final obstruents
   Cf. *Plut* 'blood', *Schuos* (for **Schnos*) 'fiancée', *Rinck* 'ring'< PGmc. **blōđą*, **snuzō*, **hringaz* (but *Tag* 'day' < PGmc **dagaz*) and see Stearns (1978, pp. 94, 96, 97) and Grønvik (1983, pp. 46–47).
4. Occlusion of *[ð] > [d]
   Cf. *fyder* 'four' < PGmc. **feđwōr* ~ **feđur-* or *Plut* 'blood' < PGmc. **blōđą* (with final devoicing, see no. 3), contrasting with ⟨tz⟩ [þ] in *Goltz* 'gold', *Statz* 'land' < PGmc. **gulþą*, **staþaz* (Stearns, 1978, p. 113).
5. Apocope of **a* in final syllables
   See the forms above under nos. 1, 3, and 4.

c. Potentially shared innovations:

6. Nonlow reflex of PGmc. **ē* (> BGoth. *ē*, late *ī*, CGoth. *i*; see no. 15)
7. Holtzmann's Law: PGmc. **jj* > *ddj*
   CGoth. *Ada* 'egg' would correspond to BGoth. *addi** or pl. *addja** < PGmc. **ajją*, pl. **ajjō*. The change is well established for Bible Gothic, e.g., gen. *twaddjē* 'two' < PGmc. **twajjǭ* (ON *tveggja*, OHG *zweio*).

d. Changes attested in Bible Gothic, but not Crimean Gothic:

8. Phonemic merger of **e* and **i*
9. 'Breaking' (i.e., lowering) of /i/ and /u/ to *ai* [ɛ] and *au* [ɔ] respectively, before *r*, *h*, *ƕ*.
   The absence of these developments in Crimean Gothic was seen already in the nineteenth century.[17] For the former, cf. *Reghen* 'rain', *Schuuester* 'sister' < PGmc. **regną*, **swestēr* vs. BGoth. *rign*, *swistar*; for the latter, cf. *Thurn* 'door', **vvurt* (in the formula *Iel vburt* 'may it be well' for **Iel vvurt*) < PGmc. **dur-*, 3sg. subj. pret. **wurđī* vs. BGoth. *daur*, *waurþi* with lowering.

[16] So rather than from the combining form **feđur-* (Stearns, 1978, p. 136; Grønvik, 1983, pp. 27–29). See Stiles (1985, p. 19), though **feđur-* need not be Northwest Germanic.

[17] See Loewe (1896, pp. 157–158), Stearns (1978, pp. 110 & 118), Cercignani (1980, pp. 211–212), and Fulk (2018, p. 20).

e. Changes attested in Crimean Gothic, but not Bible Gothic:

10. Loss of PGmc. **h*-
CGoth. **h*- > *Ø*- not only before sonorants (e.g., *Rinck* 'ring' < PGmc. **hringaz*), but also before vowels. In the latter, Busbecq added an etymological ⟨h⟩ in words that he recognized as Germanic, hence in *Hus* 'house', *Hoef* 'head', *Handa* 'hand', but not *Ano* 'hen, chicken', *Ael* 'stone', *Ieltsch* 'alive, healthy' (BGoth. *hana*, *hallus*, *hails*).[18] The Iranian borrowing *Hazer* [x]- 'thousand' shows that the loss must have been relatively early (Kim, 2022, p. 87).
11. Unrounding of /gʷ/ to /g/ in CGoth. *Singhen* 'sing' < PGmc. **singʷanq̨* (BGoth. *siggwan*)
This easily repeatable change was surely independent of that in West Germanic (OE, OS, OHG *singan*), as admitted by Grønvik (1983, p. 49; cf. Stearns, 1978, p. 114). OFris. *siunga* shows that the unrounding was not proto-West Germanic in any case.
12. Lowering of PGmc. **u* > **o* before **a*
Along with retention of the contrast between PGmc. **e* and **i* (nos. 8 & 9), this has long been taken as proof of the (North)West Germanic affiliations of Crimean Gothic.[19] However, not only can a parallel change not be ruled out for an earlier stage of Bible Gothic prior to the 'breaking' that (re)partitioned [o] and [u] along the same lines as [e] and [i] (Nielsen, 1986, p. 68), but I am not aware of any cogent arguments that lowering of **u* to *[o] could not have begun already in proto-Germanic.
13. Reduction of unstressed vowels to [ə][20]
An innovation found in late Bible Gothic,[21] as well as the great majority of medieval and modern Germanic languages, of no value for subgrouping.

---

[18] See Loewe (1896, pp. 147–148) and Stearns (1978, pp. 59, 82, 95).

[19] See Loewe (1896, pp. 157–158) and Grønvik (1983, p. 56).

[20] Represented variously as *a*, *e*, *i*, *o*, *u* in the speech of Busbecq's main informant, whose native language was Crimean Greek. See Loewe (1896, pp. 136 & 141–143), Stearns (1978, pp. 54–55 & 90–91, 1989, pp. 179–180), and Grønvik (1983, pp. 23 & 35–36).

[21] See Jellinek (1926, pp. 96–97) on fluctuation in linking vowels of compounds, as well as in final syllables.

f. Parallel innovations in Bible Gothic and Crimean Gothic:

14. Monophthongization of PGmc. **ai*, **au* > BGoth. [ɛː], [ɔː], CGoth. /e/, /o/
This could be placed under (c), but monophthongization was probably a recent change in Wulfila's Bible translation.[22] For Crimean Gothic, see *Iel* 'life, health', *Ieltsch* 'alive, healthy' < PGmc. **hailą*, **hailaz* (BGoth. *hail(s)*), *Oeghene* 'eyes', *Hoef* 'head' < PGmc. **augōnō*, **haubidą* (BGoth. *augona*, *haubiþ*).
15. Raising of **ē*, **ō* > [iː], [uː] in late Bible Gothic and in Crimean Gothic
For confusion of *ei*, *e*, *i* and *u*, *o* in Bible Gothic, cf. C 4.14 *leikeis*, L 1.5 *qeins* for *lekeis* 'physician', *qens* 'wife' and conversely L 20.10 3pl. subj. pret. *gebena* for *gebeina* 'would give', Mc 11.32 3pl. pret. *uhtedun* for *ohtedun* 'feared';[23] also Ostrogothic proper names from sixth-century Italy such as *Dumarit* (for BGoth. **Dōmarēþs*) and the ninth-century Codex Vindobonensis with *aiwaggeljo*, *þo* glossed *euangeliū*, *thuo̯*. The Crimean Gothic evidence is unambiguous: cf. *Mine* 'moon', *Schlipen* 'sleep', *Plut* 'blood', *Bruder* 'brother' < PGmc. **mēnan-*, **slēpaną*, **blōdą*, **brōþer-* (BGoth. *mēna*, *slēpan*, *blōþ*, *brōþar*).

The only likely shared innovations are the nonlow reflexes of PGmc. **ē*, which may rather be a retention; and the Holtzmann's Law treatment of PGmc. **jj*, which is noteworthy, but not so idiosyncratic, since it probably took place independently in North Germanic (giving ON *ggj*) and has numerous crosslinguistic parallels.[24]

In morphology, an innovation shared by Bible Gothic and Crimean Gothic is pronominal neut. nom./acc. sg. *-ata* (CGoth. *Atochta* 'bad', *Gadeltha* 'beautiful', *Vvichtgata* [for **VVitgata*] 'white', BGoth. *þata*, *blind-ata*; Stearns, 1978, p. 103), contrasting with ON *-t*, OHG *-aȥ* <

[22] On the value of BGoth. ⟨ai⟩, ⟨au⟩, see the references and discussion in Miller (2019, pp. 39–43). The form **hailag** on the golden ring of Pietroassa (first half of 5th c.) appears to preserve PGmc. **ai* (Nedoma, 2010, pp. 29–31 & 43, 2017, p. 879), but the inscription may not even be East Germanic (Snædal, 2011b, pp. 238–242; cf. Miller, 2019, p. 7).

[23] See Jellinek (1926, pp. 45–46 & 85–86), Krause (1968, pp. 37 & 78–80), Marchand (1973, pp. 50–53), and Braune and Heidermanns (2004, pp. 31 §7[2] & 34 §12[1]).

[24] See Grønvik (1983, p. 46) and Bousquette & Salmons (2017, pp. 388–389) on Faroese and Modern German dialects. For other examples, see Kümmel (2007, pp. 159–161).

PGmc. *-*at*.[25] Pace Grønvik (1983, pp. 36–38), these endings cannot be reconciled by reconstructing PGmc. *-*atǭ*, and even if one wished to invoke the masc. acc. sg. as a model (cf. BGoth. *þana*, *blind-ana*, OE *þone*, *gōd-ne* < PGmc. *-*anǭ*), there are no grounds for projecting a variant *-*atǭ* back to the proto-Germanic stage.[26]

In the lexicon, most divergences can be understood as accidents of attestation and/or generalization of different proto-Germanic items.[27] Noteworthy are the apparent Verner's Law alternants in CGoth. *Alt* 'old', *Plut* 'blood' < PGmc. **aldaz*, **blōđą* beside BGoth. *alþeis*, *blōþ* (GEN *blōþis*) < PGmc. **alþ-*, **blōþą* (Stearns, 1978, p. 113) and retention in CGoth. *geen* 'go' of a reflex of PGmc. **gai-* ~ **gā-* < **gaji-* ~ **gaja-* < (post-) PIE **ĝʱh₁-i̯é/ó-*.[28] The coexistence of this present stem and BGoth. *gaggan* is paralleled in West Germanic (OE, OFris., OS *gān*, OHG *gān* ~ *gēn* beside OE, OS, OHG *gangan*, OFris. *ganga*), as well as North Germanic (OSwed., ODan. *gā* vs. OIcel. *ganga*).[29]

In sum, the available evidence argues against identification of Crimean Gothic with Northwest Germanic and in favor of a close relationship with Bible Gothic.[30] The few sound changes shared by Bible Gothic and Crimean Gothic are either retentions (PGmc. **ē* > BGoth. *ē*, late *ī*, CGoth. *i*) or not especially unusual (PGmc. **jj* > BGoth. *ddj*, CGoth. *d*), but pronominal neut. nom./acc. sg. -*ata* is almost certainly a common innovation. Since Crimean Gothic escaped the Bible Gothic merger of PGmc. **e* and **i*, the ordered sequence of monophthongization of **ai*, **au* followed by raising of **ē*, **ō* must have spread across already distinct dialects.[31]

---

[25] The preterite verb forms *VVarthata* 'you, he made' and *Malthata* 'I say' (recte: 'I said') are also generally interpreted as containing the neut. acc. sg. pron. **ita* or **þata* (cf. BGoth. *ita*, *þata*; Stearns, 1978, pp. 102, 106, 114–115).

[26] Thus Nielsen (1986, p. 66). See also Stearns (1978, pp. 114 & 119) and Ganina (2011, p. 226).

[27] See Stearns (1978, pp. 115–117) and Ganina (2011, pp. 227–229).

[28] See Thórhallsdóttir (1993, pp. 35–37) and Ringe (2017, p. 295) pace Seebold (1970, p. 216) and Bammesberger (1986, p. 116), who set up a full-grade **gǣ-ja-* (**gē-ja-*).

[29] See Stearns (1978, pp. 116–117), despite the doubts of Grønvik (1983, p. 60) and Ganina (2011, pp. 123–124).

[30] Cf. Krause (1968, p. 25), Molinari (1975, pp. 116–118), Stearns (1978, pp. 118–120), van Bree (2016, pp. 38–39), Nedoma (2017, p. 880 'a late EGmc. dialect'), and Miller (2019, p. 6).

[31] Even under the West Germanic hypothesis of Crimean Gothic, this parallel development would hardly have to be ascribed to 'later Gothic/CG contact' (pace Nielsen, 1986, p. 66).

What does not emerge from this discussion is whether these few shared innovations suffice to posit an East Germanic clade comprising Bible Gothic, Crimean Gothic, and perhaps other languages of the early centuries AD. To answer that question, we must now turn to the fragmentary records of Vandalic (§5) and Burgundian (§6).

5 Vandalic

Hartmann (2020), building upon Wrede (1886), Francovich Onesti (2002, pp. 133–202), Reichert (2009), and others, has provided an updated description of Vandalic together with statistical analyses of the development of individual proto-Germanic phonemes. As a result, it is now possible to list with some confidence the features of Vandalic and classify them along the same lines as for Crimean Gothic in §4.[32]

a. Archaisms:

1. Retention of PGmc. **z*
   See the various forms in *Gais-*, *Geis-*, *Ges-*, *Gis-*, Γειζ-, Γεζ-, Γιζ-, etc. < PGmc. **gaiza-* 'spear' (Hartmann, 2020, pp. 75–77 & 129).
2. Retention of PGmc. **ai*, **au* (see no. 11)
   Cf. *Gais-* < PGmc. **gaiza-* 'spear', *Baudus*, [*M*]*ero-baudes* < PGmc. **bauđa-* 'master'. Proper names such as *Gaisericus* were thus not Gothic proper, since the proto-Germanic diphthongs were monophthongized in Bible Gothic; furthermore, the form *eils* 'hail!' < PGmc. **hailaz* supports the identification of the so-called Gothic epigram as Vandalic.
3. Raising of **i* < PGmc. **e* in unstressed position and before **i*
   Both changes are attested in *Sigis-teus* < PGmc. (**segaz-* ~) **sigiz-* 'victory'; for raising in unstressed position, see also *Agis-ild* < PGmc. (**agaz-* ~) **agiz-* 'fear', for raising before **i*, the famous name *Stilic*(*h*)*o* < **stel-ik-an-*.[33]

[32] Most of these have also been identified by Francovich Onesti (2013, pp. 188–191); the few disagreements are marked below. The discussion of Reichert (2009, pp. 89–115) is undermined by his assumption that 'Wandalisch-Gotisch' and Bible Gothic were essentially identical, i.e., the Vandals spoke 'ein ziemlich reines Gotisch' (115).

[33] Variants in *stel-* do occur, but are far outnumbered by those in *stil*(*l*)-; of the 58 inscriptional tokens listed by Hartmann (2020, pp. 29–31) that preserve the vowel, 51 contain ⟨i⟩. 'Victory' and 'fear' have been remodeled in all Germanic languages, but the reflexes clearly point to original *z*-stems; see Ringe (2017, pp. 310–311).

Although these forms do not prove retention of *e ~ *i allophony, they do support a proto-Germanic date for raising, since Bible Gothic has eliminated the phonemic contrast of *e and *i (see n. 7). Pace Francovich Onesti (2013, p. 189), the distribution of Vand. ⟨e⟩ and ⟨i⟩ does not support a Bible Gothic-style merger and redistribution; see the statistical analysis of Hartmann (2020, pp. 35–41).

b. Typologically common changes shared with other Germanic languages:

4. Devoicing of word-final obstruents
Attested for PGmc. **z* and **đ* [ð], cf. *-geis* < PGmc. **-gaizaz* 'spear', *-mut*, *-muth* [-muːθ] < PGmc. **-mōđaz* 'mind, anger' (Hartmann, 2020, pp. 99–100, 112–113, 118).
5. Apocope of final vowels
6. Loss of **-z*
Evidence for these changes comes from names which have lost their final syllable, e.g., those in *-geis*, *-uult*, *-ric* (*-ricc*, *-rich*, -ρικ, -ριχ) for PGmc. **-gaizaz* 'spear', **-wulþuz* 'glory', **-rīkaz* 'ruler'.[34] Forms such as *Hildeguns*, *Th*[*ra*]*sa-muns* ~ *Thrasa-muds* < PGmc. **-gunþiz* 'battle', **-mundaz* 'protection' and *eils* < PGmc. **hailaz* show that apocope occurred first.
7. Debuccalization of PGmc. **h* [x] > [h] and loss
See Hartmann (2020, pp. 69–74, 80, 99); the data is unreliable, since *h* had been lost in contemporary spoken Latin (and long before in Greek), but note variants such as *Hildirix* ~ *Ilderich* (Jordanes) and *Ari-fridos*, *Aria-rith* < PGmc. **harja-* 'army', *eils* < PGmc. **hailaz*.[35]

c. Potentially shared innovations:

8. Nonlow reflex of PGmc **ē*
Vand. *ē* ⟨e⟩ is assured, e.g., in [*M*]*ero-baudes*, *-mer*, -μερ, *-mir* < PGmc. **mērijaz* 'famous'. On raising to *ī*, see no. 12.

---

[34] See Hartmann (2020, pp. 103–104 & 107). Francovich Onesti (2013, p. 189) notes that royal names on coins usually retain the ending, e.g., *Hildirix*, *Thrasamuds*, though we do find *Geilamir* (CCVan. 15) and *Gunthamund* (CCVan. 8); whereas inscriptions usually omit the *-s*, e.g., *Vilimut*, *Beremut* (Carthage), Φριδεριχ (Sitifis), *Gesiric* (Sufetula), *Sindivult* (Tipasa), but *Hildeguns* (Mactar). This distribution suggests that *-s* was associated with formal language, as does the restriction of *Hunirix* to official titles vs. *Huniricus* elsewhere in the history of Victor of Vita (Wagner, 1984, pp. 151–152, 2002, pp. 263–264).

[35] This change may, but hardly need reflect contact with spoken Latin or 'Romanisation', as claimed by Francovich Onesti (2002, p. 201, 2013, p. 191) and Hartmann (2020, pp. 73–74).

d. Changes attested in Vandalic but not (Bible) Gothic:

9. Medial *_ai_ > _a_ in PGmc. *_amaitijōn-_ > αμματ- 'ant' (?)
This innovation is absent from both Bible Gothic and Crimean Gothic (cf. CGoth. _Miera_ 'ant' with _(i)e_ < *_ai_); see Hartmann (2020, pp. 102–103 & 126).

e. Changes attested in (Bible) Gothic, but not Vandalic:

10. PGmc. *_ww_ > BGoth. _ggw_[36] in _triggws_ 'true, faithful', _triggwa_ 'covenant' < PGmc. *_trewwaz_, *_trewwō-_
Judging by _triova_ < PGmc. *_trewwō-_, Holtzmann's Law did not apply to *_ww_ in Vandalic (Hartmann, 2020, pp. 101–102, 117).

f. Parallel innovations in Bible Gothic/Crimean Gothic and Vandalic

11. Monophthongization of _ai_ > _ei_ > _ē_ and of _au_ > _ō_ (see no. 2)
Hartmann (2020, pp. 46–55, 106, 108) shows that this was a change in progress, with monophthongization more frequent after ca. 550; cf. the variants _Gaisericus, Geisericus, Gesiric._[37]
12. Raising of _ē, ō_ > _ī, ū_
Cf. _-rid, -rit, -rith_ < PGmc. *_-rēđaz_ 'advice' (BGoth. _garēds*_ 'honest, proper'), _bluma-_ < PGmc. *_blōmō-_ 'flower' (BGoth. _blōma_) and see Francovich Onesti (2002, p. 196) and Hartmann (2020, pp. 42–43, 44–45, 105–106).
13. Weakening of unstressed vowels
Note fluctuation in the stem vowel of compound first members, e.g., _Gaise-/Geise-, Gaisi-/Geisi-_ < PGmc. *_gaiza-_ 'spear' or _Trasa-, Trase-, Trasi-_ < PGmc. *_þrasa-_ 'dispute' (Hartmann, 2020, pp. 90–94).
14. Voicing of word-internal *_þ_
Cf. _Fridi, Frid-, -frida,_ Φριδε- [frið-] < PGmc. *_friþuz_ 'peace' (Hartmann, 2020, p. 104).

---

[36] I assume that this spelling represented [ggʷ] (Kümmel, 2007, p. 160) or perhaps [ɣɣʷ], as [ŋgw] (Snædal, 2011a) would be phonetically unlikely as an outcome of *_ww_.

[37] See also Francovich Onesti (2002, pp. 196–197). Wagner (2002, pp. 264–265) concludes that diphthongs were retained in the high register of 'Wulfilan' church language, but this assumes identity of Vandalic and Gothic and is contradicted by the prayer formula _froia arme_ (see below).

The picture that emerges is comparable to that for Crimean Gothic, except that points of contact with Bible Gothic are even fewer.[38] The only potentially shared innovation is the nonlow reflex of PGmc. **ē*, if this is not, in fact, an archaism. Monophthongization and raising of mid vowels are paralleled in late Bible Gothic and Crimean Gothic, but probably occurred contemporaneously or in reverse order (**ē*, **ō* > *ī*, *ū*, then **ai*, **au* > **ē*, **ō*, i.e., a 'pull chain').[39] Voicing of medial **þ*, which along with final devoicing erased the contrast of /þ/ and /d/ outside word-initial position, may be shared with Crimean Gothic (cf. *Bruder* 'brother' < PGmc. **brōþer-*), but also occurred in Old English and North Germanic. Apocope and loss of word-final **-z* are found in West Germanic, as is retention of **ww* in **treww-* (cf. OHG *triuwa*), but these changes are of little value for subgrouping (Hartmann, 2020, pp. 121–123); the former also occur in sixth-century Ostrogothic names such as *Dumerit*, *Angelfrit*, *Ebremud*.[40]

Morphological isoglosses are few, since most of the data consists of proper names with patently Latin or Greek endings (Hartmann, 2020, pp. 88–95).[41] In the formula *froia arme* 'domine miserere' corresponding to BGoth. *frauja armai*,[42] nom. sg. *froia* shares the ending of BGoth. *-a* < PGmc. **-ō̄* and Ostrogothic names such as *Tanca* or *Merila*, but this is likely to be an archaism vis-à-vis OE *-a*, OHG *-o* < (post-)PGmc **-ǭ*.[43] 2sg. impv. *arme* < **armai* confirms that the Class 3 weak verbs had a stem in **-ai-* in the '*e*-forms', but whether this alternated with **-a-* as in BGoth.

---

[38] Cf. the assessment of Hartmann (2020, pp. 111–119).

[39] See Hartmann (2020, pp. 105–106, 116, 118–119), though I disagree that monophthongization 'seems unlikely … to occur independently' (116).

[40] See Wagner (1984, pp. 145–150, 2002, pp. 262–264), Reichert (2009, pp. 111–112), and Francovich Onesti (2013, pp. 189 & 190). The fluctuation in Ostrogothic *Triggva*, *Trigguilla* ~ *Triwa*, *Triwila* raises the possibility that occlusion of **ww* was variable in Gothic dialects, but Wagner (2003) argues that the spellings with *-w-* are hypercorrect for /gw/.

[41] Francovich Onesti (2002, p. 196, 2013, pp. 181 & 189) interprets the first element of *Vandalirice* 'ruler of the Vandals' as containing a gen. pl. ending matching BGoth. *-ē*, but this is highly uncertain (Hartmann, 2020, p. 89).

[42] See Tiefenbach (1991, pp. 259–265) and Hartmann (2020, p. 85); on the manuscript transmission, see Tiefenbach (1991, pp. 252–259 & 265–268). For Reichert (2009), who believes that PGmc **ai*, **au* were retained in spoken Gothic and Vandalic (90–95), the monophthongs must reflect local Latin pronunciation (112–115).

[43] On the complex prehistory of the *n*-stem nom. sg. endings, see Jasanoff (2002).

(3sg. *habaiþ*, 3pl. *haband* 'have') or was generalized as in OHG (3sg. *habēt*, 3pl. *habēnt*) cannot be determined. In the lexicon, the main agreement with Bible Gothic is *ia* 'and' in the Vandalic epigram, corresponding to BGoth. *jah*.[44]

6 Burgundian

The evidence has most recently been analyzed by Hartmann & Riegger (2022; hereafter HR); among their sources is the useful comparative study of Burgundian and Ostrogothic names by Francovich Onesti (2008; hereafter FO8). Once again, features are grouped according to their value for subgrouping.

a. Archaisms:

1. Retention of PGmc *z
   In addition to masculine names in *-s* < *-*z* (no. 6), see, e.g., *Gaisse-fredo* < PGmc. **gaiza-* 'spear'.
2. Retention of PGmc. **h* as [x] (?)
   A velar value is suggested by *Franno* < PGmc. **hraƀnaz* 'raven', which recalls Old French borrowings like *flank* 'flank' ← Franconian *[x]*lank-* (FO8 278; HR 53–54; cf. Ringe, 2017, p. 244; Stiles, 2017, p. 892).
3. Retention of nasality in PGmc. **anh*
   This remarkable archaism is attested in *Hanha-valdus* < PGmc. **hanhaz* 'heel' (FO8 278; HR 55 & 61–62). The spelling ⟨anh⟩ stands for [ã:h], which yielded /a:h/ in all other Germanic languages, e.g., Goth., OHG *hāhan* 'hang' < PGmc. **hanhanq̨*.
4. Retention of PGmc. **ai*, **au*
   See *Aisa-berga*, *Gaisse-fredo*, *Austerius*, *Baud-ulfum* < PGmc. **aizō* 'fear', **gaiza-* 'spear', **austrą* 'east', **bauđa-* 'master' (FO8 277; HR 55). Also, the runic inscription on the Charnay fibula (6th c.), if actually Burgundian, reads *uþfnþai* /unþafinþai/ 'may discover' with 3sg. subj. *-ai* < PGmc. *-*ai* (Nedoma, 2010, pp. 38–41, 43, 44).

[44] The exact interpretation and context of the epigram are much debated: see Scardigli (1974), Snædal (2009b), and Hartmann (2020, pp. 85–87), to which add Ganina (2008) and Kleiner (2018).

5. Raising of PGmc. *_e_ > *_i_ in unstressed position and before *_i_ (?)
The evidence is inconsistent, with variants such as _Gibica_ ~ _Gebeca_ ← PGmc. *_geƀō_ ‘gift’ arguing against a Bible Gothic-style general raising of *_e_ (HR 45–49; pace FO8 276). Names like _Leudis_, _Reudilo_ < PGmc. *_liuđiz_, *_reuđil-_ and _Aga-theus_ beside _Ale-thius_ < PGmc. *_þewaz_ ‘servant’ suggest that *_iu_ merged with *_eu_.

b. Typologically common changes shared with other Gmc languages:

6. Devoicing of word-final obstruents (?)
Cf. _Aga-theus_, _Gund-ulfus_ < PGmc. *_þewaz_ ‘servant’, *_wulfaz_ ‘wolf’, though their value is minimal given the certainty of Latin influence. HR (53) deem devoicing ‘unlikely to be a general rule’ in light of, e.g., _odofrid_ < PGmc. *_friþuz_, but these would not be exceptions if devoicing was followed by apocope.
7. Apocope of *_a_ in final syllables
Cf. _Conia-rici_, _Gudo-mar_ < *_kunja-rīką_, *_-marhaz_ (HR 51). The absence of forms with deleted vowel and retained consonant (like Vand. _eils_, _-guns_; see §5, no. 6) might imply that loss of *_-z_ preceded apocope as in West Germanic (Ringe & Taylor, 2014, pp. 45–46).

c. Potentially shared innovations:

8. Nonlow reflex of PGmc. *_ē_
Burg. _ē_ ⟨e⟩ is assured, e.g., in _Baldo-merus_, _Filo-mere_ < PGmc. *_-mērijaz_ ‘famous’, _Balda-redum_ < PGmc. *_-rēđaz_ ‘advice’ (FO8 276; HR 55 & 58).

d. Changes attested in Burgundian and/or Crimean Gothic, but not Bible Gothic:

9. Loss of PGmc. *_h-_
Cf. _Ari-gunde_ vs. _Anda-hari_ < PGmc. *_harja-_, although orthographic interference from Latin must be reckoned with (cf. HR 52, who consider the phenomenon to be ‘graphematic’).
10. Lowering of PGmc. *_u_ > *_o_ before *_a_
Attested, if inconsistently, including before consonants other than *_r_ (HR 49–50): cf. _Ebro-vaccus_ < PGmc. *_eƀuraz_ ‘boar’, _Gond-ulfus_ ~ _Gunda-harium_ < PGmc. *_gunþiz_ ‘battle’, _morgine-giba_ < PGmc. *_murginaz_ ‘morning’.

11. Raising of *ē > ī
    Attested in, e.g., *Wada-miris*, *Balda-ridus* < PGmc. **-mērijaz* 'famous', **-rēđaz* 'advice' (beside *Baldo-merus*, *Balda-redum*; FO8 276; HR 55).
12. Weakening of unstressed vowels
    This may be observed in compounds, e.g., *Balda-redum* ~ *Balde-radus* < PGmc. **balþa-* 'strong', *Vilie-meris* ~ *Vili-meris* < PGmc. **wilja-* 'will', *Frede-mundi* ~ *Fridi-gernus* < PGmc. **friþu-* 'peace' (FO8 277; HR 50–51 & 58).

In comparison with Gothic and Vandalic, Burgundian retains proto-Germanic diphthongs and, notably, nasality in PGmc. **anh*.[45] With them it shares loss of *h-*, raising of **ē*, variable apocope, and weakening of unstressed vowels, all of which could have occurred independently or spread by diffusion. Pace HR (59–60, 63, 65), there are no changes clearly shared with Bible Gothic, since conditioned raising of **e* > **i* is already proto-Germanic, and lowering of **u* > [o] could be, as well.[46] On the morphological side, both *ā*-stems and *n*-stems show a confusion of endings (respectively *-a* ~ *-o* and *-on*, *-o*, *-a*; HR 56–57 & 62), but the prevalence of hypocoristics in masc. *-a* and fem. *-o* (e.g., *Athala*, *Vulfie*; *Agano*, *Valho*; FO8 274 & 279) suggests that these are the *n*-stem nom. sg. endings matching BGoth. *-a* and *-ō*.

7 Conclusion: Doing Away with 'East Germanic'

We have seen that the phonological innovations linking Crimean Gothic, Vandalic, and Burgundian to Bible Gothic are extremely few: the reflex of PGmc. **ē* as a mid vowel vs. NWGmc. **ā*, which may rather be an archaism; and fortition of PGmc. **jj* > BGoth. *ddj*, CGoth. *ada* 'egg(s)'.

[45] This is 'probably the latest phonological innovation shared by all the attested Germanic languages, and as such it could have spread through an already well-differentiated dialect continuum' (Ringe, 2017, pp. 174–175). Additionally, HR (57) observe that the fluctuation of ⟨morgane⟩- and ⟨morgine⟩- could continue PGmc. **murgana-* ~ **murgina-* 'morning' (cf. BGoth. *maurgins* vs. OHG *morgan*; Ringe & Taylor, 2014, p. 19), but this could, of course, simply reflect weakening of unstressed vowels.

[46] See n. 7 and §4 no. 12.

Crimean Gothic also shares one morphological feature with Bible Gothic (pronominal neut. nom./acc. sg. *-ata*), which is consistent with a closer relationship between them, specifically with the view that Crimean Gothic is descended from an Ostrogothic variety (Stearns, 1978, pp. 118–120; Ganina, 2011, pp. 235–236). The raising of long mid vowels is shared by these languages, but, since it is late in Bible Gothic and Burgundian, it can, at most, be considered an example of diffusion or parallel innovation, as may monophthongization of PGmc. **ai*, **au* and weakening of unstressed vowels.[47] With these exceptions, the entire array of 'East Germanic' features is better labeled 'pre-(Bible) Gothic'; there is no way of knowing whether such idiosyncrasies as the phonemic merger of PGmc. **e* and **i*, shift of PGmc. **fl-* > *þl-*, Thurneysen's Law, masc./neut. gen. pl. *-ē*, or productivity of the adverb suffix *-ba* affected all 'Gothic' varieties, let alone the other languages traditionally ascribed to East Germanic.

I conclude that, in the current state of knowledge, East Germanic should be viewed not as a subgroup, but as a peripheral set of varieties that lost contact early on with the rest of Germanic and, therefore, did not participate in any of the Northwest Germanic innovations or later changes, such as umlaut, that diffused through the diversifying Northwest Germanic dialect continuum. Earlier doubts about the validity of East Germanic arose from the paucity of evidence from languages other than Bible Gothic, but recent research on Crimean Gothic, Vandalic, and Burgundian has established an actual basis for the conclusion that 'an East Germanic clade with a common protolanguage did not exist' (Hartmann, 2020, p. 120).[48]

This conclusion has three consequences. First, the label 'East Germanic' has no cladistic value and should, at most, be used as a cover term for the 'speech communities at the eastern rim of the Germanic-speaking area' (HR 66; cf. Hartmann, 2023, pp. 189–192), which, with the *Völkerwanderung*, diversified into a dialect continuum stretching across southern Europe and North Africa by the middle of the first millennium

---

[47] As already intimated by Jellinek (1926, p. 14); cf. Braune and Heidermanns (2004, p. 4: 'man wird vielfach mit jüngerer gegenseitiger Beeinflussung zu rechnen haben'). Wagner (2002) refers to these changes as 'spätostgermanisch' and raising of **ē* > *ī* and **ō* > *ū* as 'gemeinspätostgermanisch' (265[35]).

[48] This is now supported by the computational models of Hartmann (2023, pp. 186–187).

AD.[49] Out of this continuum emerged the varieties that became Bible Gothic, Crimean Gothic, Vandalic, and Burgundian, although they remained in contact—and perhaps shared in changes such as raising of long mid vowels—at least until the downfall of the Vandal and Ostrogothic kingdoms. Second, one should no longer force into the straitjacket of Bible Gothic other indirect evidence for spoken eastern Germanic of the early centuries AD, above all loanwords from and into neighboring languages such as Romance or Slavic. To take just one example, PSlav. **šelmu* 'helmet' (OCS *šlěmŭ*) ← Gmc. **xelm-* could not have been borrowed from BGoth. *hilms*, but this hardly excludes a source in another 'East Germanic' language.[50]

Finally, our finding implies that after the ancestors of the Goths, Vandals, Burgundians, and other 'East Germanic' groups migrated east of the Oder/Odra to the southern Baltic coast and Vistula valley in the final centuries BC, thereby losing contact with Northwest Germanic, they did not form a speech community of sufficient cohesion and duration for innovations to spread uniformly. This is not surprising in historical terms: archaeological records indicate that the Goths began moving to the southeast already in the second century AD as part of the Wielbark culture, and by the third century were playing a major role in the Chernyakhov culture on the Black Sea coast; while the Vandals, who were associated with the Przeworsk culture, undertook a separate migration to the southeast in the second century. Meanwhile, Northwest Germanic remained intact long enough to undergo several changes together, including those such as *i*-umlaut, that clearly spread through a differentiated dialect continuum (§1).

This convergence of linguistics and (pre)history will surely be welcomed by our honorand, who has long promoted interdisciplinary approaches to the linguistic prehistory of Europe and diversification of the Indo-European family.[51] The *Stammbaum* for Germanic that best fits the available data is thus:

---

[49] They thus offer an interesting parallel to Continental Celtic, which likewise encompassed a speech continuum including multiple dialect areas. See Eska, this volume.

[50] See Cercignani (1980, p. 209[11]) pace Pronk-Tiethoff (2013, p. 95: '[t]he word must, therefore, have been borrowed from West Germanic').

[51] See in particular Anthony & Ringe (2015).

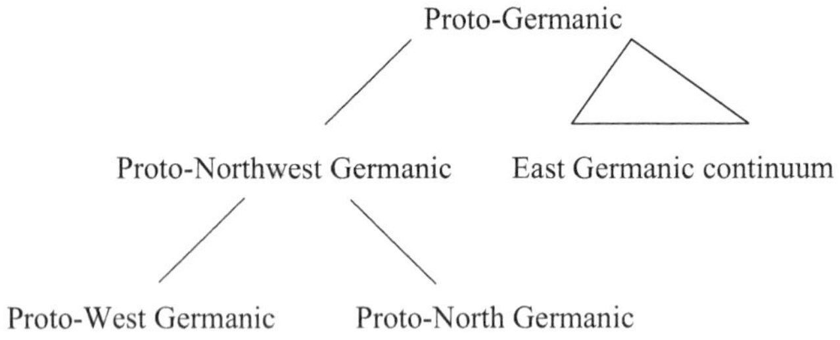

References

ANAE = Labov, W., Ash, S., & Boberg, C. (2006). *The atlas of North American English. Phonetics, phonology and sound change*. Mouton de Gruyter.

Anthony, D. W., & Ringe, D. (2015). The Indo-European homeland from linguistic and archaeological perspectives. *Annual review of linguistics, 1*, 199–219.

Bammesberger, A. (1986). *Der Aufbau des germanischen Verbums*. Winter.

Bousquette, J., & Salmons, J. (2017). Germanic. In M. Kapović (Ed.), *The Indo-European languages*[2] (pp. 387–420). Routledge.

Braune, W., & Heidermanns, F. (2004). *Gotische Grammatik*[20]. Niemeyer.

Campbell, L. (2021). *Historical linguistics. An introduction*[4]. The MIT Press.

Cercignani, F. (1980). Alleged Gothic umlauts. *Indogermanische Forschungen, 85*, 207–213.

Clackson, J. P. T. (2007). *Indo-European linguistics. An introduction*. Cambridge University Press.

Francovich Onesti, N. (2002). *I Vandali. Lingua e storia*. Carocci.

Francovich Onesti, N. (2008). Ostrogothic and Burgundian personal names in comparison. A contrastive study. In A. Greule, H.-W. Herrmann, K. Ridder, & A. Schorr (Eds.), *Studien zu Literatur, Sprache und Geschichte in Europa. Wolfgang Haubrichs zum 65. Geburtstag gewidmet* (pp. 267–280). Röhrig Universitätsverlag.

Francovich Onesti, N. (2013). Tracing the language of the Vandals. In *Goti e Vandali. Dieci saggi di lingua e cultura medievali* (pp. 179–195). Artemide.

Fulk, R. D. (2018). *A comparative grammar of the early Germanic languages*. John Benjamins.

Ganina, N. A. (2008). Inter eils goticum. In *Germanistika. Skandinavistika. Istoričeskaja poètika (k dnju roždenija O. A. Smirnickoj)* (pp. 43–51). MAKS.

Ganina, N. A. (2011). *Krymsko-gotskij jazyk*. Aletejja.
Grønvik, O. (1983). *Die dialektgeographische Stellung des Krimgotischen und die krimgotische* cantilena. Universitetsforlaget.
Grønvik, O. (1998). *Untersuchungen zur älteren nordischen und germanischen Sprachgeschichte*. Peter Lang.
Hartmann, F. (2020). *The Vandalic language—Origins and relationships*. Winter.
Hartmann, F. (2023). *Germanic phylogeny*. Oxford University Press.
Hartmann, F., & Riegger, C. (2022). The Burgundian language and its phylogeny. A cladistical investigation. *NOWELE, 75*, 42–80.
Heather, P. (1996). *The Goths*. Blackwell.
Hoenigswald, H. (1960). *Language change and linguistic reconstruction*. The University of Chicago Press.
Hoenigswald, H. (1966). Criteria for the subgrouping of languages. In H. Birnbaum & J. Puhvel (Eds.), *Ancient Indo-European dialects* (pp. 1–12). University of California Press.
Jasanoff, J. H. (2002). The nom. sg. of Germanic *n*-stems. In A. R. Wedel & H.-J. Busch (Eds.), *Verba et litterae. Explorations in Germanic languages and German literature (Festschrift for Albert L. Lloyd)* (pp. 31–46). Linguatext.
Jellinek, M. H. (1926). *Geschichte der gotischen Sprache*. De Gruyter.
Kim, R. I. (2022). Crimean Gothic *sada* 'hundred', *hazer* 'thousand'. *NOWELE, 75*, 81–94.
Klein, J., Joseph, B., & Fritz, M. (Eds.). (2017–2018). *Handbook of comparative and historical Indo-European linguistics*. De Gruyter Mouton.
Kleiner, Y. (2018). Another hypothesis concerning the grammar and meaning of *Inter eils goticum*. *NOWELE, 71*, 236–248.
Krause, W. (1968). *Handbuch des Gotischen³*. C. H. Beck.
Kümmel, M. (2007). *Konsonantenwandel. Bausteine zu einer Typologie des Lautwandels und ihre Konsequenzen für die vergleichende Rekonstruktion*. Reichert.
Leskien, A. (1876). *Die Declination im Slavisch-Litauischen und Germanischen*. Hirzel.
Loewe, R. (1896). *Die Reste der Germanen am Schwarzen Meere. Eine ethnologische Untersuchung*. Niemeyer.
Marchand, J. W. (1970). Gotisch. In L. E. Schmitt (Ed.), *Kurzer Grundriss der germanischen Philologie bis 1500 i, Sprachgeschichte* (pp. 94–122). de Gruyter.
Marchand, J. W. (1973). *The sounds and phonemes of Wulfila's Gothic*. Mouton.
Miller, D. G. (2019). *The Oxford Gothic grammar*. Oxford University Press.

Molinari, M. V. (1975). Considerazioni sul gotico di Crimea. *Incontri linguistici, 2*, 97–118.
Nakhleh, L., Warnow, T., Ringe, D., & Evans, S. N. (2005). A comparison of phylogenetic reconstruction methods on an Indo-European dataset. *Transactions of the Philological Society, 103*, 171–192.
Nedoma, R. (2010). Schrift und Sprache in den ostgermanischen Runeninschriften. In *NOWELE* 58/59 (= *The Gothic language. A symposium*, ed. H. F. Nielsen & F. T. Stubkjær), pp. 1–70.
Nedoma, R. (2017). The documentation of Germanic. In J. Klein, B. Joseph, & M. Fritz (Eds.), 2017–2018: ii 875–888.
Nielsen, H. F. (1986). Review of Grønvik (1983). *Beiträge zur Geschichte der deutschen Sprache und Literatur, 108*, 65–70.
Nielsen, H. F. (1989). *The Germanic languages. Origins and early dialectal interrelations*. University of Alabama Press.
Nielsen, H. F. (2017). The phonological systems of Bible Gothic and Crimean Gothic compared. In J. Krüger et al. (Eds.), *Die Faszination des Verborgenen und seine Entschlüsselung. Rāði sāʀ kunni. Beiträge zur Runologie, skandinavistischen Mediävistik und germanischen Sprachwissenschaft* (pp. 277–290). De Gruyter.
Penzl, H. (1972). *Methoden der germanischen Linguistik*. Niemeyer.
Pronk-Tiethoff, S. (2013). *The Germanic loanwords in Proto-Slavic*. Rodopi.
Reichert, H. (2009). Sprache und Namen der Wandalen in Afrika. In A. Greule & M. Springer (Eds.), *Namen des Frühmittelalters als sprachliche Zeugnisse und als Geschichtsquellen* (pp. 43–120). De Gruyter.
Ringe, D. (2012). Cladistic principles and linguistic reality. The case of West Germanic. In P. Probert & A. Willi (Eds.), *Laws and rules in Indo-European* (pp. 33–41). Oxford University Press.
Ringe, D. (2017). *From proto-Indo-European to proto-Germanic²*. Oxford University Press.
Ringe, D., & Eska, J. F. (2013). *Historical linguistics. Toward a twenty-first century reintegration*. Cambridge University Press.
Ringe, D., & Taylor, A. (2014). *The development of Old English*. Oxford University Press.
Ringe, D., Warnow, T., & Taylor, A. (2002). Indo-European and computational cladistics. *Transactions of the Philological Society, 100*, 59–129.
Roberge, P. (2020). Contact and the history of Germanic languages. In R. Hickey (Ed.), *The handbook of language contact²* (pp. 323–343). Wiley-Blackwell.

Rübekeil, L. (2017). The dialectology of Germanic. In J. Klein, B. Joseph, & M. Fritz (Eds.), 2017–2018: ii 986–1002.

Scardigli, P. (1974). Das sogenannte gotische Epigramm. *Beiträge zur deutschen Sprache und Literatur, 96*, 17–32.

Seebold, E. (1970). *Vergleichendes und etymologisches Wörterbuch der germanischen starken Verben*. Mouton.

Snædal, M. (2009a). Ostgermanische Morphologie. *Chatreššar, 10*, 147–167.

Snædal, M. (2009b). The 'Vandal' epigram. In F. D. Raschellà, F. Ferrari, & V. Micillo (Eds.), *Lingua e cultura dei Goti* (pp. 181–214). Prometheus.

Snædal, M. (2011a). Gothic <ggw>. *Studia linguistica Universitatis Iagellonicae Cracoviensis, 128*, 145–154.

Snædal, M. (2011b). The runic inscriptions from Kovel and Pietroassa. In P. Lendinara, F. D. Raschellà, & M. Dallapiazza (Eds.), *Saggi in onore di Piergiuseppe Scardigli* (pp. 233–243). Peter Lang.

Stearns, M. D., Jr. (1978). *Crimean Gothic. Analysis and etymology of the corpus*. Anma Libri.

Stearns, M. D., Jr. (1989). Das Krimgotische. In H. Beck (Ed.), *Germanische Rest- und Trümmersprachen* (pp. 175–194). De Gruyter.

Stiles, P. V. (1985). The fate of the numeral '4' in Germanic (1). *NOWELE, 6*, 81–104.

Stiles, P. V. (2013). The pan-West Germanic isoglosses and the sub-relationships of West Germanic to other branches. *NOWELE, 66*, 5–38.

Stiles, P. V. (2017). The phonology of Germanic. In J. Klein, B. Joseph, & M. Fritz (Eds.), 2017–2018: ii 888–912.

Thórhallsdóttir, G. (1993). *The development of intervocalic* *j *in proto-Germanic*. PhD dissertation, Cornell University.

Tiefenbach, H. (1991). Das vandalische *Domine miserere*. *Historische Sprachforschung, 104*, 251–268.

van Bree, C. (2016). *Gotische grammatica. Inleiding, klankleer*^{2}. Universiteit Leiden.

Wagner, N. (1984). Zum *-s*-losen Nominativ Singular des Maskulinums im späten Ostgotischen. *Beiträge zur Namenforschung N.F., 19*, 145–154.

Wagner, N. (2002). Gaisericus und Gesiric. Zu *ai* und *au* im späteren Ostgermanischen und bei Wulfila. *Beiträge zur Namenforschung N.F., 37*, 259–270.

Wagner, N. (2003). *Triggvilla**, *Tragvila** und *Triwila**. Zu *-ggv-* : *-w-* in zwei Ostgotennamen. *Beiträge zur Namenforschung N.F., 38*, 275–279.

Wrede, F. (1886). *Über die Sprache der Wandalen*. Trübner.

3

Progress on Constructing Phylogenetic Networks for Languages

Tandy Warnow, Steven N. Evans, and Luay Nakhleh

1 Introduction

The evolutionary history of a collection of languages is fundamental to many questions in historical linguistics, including the reconstruction of proto-languages, estimates of dates for diversification of languages, and determination of the geographical and temporal origins of Indo-Europeans (Gray et al., 2009; Haak et al., 2015; Chang et al., 2015). These phylogenetic trees can be estimated from linguistic characters,

T. Warnow (✉)
University of Illinois, Urbana-Champaign, Urbana, IL, USA
e-mail: warnow@illinois.edu

S. N. Evans
University of California at Berkeley, Berkeley, CA, USA
e-mail: evans@stat.berkeley.edu

L. Nakhleh
Rice University, Houston, TX, USA
e-mail: nakhleh@rice.edu

J. F. Eska et al. (eds.), *The Method Works*,
https://doi.org/10.1007/978-3-031-48959-4_3

including morphological, typological, phonological, and lexical characters (Dunn et al., 2005; Nichols & Warnow, 2008; Calude & Verkerk, 2016; Goldstein, 2020, 2022).

There are many methods for estimating phylogenetic trees, including parsimony criteria, distance-based methods, and likelihood-based techniques based on parametric models of trait evolution, and the relative strengths of these methods and how they depend on the properties of the data have been explored using both real-world and simulated datasets (Ringe et al., 2002; Rexová et al., 2003; McMahon & McMahon, 2006; Barbançon et al., 2013). Yet it is well known that languages do not always evolve purely via descent, with "borrowing" between languages requiring an extension of the Stammbaum model to a model that explicitly acknowledges exchange between languages (Nakhleh et al., 2005; Atkinson et al., 2005; Boc et al., 2010; Nelson-Sathi et al., 2011; Skelton, 2015).

One graphical model that has been used explicitly for language evolution is composed of an underlying genetic tree on top of which there are additional contact edges allowing for borrowing between communities that are in contact (Nakhleh et al., 2005; Boc et al., 2010). This type of graphical model has been studied in the computational phylogenetics literature, where it is referred to as a "tree-based phylogenetic network" (Francis & Steel, 2015).

The estimation of phylogenetic networks is very challenging, both for statistical reasons (i.e., potential non-identifiability) and for computational reasons (see discussion in Cao et al., 2019); although tree-based phylogenetic networks are a restricted subclass of phylogenetic networks, there are still substantial challenges in estimating these phylogenetic networks, as discussed in Gambette et al. (2012) and Keijsper & Pendavingh (2014).

As difficult as it is to estimate a tree-based phylogenetic network, the estimation of a dialect continuum represents an even larger challenge, and the interpretation of a dialect continuum is also difficult (Nichols & Warnow, 2008; Jacques & List, 2019). However, at least for language families such as Indo-European, tree-based phylogenetic networks may suffice (Nakhleh et al., 2005) and hence are the focus of this chapter.

The inference of phylogenetic networks depends on the graphical model (i.e., tree, tree-based phylogenetic network, etc.) and also on the stochastic model of character evolution. Examples of relevant character evolution models include the Stochastic Dollo with Lateral Transfer model in Kelly & Nicholls (2017), which models presence/absence of cognate classes (i.e., binary characters) with borrowing, and a model for multi-state character evolution in Warnow et al. (2006), which also allows for borrowing. When the phylogenetic network is tree-based, we may seek to estimate just the genetic tree (i.e., the tree in the tree-based phylogenetic network) or we can seek to estimate the entire topology of the phylogenetic network itself, which would include the location of the contact edges.

In this study, we address the challenge of estimating the phylogenetic network topology under an extension of the model proposed in Warnow et al. (2006), which we will refer to as the WERN 2006 model to acknowledge the four authors of the model (Warnow, Evans, Ringe, & Nakhleh).

In the WERN 2006 model, the graphical model is a tree-based phylogenetic network so that the underlying genetic tree is rooted and binary and the non-tree edges represent contact between language groups and are bi-directional. Characters can evolve down the underlying genetic tree or can use one or more contact edges. However, if a character evolves using a contact edge so that a state is borrowed into a lineage via that contact edge, then the borrowed state replaces the state already in the lineage. Thus, every character evolves down some rooted tree contained within the rooted network. The WERN 2006 model includes numeric parameters that govern the probability of change, and these parameters depend on the type of character, which may be phonological, morphological, or lexical. While the phonological characters have two states, 0 and 1, indicating presence-absence of a sound change and 0 indicating the ancestral state, the other characters can exhibit any number of states on the languages and so are called "multi-state" characters. The WERN 2006 model allows for homoplasy in character evolution (i.e., parallel evolution or back-mutation, see Fig. 3.2), provided that the homoplastic character states are known (in other words, we know which character states can arise as a result of either parallel evolution or back-mutation).

Our WERN 2023 model modifies the WERN 2006 model as follows. First, under the WERN 2023 model, we allow for any number of homoplastic states, as long as these states are known in advance. We require that the probability of homoplasy for the root state be strictly less than 1 for all non-binary characters. We also allow for some characters to not exhibit any homoplasy, but the probability of a character being homoplasy-free is a parameter x that can be any value between 0 and 1 (i.e., $0 \leq x \leq 1$). The special case where $0 < x$ means that the probability of a random character being homoplasy-free is strictly positive; when this special case holds, we will be able to use this information fruitfully.

In this chapter, we show that we can estimate the unrooted topology of any WERN 2023 model phylogenetic network in a statistically consistent manner, provided that the cycles in the phylogenetic network are vertex-disjoint, which will ensure that the phylogenetic network is level-1 (Choy et al., 2004; Gusfield et al., 2004) and each cycle contains at least six vertices. The key to constructing these unrooted topologies is the inference of the unrooted quartet trees displayed by trees contained within the phylogenetic network, and these can be easily constructed from the fact that we have identifiable homoplasy. Finally, we also show that if homoplasy-free characters have positive probability, then we can identify the rooted topology of such a phylogenetic network.

The rest of the chapter is organized as follows. We begin with a high-level description of the new model we propose, followed by an algorithm for estimating the unrooted phylogenetic network and then an algorithm for rooting that unrooted topology. We state the theoretical guarantees for the algorithms, but leave the proofs in the appendix. We finish with a discussion of the implications for the theoretical results we provide, and the issues when trying to estimate these phylogenetic networks in practice.

2 Mathematical Foundations

This section introduces the basic mathematical concepts and results, but we direct the interested reader to Warnow (2017) and Gusfield (2014) for additional context.

3 Basic Terminology

The tree-based rooted phylogenetic networks N we consider are formed by taking a rooted binary tree T (with root r) and adding edges to the tree (see Fig. 3.1) so that no two cycles share any vertices. The edges within the rooted tree are directed away from the root toward the leaves, but the additional edges represent borrowing and so are bi-directional. To ensure

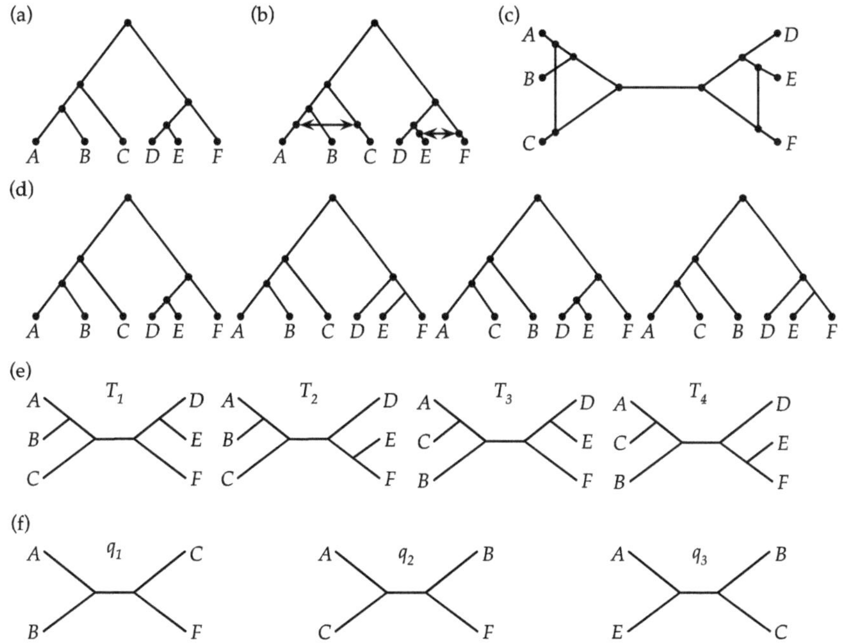

Fig. 3.1 Panel (a) shows a genetic tree with leafset *{A, B, C, D, E, F}*. Panel (b) shows the tree-based phylogenetic network formed by adding two contact edges to the genetic tree. Panel (c) shows an unrooted version of the rooted network in (b). Panel (d) shows all four rooted trees contained inside the rooted network from (b), with the first being the genetic tree from (a). Panel (e) shows the unrooted versions of the rooted trees in (d). Panel (f) shows three quartet trees; q_1 is displayed in T_1 and T_2, but not in T_3 or T_4; q_2 is displayed in T_3 and T_4, but not in trees T_1 or T_2; and q_3 is not displayed in any of these trees. Because q_1 and q_2 are each displayed by at least one tree in the network, the set $Q(N_r)$ of all quartet trees displayed by trees in the network N will contain both q_1 and q_2, but will not contain q_3

identifiability, throughout this chapter we will constrain the phylogenetic network topology so that the smallest cycle in the unrooted network has at least six vertices; for example, the unrooted network in Fig. 3.1(c) has two cycles, each with four vertices. Moreover, when we say that the phylogenetic network N is level-1, we will specifically mean that all cycles have at least six vertices.

We let S denote the set of languages for which we wish to construct the true phylogenetic network, N. We use linguistic characters to estimate this network and let $\alpha(L)$ denote the state of language L for character α. Recall that we say that a character exhibits *homoplasy* on a tree T if it is not possible to assign labels to the internal vertices so that the character evolves without back-mutation or parallel evolution (Fig. 3.2). Furthermore, every rooted network defines a set of rooted trees (Fig. 3.1) and every character evolves down one of the trees within the network. We say that a character evolves without homoplasy on a network if it is homoplasy-free on at least one of the trees inside the network; conversely, a character exhibits homoplasy on a phylogenetic network if it exhibits homoplasy on every tree within the network.

We can also consider the rooted trees in the network as unrooted trees, in which case they can be used to define quartet trees. Thus, we will say that the unrooted tree T displays a quartet tree $uv|xy$ if T has an edge e that separates leaves u, v from leaves x, y (see Fig. 3.1). The set of all quartet trees displayed by any tree contained inside the network N is referred to as $Q(N_r)$.

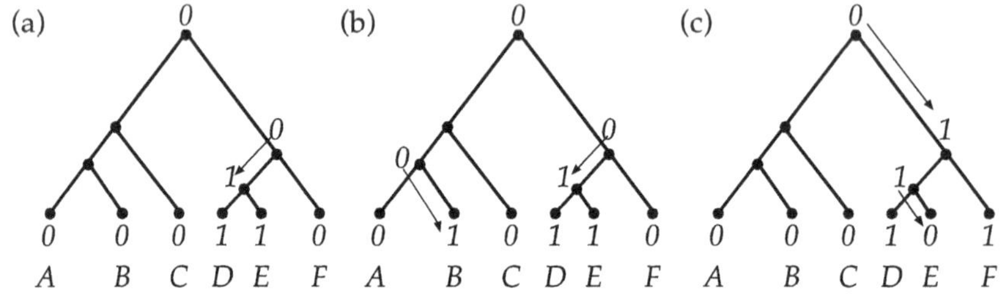

Fig. 3.2 Character evolution on a rooted tree. Panel (a) shows evolution without any homoplasy, panel (b) shows homoplasy due to parallel evolution (i.e., two 0→1 transitions), and panel (c) shows homoplasy due to back-mutation (note the 1→0 transition, where 0 is the ancestral state)

4 Constructing the Unrooted Network Topology

In this chapter, the phylogenetic network N consists of an underlying genetic tree on top of which there are borrowing edges, the cycles that are created have at least six vertices and are vertex-disjoint, and we assume that the characters evolve down N under the WERN 2023 model. Here we describe a method that is based on computing quartet trees for constructing the unrooted topology of the phylogenetic network.

4.1 *Quartet Tree Calculator* (*QTC*). Constructing $Q(N_r)$

We begin with a description of the *QTC* method (*Quartet Tree Calculator*) for computing quartet trees. Recall that we assume we know which of the states are homoplastic. Let α be a character and assume states 1 and 2 are both non-homoplastic. Now suppose that we have four languages a, b, c, d such that $\alpha(a) = \alpha(b) = 1$ and $\alpha(c) = \alpha(d) = 2$. Then, we add quartet tree $ab|cd$ to our estimate of $Q(N_r)$. We compute these quartet trees for every character α in turn, thus defining a set of quartet trees that we will refer to as Q, the output of *QTC*.

Theorem 1 *Let N be a rooted phylogenetic network, and let characters evolve down N under the WERN 2023 model, and let Q be the output of* QTC. *Then every quartet tree in Q will be in* $Q(N_r)$. *Furthermore, as the number of characters increase, with probability converging to* 1, *every quartet tree in* $Q(N_r)$ *will appear in Q. Thus,* QTC *is a statistically consistent estimator of* $Q(N_r)$.

The proof of this theorem is given in the appendix.

4.2 Quartet-Based Topology Estimator

We now present *QBTE* (*Quartet-Based Topology Estimator*), our method for constructing an unrooted network topology, using the quartet trees calculated using *QTC*. By Theorem 1, *QTC* will return $Q(N_r)$ with probability going to 1 as the number of characters increases. Hence, to estimate the unrooted topology of a phylogenetic network N, it suffices to use a method that can take unrooted quartet trees as input, provided that it is guaranteed to return the unrooted topology of N when given $Q(N)$.

A natural candidate is the algorithm from §7.1 of Gambette et al. (2012), which correctly constructs the unrooted topology of level-1 networks N given $Q(N)$, the entire set of quartet trees consistent with the network, and does so in polynomial time. However, $Q(N_r)$ is in general a proper subset of $Q(N)$, and so we cannot use the algorithm from Gambette et al. (2012) as is. Therefore, we have modified the algorithm, as we describe in Warnow et al. (2023) https://arxiv.org/abs/2306.06298. Hence, we propose the following two-phase technique to estimate the unrooted topology of N.

4.3 *QBTE*: Constructing the Unrooted Network Topology

- Construct a set of quartet trees Q from the input M character dataset, using the *QTC* method.
- Apply the modification of the algorithm from Gambette et al. (2012) provided in Warnow et al. (2023) https://arxiv.org/abs/2306.06298 to Q to produce an estimate of the unrooted topology of N.

Theorem 2 *The* QBTE (Quartet-Based Topology Estimation) *method is statistically consistent for estimating the unrooted topology of the network N under the WERN 2023 model when the rooted network N is a level-1 network where all cycles have length at least six; furthermore, QBTE runs in polynomial time.*

The proof is provided in the appendix.

4.4 *Root-Network*: Rooting an Unrooted Level-1 Network

Here we present *Root-Network*, a method for rooting an unrooted level-1 phylogenetic network. Thus, the input to *Root-Network* will be the unrooted network N and the set C_0 of homoplasy-free phonological characters that exhibit both states 0 and 1 at the leaves of *N*. If C_0 is empty, we mark every edge as being able to include the root, and otherwise we will process the edges to determine which edges are infeasible as root locations. At the end of processing all the homoplasy-free phonological characters, any edge that is not determined to be infeasible considered a feasible root location.

When an edge $e = (a, b)$ is used as the root location, it is subdivided through the introduction of a new vertex v_e so that the edge (a, b) is replaced by a path of length two containing two edges: (a, v_e) and (v_e, b). The vertex v_e is then the root of the tree that is produced. Since these characters in C_0 exhibit both states and because 0 is the ancestral state, making *e* contain the root is equivalent to saying that the state of v_e is 0 for every character in C_0. Hence, determining if v_e can be the root for a given character $\alpha \in C_0$ is equivalent to saying that v_e can be labeled 0 without losing the homoplasy-free property for α.

Root-Network determines which edges cannot contain the root by processing each character from C_0 in turn. All edges are initially colored green, and any edge that is discovered to not be able to contain the root for some character is colored red. Under the assumptions of the algorithm, at the end of the algorithm there will be at least one edge that is not colored red. The set of edges that are green constitutes the set of edges that can contain the root and will be returned by the algorithm.

Handling cut edges. An edge whose deletion splits the network into two components is referred to as a "cut edge." If *e* is a cut edge in the network, then it is easy to tell if it should be red or green. Removing a cut edge *e* splits the leafset into two sets, *A* and *B*. If any character exhibits state 1 on leaves in both *A* and *B*, then *e* must be colored red, and otherwise it remains green. We note that it is not possible for both 0 and 1 to appear on both sides of *e*, since that is inconsistent with homoplasy-free evolution.

Processing edges in cycles. All edges that are not cut edges are in cycles, and because we are working with a level-1 network, any such edge is in exactly one cycle. Here we show how to color the edges that are in cycles.

Let γ be a cycle in *N*, and assume it has *k* vertices. If we were to remove all the edges in the cycle, the network would split into exactly *k* components, since all cycles in N are vertex-disjoint. Consider a single character in C_0 and the states of this character at the leaves in each of the components defined for γ. We split the components into three sets: the set $A(0)$ of components all of whose leaves have state 0, the set $A(1)$ of components all of whose leaves have state 1, and the set $A(0, 1)$ of components where at least one leaf has state 0 and at least one leaf has state 1. Each vertex in γ belongs to exactly one component, and so we can label the vertices of γ according to the type of component they belong to (i.e., $A(0)$, $A(1)$, or $A(0, 1)$). We note that γ has at most one vertex labeled $A(0, 1)$, as otherwise the character cannot evolve without homoplasy. We use this to determine if we should recolor the edges in γ as follows:

- If there is one vertex in γ labeled $A(0, 1)$, then we color red any edge incident with a vertex labeled $A(1)$.
- If there are no vertices in γ labeled $A(0, 1)$, then we color red any edge both of whose endpoints are labeled $A(1)$.

We perform this processing for every character, thus recoloring some edges in γ red. Any edge that remains green throughout this process is returned by *Root-Network*.

Theorem 3 *Let N be the true unrooted level-1 network and let C_0 denote the set of homoplasy-free phonological characters that exhibit both* 0 *and* 1 *at the leaves of N. Rooting N on any edge returned by* Root-Network *will produce a rooted network on which all characters in C_0 can evolve without homoplasy, and the edge containing the true location of the root will be in the output returned by* Root-Network. *Furthermore, when given the unrooted topology of the true phylogenetic network as input,* Root-Network *is a statistically consistent estimator of the root location under the assumption that the probability of homoplasy-free phonological characters is positive.*

The proof for this theorem is in the appendix. As a corollary, we have:

Corollary 1 *The two-stage method of* QBTE *followed by* Root-Network *is statistically consistent for estimating the rooted topology of the network N under the WERN 2023 model, when the rooted network N is a level-1* *network without any cycles of size less than six and the probability of homoplasy-free phonological characters is positive. Furthermore, this two-stage method runs in polynomial time.*

The proof follows easily from Theorems 2 and 3.

5 Practical Considerations

We have described (1) *QBTE*, a method for constructing the unrooted topology of a level-1 phylogenetic network from characters, and (2) *Root-Network*, a method for rooting the resultant topology of the level-1 network. Each of these methods has strong theoretical guarantees of statistical consistency. However, these guarantees do not imply good, or even reasonable, accuracy on finite data, such as can occur when the input is of insufficient quantity or does not evolve under the assumptions of the theorems (e.g., down a level-1 network with known homoplastic states).

Therefore, we ask: *what are the consequences for estimating the network from real-world languages, given these caveats?* It is important to realize that the guarantees for the *QBTE* algorithm depend on *QTC* correctly returning the entire set of quartet trees $Q(N_r)$, as our modification of the algorithm from Gambette et al. (2012) depends on having this entire set for constructing the unrooted network topology. Moreover, *QBTE* also requires that the characters evolve down a level-1 network. Even if the assumptions of the character evolution are valid, so that the characters evolve down a level-1 phylogenetic network under the WERN 2023 model, some of the quartet trees in $Q(N_r)$ may fail to appear in the output from *QTC*, which will violate the requirements for *QBTE* to return a network. Furthermore, if the assumptions regarding character evolution are invalid, then some of the quartet trees produced by *QTC* may be incorrect (e.g., they may be quartet trees not displayed in the phylogenetic network). Finally, it may be that the characters evolve down a phylogenetic network that is more complex than a level-1 network. In each of these cases, the most likely outcome is that *QBTE* will fail to return anything.

Given the likely limitations of all three methods, we consider an alternative approach. Instead of estimating the unrooted network topology directly, we propose to estimate the unrooted genetic tree first, perhaps using quartet trees, then (if desired) root the genetic tree and add in the contact edges. For example, such an approach was used in Nakhleh et al. (2005) to produce a perfect phylogenetic network for Indo-European.

5.1 Genetic Tree Estimation (Heuristic)

- Step 1: Construct a set Q of quartet trees using the *QTC* technique.
- Step 2: Build a tree T for L from Q, using quartet amalgamation methods that construct trees on the full leafset from sets of estimated quartet trees; examples include ASTRAL (Mirarab et al., 2014), Quartets MaxCut (Snir & Rao, 2012), and Quartet FM (Reaz et al., 2014), which do not require that all the quartet trees be correct nor that the set contain a quartet tree for every four-leaf subset of the leafset.

Note that quartet amalgamation methods typically try to solve the *Maximum Quartet Support Supertree* problem, where the output is a tree that agrees with as many quartet trees in the input as possible. Because these quartet amalgamation methods will return trees even under adverse conditions (e.g., where many quartet trees have errors), this type of approach is guaranteed to return a tree T provided that the set Q of quartet trees produced by *QTC* contains quartets that cover the leafset. This condition is much easier to achieve than what is required for our level-1 network estimation method, *QBTE*. Moreover, when the quartet amalgamation method uses polynomial time (which is true of many such methods), this approach uses polynomial time. Hence there are several empirical advantages to this approach over *QBTE*.

6 Future Work

This study suggests several directions for future work. For example, we recognized practical limitations of *QBTE*, our proposed method for estimating the unrooted phylogenetic network topology: although it is provably statistically consistent under the WERN 2023 model, assuming that the phylogenetic network is level-1, in practice it may fail to return any network topology for a given input. Hence, it has limited practical use for analyzing real-world data. Therefore, the most important future work is to determine whether there are methods that are provably statistically consistent for estimating the topologies of these tree-based phylogenetic networks that are also of practical benefit. The approach we suggest of estimating the genetic tree first is worthwhile, but we do not yet have any proofs of statistical consistency for that estimation using quartet amalgamation methods.

Another technique that might lead to phylogenetic network estimation methods that are of practical benefit would seek to modify the algorithms used for *QBTE* so that they are guaranteed to return network topologies even when the conditions for exact accuracy do not apply. Such extensions could potentially be implemented by seeking level-1 network topologies that agree with the maximum number of input quartet trees.

Finally, another direction for future work is to determine whether more complex graphical models (e.g., level-2 phylogenetic networks) are identifiable under the WERN 2023 model, and whether level-1 phylogenetic networks are identifiable under character evolution models that are more complex than the WERN 2023 model. Future work is needed to explore these different possibilities.

Acknowledgments The authors wish to thank Don Ringe for the inspiration we experienced in working with him over these decades. TW also thanks the Grainger Foundation for support of this research.

7 Appendix

We restate and then sketch proofs for Theorems 1–3.

Theorem 1 *Let N be a rooted phylogenetic network, and let characters evolve down N under the WERN 2023 model, and let Q be the output of* QTC. *Then every quartet tree in Q will be in $Q(N_r)$. Furthermore, as the number of characters increase, with probability converging to* 1, *every quartet* *tree in $Q(N_r)$ will appear in Q. Thus,* QTC *is a statistically consistent estimator of $Q(N_r)$.*

Proof We begin by showing that every quartet tree placed in Q is also in $Q(N_r)$. Recall that quartet tree $uv|xy$ is included in Q if and only if some character α is found such that $\alpha(u) = \alpha(v) \neq \alpha(x) = \alpha(y)$ and the states $\alpha(u)$, $\alpha(x)$ are non-homoplastic. This character evolves down some tree T contained inside the network. Moreover, since the states exhibited at u, v, x, y are non-homoplastic, there is a path in T connecting u and v and another path connecting x and y and these two paths do not share any vertices. Hence, the quartet tree $uv|xy$ is in $Q(N_r)$.

We now show that in the limit, every quartet tree in $Q(N_r)$ is also in Q. Let $ab|cd$ be a quartet tree in $Q(N_r)$. Hence, there is a rooted tree T contained in N that induces this quartet tree (when T is considered as an unrooted tree). With positive probability, a character will evolve down T. Without loss of generality, assume a and b are siblings in the rooted version of T, so that their least common ancestor, $lca_T(a, b)$, lies strictly below the root of the tree T.

Since a and b are siblings, there is an edge e above $lca_T(a, b)$ within T. It follows that the probability that a random character evolves down T, selecting a non-homoplastic state at the root, and then changing on e, but on no other edge in T, is strictly positive. Note that for any such character α, we have $\alpha(a) = \alpha(b)$ and $\alpha(c) = \alpha(d)$ where $\alpha(a)$ and $\alpha(b)$ are different and both are non-homoplastic states. In such a case, Q will include quartet tree $ab|cd$. Thus, in the limit as the number of characters increases, with probability converging to 1, Q will contain every quartet tree in $Q(N_r)$.

Since in the limit $Q \subseteq Q(N_r)$ and $Q(N_r) \subseteq Q$, it follows that $Q = Q(N_r)$ with probability converging to 1.

Theorem 2 *The* QBTE (Quartet-Based Topology Estimation) *method is statistically consistent for estimating the unrooted topology of the network N under the WERN 2023 model when the rooted network N is a level-1 network where all cycles have length at least six; furthermore,* QBTE *runs in polynomial time.*

Proof By Theorem 1, we have shown that as the number of characters increases, we can construct $Q(N_r)$. Due to space constraints, we direct the reader to Warnow et al. (2023) https://arxiv.org/abs/2306.06298 for the rest of the proof.

Theorem 3 *Let N be the true unrooted level-1 network and let* C_0 *denote the set of homoplasy-free phonological characters that exhibit both* 0 *and* 1 *at the leaves of N. Rooting N on any edge returned by* Root-Network *will produce a rooted network on which all characters in* C_0 *can evolve without homoplasy, and the edge containing the true location of the root will be in the output returned by* Root-Network. *Furthermore, when given the unrooted topology of the true phylogenetic network as input,* Root-Network *is a statistically consistent estimator of the root location under the assumption that the probability of homoplasy-free phonological characters is positive.*

Proof We sketch the proof due to space constraints. It is straightforward to verify that an edge is colored red for a character α if and only if subdividing the edge and labeling the introduced node by 0 for α makes α homoplastic on every tree contained within the network. Furthermore, it is not hard to see that if we root the network on any edge that remains green throughout *Root-Network*, then all characters in C_0 will be homoplasy-free. As a result, the first part of the theorem is established.

For the second part of the theorem, if the probability of homoplasy-free phonological characters is positive, then with probability converging to 1, for every edge in the true network, there is a character α that changes on the edge, but on no other edge; hence, α will be non-constant and homoplasy-free. Let e_1 and e_2 be the two edges incident to the root, and suppose the input set of characters contains α_1 and α_2 homoplasy-free characters that change on e_1 and e_2, respectively, then these two characters will mark as red every edge below e_1 and e_2. In the unrooted topology for N, the root is suppressed and edges e_1 and e_2 are merged into the same single edge, e. Hence, when *Root-Network* is applied to the unrooted topology for N, if characters α_1 and α_2 are in the input, then the only edge that is not colored red will be the edge e containing the suppressed root.

In conclusion, since the probability of homoplasy-free phonological characters is strictly positive, as the number of such characters increase, the probability that every edge other than the root edge will be red will converge to 1. Thus, *Root-Network* will uniquely leave the single edge containing the suppressed root green, establishing that it is statistically consistent for locating the root in the network.

References

Atkinson, Q., Nicholls, G., Welch, D., & Gray, R. (2005). From words to dates. Water into wine, mathemagic or phylogenetic inference? *Transactions of the Philological Society, 103*, 193–219.

Barbançon, F., Evans, S. N., Nakhleh, L., Ringe, D., & Warnow, T. (2013). An experimental study comparing linguistic phylogenetic reconstruction methods. *Diachronica, 30*, 143–170.

Boc, A., Di Sciullo, A. M., & Makarenkov, V. (2010). Classification of the Indo-European languages using a phylogenetic network approach. In H. Locarek-Junge & C. Weihspages (Eds.), *Classification as a tool for research* (pp. 647–655). Springer.

Calude, A. S., & Verkerk, A. (2016). The typology and diachrony of higher numerals in Indo-European. A phylogenetic comparative study. *Journal of Language Evolution, 1*, 91–108.

Cao, Z., Zhu, J., & Nakhleh, L. (2019). Empirical performance of tree-based inference of phylogenetic networks. In K. T. Huber & D. Gusfield (Eds.), *19th International Workshop on Algorithms in Bioinformatics (WABI 2019)*, vol. 143 of *Leibniz International Proceedings in Informatics (LIPIcs)*, 21: 1–21:13. Schloss Dagstuhl–Leibniz-Zentrum fuer Informatik.

Chang, W., Hall, D., Cathcart, C., & Garrett, A. (2015). Ancestry-constrained phylogenetic analysis supports the Indo-European steppe hypothesis. *Language, 91*, 194–244.

Choy, C., Jansson, J., Sadakane, K., & Sung, W.-K. (2004). Computing the maximum agreement of phylogenetic networks. *Electronic Notes in Theoretical Computer Science, 91*, 134–147.

Dunn, M., Terrill, A., Reesink, G., Foley, R. A., & Levinson, S. C. (2005). Structural phylogenetics and the reconstruction of ancient language history. *Science, 309*(5743), 2072–2075.

Francis, A. R., & Steel, M. (2015). Which phylogenetic networks are merely trees with additional arcs? *Systematic Biology, 64*, 768–777.

Gambette, P., Berry, V., & Paul, C. (2012). Quartets and unrooted phylogenetic networks. *Journal of Bioinformatics and Computational Biology, 10*(04), 1250004.

Goldstein, D. (2020). Indo-European phylogenetics with R. A tutorial introduction. *Indo-European Linguistics, 8*, 110–180.

Goldstein, D. (2022). Correlated grammaticalization. The rise of articles in Indo-European. *Diachronica, 39*, 658–706.

Gray, R. D., Drummond, A. J., & Greenhill, S. J. (2009). Language phylogenies reveal expansion pulses and pauses in Pacific settlement. *Science, 323*(5913), 479–483.

Gusfield, D. (2014). *ReCombinatorics. The algorithmics of ancestral recombination graphs and explicit phylogenetic networks*. MIT Press.

Gusfield, D., Eddhu, S., & Langley, C. (2004). Optimal, efficient reconstruction of phylogenetic networks with constrained recombination. *Journal of Bioinformatics and Computational Biology, 2*, 173–213.

Haak, W., Lazaridis, I., Patterson, N., Rohland, N., Mallick, S., Llamas, B., Brandt, G., Nordenfelt, S., Harney, E., Stewardson, K., et al. (2015). Massive migration from the steppe was a source for Indo-European languages in Europe. *Nature, 522*(7555), 207–211.

Jacques, G., & List, J.-M. (2019). Save the trees. Why we need tree models in linguistic reconstruction (and when we should apply them). *Journal of Historical Linguistics, 9*, 128–167.

Keijsper, J. C. M., & Pendavingh, R. A. (2014). Reconstructing a phylogenetic level-1 network from quartets. *Bulletin of Mathematical Biology, 76*, 2517–2541.

Kelly, L. J., & Nicholls, G. K. (2017). Lateral transfer in stochastic Dollo models. *The Annals of Applied Statistics, 11*, 1146–1168.

McMahon, A., & McMahon, R. (2006). Why linguists don't do dates. Evidence from Indo-European and Australian languages. *In Forster & Renfrew, 2006*, 153–160.

Mirarab, S., Rezwana Reaz, M. S., Bayzid, T. Z., Shel Swenson, M., & Warnow, T. (2014). ASTRAL. Genome-scale coalescent-based species tree estimation. *Bioinformatics, 30*(17), i541–i548.

Nakhleh, L., Ringe, D., & Warnow, T. (2005). Perfect phylogenetic networks. A new methodology for reconstructing the evolutionary history of natural languages. *Language*, 382–420.

Nelson-Sathi, S., List, J.-M., Geisler, H., Fangerau, H., Gray, R. D., Martin, W., & Dagan, T. (2011). Networks uncover hidden lexical borrowing in Indo-European language evolution. *Proceedings of the Royal Society B: Biological Sciences, 278*(1713), 1794–1803.

Nichols, J., & Warnow, T. (2008). Tutorial on computational linguistic phylogeny. *Language and Linguistics Compass, 2*, 760–820.

Reaz, R., Shamsuzzoha Bayzid, M., & Sohel Rahman, M. (2014). Accurate phylogenetic tree reconstruction from quartets. A heuristic approach. *PloS One, 9*(8), e104008.

Rexová, K., Frynta, D., & Zrzavý, J. (2003). Cladistic analysis of languages. Indo-European classification based on lexicostatistical data. *Cladistics, 19*, 120–127.

Ringe, D., Warnow, T., & Taylor, A. (2002). Indo-European and computational cladistics. *Transactions of the Philological Society, 100*, 59–129.

Skelton, C. M. (2015). Borrowing, character weighting, and preliminary cluster analysis in a phylogenetic analysis of the ancient Greek dialects. *Indo-European Linguistics, 3*, 84–117.

Snir, S., & Rao, S. (2012). Quartet MaxCut. A fast algorithm for amalgamating quartet trees. *Molecular Phylogenetics and Evolution, 62*, 1–8.

Warnow, T. (2017). *Computational phylogenetics: An introduction to designing methods for phylogeny estimation*. Cambridge University Press.

Warnow, T., Evans, S. N., Ringe, D., & Nakhleh, L. (2006). A stochastic model of language evolution that incorporates homoplasy and borrowing. *In Forster & Renfrew, 2006*, 75–90.

Warnow, T., Evans, S. N., & Nakhleh, L. (2023). Progress on constructing phylogenetic networks for languages. *arXiv Preprint arXiv:2306.06298*.

Part II

Linguistic Reconstruction

4

Rethinking Stang's Law, with a Note on Gk. πότνια

Jay H. Jasanoff

1 Introduction

Stang's Law (Mayrhofer, 1986: 163–164) is the inner-PIE sound change by which pre-PIE word-final *_-Vu̯m(s)_ and *_-VHm(s)_ gave PIE *_-V̄m(s)_, with subsequent reduction of *_-V̄ms_ to *_-V̄s_.[1] In his original formulation of the rule (1965), Stang was chiefly concerned with the sequence *_-u̯m(s)_, and specifically with the acc. sg. and pl. forms of the words for 'sky' and 'cow' (Ved. acc. sg. _dyā́m_ (cf. Gk. Ζῆν), _gā́m_ (cf. Gk. (Dor.) βῶν), acc. pl. _gā́ḥ_ (cf. Gk. (Dor.) βῶς) for theoretically expected *_dyávam_ < *_di̯éu̯m̥_, *_gā́vam_ < *_g^{w}óu̯m̥_, *_gā́vaḥ_ < *_g^{w}óu̯m̥s_). The extension of the rule to *_-Hm(s)_ sequences, as in the _ā_-stem acc. sg. and pl. in *_-ah$_2$m_, *_-ah$_2$ms_ (> Ved.

Thanks to Ron Kim, Alan Nussbaum, and Patrick Stiles for helpful suggestions and corrections. All errors, of course, are my own.

[1] The simplification of *_-V̄ms#_ to *_-V̄s#_ is independently motivated; cf. Ved. nom.-acc. sg. _mā́ḥ_ 'flesh' < *_mḗm̥s_ beside _mām̥sá-_ 'id.' < *_mēms-ó-_ (Mayrhofer, 1986: 163[277]). On the basis of assumptions I do not share, Stang's Law is rejected altogether by Pronk (2016).

J. H. Jasanoff (✉)
Harvard University, Cambridge, MA, USA
e-mail: jasanoff@fas.harvard.edu

J. F. Eska et al. (eds.), _The Method Works_,
https://doi.org/10.1007/978-3-031-48959-4_4

-ām, *-āḥ*; see below), was very much an add-on to Stang's main discussion, taking up only eight lines. It is this 'laryngeal' part of Stang's Law, which we will call SL_H, that will occupy us here.

The correctness of SL_H for the acc. sg. and pl. of *ā*-stems (i.e., stems in **-eh₂-*) is beyond question. In the acc. sg., monosyllabic **-ām*, without a laryngeal hiatus or equivalent prosodic feature, is preserved in Indo-Iranian (Ved. *-ām*, Av. *-ąm*), Greek (-ήν, not *-ῆν or *-ῆ (as if < **-áHm̥*)), and Germanic (Goth., OHG *-a* (< bimoric **-ō^N*), not **-o* (< trimoric **-ō̄^N*)). Only in Lithuanian, where the ending is non-acute ('circumflex') *-ą*, as if from pre-Baltic non-acute **-ān*, and not shortened **-à* (**-ą́*) < acute **-ā̰n*,[2] does the ending look like it might have been contracted from disyllabic **-aHm̥*. But this is an illusion. The non-acuteness of the Lithuanian ending was probably taken over by analogy from the phonologically regular non-acuteness of the acc. sg. of *i-*, *u-*, and *o*-stems (*-į*, *-ų*, *-ą* < **-in*, **-un*, **-on*; cf. Jasanoff, 2017: 135–137). In the plural, monosyllabic nasalless **-ās* is preserved in Indo-Iranian (Ved. *-āḥ*, Av. *-å*), Germanic (Goth. *-os*), and Lithuanian (illative pl. *-ósna* < pre-Balt. **-ā̰s*).[3] Gk. -ᾱς/-ανς, copying the *o*-stem ending -ους/-ονς, is an obvious innovation.

2 Other Accusatives

When we move from *ā*-stems to *ī*- and *ū*-stems, the picture becomes more complicated. In Indo-Iranian, as is well known, there are two kinds of derived *ī*-stems, the so-called *devī-* and *vr̥kī*-types. *devī*-stems have an asigmatic nom. sg. and an ablauting proterokinetic suffix *-yā-/-ī-* < **-i̯eh₂-/*-ih₂-*; *vr̥kī*-stems have a sigmatic nom. sg. and an apophonically inert *-ī-* (*-i(y)-*) < **-ih₂-*.[4] Root nouns of the type *dhī́-* 'thought' follow the *vr̥kī-* pattern. Representative forms are the following:

[2] Cf. *ā*-stem instr. sg. *-a*, *-à*, with shortening and automatic denasalization by Leskien's Law, but *-ąja*, *-ąja* in definite adjectives. The ending in this case goes back to acute **-ā̰N*, apocopated from **-āmi*.

[3] The Lithuanian illative consists historically of an archaic form of the accusative suffixed by a postposition. The form of the Baltic (and Balto-Slavic) ending is a perennial topic of dispute. Kim (2019: esp. 14–16) gives an excellent overview.

[4] I follow the standard view that the laryngeal in *vr̥kī*-stems was **h₂*. Nothing will depend on this assumption in what follows.

(1)

	sg.	pl.	sg.	pl.
nom.	*deví* 'goddess'	*devī́ḥ*	*vr̥kī́ḥ* 'she-wolf'	*vr̥kíaḥ*
acc.	*devī́m*	*devī́ḥ*	*vr̥kíam*	*vr̥kíaḥ*
gen.	*devyā́ḥ*	*devī́nām*	*vr̥kíaḥ*	*vr̥kī́nām*
dat.	*devyái*	*devī́bhyaḥ*	*vr̥kíe*	*vr̥kī́bhyaḥ*

The accusative forms in the two declensions are conspicuously different. In the acc. sg., *devī́m* is the expected output of **-ih₂m* by SL_H, while *vr̥kíam* (< **-ih₂m̥*) stands as an apparent counterexample to the rule. Standard opinion takes the *-iam* of *vr̥kíam* to be analogical, restored from 'correct' **-īm* to **-iHm̥* (vel sim.) under the influence of the recurrent **-iH-* of the other case forms. In principle, there is no reason why this might not be true. But, logically speaking, the opposite could also be the case: if PIE **-ih₂m* had for some reason *not* been subject to SL_H, and had rather given **-iHm̥/-iam* by sound change, *-īm* could easily have been generated by analogy to the *ā*-stem ending *-ām*:

(2) nom. sg. *sénā* 'weapon' : acc. sg. *sénām* :: nom. sg. *deví* : acc. sg. ***devī́m.***

Under the latter scenario, the acc. sg. *vr̥kíam* would not have been remade to **vr̥kī́m* because its sigmatic nom. sg. (*vr̥kī́ḥ*) would have 'protected' it from the influence of the *ā-* and *devī*-stems.[5] The situation is similar in the acc. pl. Here the *devī*-ending *-īḥ* conforms to SL_H (**-ih₂ms* > **-īms* > **-īs*), while the *vr̥kī*-ending (*-iaḥ*) could have been analogically restored. On the other hand, if **-iaḥ*, rather than *-īḥ*, had been the phonologically regular reflex of the acc. pl. in **-ih₂ms*, there is almost no chance that this ending would have been able to survive alongside the nom. pl. in *-īḥ*; the identity of the nom. pl. and acc. pl. in *ā*-stems (nom. pl. *sénāḥ* = acc. pl. *sénāḥ*) would almost certainly have imposed *-īḥ* in the acc. pl., as well.[6]

---

[5] And indeed, the presence of an *-s* in the nom. sg. eventually came to be a synchronic 'trigger' for the non-application of SL_H even in descriptive *ā*-stems. We thus find, e.g., acc. sg. *pánthaam* 'path' (nom. *pánthāḥ*), *rathesṭhā́am* 'standing in a chariot' (nom. *-ṣṭhā́ḥ*), etc.

[6] Note that the nom. pl. in *-īḥ* is itself analogical. The *devī*-stem pattern nom. pl. *-īḥ* = acc. pl. *-īḥ* simply copies the *-āḥ* = *-āḥ* pattern of *ā*-stems.

The evidence of *ī*-stems in Indo-Iranian is thus consistent with the unmarked assumption that SL_H applied to all sequences of the form *-*VHm*(*s*), regardless of the identity of the vowel that preceded the laryngeal. But it is equally compatible with the possibility that only the non-high vowels **e*, **a*, and **o* triggered the rule. Why this more restricted formulation—'Limited SL_H', as we shall call it—should have a claim to our attention will emerge below.

The only other branch of the family with a relevant distinction between *devī*- and *vr̥kī*-stems is Greek. *devī*-stems are ubiquitous in Greek, where they productively make feminines to consonant stems of every kind, including active participles (-οντ-, f. -ουσα < *-*onti̯a* < *-*ont-ih*$_2$), *s*-stems (*-εh-, f. -εια < *-*ehi̯a* < *-*es-ih*$_2$), and various other formations (e.g., f. -αινα < *-*n̥i̯a* < *-*n-ih*$_2$). In theory, the acc. sg. forms of these stems ought to reveal the regular Greek treatment of the sequence *-*ih*$_2$*m*. But the phonological reflex of *-*ih*$_2$*m* in *devī*-stems, which could in principle have been either *-ῑν (with SL_H) or *-ια[ν] (without SL_H), was systematically replaced by analogical -$^{(j)}$αν in Greek, with -ν mechanically added to the -$^{(j)}$α of the nom. sg. (-ουσαν, -ειαν, -αιναν, etc.). Evidence for an acc. sg. in *-ῑν is probably to be seen in nouns of the type ἀκτίς, -ῖνος 'ray', ὠδίς, -ῖνος 'travail; pangs', γλωχίς, -ῖνος 'projecting point', etc. (Schwyzer, 1939: 465), where the accusative was taken as the starting point for the creation of a new oblique stem in -ῑν-. These, however, are the Greek counterpart of *vr̥kī*-stems, with -ῑς < *-*ih*$_2$*s* in the nom. sg. Nouns of this type, if they had not inherited acc. sg.'s in -ῑν directly from PIE, would have been under heavy pressure to acquire them by analogy to, e.g., the short *i*-stems (πόλις : πόλιν :: ἀκτῑ́ς : ἀκτῑ́**ν**).[7]

The remains of *ī*-stems in the other branches add nothing to the discussion. In Germanic, the *devī*-type is represented by words like Goth. *mawi*, gen. *maujos* 'girl' and *þiwi*, gen. *þiujos* 'maidservant'. These have been rebuilt in Germanic as *jō*-stems (i.e., *i̯ā*-stems) with a synchronically irregular nom. sg. in *-*ī*; their acc. sg.'s end in remade *-ja* < *-*jō*^{N}, as if < *-*i̯eh*$_2$*m*. The same treatment—extension of *i̯ā*-stem inflection to the accusative—can be observed in Celtic (OIr. *Brigit* 'Bridget' < *-*n̥tī*, gen.

[7] So too the root nouns (ϝ)ῑ̆ς, (ϝ)ῑ̆ν 'strength' (cf. Lat. *uīs*, *uim*), λῑ́ς, λῖν 'lion', and κῑ́ς, κῖν 'corn borer'.

Brigte < **-n̥t(i)i̯ās*, acc. *Brigti* < **-n̥t(i)i̯ān*), Baltic (Lith. *marti* 'daughter-in-law' < **-tī*, gen. *marčiõs* < **-ti̯ās*, acc. *mar̃čią* < **-ti̯ān*), and Slavic (OCS *bogynji* 'goddess', acc. *bogynjǫ* < **-ni̯ān*). The acc. pl. forms in these languages are equally uninformative.

In *ū*-stems, the forms of the accusative tend if anything to argue for the restricted version of SL_H. All *ū*-stems in Indo-Iranian pattern like *vr̥kī*-stems, with **-uu̯am*, not **-ūm*, in the acc. sg.:[8]

(3)		sg.	pl.
	nom.	*tanū́ḥ* 'body'	*tanúaḥ*
	acc.	*tanúam*	*tanúaḥ*
	gen.	*tanúaḥ*	*tanū́nām*
	dat.	*tanúe*	*tanū́bhyaḥ*

On the Iranian side, compare YAv. *tanuš*, acc. OAv. *tanuuə̄m* (also *-ūm* = *-uu̯əm*),[9] gen. OAv. *tanuuō*, dat. YAv. *tanuiie*, etc. Root nouns in *-ū-* follow the same declension: Ved. *bhū́ḥ*, *-bhúvam*, *-bhúvaḥ*; OAv. *fšᵊra-tuš* 'joy-strengthening', *-tūm* (= *-tuu̯əm*), *-tuuō*. It is noteworthy that there is no *ū*-stem analogue of the *devī́*-type in the oldest Indo-Iranian. Vedic forms of the type acc. *tanū́m*, gen. *tanvā́ḥ*, dat. *tanvái*, etc. only begin to appear in the later saṃhitās.

The *ū*-stems of Greek, many of which are root nouns, predictably pattern like ἀκτῑ́ς, with -ῡς in the nom. sg. and -ῡν in the acc. sg. (cf., e.g., χέλῡς, -ῡν 'turtle'; ἰχθῦς, -ῡν 'fish'; ὀφρῦς, -ῡν 'eyebrow'; σῦς/ὗς, σῦν/ὗν 'pig'). The acc. sg.'s in -ῡν seemingly conform to SL_H, but, like the accusatives in *-ῑν, are too easily explained by analogy to be of any probative value. Of mild interest are the variant Homeric acc. plural forms ἰχθύας, ὀφρύας, violating SL_H, beside normal ἰχθῦς, ὀφρῦς. These too, however, need not be anything more than analogical pendants to the corresponding nominatives (ἰχθύες, ὀφρύες).[10]

[8] Standing apart is the word for 'tongue' (Ved. *jihvā́-*, *juhū́-*; YAv. acc. sg. *hizuuąm*, gen. sg. *hizuuō*, etc.), probably pointing to an original hysterokinetic paradigm in **-u̯éh₂-/-uh₂-´* (EWAia 591–592).

[9] Cf. Hoffmann & Forssman (2004: 128). No great weight can be attached to OP acc. sg. *tanum*.

[10] Compare the similarly split picture in Italic, where Umbrian acc. sg. *sim* 'pig' < **sūm*, acc. pl. *sif* are at odds with Lat. *suem*, *suēs*.

The remaining IE branch with conspicuous *ū*-stems is Slavic. Here the declension is exactly the same as in Indo-Iranian:

(4)	sg.	pl.
nom.	*svekry* 'mother-in-law'	*svekrъve*
acc.	*svekrъvь*	*svekrъvi*
gen.	*svekrъve*	*svekrъvъ*
dat.	*svekrъvi*	*svekrъvamъ*

Although the possibility that Indo-Iranian and Slavic innovated separately cannot be logically excluded, the segment-for-segment match of OCS nom. sg. *svekry*, acc. *svekrъvь* with Ved. nom. sg. *śvaśrū́ḥ* 'id.,' acc. sg. *śvaśrúam* has the unmistakable flavor of an inheritance.[11]

3 Limited SL$_H$

In what follows, I will argue for Limited SL$_H$, i.e., the version of the rule that holds that pre-PIE **-eHm(s)*, **-aHm(s)*, and **-oHm(s)* gave **-ēm(s)*, **-ām(s)*, and **-ōm(s)*, respectively, while **-iHm(s)* and **-uHm(s)* were realized as **-iHm̥(s)* and **-uHm̥(s)*. The phonetic rationale for the difference in treatment between the two kinds of sequences would have been rooted in the well-documented lowering effect of guttural (= uvular, pharyngeal, and laryngeal) consonants on neighboring vowels.[12] A relevant process is found in Biblical Hebrew, where the vowels *ī* and *ū* develop an epenthetic *a* before a voiceless laryngeal [h] or pharyngeal [ħ] fricative in the same syllable: cf., e.g., *rūaḥ* 'spirit' < **rūḥ*, *mašīaḥ* 'messiah' < **mašīḥ*.[13] An inner-PIE tendency to realize the sequences **-iHm* and **-uHm* as [-i^{ə}Hm] and [-u^{ə}Hm], with a lowering or centralizing off-glide, would have made it less likely for a speaker to misparse the laryngeal in these groups as a

[11] So too *ljuby*, *-ъve* 'love', *žely*, *-ъve* 'turtle' (= Gk. χέλῡς), *kry*, *krъve* 'blood', etc. The forms *ljuby* and *prěljuby* in the expression *(prě)ljuby (sъ)tvoriti/dějati* 'commit adultery' are not *ū*-stem accusatives; pre-Slavic acc. sg. **-ūn*, like the **-ūn* (< **-ōn* < **-ōm*) of the gen. pl., would in my view have given OCS *-ъ*. For discussion and a new proposal, see Majer (2020: 94–97).

[12] See, e.g., Rose (1996), with references.

[13] Compare also the breaking of *-e-* to *-eo-* before *-h-* in Old English (e.g., **sehan* > **seohan* > *sēon* 'see'), although Old English lacks pharyngeals.

mora of length, and hence as an extension of the preceding vowel, than in the low-vowel sequence **-aHm* [-aHm], where there was no epenthesis.

We have now seen the ways in which the accusative ending **-m* and its plural **-ms* combine with laryngeal-final nominal stems. What has yet to be discussed is the verbal side of the picture: how present and aorist stems ending in **-VH-* interact with the homophonous 1sg. verbal ending **-m*. Unsurprisingly, the rule applies just as well in verbs as in nouns when the vowel before the laryngeal is non-high. Thus, in Indo-Iranian we find indicatives and injunctives of the type Ved. 1sg. aor. *ádhām* (: *dhā-* 'put'), *sthām* (: *sthā-* 'stand'), impf. *ádadām* (: *dā-* 'give'), *ā́śnām* (: *aś-* 'eat'), YAv. pres. inj. *daδąm* (: *dā-* 'put, give'), almost all with monosyllabic *-ām*.[14] Similar forms are found in Greek, although here there is no way to know whether the long vowel in, e.g., 1sg. aor. ἔστᾱν 'I stood', ἔγνων 'I recognized/know', or ἐμάνην 'I went mad' was 'acute', as predicted by SL_H (cf. acc. sg. -ήν), or 'circumflex', i.e., contracted across a laryngeal hiatus. A more interesting further case comes from Germanic. The origin of the Germanic dental ('weak') preterite is contested, but there is near-unanimous agreement that the ending of Runic Norse 1sg. *tawido* 'I made' and its congeners (cf. Goth. *tawida*, ON *-ða*, OHG *-ta*, OE *-de*) goes back to a proto-Germanic ending **-dō^N*, with the same bimoric final vowel as in the acc. sg. of *ā*-stems (cf. §1). Whatever the route by which it entered the weak preterite paradigm, the ending **-dō^N* can only have been taken from a 1sg. secondary form of **dʰeh₁-* 'put, do', such as a 1sg. impf. **dʰédʰeh₁-m* or **dʰédʰoh₁-m*, or an aorist **dʰéh₁-m*.[15]

Turning to the sequences **-iHm* and **-uHm*, a conspicuous case of the latter is found in the non-ablauting root aorist of the root **bʰuH-* 'become'. The underlying PIE 1sg. was **bʰuH-m*, continued in Gk. ἔφῡν (: 2sg. ἔφῡς, 3sg. ἔφῡ) and Ved. *(a)bhuvam* (: 2sg. *ábhūḥ*, 3sg. *ábhūt*). Between Greek and Vedic there can be little doubt as to which is phonologically regular and which is analogical. Given the existence of the pattern ἔστᾱν, -ᾱς, -ᾱ, a new 1sg. ἔφῡν could have been created in Greek at

[14] The one Rigvedic exception is *daam* 'I gave' X.49.1, from a verb (*dā-*) whose monosyllabic injunctive forms all have the property—not shared, interestingly, with the corresponding forms of *dhā-* 'put'—that they can be read disyllabically (2sg. *dāḥ* ~ *daaḥ*, 3sg. *dāt* ~ *daat*).

[15] The origin of the *o*-timbre is a separate and much-discussed issue. The case for a phonological development **-eh₁m* > **-ē^N* > **-ō^N* is made by Ringe (2006: 192–196).

any time. Ved. *abhuvam*, on the other hand, is synchronically isolated in its paradigm; it is not obvious how or why it would have replaced phonologically correct **ábhūm* if such a form had ever existed.[16] The simplest assumption is that the PIE syllabification was **b^huH-m̥*.

The best evidence for the treatment of underlying **-iHm* comes from the optative. The mark of the PIE optative was an ablauting suffix **-i̯eh$_1$-*/**-ih$_1$-*. The forms of interest for our purposes here are those in which the zero grade **-ih$_1$-* combined with the 1sg. ending **-m*. Such combinations would have been proper to the optative of Narten presents and other athematic formations where the root was consistently accented. Two conspicuous 'Narten optatives' are the Latin present subjunctives *edim*, *-īs*, *-it*, etc. (: *edō* 'eat' < **h$_1$ḗ̆d-*) and *uelim*, *-īs*, *-it*, etc. (: *uolō* 'want' < **u̯ḗ̆lh$_1$-*). Superficially, the appearance of *-im* rather than **-iem* (< **-ih$_1$-m̥*) in these forms would seem to argue for the traditionally assumed SL$_H$ development *-im* < **-īm* < **-ih$_1$-m*. But this impression is illusory. The *-im* of *edim* and *uelim* is probably analogical, with the same substitution of *-i-* for phonologically regular **-ie-* as must be assumed in any case for the 3pl. forms *edint*, *uelint* (for **edient*, **uelient* < **-ih$_1$-ent*).[17] A better approximation to the phonologically regular reflex of **u̯elh$_1$-ih$_1$-m* can be seen in the corresponding Germanic 1sg. forms, represented by Goth. *wiljau* 'I want' (2sg. *wileis*, 3sg. *wili*) and OHG *willu*/OS *williu*/OE (Anglian) *willo*. The starting point for these was a 1sg. opt. **u̯elh$_1$-ih$_1$-m̥*, which developed through a stage **welijun* to give PGmc. **wilju^N*. In Gothic this was lightly remade to *wiljau* by replacing the final **-u^N* by **-au^N*, the corresponding 1sg. opt. ending in thematic stems (see below). In West Germanic, the preform **willju* is commonly said to have been remade as a class I weak present in **-ju* < **-jō*. This is no doubt true in a synchronic sense; early West Germanic speakers who said **willju* would surely have analyzed the ending as that of a normal 1sg. indicative. But

---

[16] Nothing can be concluded from the corresponding forms in the other languages, notably Lat. 1sg. perf. *fuī*, with a new ending, and OCS 1sg. aor. *byxъ*, remade as an *s*-aorist.

[17] The same is true of the type *faxim*, *iussim*, etc.—historically the optative of a Narten desiderative *s*-present (Jasanoff, 2019: 18).

there is no need to posit an actual *refashioning* of **wilju*^{N} to **wiljō* (vel sim.), since PGmc. **wilju*^{N} would have given WGmc. **willju* directly.[18]

A further location where the vocalization pattern *-*ih*$_1$-*m̥* can be observed, albeit indirectly, is in the optative of the *s*-aorist in Greek. The status of the *s*-aorist at the PIE level is notoriously controversial. According to one view, the classically reconstructed *s*-aorist was a fully formed category in the protolanguage; according to another, it developed from an earlier 'presigmatic' paradigm after the separation of Anatolian and Tocharian from the rest of the family.[19] The question is not relevant for Greek, where it is generally agreed that by the time Greek left the family the *s*-aorist was a fully sigmatic Narten-ablauting formation of the type **u̯ḗǵ*^{h}-*s*-/**u̯éǵ*^{h}-*s*- (: **u̯éǵ*^{h}-'convey'; cf. Cyprian 3sg. ϵϝϵξϵ 'brought'). Such aorists would have had root accent with zero grade of the suffix in the optative (**u̯éǵ*^{h}-*s*-*ih*$_1$-). A few conservative forms of this type are actually attested in the Central Cretan dialect: 3sg. δικακσιε 'may judge', κοσμησιε 'may serve as *kosmos*' (Drerus, 7th c.), 3pl. ϝερκσιεν 'may perform' (Gortyn, 5th c.). The last of these is the phonologically correct reflex of the regular 3pl. **u̯érg*-*s*-*ih*$_1$-*ent*.[20] In the less straightforward case of the 3sg., the sequence -σιε is obviously not the direct continuant of *-*s*-*ih*$_1$-*t*. But this is because, as in the indicative (cf. 3sg. ἔλυσε, not *ἔλυς < *-*s*-*t*), Greek has substituted -ε for the zero ending that would have resulted from the loss of word-final *-*t*. The athematic 3sg. in -ε is never found in isolation; it is part of an alphathematic 'package' with two other endings, the 1sg. in -α and the 2sg. in -ας. It is safe to assume that the 1sg. corresponding to -σιε, even if unattested, ended in *-σια. This *-σια was the phonological reflex of *-*s*-*ih*$_1$-*m̥*, with the syllabification pattern mandated by Limited SL$_H$.[21]

---

[18] No light is shed on the original form of the 1sg. by OCS *po-veljǫ* 'I command' (2sg. -*iši*, etc.), likewise a remade optative.

[19] The Tocharian data are crucial on this point. For contrasting views, see, e.g., Ringe (1990) and Jasanoff (2019: 37–39).

[20] The later (4th c.) διαλυσιαν 'may dissolve'(?), if indeed an optative (cf. Bile, 1988: 235–237), would show the substitution of the 'normal' alphathematic ending -αν for older -εν.

[21] I no longer support the idea (Jasanoff, 1991: 117) that the *-α of *-σια and the -ε of -σιε were the PIE *h*$_2$*e*-conjugation endings *-*h*$_2$*e* and *-*e*, respectively. Outside the Cretan dialect, the -*si*- of these forms was replaced by -*sei*-. Exactly how this happened is disputed; see Rix (1976: 232–233) and Jasanoff (1991: 118–119) for different possibilities.

Surprisingly, perhaps, the syllabification *-ih$_1$-m̥ also has to be assumed for the best-attested optative formation of all, the thematic optative in *-o-ih$_1$-. An important discovery of the past half-century, due originally to Hoffmann (1976: 615[12]), is that the combination of the optative suffix *-ih$_1$- with the thematic vowel *-o- remained disyllabic in PIE. This is most clearly seen in the 3pl. forms:

(5) Ved. *bháreyuḥ* for *-eyan < *-ai̯i̯ant < *-o.i(i̯)ent < *-oïh̸$_1$ent (not *-ayan < *-oi̯h̸$_1$ent)[22]
Gk. φέροιεν < *-o.i(i̯)ent < *-oïh̸$_1$ent (not *-οεν < *-oi̯h̸$_1$ent)

While it is theoretically possible that Indo-Iranian and Greek could have independently restored the prevocalic diphthong from the rest of the paradigm (i.e., *-ayan → *-eyan/-eyuḥ; *-οεν → -οιεν), nothing of the kind happened in other Vedic paradigms of the same structure (cf., e.g., 3sg. *ábibhet* 'feared', pl. *ábibhayuḥ*, not *-eyuḥ). The matter is settled in favor of disyllabicity by the reflex of the thematic optative in Slavic. Optatives regularly yield imperatives in Slavic; cf. OCS 2sg. impv. *vedi* 'lead!' < *-ois, 3sg. *vedi* < *-oit (: pres. *vedǫ*). Forms of this type were accented on the final syllable in Late Common Slavic (*vedí)—showing, as I have argued elsewhere (Jasanoff, 2017: 186–188), that their pre-Slavic prototypes were trisyllabic (*u̯édʰoïh$_1$s, *u̯édʰoïh$_1$t).

The 1sg. of the thematic optative was thus made by adding *-m to disyllabic *-oïh$_1$-. In keeping with Limited SL$_H$, the resulting sequence was vocalized *-oïh$_1$m̥. No fewer than three languages attest to this syllabification:

(6) Ved. *bháreyam* < *-ai̯i̯a[m] < *-o.i(i̯)m̥ < *-oïh$_1$m̥
Gk. (Arc.) εξελαυνοια[23] 'I would drive out' < *-o.i(i̯)m̥ < *-oïh$_1$m̥
Goth. *bairau* < *-au^N < *-ajun[24] < *-aijun < *-o.i(i̯)m̥ < *-oïh$_1$m̥

[22] The corresponding Avestan ending (*-aiiən*) is ambiguous between *-ai̯i̯ant and *-ai̯ant, but Sogdian *-ēnd*, if not analogical, points to the former; cf. Tedesco (1923: 299–300).

[23] Elsewhere replaced by -οιμι.

[24] Intervocalic *-ij- ~ *-jj-, which would have led to *Verschärfung* after a stressed vowel (cf. Goth. *twaddje*, ON *tveggja* 'duorum' < *twaijō̄^{N}), was simplified to *-j- and lost when the preceding vowel was unaccented. The same development is seen in the corresponding 3pl. ending *-aina* < *-ajin- < *-aijin- < *-o.i(i̯)ent < *-oïh$_1$ent.

Perhaps owing to the relative frequency of these forms, the final sequence _*-Hm̥_ (< _*-h_1m̥_) came to be seen as an essential feature of the 1sg. optative in Indo-Iranian, leading to the extension of disyllabic readings even into the hysterokinetic optative 1sg. in _*-i̯ā́m_ < _*-i̯éh$_1$-m_, where Stang's Law would properly have applied. This may be the best explanation for forms like OAv. _x́iiə̄m_ 'I may be' (= Ved. _syā́m_), with disyllabic _-ə̄-_,[25] and Ved. _dheyām_ (_-yaa-_) 'I would put'.[26]

4 πότνια vs. δέσποινα

The discovery that Stang's Law did not apply to sequences of the type _*-iHm(s)_ and _*-uHm(s)_ has ramifications beyond the forms we have discussed so far. A well-known problem that can now be laid to rest is the relationship between the Greek words πότνια and δέσποινα, both meaning 'mistress'. Uncompounded πότνια is an inherited _devī_-stem, the cognate of Ved. _pátnī-_ and YAv. _paθnī-_ 'id.'. Within their respective traditions, πότνια and _pátnī-_ serve as feminines to the masculine _i_-stem _*póti-_ 'lord, master' (Gk. πόσις, Ved. _páti-_, Av. _paiti-_, etc.). The synchronically unmotivated _*-n-_ shows that the feminine _*pótnih$_2$-_ is inherited. But the selfsame stem _*pótnih$_2$-_, with a different phonological treatment, is also seen in δέσποινα < _*-poni̯a_ < _*-potni̯a_, properly a genitive + noun phrase _*dém-s pótnih$_2$_ 'mistress of the house', parallel to Ved. (nom. sg.) _pátir dán_, univerbated _dámpati-_ (cf. Gk. δεσπότης) 'master'. The reason for the twofold treatment—_*-tnii̯a_ in πότνια but _*-tni̯a_ in -ποινα—is a mystery. Word-final sequences of the form _*(-)CRih$_2$_ sometimes appear with what appears to be an epenthetic _*-i-_ in Greek; cf., e.g., μία 'one (f.)' < _*smii̯a_ for expected _*smi̯a_ < _*smih$_2$_, or the feminine agent nouns in -τρια (Myc. _-ti-ri-ja_, _-ti-ra$_2$_) < _*-trii̯a_ for expected _*-tri̯a_ < _*-trih$_2$_. The rule governing the putative epenthesis in these cases, however, is extremely difficult to pin down. The general phenomenon of _*-ii̯a_ seemingly taking the place of _*-i̯a_ is exhaustively, but inconclusively, surveyed by Peters

[25] Cf. Hoffmann & Forssman (2004: 71, 202). The scansion recurs in the 1sg. root aorist opt. _diiąm_ (ibid., 226).

[26] Cf. Jamison (1999) and Catt (2016, with literature), correcting my earlier advocacy (Jasanoff, 1991: 102) of a scansion _*dhaïyām_ < _*d^heh$_1$-i̯eh$_1$-_.

(1980: 127–286). For the specific case of πότνια : -ποινα, Peters discusses the possibility of a difference between formal/lento and informal/allegro speaking styles: 'epenthesized' *_-tnii̯a_, he suggests, may have been proper to formal speech, while *_-tni̯a_ (> *_-ni̯a_) was the corresponding fast-speech form (147). It is easy to see, however, that this is not really a solution at all. The metrical and formulaic profiles of the two words are not the same, but there is nothing 'formal' about πότνια or 'informal' about δέσποινα.[27]

In fact, the answer to the 'πότνια problem' is not phonological, but morphological. As we have seen, the productive types of _devī_-stems in Greek have phonologically regular nominatives (-ουσα < *_-onti̯a_ < *_-ontih_$_2$, -αινα < *_-n̥i̯a_ < *_-nih_$_2$, etc.) and analogical accusatives (-ουσαν, -αιναν = -ουσα, -αινα + -ν). δέσποινα conforms to this pattern: nom. sg. -ποινα < *_-poni̯a_ < *_-potni̯a_ is phonologically regular; acc. sg. -ποιναν is analogical (-ποινα + -ν). But this raises the question: what would have been the phonologically regular acc. sg. corresponding to nom. sg. *-ποινα? According to Limited SL$_H$, the expected reflex of *_pot-nih_$_2$_m_ would have been trisyllabic *_pótnih_$_2$_-m̥_, which would have given *πότνια (→ πότνιαν). If this was the origin of acc. sg. πότνιαν, as I would maintain it was, the obvious explanation for the nom.-voc. sg. πότνια is that it was a back-formation from the accusative.

The problem of πότνια thus opens the way to a new approach to the 'epenthesis' phenomenon more generally. Since virtually all the forms exhibiting the *(-)_CRii̯a_ treatment are _devī_-stems,[28] it is tempting to think that the difference between, e.g., an ordinary motivated feminine of the type δράκαινα 'she-dragon' (< *_-kn̥i̯a_ < *_-kni̯a_ (not *_-knii̯a_)) and the agent nouns in -τρια (< *_-trii̯a_ (not *_-tr̥i̯a_ < *_-tri̯a_)) had nothing to do with the precise formulation of a set of sound changes, but was rather a function of whether it was the original nom. sg. or acc. sg. that imposed its phonology on the final paradigm. A full exploration of this question would go beyond the bounds of the present discussion, but it promises to be a productive direction for further study.

---

[27] A fast-speech explanation for the specifically vocative (later also nominative) form πότνα, on the other hand—either as a syncopated form of πότνια or a cluster-simplified version of earlier *_pótni̯a_—would make excellent sense.

[28] The only conspicuous exception is τρία '3' (nt. pl.) < *_trih_$_2$, where many factors would have conduced to setting aside a phonologically regular *ταῖρα < *_tr̥i̯a_ < *_tri̯a_.

References

Bile, M. (1988). *Le dialecte crétois ancien. Étude de la langue des inscriptions, recueil des inscriptions postérieures aux IC*. Librairie orientaliste Paul Geuthner.

Catt, A. A. (2016). On the scansion of the sequence *-eyā-* in the Vedic root aorist optatives. *Journal of Indian and Buddhist studies, 64*, 1067–1073.

EWAia = Mayrhofer, M. (1986–2001). *Etymologisches Wörterbuch des Altindoarischen*. Winter.

Hoffmann, K. (1976). Prateritaler Optativ im Altiranischen. In J. Narten (Ed.), *Aufsätze zur Indoiranistik* (pp. 605–619). Reichert.

Hoffmann, K., & Forssman, B. (2004). *Avestische Laut- und Flexionslehre²*. Institut für Sprachen und Literaturen der Universität Innsbruck.

Jamison, S. W. (1999). Once more, yet again, the Vedic type *dheyām* revisited. Metrical marginalia to a persistent problem. In H. Eichner & H. Luschützky (Eds.), *Compositiones Indogermanicae in memoriam Jochem Schindler* (pp. 165–181). Enigma.

Jasanoff, J. H. (1991). The ablaut of the root aorist optative in Proto-Indo-European. *Münchener Studien zur Sprachwissenschaft, 52*, 101–122.

Jasanoff, J. H. (2017). *The prehistory of the Balto-Slavic accent*. Brill.

Jasanoff, J. H. (2019). The sigmatic forms of the Hittite verb. *Indo-European linguistics, 7*, 13–71.

Kim, R. I. (2019). North Slavic *-ě* vs. South Slavic *-ę*. A problem of forward reconstruction. *Journal of Slavic linguistics, 27*, 1–26.

Majer, M. (2020). Slavic **ljuby* and the heterogeneity of the inflectional class in **-y*. *Indogermanische Forschungen, 125*, 79–104.

Mayrhofer, M. (1986). *Lautlehre (Segmentale Phonologie des Indogermanischen)*. In *Indogermanische Grammatik* (Bd. I, pp. 73–181). Winter.

Peters, M. (1980). *Untersuchungen zur Vertretung der indogermanischen Laryngale im Griechischen*. Verlag der Österreichischen Akademie der Wissenschaften.

Pronk, T. (2016). Stang's Law in Baltic, Greek and Indo-Iranian. *Baltistica, 51*, 19–35.

Ringe, D. (1990). The Tocharian active *s*-preterite. A classical sigmatic aorist. *Münchener Studien zur Sprachwissenschaft, 51*, 183–242.

Ringe, D. (2006). A sociolinguistically informed solution to an old historical problem. The Gothic genitive plural. *Transactions of the Philological Society, 104*, 167–206.

Rix, H. (1976). *Historische Grammatik des Griechischen. Laut- und Formenlehre*. Wissenschaftliche Buchgesellschaft.

Rose, S. (1996). Variable laryngeals and vowel lowering. *Phonology, 13*, 73–117.

Schwyzer, E. (1939). *Griechische Grammatik i, Allgemeiner Teil. Lautlehre. Wortbildung. Flexion*. C. H. Beck.

Stang, C. S. (1965). Indo-européen **g^{w}ōm, *d(i)i̯ēm*. In *Symbolae linguisticae in honorem Georgii Kuryłowicz* (pp. 292–296). Zakład Narodowy im. Ossolińskich.

Tedesco, P. (1923). *a*-Stämme und *aya*-Stämme im Iranischen. *Zeitschrift für Indologie und Iranistik, 2*, 281–316.

5

The Sources of the *-*ono*- 'god' Suffix

Lionel S. Joseph

In the collection that follows, I will begin each suffixal class with the Celtic names in alphabetical order, followed by Italic names, and finally one Lithuanian and two Vedic names in the last section.

1 *n*-stem

(1) British *Abona* 'Avon' (Jackson, 1953, pp. 89 & 272; Zair, 2012, p. 215); derived from the *n*-stem so **abon-ā*, a thematized *n*-stem (pace Watkins, 1973, p. 80).[1] This is especially interesting because most of the examples that follow are **no*-stems.

I am grateful to Brian Drayton, H. Craig Melchert, Alan Nussbaum, and Michael Weiss for valuable discussions of this essay. Special thanks to Craig for guiding me through the turbulent waters of the Anatolian word for 'river'. Remaining opinions and errors are of course mine.

[1] Ptolemy [second century CE] knows of Αβος as the name for the River Humber, so **abonā* cannot be excluded. Watkins (1973, p. 87) compares Hitt. -*ḫapa*- in compounds.

L. S. Joseph (✉)
William James College, Newton, MA, USA
e-mail: lionel_joseph@alum.williamjames.edu

J. F. Eska et al. (eds.), *The Method Works*,
https://doi.org/10.1007/978-3-031-48959-4_5

Alan Nussbaum (personal communication, 16 April 2023) derives Italo-Celt. *_ab-_ from an archaic oblique pl. *_$h_2$ep-$b^{ɦ}$i(s)_ > *_$h_2$eb-$b^{ɦ}$i(s)_ to the root noun we have in Indo-Iranian (IEW 51). 'To the waters' and 'in the waters' would, of course, have been very frequently used forms of this word.

The second laryngeal is established by Anatolian: Hitt. dir. _ḫa-pa-a_ KUB 13.3 3.29, 32 (Watkins, 1973, p. 82)[2]; Cun. Luv. nom. sg. _ḫa-a-pi-iš_ KUB 35.108, etc. (thanks to Craig Melchert for this citation).

In addition to the Anatolian evidence, the initial laryngeal is confirmed by consistent lengthening in Sanskrit before *_-h_2p-_ as a second compound member—let one stand for many: _dvīpá-_ 'island' < *'having two waters around it' < *_dwi-h_2p-o-_. Many more examples at IEW 51.

I will not summarize the controversy over *_$h_2$ep-_ versus *_h_2e$b^{ɦ}$-_, especially since I do not control the Anatolian data. If there were an obvious way to reconcile these two forms in a single paradigm, it would have been published long ago. However, because Oettinger (2017) has recently proposed that what I call an n-stem was originally formed from the Hoffmann possessive suffix *_-$h_1$on-_ (formerly *_-$h_3$on-_; Hoffmann, 1955; Haudry, 1981), I will need to touch on his arguments. Oettinger (594) defines *_$h_2$ep-_ as '(fliessendes) Wasser', presumably as opposed to *_u̯od-r̥_ 'water as a substance' (my definition), a useful distinction which goes back to Meillet (1920).[3] Oettinger then reconstructs *_$h_2$ep-$h_3$on-_ '(fliessendes) Wasser habend', with the additional claim that *_ph_3_ became *_b_ in Anatolian, and by implication in Celtic, as well. That idea goes back to Hamp (1972). Now that we reconstruct the Hoffmann suffix as *_-$h_1$on-_, that explanation no longer holds water.

As Zair (2012, p. 215) points out, the only real evidence within Italo-Celtic for the sound change (voicing assimilation?) is OIr. _ibid_ 'drinks' < *_pi-ph_3-e-_: Lat. _bibō_ 'drink'. However, _-b-_ also occurs in this verb in Sanskrit and Armenian (EDLIL 72), making it likely that the sound change, if that is what it is, had already occurred in the parent language.

---

[2] This citation is important because 'river' is usually written with the Sumerogram ÍD.

[3] In his attempt to explain why PIE has two words each for 'fire' and 'water'. Thanks to Alan Nussbaum and Michael Weiss for this reference.

For our purposes, the input into Italo-Celtic would have been **abon-*, which could only have been interpreted as an *n*-stem in Celtic (and remade into an *i*-stem **abn-i-* in Italic, yielding Lat. *amnis* 'river').

(2) MW *Gwydion*, the hero of the Fourth Branch of the Mabinogi, is ambiguous. The name could continue **wition-o-* (derived from the oblique cases of a complex *n*-stem that we see in W *Iwerddon* 'Ireland' beside the old nominative *Iwerydd* < Brit. **īweri̯i̯ī* < **piH-u̯er-i̯i̯ō(n)* = OIr. *íriu* 'land, earth'; Jackson, 1953, pp. 385 & 472; Thurneysen, 1946, p. 212), or **witi-ono-*. For a slightly different analysis of *Iwerydd*, see Zair (2012, p. 107).

2 *o*-stem

(3) Gaul. *Belenos, Belinos*, associated with Apollo. While these names have been taken to mean 'bright, shining', I agree with DLG 72 that they are better understood as containing the root **bel-* 'strong'.[4] Since a simple thematic *Belos* is also attested, and is supported by Skt. *bálam* 'strength' RV+,[5] *Belenos* would appear to continue **bele-no-*. *Belinos* reminds one of Skt. *bálin-* RV+ 'strong', so **belin-o-* would be the 'strong one'. There is even a superlative *Belisama* 'strongest goddess', and Ptolemy refers to the estuary of the *Belisama* (Jackson, 1953, p. 266; variously identified with the Ribble or the Mersey), which establishes a Gaulish-British connection.

Since we have both a positive (*Belos*) and a superlative (*Belisama*), do we have any trace of a comparative? I would make the highly speculative suggestion that we do, in the name of Beli Mawr, the mythical ancestor of the folk of Gwynedd. His name is a close match with the Skt. comparative *bálīyas* 'stronger', though I would expect ˣ*Belidd* in Welsh given *pridd* 'clay' < *k^{w}*r̥̄́i̯at-s*, and anyway *-īyas* is not how Celtic makes comparatives. Still, the similarity is striking.

[4] A supposed connection to henbane has been firmly debunked by Prósper (2017).

[5] The older literature says that this is for **válam* and goes with Lat. *valor*, but I see no reason to accept this.

(4) Gaul. *Damona* (whether she is the goddess of oxen or deer; DLG 135).[6]
(5) Gaul. *Deuona* < Celt. **deiwo-nā*; cf. Celtib. **Teiuo**- (DLG 142–143).
(6) Gaul. *Epona* 'Horse Goddess' (67 attestations) can only be from Celt. **ekwo-nā* (DLG 163).
(7) W *Mabon ap Modron* 'divine son, son of divine mother' has to be *$mak^{w}o$-no-*, there being no root noun. Common Insular Celtic only had an *o*-stem *$mak^{w}(k^{w})o$-*, as Ogam gen. MAQQI shows.
(8) MW *Teyrnon* < **tigernonos* (Jackson, 1953, p. 279). The title was Common Celtic: OIr. *tigern* 'lord' *o*-masc., CIIC 206 TIGIRN with apocope (McManus, 1997, p. 107); Gaul. *Castrum Tigernum* (mod. Thiers). LÉIA T–63 connects the Iranian royal name Τιγρανης, which is probably related to the River Tigris.
(9) Lat. *Bellōna* 'war goddess'; both Pinault (1987) and EDLIL 70 reconstruct **duenelo-nā* with syncope (so EDLIL 73). However, the goddess has a long *-ō-* and, therefore, we will reconstruct *$*duenelo\text{-}h_1neh_2$* with the Herrschersuffix (Rix, 1981).[7] The Old Latin form of the genitive is attested as DVELONAI (SC de Bacch. 3; LEW i 100).

To call the war goddess the 'good (**dueno-*) goddess' is evidently apotropaic (like, at a lower register, calling the fairies the 'good folk'). 'Good god(dess)' is probably a universal: cf. Lat. *Bona Dea* and OIr. *Dag-da* 'Good God'.[8] For the **-l-* suffix in a divine name, cf. Thracian *Zemele* 'Mother Earth' < $*d^{h}\hat{g}^{h}em\text{-}el\text{-}eh_2$; Hitt. ^{DINGIR}*ḫapaliya-* 'river god' < $*h_2ep$-*el-i̯o-* (though EDLIL 73 prefers to see it as a diminutive in **duenelo-*). Cf. Hom. Νεφελ-ηγερέτα Ζεῦς 'Zeus the Cloud-Gatherer'.

[6] It is interesting that Bona Dea was also called Damia, and that the pregnant sow which was sacrificed to her was called *damium*. Only women could take part in Damia's mysteries, which reminds us of the special status of women in the Thesmophoria, sacred to Demeter Thesmophoros, part of which featured seeds being planted in the rotting remains of sacrificed pigs (Detienne, 1989). Both Bona Dea and Maia had their festival on May-Day (Scullard, 1981, p. 116), so it may be that they are two names for the same goddess.

[7] Formerly reconstructed with $*h_3$ like the Hoffmann suffix, of which it is a thematic derivative. Thanks to Michael Weiss for clarifying this point. The roots of the Herrschersuffix go back to Wolfgang Meid's 1955 Tübingen doctoral dissertation and his 1957 article based upon it.

[8] Other examples include Vedic Rudra-Śiva < *śivá-* 'kindly', which he hardly is as Śiva the Destroyer; the Furies becoming the Eumenides 'gracious ones' and receiving cult in Athens.

(10–11) Lat. *Faunus* (Enn.+) 'favorable/merciful god' appears to belong here, as does *Favōnius* 'West Wind', the harbinger of the favorable season of spring (Cato, *Agr.* 50.1) (EDLIL 205–206); root $*b^{ɦ}h_2u$- 'be favorable'. The connection with Lat. *favēre* was already made by the ancient authors (Bonnefoy, 1981/1992, p. 126), but LIV^2 148 prefer to derive it from $*d^{ɦ}eu$- 'run, hurry' (for extensive earlier literature, see LEW 464–466).

Faunus probably continues $*b^{ɦ}h_2$u̯o-no-. There are several possibilities for *Favōnius*; I prefer $*b^{ɦ}h_2$u̯o-$h_1$nio- based on the Herrschersuffix. OIr. *búan* 'good, favorable' = MW *bun* 'maiden, sweetheart' continue $*b^{ɦ}h_2$ou̯-no-/ā, similar to Umb. *fons* 'merciful' if < $*b^{ɦ}h_2$ou̯-ni-. For the semantics of W *bun*, cf. OLat. *favea* (Plautus) 'maidservant'.

(12) Lat. *Pōmōna*, the goddess of fruit, could belong here if her name is derived from *pōmum* 'fruit(-tree)', as seems likely (EDLIL 479). Formally, *Pōmōna* looks like she contains the Herrschersuffix $*\text{-}h_1n\text{-}o$- (formerly $*\text{-}h_3n\text{-}o$-) to make divine names (she is already on the list compiled by Meid, 1957).

I believe that she was the model for *Būbōna*, the Cow Goddess, uniquely attested in Augustine *De civ. Dei* 4.34 (soon after 410 CE). *Būbus* is attested at Tacitus, *Germania* 40. Although she does not appear to be old, *Būbōna* may show that new divine names with this shape could still be formed well into the Late Roman period.

(13) Lat. *Orbōna*, the goddess invoked for protection against/comfort after the loss of a child (Pliny, *Nat. hist.* 2.16) is, of course, derived from *orbus* 'bereaved', the 'orphan' word, so $*h_3orb^{ɦ}o\text{-}h_1neh_2$.[9] (Not discussed by Scullard, 1981.)

(14) Umb. **Vesuna**: Weiss (2010, p. 240) accepts Waanders' (2003) connection with *u̯etes-* 'year' and reconstructs *u̯etsōna* 'Lady of the (current) year'. A *u̯ets-o-* 'having one year' was specialized to mean 'yearling calf' in Ved. *vatsá-*, but Weiss argues convincingly that **Vesuna** is not a calf goddess, but a year goddess. We will reconstruct *u̯ets-o-h_1neh_2.

[9] *Juno Populōn(i)a* belongs here formally, but since we do not have evidence that she was a separate divinity, I do not list her as such. Cf. IVNONI REGINAE POPULONAE DEAE PATRIAE (CIL iii 1075).

(15) A related *s*-stem derivative may be the Latin goddess name *Angerōna*, whose festival day was 21 December, the 'narrowest' day of the year. Many cultures have special rituals to ensure that the days will stop getting shorter and shorter, so a goddess whose name referred to narrowness with the neuter *s*-stem attested in Ved. *áṁhas-* 'fear, distress', Lat. *angor* 'anguish; suffocation', and ultimately Germ. *Angst*, would make perfect sense (Weiss, 2010, p. 238[362]). *Angerōna* is depicted with her mouth bound shut (*ore obligato*; Scullard, 1981, p. 209); she knows the secret name of Rome, but will not reveal it![10]

3 *ā*-stem

(16) Gaul. *Sequana* 'Seine' (note that it comes from a '*q*-Gaulish' dialect).

(17) Lat. *Silvānus*, the god of woodlands (*silva*) and uncultivated lands generally. For all of these **-āno-*/*-ānā* god names, I reconstruct **-ā-* h_1*no-*/*-*h_1*nā*, an idea that can be traced back to Meid (1957), but which in its current form I owe to Alan Nussbaum (personal communication).

(18) Lat. *Volcānus* < **wolkā-*h_1*no-* (West, 2007, p. 268). West compares Ved. *Ulkā́* 'flame' (of Agni; RV 4.4.2); *Volcānus* would presumably be a vr̥ddhi derivative. Schrijver (1991a, p. 470) explains that this did not become **Valcānus* because it was Italic **welkāno-* when the sound change **#wo-* > *#wa-* operated.

4 **-ono-/ā* made to a consonant stem

(19) MW *Gofannon* < **gobann-ono-*, one of the sons of Dôn (see Evans, 1967, pp. 350–351; DLG 182; Blažek, 2008 for the many derivatives of this word for 'smith').[11] The geminate *-nn-* is almost always found[12]: e.g., *Gobannitio*, who tried to hold Vercingetorix back from rebelling against the Romans (Evans, 1967, p. 350); *Gobannilo*; also in the British place

[10] It may be Amor, Roma spelled backwards!

[11] On the magical powers of the smith god in early Irish tradition, see Carey (2019).

[12] The only exception to the geminate spelling that I know of is the Gaulish god name GOBANO (Bern; de Bernardo-Stempel, 2003, pp. 49–50 and Fellmann, 2004, pp. 747–748).

name *Gobannio* 'Smithy' (Antonine Itinerary; Thurneysen, 1946, p. 209), which survives in the Welsh place name *Abergafenni* (Hamp 1988).[13] For Old Irish, cf. *gobae* ⁊ *goibenn* (OM 665). Its presence in Insular Celtic argues against its being an instance of de Bernardo Stempel's (2010, p. 75) posttonic gemination in Continental Celtic. Gaul. instr. pl. GOBEDBI (Alise-Sainte-Reine) is presumably a parallel formation **gobet-* (so DLG 182 concludes) like **nemet-* 'sacred space', above. It is tempting to try to combine the two forms, and **gobat-no-* > *Gobanno-* would work for Gaulish, and may even be attested as a god name: DEO COBANNO (Fontenay-près-Vézelay; Blažek, 2008, p. 70) 'to the Smith God', but it will not work for British, as e.g., W *edn*, OCorn. *hethen* 'bird' < **pet-no-* show.

Based on Thurneysen (1946, p. 209), the assertion that *gobann-* continues **gobenn-* is often repeated in the literature (including Blažek, 2008, p. 67; DLG 182 reconstructs **goben-* without explanation). The rationale is presumably forms like the mythological name *Goibniu* and *Goibne Goba*, Corm. Y 83–84.975, which have palatalized /b^j/. However, as I have shown (Joseph, 1990), Goid. **a* developed a higher allophone before **-n#*, which had the properties of palatalizing a preceding consonant before it was lost by apocope, but without raising a preceding vowel (for an improved statement of this rule, see Schrijver, 1991b). McCone (1996) has accepted it and has further generalized it to both apocope and syncope of **a* /_**nC* (as here) and **ns*. Thus, the longer form of the word for 'smith' was uniquely **gobann-*, which could continue proto-Celtic **g*$^{(ɦ)}$*ob*$^{(ɦ)}$*-n̥n-* or **g*$^{(ɦ)}$*ob*$^{(ɦ)}$*-n̥d-n-*. Hamp (1988, p. 54) advances a very similar reconstruction: **g*$^{(ɦ)}$*ob*$^{(ɦ)}$*-n̥t-n-* (see Blažek, 2008, p. 71 for discussion).[14]

---

[13] For the geminate, cf. Hitt. *šiuanna-* 'divinus' (Watkins, 1973, p. 80), contrasting with Hitt. gen. sg. *šiunaš* 'of a god', Lyd. *ciwvali-* 'divine', both built on the Anatolian accusative **dyű́n* (Melchert, 2019, p. 243[15]). I do not know what to make of the *-nn-* in Gaul. *Cernunnos*, the Stag God (Watkins, 1999; Oettinger, 2017).

The only exception to the geminate spelling that I know of is the Gaulish god name GOBANO (Bern; de Bernardo Stempel, 2003, pp. 49–50; Fellmann, 2004, pp. 747–748).

[14] However, I recently (Joseph, 2023) made an extensive collection of Celtic *nt*-stems ($n = 42$), and none of them shows an unambiguous R(o); the u-diphthongs in **loukent* 'lightning' and *noudont-* (*Núadu*) are ambiguous, since they could continue **eu* or **ou*. I have changed my analysis of OIr. *snáthat* 'thread' (§22); I now believe that it continues **sn̥h*$_1$*-to-nt-* *'having spun [thread]', so it has no bearing on R(o).

I find it strange that the Irish female saint Gobnait (honored on 11 February according to the *Félire*) is not included in this discussion. She is a mytho-historical character who is supposed to have lived in the sixth century and whose church was in Baile Bhuirne, Co. Cork (where the ruins of an eleventh-century church still survive). She is the patroness of bee-keeping and ironworking, and when the grounds of her church were excavated, traces of an ironworking establishment were found. Given her name, which continues pre-Ir. **gobannantī*, she is probably a euhemerized smith goddess comparable to *Brigit bé goibnechta* (Corm. 8) 'Brigit woman of smithcraft', who was also the patroness of blacksmiths.

As Blažek makes clear, the problem with 'smith' is that there are too many possible etymologies. My personal opinion, and it is no more than that, is that the root is **g^hab-* with basic **a* and the rare, but real, phoneme **b*. Since I believe that PIE had primary **a/o* ablaut as well as **e/o* ablaut, **g^hab-/g^hob-* is not a problem for me so long as R(o) can be motivated. Within Italo-Celtic, I would compare Lat. *habilis* 'handy' with MW *geueil*, MBret. *gouel* 'smithy' (DGVB 177). In the best study of the unresolved question of whether final **-i* causes *i*-affection in British, Schrijver (1995, pp. 265–268) concludes that our strongest examples involve **e*, so Brit. **gobeli-* for *geueil*. Italic **habeli-* would, of course, fit *habilis* perfectly because of medial vowel weakening in open syllables (Weiss 2020, p. 126). A probable external cognate is Lith. *Gabie*, the pre-Christian fire god, discussed in detail by Blažek (2008, p. 75): 'Fire is called *ugnis* in the current language and in solemn speech *gabija*'.

While I have just argued for inherited **a/o* ablaut, there are at least two other possible explanations: one phonological and one morphological (Nussbaum, 2004; Vine, 2011), and I do not yet see a principled way to judge between them.

a. The phonological possibility is that in Italo-Celtic there was a phoneme /ɔ/ (whether from **a* or **o*) which developed into Italic **a* and Celt. **o* under some circumstances. Although the sample is miniscule, it is noteworthy that in all five of the pairs in which Celtic has *-o-* and Latin has *-a-*, Celt. *-o-* is always in a labial (i.e., rounding) environment: four pairs are well-known (Thurneysen, 1946, p. 51; Schrijver, 1991a, pp. 459–460), and I am proposing to add a fifth in *gobae*.

1. OIr. *muir* 'sea' : Lat. *mare*, neut. *i*-stem with initial *m*-.
2. OIr. *loch* 'lake' : Lat. *lacus*, neut. *u*-stem in early Irish, which provides the labial.[15]
3. OIr. *buide* 'yellow' : Lat. *badius* 'bay-colored', initial Italo-Celt. **b*-.
4. W *morwyn*, OCorn. *moroin* 'girl, maiden' < Brit. **morēnā* prob. < **mori-gneh*$_2$: Lat. *marītus* 'husband' < *'has the maiden'; outside of Italo-Celt., Lith. *Martì* 'girl; bride (who has not yet had children)' < **mor-t-ih*$_2$ (EDLIL 365).[16] For Vine's (2011, p. 266) morphological explanation, which I find very convincing, see below.
5. OIr. *gobae* 'smith': Lat. *habilis* as above, proposed root **g^hob-/g^hab-* ending in *-*b*.

Schrijver (1991a, pp. 475–476) tries to explain *lacus* by an unrounding rule **o* > *a* / l_CV attributed to the velar quality of **l*. However, as he himself acknowledges, the conditioning environment for this hypothetical sound change must be further restricted to / #l_CV because of *locus* 'place' < **stloko*- and *loquor* 'speak' < **tlok^w*-. Too ad hoc to be retained.

Two apparent exceptions, one of which involves a labial, can be readily explained: Celt. **karn*- : Italic **korn*- 'horn' simply show the two different outcomes of **k̑r̥n*- in the two branches. Galat. Κάρνον (Hsch.), Gaul. καρνυξ 'trumpet'; MW *carn* 'hoof', OBret. *carn* gl. 'ungula caballi', are all lautgesetzlich from proto-Celt. **kr̥n-o-/u*-, as is Lat. *cornū* 'horn' < **kr̥n-u*. MW *ascwrn*, OCorn. *ascorn* gl. 'oss', Bret. *askorn* lit. 'bone[-horn]' continue *o*-grade Celt. **ast-korn*- (EDLIL 136; EDPC: 190–191; Nussbaum, 1986; Schrijver, 1995, p. 53).

OIr. *maraid* 'remains' clearly corresponds to Lat. *mora* 'delay' (EDLIL 388), but *maraid* is a *tudati*-present **mr̥H-e*-; we see the effect of the laryngeal in Skt. *mūrtá*- 'congealed'. *Mora* continues **morH-eh*$_2$ (Schrijver, 1991a, pp. 110 & 216), so, as Schrijver points out, the laryngeal closes the syllable, preventing the sound change **mo*- > *ma*-, **wo*- > *va*- in an

[15] To my knowledge, OIr. *lacho*, *lachu* 'duck' (*n*-stem, as is shown by *lachnach* 'abounding in ducks') < **lakon*- has not been discussed in this context. While the duck as 'belonging to the lake' makes sense semantically, *lach*- rather than *loch*- would have to be explained.

[16] I will draw the veil of discretion over Skt. *márya*- 'young man' = YAv. *mairiia*- 'scoundrel, villain'.

open syllable (474).[17] Other examples include *mola* 'ground grain; grindstone' < **molh₁-eh₂* and *vorāre* 'swallow', *carnivorus*, which presuppose **gʷorh₃-o-/-eh₂*; cf. Lith. *gérti* 'swallow' with acute.

However, Vine (2011, pp. 267–283) offers a strong challenge to this proposed sound change, and suggests that the reverse may have been true: that, at least for **mo- > ma-*, the conditioning environment may have been a closed syllable.

b. A morphological possibility (Nussbaum, 2004, further developed by Vine, 2011) depends upon the recognition that the Italo-Celtic word for 'sea' originally had an acrostatic paradigm nom. **móri*, gen. *méri-s. This archaic paradigm was vulnerable to replacement by a 'neo-proterokinetic' paradigm **móri*, **mr-éis* or the like, which developed a Lindeman variant **mr̥réis* (or **mr̥rés*). Vine discusses the further development for such a sequence in Italic, but for our purposes, it is enough to say that it could have become *mar-*, which would then have been generalized throughout the paradigm, giving nom. *mare*. One advantage of this very plausible explanation is that it does not require new assumptions about the prehistory of Italo-Celtic phonology.

This line of reasoning also leads to a convincing explanation for Lat. *marītus* 'husband': Vine (2011, p. 266) starts from an acrostatic abstract **móri-s*, gen. **méri-s* 'youth', (except for its animate gender, a homophone of the neuter word for 'sea'). As he points out, *youth* 'young-ness' > *youth* 'young man' is straightforward. The same change of inflectional class as in 'sea' would have taken place, yielding a new derivational base **mari-*, the instrumental of which would have been **mari-h₁* 'with youth' = 'young'.

As Vine (2011, p. 266[18]) recognizes, following a suggestion of Oettinger, the heroine of this derivational chain is the marriageable maiden, the *nūbilis*, and the *marītus*, as above, is the one who 'has the maiden'.

(20) Gofannon's brother *Amaethon*, the divine ploughman, has a name derived from MW *amaeth* 'ploughman' < **amb-ag-to-*, the one who leads the plough animals back and forth (**amb*[*i*]-) across the field = Gallo-Lat. *ambactus* (EDLIL 31), so his name is a *no*-stem derivative to a thematic

[17] Schrijver (1991a, pp. 454–465) has an impressively thorough collection of Latin words that show **mo- > ma-* and **wo- > va- in an open syllable* where there is no evidence for a laryngeal (465).

stem. In CO 22.585–587, the divine smith and the divine ploughman are brought together, since Gofannon keeps his ploughshares sharp only for a rightful king (*urenhin teithiawc*).[18]

(21) Gaul. *Matrona* 'Marne', and W *Modron* 'Great Mother' < **mātr-onā*. If Marne means 'Mother of Waters', cf. Algonquian *Misi-ziibi* 'Mississippi River' < 'Father of Waters'. The unique Gaulish *Bratronos* (Néris-les-Bains) appears to be a personal name rather than a god name (Evans, 1967, p. 314; DLG 85), as does *Ateronios* (DLG 58).[19]

(22) Gaul. *Nemetona*, the partner of Loucetius and goddess of the Nemetes (LÉIA N–9), is probably to be segmented **nem-et-onā*, given athematic Nemetes and *Silua quae vocatur Nemet* (ACS ii 708–713). Thematic **Nemeton* would probably have been written as such, as in Galat. *Drunemeton* 'oak sanctuary' (Strabo) and numerous other examples given in ACS.

(23) MW *Rhiannon* 'Great Queen' < Brit. **rīgant-onā*. Note that the Herrschersuffix is not obligatory in this formation.

(24) Gaul. *Đirona*, *Sirona* 'Star Goddess' < Celt. **stēr-onā* (DLG 282) was worshipped throughout the central and eastern Continental Celtic lands, but not in Iberia, the British Isles, or Ireland. She was associated with Apollo as god of healing, and was depicted with eggs and a snake, and wearing a diadem with a star. Formally, the lengthened grade in her name matches Lat. *stella* 'star' < Italic **stēr-olā*, as Romance forms like Fren. *étoile* show.

5 *i*-stem

(25–26) W *Hafren*, OE *Sæfern*, Mod. *Severn* < Brit. **Sabrinā* (Jackson, 1953, pp. 519 & 576). Note that the *-*i*- is not lengthened, so this is not an instance of the Herrschersuffix. Contrast Lat. *Tiberīnus*, which is: OLat. *Pater Tiburine tuo cum flumine sancto* (Ennius, *Ann.* 54) 'O Father Tiber with your holy flood'. These, together with Gaul. *Matrona* 'Marne' and *Sequana* 'Seine', make a little family of river names.

[18] On the relationship between the legitimate king and the fruitful land, see Joseph (2021).

[19] Modron is connected with a shadowy figure Euron in *Kat Godeu* 'Battle of the trees' (LPBT 182.167–168). Koch (1989) suggests that Euron was a misspelling of **Uuron* < Brit. **wironos* 'divine man' (or 'hero'), a potential consort for Modron. However as Haycock (2015, p. 226) points out, *Eur-* 'golden' is a common first element in female names, so that is probably what we have here.

(27) Lat. *Lūcīna*, as *Juno Lucina*, the goddess of childbirth (the one who brings children into the light; Scullard, 1981, p. 85). LOVC- in early inscriptions, e.g., CIL 1^2 359. **louki-$h_1$neh$_2$*. For the root in another god name, cf. Gaul. *Leucetius*, *Loucetius*, an epithet of Mars (DLG 200). We see the *i*-stem in the Gaulish personal names *Loucis*, *Loucita*, and in Lat. *lūx lūcis* (Ennius+), *i*-stem, OPruss. *Luckis* 'light', etc.

The vast literature concerning the etymology of Lat. *Quirīnus* is beyond the scope of this study (see EDLIL 509–510; a Sabellic loanword?).

6 *u*-stem

(28) Thanks to the work of de Bernardo Stempel (2010) on posttonic gemination in Continental Celtic, the *-nn-* in Gaul. *Cernunnos*, the Stag God (Watkins, 1999; Oettinger, 2017),[20] can now be explained as continuing Celt. **kérnu-Hno-*, with the word for 'horn' that is cognate with, e.g., Lat. *cornu* (Nussbaum, 1986). Exact equivalents of Cernunnos are not found in Insular Celtic, but Conall *Cernach* is certainly to be compared: in *Táin bó Fraích*, he has to attack a serpent which is guarding a fort (TBF 14.360–361). However, instead of fighting back, the serpent becomes small and gentle, and hops into his girdle: ⁊ *ní dergéni nechtar de olc fria chéile* (TBF 15.375–376) 'and neither harmed the other'! This otherwise inexplicable episode matches the depiction of Cernunnos in the Autun bronze, in which two serpents are entwined around his waist (Bober, 1951, p. 15).

(29) Gaul. MEDVNA (CIL xiii 7667: Bad Bertrich, Rhineland-Palatinate, noted since Roman times for its healing hot spring) has two goddess names, one of whom is *Meduna*. She is evidently **med^{h}u-nā*, the goddess of sovereignty who confirms the rightful king with a drink (Joseph, 2021, pp. 156–157).

(30) Lat. *Fortūna*, the goddess of good luck < **b^{h}r̥tu-$h_1$neh$_2$* (after EDLIL 236). Weiss (2020, p. 310) suggests that all three of these Latin god names may be deinstrumental, which comes to the same thing, since the

[20] The spelling is seen most clearly in the relief in the Cluny Museum. Today only]ERNVNNOS is visible, but Bober (1951, p. 14), in her comprehensive study of representations of the god, assures us that CERNVNNOS is clear from eighteenth-century drawings.

Herrschersuffix is taken to be derived from the instrumental case (Haudry, 1981).

(31) Lat. *Neptūnus* certainly belongs here, whichever etymology we accept, since the base is a *tu*-stem, probably **neb*^{ɦ}*-tu-* 'moistening'[21] (EDLIL 406; so Rix, 1981, p. 123 **neb*^{ɦ}*-tu-*h_3*n-o-*; I would prefer **neb*^{ɦ}*-tu-*h_1*no-*). Despite Dumézil's (1995, p. iii 40) intriguing connection with OIr. *Nechtan Scéne* 'Nechtan of the Knife',[22] the guardian of the Well of Wisdom (like Old Norse Mimir), the equation is not perfect, because a medial *-u-* would raise **e* to ^{x}Nichtan, so **neb*^{ɦ}*-to-no-* for Irish. Still, the fact that Nechtan is the guardian of a magical well does associate him with the power of waters. Note, however, that **neb*^{ɦ}- loses the connection with Ved. *Apā́m Nápāt* = Av. *Apąm Napāt* 'Descendant of Waters', which Dumézil offered as his tertium comparandum.

The clearest evidence for the original form of this god name in Celtic comes from British and Pictish: the Pictish king lists (Anderson, 1950) begin to move out of myth into history in the fifth century, and the king in which we are interested is *Nectan I Morbet* 'the Great' *mac Erp* (r. 456–480, a more reasonable reign than those of some of his predecessors, who supposedly reigned for as much as a century). While Nectan I may have been a real person, it is his name that holds our attention. Although it matches OIr. *Nechtan*, there is an Ogam inscription from Shetland that may preserve an older spelling. The Lunnasting Stone has **NEHHTONS**, and Rodway (2020, p. 179) compares **NECTON** (Aberdeenshire), and with the later change of **x* to *-i-*, NEITANO (Peebles) and Bede's *Naiton*. What is, of course, striking is that three of these four early attestations agree on *-on-* rather than *-an-*.

The Latin notice of Nechton's death is not probative, since Nectonius could be a Latinization: *optulit igitur Nectonius magnus filius Wirp* [*Eirp*], *rex omnium provinciarum Pictorum*. Since we are interested in possible connections between Nechton and waters, note that his name survives in the river name Nethan Water, a tributary of the Clyde which flows from

[21] Following *LIV*^{2} 448, Melchert (2019, p. 245) glosses the root **neb*^{ɦ}- 'become cloudy; become damp'.

[22] Attempts to connect his name with *scén* 'terror' fail on morphological grounds: *scén* is an *o*-stem, so no case form in its paradigm ends in *-e*.

East Ayrshire to South Lanarkshire. There is also the village of Cambusnethan (earlier *Kamysnethyn*) in Lanarkshire on the Clyde, which clearly means 'Nechtan's riverbend'.

Turning to Welsh, the ancestor of the folk of Gwynedd is Beli Mawr, and in the second of the prophecies of Taliesin (Haycock, 2013, p. 48), *Beli wirawt* 'Beli's liquor' is a kenning for the sea. The collocation is likely to be old, because it contains the archaic word for 'drink; liquid' *$^*weh_1$-r* discussed by Watkins (2009, p. 226). As Haycock says, the name Beli recurs several times in Welsh tradition. The iteration that is of interest to us is Beli fab Nwython, where Nwython is just the modernized spelling of Pictish Nechton with which we started (right down to *-on* rather than *-an*; Koch, 1997, p. lxxxi). The full context is Eugein map Beli map Neithon, in the Strathclyde pedigree (mid-seventh century, Harl. Gen. §5; Koch, 1997, p. 154). Beli, whose liquor is the sea, is thus the son of the Celtic god of waters who we can now confidently call **Neptonos*.

(32) Lat. *Portūnus*, the god of harbors < **pr̥tu-$h_1$no-* (Oettinger, 2017, p. 594, with my updated reconstruction).
(33) OLith. *Perkúnas* 'thunder (god)' = Latv. *Pḙrkuôns* < *u*-stem. EDLIL 507 believes that these words are not related to the word for 'oak', **perk^{w}u-*; however, given the evidence assembled by Nagy (1990, pp. 182–201) about the sacred character of an oak struck by lightning, I think that the connection should be retained.
(34) Ved. *Dámūnas-*, which Pinault (2000, p. 78) translates 'bénéficiare de la maison', belongs here formally: it is most easily derived from **demu-$h_1$no-s-* with the Herrschersuffix. Since it is most frequently used to refer to Agni, I would suggest that in origin it too was a god name: *Agni Damūnas*.

**demu-* is attested in Slavic (OCS *domъ* 'house') and Latin (first in Plautus, *Mil.* 126 as the hapax *domū* 'away from home'). As Pinault (2000, p. 88) points out, a **domu-$h_3$no-s-* (now **domu-$h_1$no-s-*) would give *ˣdā́mūnas-* by Brugmann's Law. He solves this by the ingenious suggestion that *dámūnas-* starts from a Lindeman variant **dm̥m-u-*, made from the weak stem of Gk. δμώς, gen. δμωός 'servant' < *'belonging to the house' (89). As noted above, it may be simpler to reconstruct an acrostatic paradigm **domu-* : **demu-* like Gk. γόνυ : Lat. *genu* 'knee'. We already know that the root noun made acrostatic **dom* : **dem*.[23]

(35) Ved. *Váruṇa-*: The etymology of his name has been much discussed. A *u*-stem is attested in Baltic: Lith. *Virvė*, Latv. *Vìrve* 'rope' (IEW 1150). Does he 'bind' the agreement that his fellow god Mitra 'establishes'? This raises an interesting alternative for Gwydion: in Joseph & Drayton's (2020/2021) discussion of early Irish tree names, we translate the poem which begins by calling honeysuckle *Airdrīg fedha Fáil* 'high king of the wood of Fál' because it binds every tree just as a high king binds every lesser king (66). OIr. *féithlenn* 'honeysuckle' gives us **féith* 'bind' < Goid. **weitā*, which could align Gwydion functionally with Váruṇa.

7 Conclusion

Only five or six of the 34 names we have considered are derived from **-ono-/ā* suffixes added to consonant stems. Divine names in **-no-/ā* are, therefore, a heterogeneous group which does not have a single source. The original nucleus probably included both *-no*-suffixes added to thematic stems and thematized *n*-stems, from which a new suffix **-ono-/ā* was extracted by resegmentation and added to athematic stems.

References

ACS = Holder, A. (1896–1913). *Alt-celtischer Sprachschatz*. B. G. Teubner.

Anderson, M. O. (1950). The lists of kings. II. Kings of the Picts'. *Scottish Historical Review, 29*, 13–22.

Blažek, V. (2008). Celtic 'smith' and his colleagues. In A. Lubotsky, J. Schaeken, & J. Wiedenhog (Eds.), *Evidence and counter-evidence. Essays in honour of Frederik Kortlandt i, Balto-Slavic and Indo-European linguistics* (pp. 67–85). Rodopi.

[23] Pinault's analysis of Lat. *dominus* 'master; householder' and his attempt to derive the Hoffmann suffix from a verbal noun meaning 'benefit', fascinating as they are, are beyond the scope of this study.

Bober, P. F. (1951). Cernunnos. Origin and transformations of a Celtic divinity. *American Journal of Archaeology, 55*, 13–51.
Bonnefoy, Y. (Ed.). (1992). *Roman and European mythologies* (W. Doniger et al., Trans.). University of Chicago Press. Original work published in 1981.
Carey, J. (2019). *Magic, metallurgy and imagination in medieval Ireland. Three studies*. Celtic Studies Publications.
CIIC = Macalister, R. A. S. (1945–1949). *Corpus inscriptionum insularum Celticarum*. Stationery Office.
CIL = Mommsen, T, et al. (1853). *Corpus inscriptionum Latinarum*. Georg Reimer.
CO = Bromwich, R., & Simon Evans, D (Ed.). (1992). *Culhwch ac Olwen. An edition and study of the oldest Arthurian tale*. University of Wales Press.
Corm. Y = Meyer, K. (Ed.). (1912). *Sanas Cormaic. An Old-Irish glossary*. Halle a.S.: Niemeyer / Dublin: Hodges, Figgis.
De Bernardo Stempel, P. (2003). Die sprachliche Analyse Keltischer Theonyme. *Zeitschrift für celtische Philologie, 53*, 41–69.
De Bernardo Stempel, P. (2010). Die Geminaten des Festlandkeltischen. In K. Stüber, T. Zehnder, & D. Bachmann (Eds.), *Akten des 5. deutschsprachigen Keltologen-Symposiums, Zürich, 7–10. September 2009* (pp. 65–87). Praesens.
Detienne, M. (1989). The violence of wellborn ladies. Women in the Thesmophoria. In M. Detienne & J.-P. Vernant (Eds.), *The cuisine of sacrifice among the Greeks* (pp. 129–147). University of Chicago Press.
DGVB = Fleuriot, L. (1964). *Dictionnaire des gloses en vieux breton*. C. Klincksieck.
DLG = Delamarre, X. (2003). *Dictionnaire de la langue gauloise. Une approche linguistique du vieux celtique continental*^{3}. Éditions Errance.
Dumézil, G. (1995). *Mythe et épopée*. Éditions Gallimard.
EDLIL = De Vaan, M. (2008). *Etymological dictionary of Latin and the other Italic languages*. Brill.
EDPC = Matasović, R. (2008). *Etymological dictionary of proto-Celtic*. Brill.
Evans, D. E. (1967). *Gaulish personal names. A study of some Continental Celtic formations*. Clarendon Press.
Fellmann, R. (2004). Gobannus, une divinité gauloise et galloromaine pratiquement inconnue (habent sua fata inscriptiones). In H. Heftner & K. Tomaschitz (Eds.), *Ad fontes. Festschrift für Gerhard Dobesch zum fünfundsechszigsten Geburtstag* (pp. 747–757). Wiener Humanistischen Gesellschaft.
Hamp, E. P. (1972). Palaic *ḫa-ap-na-aš* ‘river’. *Münchener Studien zur Sprachwissenschaft, 30*, 35–37.

Hamp, E. P. (1988). *(Aber)Gevenni. Bulletin of the Board of Celtic Studies, 35*, 53–54.

Haudry, J. (1981). La derivation en indo-européen. *L'information grammaticale, 8*, 3–11.

Haycock, M. (Ed. & Tr.). (2013). *Prophecies from the Book of Taliesin*. CMCS.

Haycock, M. (Ed. & Tr.). (2015). *Legendary poems from the Book of Taliesin*[2]. CMCS.

Hoffmann, K. (1955). Ein grundsprachliches Possessivsuffix. *Münchener Studien zur Sprachwissenschaft, 6*, 35–40.

IEW = Pokorny, J. (1959–1969). *Indogermanische etymologisches Wörterbuch*. Francke.

Jackson, K. (1953). *Language and history in early Britain. A chronological survey of the Brittonic languages 1st to 12th c. A.D.* Edinburgh University Press.

Joseph, L. S. (1990). Old Irish cú. A naïve reinterpretation. In Celtic language, Celtic culture. A festschrift for Eric P. Hamp. In A. T. E. Matonis & D. F. Melia (Eds.), (pp. 110–130). Ford & Bailie.

Joseph, L. S. (2021). Plenty as a consequence of justice in Ancient Greece and Medieval Ireland. *Studia Celtica, 55*, 151–172.

Joseph, L. S. (2023). OIr. *námae* 'enemy' and the Celtic *nt*-stems. *Ériu*, 73, 1–28.

Joseph, L. S., & Drayton, B.. (2020/2021). Trees and tradition in Early Ireland. *Studia Celtica Fennica, 17*, 54–73.

Koch, J. T. (1989). Some suggestions and etymologies reflecting upon the mythology of the Four Branches. *Proceedings of the Harvard Celtic Colloquium, 9*, 1–11.

Koch, J. T. (Ed. & Tr.). (1997). *The Gododdin of Aneirin. Text and context from dark-age North Britain*. University of Wales Press.

LÉIA = Vendryes, J., Bachellery, E., & Lambert, P.-Y. (1959–). *Lexique étymologique de l'irlandais ancien*. Dublin Institute for Advanced Studies; Centre National de la Recherche Scientifique.

LEW = Walde, A., & Hofmann, J. B. (1938–1956). *Lateinisches etymologisches Wörterbuch*[3]. Carl Winter.

LIV2 = Rix, H, et al. (2001). *Lexikon der indogermanischen Verben*. In *Die Wurzeln und ihre Primärstammbildungen*. Dr. Ludwig Reichert.

LPBT = Haycock, M. (Ed. & Tr.). (2015). *Legendary poems from the Book of Taliesin*[2]. : CMCS.

McCone, K. (1996). *Towards a relative chronology of ancient and medieval Celtic sound change*. Department of Old Irish, St. Patrick's College.

McManus, D. (1997). *A guide to Ogam*. An Sagart.
Meid, W. (1955). *Personalia mit* *-no-*Suffix*. Doctoral dissertation, Universität Tübingen.
Meid, W. (1957). Das Suffix *-no-* in Götternamen. *Beiträge für Namenforschung, 8*, 72–108 & 113–126.
Meillet, A. (1920). Les noms du 'feu' et de l' 'eau' et la question du genre. *Mémoires de la Société de Linguistique de Paris, 21*, 249–256.
Melchert, H. C. (2019). Solar and sky deities in Anatolian. In A. A. Catt, R. I. Kim, & B. Vine (Eds.), *QAZZU warrai. Anatolian and Indo-European studies in honor of Kazuhiko Yoshida* (pp. 239–249). Beech Stave Press.
Nagy, G. (1990). *Greek mythology and poetics*. Cornell University Press.
Nussbaum, A. J. (1986). *Head and horn in Indo-European*. de Gruyter.
Nussbaum, A. J. (2004). A *-t-* party. Various IE nominal stems in *-(*o*/*e*)*t*-. Paper presented at the Sixteenth Annual UCLA Indo-European Conference, Los Angeles, 5–6 November 2004.
Oettinger, N. (2017). Gall. *Cernunnos*, lat. *cornū* ›Horn‹ und heth. *Tarhunna-*; mit einer Bemerkung zu gr. πᾶς ›ganz‹. In *Usque ad radices. Indo-European studies in honour of Birgit Anette Olsen*, (Eds.) Bjarne Simmelkjær Sandgaard Hansen et al., 593–603. Museum Tusculanum Press.
OM = Moran, P. (Ed. & Tr.). (2019). *De origine Scoticae linguae (O'Mulconry's Glossary). An early Irish linguistic tract with a related glossary*. Brepols.
Pinault, G. (1987). Bellum: La guerre et la beauté. In G. Freyburger (Ed.), *De Virgile à Jacob Balde: Hommage à Mme Andrée Thill* (pp. 151–156). Université de Haute Alsace.
Pinault, G.-J. (2000). Védique *dámūnas-*, Latin *dominus* et l'origine du suffixe de Hoffmann. *Bulletin de la Société de Linguistique de Paris, 95*(1), 61–117.
Prósper, B. M. (2017). The irreducible Gauls used to swear by Belenos. Or did they? Celtic religion, henbane and historical misapprehensions. *Zeitschrift für celtische Philologie, 64*, 255–297.
Rix, H. (1981). Rapporti onomastici fra il panteon etrusco e quello romano. In G. Colonna (Ed.), *Gli Etruschi e Roma. Atti dell'incontro di studio in onore di Massimo Pallottino: Roma, 11–13 dicembre 1979* (pp. 104–126). G. Bretschneider.
Rodway, S. (2020). The Ogham inscriptions of Scotland and Brittonic Pictish. *Journal of Celtic linguistics, 21*, 173–234.
Schrijver, P. (1991a). *The reflexes of the proto-Indo-European laryngeals in Latin*. Rodopi.
Schrijver, P. (1991b). The development of Primitive Irish **aN* before voiced stop. *Ériu, 42*, 13–25.

Schrijver, P. (1995). *Studies in British Celtic historical phonology*. Rodopi.
Scullard, H. H. (1981). *Festivals and ceremonies of the Roman Republic*. Thames and Hudson.
TBF = Meid, W. (Ed.). (1974). *Táin bó Fraích* (Rev. ed.). Institute for Advanced Studies.
Thurneysen, R. (1946). In D. A. Binchy & O. Bergin (Eds.), *A grammar of Old Irish* (rev. ed.). Dublin Institute for Advanced Studies.
Vine, B. (2011). Initial **mo*- in Latin and Italic. *Münchener Studien zur Sprachwissenschaft, 65*, 261–286.
Waanders, F. (2003). *Pantoia*—A mixed salad. *Hyperboreus, 9*, 16–21.
Watkins, C. W. (1973). 'River' in Celtic and Indo-European. *Ériu, 24*, 80–89.
Watkins, C. W. (1999). A Celtic miscellany. In K. Jones-Bley, M. E. Huld, A. D. Volpe, & M. R. Dexter (Eds.), *Proceedings of the Tenth Annual UCLA Indo-European Conference, Los Angeles, May 21–23, 1998* (pp. 3–25). Institute for the Study of Man.
Watkins, C. W. (2009). The milk of the dawn cows revisited. In K. Yoshida & B. Vine (Eds.), *East and west. Papers in Indo-European studies* (pp. 225–239). Hempen.
Weiss, M. (2010). *Language and ritual in Sabellic Italy. The ritual complex of the third and fourth Tabulae Iguvinae*. Brill.
Weiss, M. (2020). *Outline of the historical and comparative grammar of Latin*[2]. Beech Stave Press.
West, M. L. (2007). *Indo-European poetry and myth*. Oxford University Press.
Zair, N. (2012). *The reflexes of the proto-Indo-European laryngeals in Celtic*. Brill.

6

The Final Glottal Stop of the Kuṛux Verb Bases

Masato Kobayashi

1 Introduction

Kuṛux and Malto are the two most northeasterly Dravidian languages, spoken in Jharkhand, West Bengal, and Odisha in India. They are close sisters and form a subgroup of their own, henceforth called Kuṛux-Malto. While the phonemes of these languages show highly regular correspondences, only Kuṛux has the glottal stop /ʔ/ as a phoneme, which sometimes corresponds to Mlt. *y*, but sometimes to zero, e.g., Kṛx. *ciʔ-* : Mlt. *ciy-* 'give', Kṛx. *nāxʔ-* : Mlt. *nēɢy-* 'breathe' vs. Kṛx. *tindʔ-* 'feed' : Mlt. *tind-* 'feed by hand'. Contact with Austroasiatic languages such as

This chapter is a modest token of my gratitude to Don for imparting his vast knowledge. When I took his classes on Indo-European historical linguistics in the late 1990s, the most difficult part for me to understand was how analogy and leveling work. I hope my argument here would meet his standards.
I thank the members of the DravLing Zoom group for their kind comments. Forms and meanings of Kuṛux verbs are taken from Grignard (1924), and those of Malto from Droese (1884) unless noted otherwise.

M. Kobayashi (✉)
University of Tokyo, Tokyo, Japan
e-mail: masatok@l-u.tokyo.ac.jp

J. F. Eska et al. (eds.), *The Method Works*,
https://doi.org/10.1007/978-3-031-48959-4_6

Mundari, which also has phonemic *ʔ*, might have played a role in the phonemicization of *ʔ* in Kuṛux, but the process is unclear. The phonemic *ʔ* of Kuṛux occurs most often at the end of a verb base. If *ʔ* is preceded by a consonant, the base-final *ʔ* surfaces only when followed by a vowel-initial suffix as in Kṛx. *tindʔ-ā* 'feed.INF'. *ʔ* also occurs in the adverbial suffixes *-ʔā* and *-ʔanā*, and morpheme-internally in a few nouns such as *ṭoŋgʔe* 'axe'.

In Dravidian languages, verb roots, nouns, and adjectives form verb bases with or without derivational suffixes, and finite and non-finite verb forms are derived by suffixation to verb bases. In many Dravidian languages, including most South Dravidian languages and Kuṛux-Malto, verb bases have idiosyncratic past stems, from which various forms such as the simple past are made. The verb base and the past stem are the principal parts of Kuṛux and Malto verb inflection, and in this chapter we give these forms together when citing a verb, e.g., 'Mlt. *ciy-* / *cic-* "to give"'.

Kobayashi & Tirkey (2017, p. 123) group Kuṛux and Malto verbs by their past stems under four classes:

(1) a. the *-y* class, such as Kṛx. *ēk-* / *īky-* 'walk' : Mlt. *ēk-* / *eky-* 'go'
 b. the *-c* class such as Kṛx. *korʔ-* / *korc-* : Mlt. *kor-* / *korc-* 'enter'
 c. the zero/geminating class such as Kṛx. *kīdʔ-* / *kīd-* : Mlt. *kīd-* / *kīd-* 'lay down'
 d. a relic class of irregular verbs with original **-t* or **-c* such as Kṛx. *on-* / *oṇḍ-* : Mlt. *ōn-* / *oṇḍ-* 'drink' (Kobayashi 2022, pp. 265 & 275)

About 60% of Kuṛux verbs ending in *ʔ* form their past stems with the suffix *-c*, while the past stems of the rest have no morpheme signaling the past, e.g., Kṛx. *korʔ-* / *korc-* 'enter' vs. Kṛx. *kīdʔ-* / *kīd-* 'lay down'.

Unlike Tamil, which has vowel-final verb bases like *pō* 'go', the verb bases of Kuṛux and Malto all end in a consonant or a consonant cluster. However, a few verb bases ending in *ʔ* in Kuṛux and *y* in Malto may be traced back to vowel-final verb roots. For example, Pfeiffer (1972, p. 28) traces the verb Kṛx. *ciʔ-* / *cicc-* and Mlt. *ciy-* / *cic-* 'give' back to PDrav. **cī*, which is supported by reflexes such as Tamil *ī* 'give to inferiors' (with loss of the initial **c*), Kolami *sī* 'give', and also by *cī* in the Kuṛux reduplicated form *cīciʔ-*. There are about ten of these monosyllabic Kṛx. -V*ʔ* : Mlt. -V*y* verb bases, which are underived, basic verbs such as the following.

(2) a. Kṛx. *hoʔ- / hocc-* : Mlt. *oy- / oc-* 'take' (DEDR 984; cf. Tamil *uy- / uytt-* 'carry, take away', Parji *uy- / uñ-* 'carry, take, take away')
b. Kṛx. *coʔ- / cōc-* : Mlt. *coy- / cōc-* 'get up' (DEDR 2867; cf. Koṇḍa *sō- / sōt-* 'to set out')
c. Kṛx. *kheʔ- / kecc-* : Mlt. *key- / kec-* 'to die' (DEDR 2426; cf. Tamil *cā- / cett-*, Parji *cay- / cañ-*, Brahui *kahing / kask* id.)

If the base-final *ʔ* in Kuṛux and *y* in Malto have a vocalic origin as Pfeiffer proposes, it explains the synchronic gap that these languages do not have verb bases ending in a vowel. Since sequences of vowels are avoided in Kuṛux and Malto, the idea that Kṛx. *ʔ* was a hiatus breaker between morphemes makes sense (Gordon 1976, p. 68: 'a morphophonemically conditioned transitional "hiatus-filler"'). And if *ʔ* occurred after a Kuṛux verb base ending in -CV, the final V would be deleted before a vowel by syncopation, leaving *ʔ* (*-CV > -CV*ʔ* > -C*ʔ* / __V).

The question remains what the precursor of Kṛx. *ʔ* was in proto-Kuṛux-Malto. Furthermore, why does Kṛx. *ʔ* sometimes correspond to Mlt. *y* and sometimes to zero? Why do some Kuṛux verb bases ending in *ʔ* form the past stem with *-c* and others with zero? In this chapter, we propose that the final *ʔ* of Kuṛux verb bases has analogical, as well as etymological, origins, and answer these questions with the following hypotheses.

(3) a. The final *V of proto-Drav. *-VV verb bases, and the proto-Dravidian denominative suffix **-i*, are reflected as *ʔ* in Kuṛux and *y* in Malto before vowel-initial suffixes.
b. The final *c* in the Kuṛux and Malto past stems has two origins. One is the proto-Dravidian past suffix **-tt* palatalized after a front vocoid **y* or **i*, as in Kṛx. *ciʔ- / cicc-* 'give' and *emʔ- / emc-* 'take a bath'. The other is a past suffix per se, as found in verbs such as Mlt. *bar- / barc-* 'come'.
c. Kuṛux extended the use of proto-Kṛx.-Mlt. **-i* to mark transitivity, and the original transitive suffix **-t(t)* was doubly marked for transitivity with *-ʔ* in verbs such as Kṛx. *kīdʔ- / kīd-* 'lay down'.
d. The pattern *ʔ / Ø* as in Kṛx. *kīdʔ- / kīd-* or *argʔ- / arg-* 'lift up' had its origin in extension of the geminating past, and then it became productive and was applied to many Kuṛux verbs.

2 Functions of the Kuṛux Base-final ʔ in Comparison with Malto

As mentioned above, many derived verb bases in Kuṛux end in *ʔ*, while the Malto cognates sometimes have *y* and sometimes zero. To understand the origin of the Kuṛux base-final *ʔ*, we first need to identify its functions. Judging from minimal pairs with *ʔ*, it is concluded that Kuṛux base-final *ʔ* serves as a denominative suffix (§2.1), as a suffix adapting borrowed verbs (§2.2), and also as a transitivizing suffix (§2.3).

2.1 Denominative Verbs with ʔ

Kuṛux has many noun-verb pairs in which *ʔ* functions as a denominative suffix, e.g., Kṛx. *aguwaʔ- / aguwāc-* 'lead' from *aguwas* 'leader', borrowed from Indo-Aryan, such as Hindi *agwānī* 'forerunner'. Malto also has denominatives derived with *-y* or *-ey*.

Of verb bases which end in Kṛx. *ʔ* and Mlt. *y* and are derived from inherited nouns, the following is the most securely reconstructible pair.

(4) Kṛx. *emʔ- / emc-* : Mlt. *amy- / amc-* 'take a bath'.

Gordon (1976, pp. 69–70) proposes that these forms are derived from the proto-Kuṛux-Malto noun **am* 'water' > Kṛx. *amm*, Mlt. *amu* and the suffix **-i*, which is reflected as *y* in Mlt. *amy-* and as *ʔ* in Kṛx. *emʔ-*, where **a* is fronted to *e* by **-i* according to Gordon. This is practically the only denominative verb which is derived from an inherited noun and is attested in both languages, and we cannot strengthen Gordon's reconstruction of **-i* with more examples. Fronting of **a* to *e* by **i* or **y* in Kuṛux-Malto is supported by a few other words,[1] even though there are

[1] Kṛx. *emsʔ- / ems-* 'be defiled' (DEDR 171; cf. Tulu *amè* 'ceremonial impurity in case of birth'); Kṛx. *kheʔ- / kecc-* : Mlt. *key- / kec-* 'die' (DEDR 2426; cf. Tamil *cā- / cett-*, Telugu *caccu*, Parji *cay- / cañ-*, Brahui *kahing / kask-*); Kṛx. *neʔ- / nēc-* 'ask for' (DEDR 3602; cf. Tamil *naya-* 'long for'). The following pairs show Kṛx. *a* vs. Mlt. *e*: Kṛx. *nāxʔ- / nāxc-* : Mlt. *nēɢy- / nēɢc-* 'breathe' (DEDR 3765; cf. Pengo *nēnj- / nēnc-*, Gadaba *nēnj-*); Kṛx. *cā̆ʔ- / cā̆c-* : Mlt. *cẽy- / ceñc-* 'stink' (cf. Droese 1884, p. 22 *ceṉy- / ceṉc-*).

examples of both Kṛx. *e* vs. Mlt. *a* and Kṛx. *a* vs. Mlt. *e*. Gordon's idea that proto-Kuṛux-Malto had a denominative suffix **-i* is tenable if we accept the sporadic fronting of **a*.

Outside Kuṛux-Malto, Kumaraswami Raja (1969, p. 87) points out that Tamil *-i*, Kannada *-isu*, and Telugu *-incu* derive verbs from nouns, as in Tamil *kātali- / -tt-* 'love' from *kātal* 'love', and is also used to adapt Indo-Aryan verbs, as in Tamil *rasi- / -tt-* 'relish' from Skt. *rasa-* 'taste', Telugu *jay-incu* 'to conquer' from Skt. *jaya-* 'victory'. If **-i* can be extracted as a proto-Dravidian denominative morpheme, and if Kuṛux and Malto have ample evidence of denominative **-i*, we can trace proto-Kuṛux-Malto denominative **-i* back to proto-Dravidian.

We looked through Kuṛux and Malto dictionaries and extracted verbs which appear to be derived from nouns, listed under (A) to (C) below.

A. *ʔ / c* type

The most common type is verbs whose bases end in Kṛx. *ʔ* : Mlt. *y* and whose past stems end in *c* in both languages.

(5)
a. Kṛx. *ghokhʔ- / ghokhc-* 'think, to think of' from *ghokh* 'thought'
b. Kṛx. *xanʔ- / xanc-* 'be pleasant to the eye' from *xann* 'eye'
c. Kṛx. *xōxʔ- / xōxc-* 'throw flat on the back' from *xōxā* 'back' vs. Mlt. *qōqey- / qōqec-* 'turn one's back' from *qōqe* 'back'
d. Kṛx. *koṛʔ- / koṛc-, koḍḍ-* 'dress the soil around young plants', probably from *koṛā* 'gardening' or from CDIAL 3934.3 **kōḍḍ-* 'dig' (cf. Bengali *koṛā* 'to dig')
e. Mlt. *oḍy- / oḍc-* 'screen, to shelter' from *oḍe* 'shelter, refuge' (possibly from CDIAL 2544 **ōṭṭā* 'shelter, screen')
f. Mlt. *sājy- / sājc-* 'adorn with ornaments' from *sāje* 'ornaments' (from CDIAL 13095; cf. Maithili *sāj* 'adornment, garments')
g. Mlt. *jaly- / jalc-* 'cast the net' from *jale* 'net' (from CDIAL 5213; cf. Hindi *jāl* 'net')
h. Mlt. *kasy- / kasc-* 'castrate' from Mlt. *kasi* 'a castrated animal'
i. Mlt. *ugley- / uglec-* 'think, think of' from *ugli* 'mind'
j. Mlt. *bansey- / bansec-* 'fish, angle' from *bansi* 'fishing hook'

There are also three adjectives which follow this pattern.

(6) a. Kṛx. *kīrnā* 'cold', *kīrʔ- / kīrc-* 'be cold'
b. Kṛx. *tīnnā* 'sweet', *tīnʔ- / tīnc-* 'be sweet', cf. Mlt. *tēni* 'honey'
c. Kṛx. *biṛnā* 'scorching heat, hot', *biṛʔ- / biḍḍ-* 'be hot' (*ḍḍ* is the geminate counterpart of *ṛ*) vs. Mlt. *biḍy- / biḍc-* 'shine'. Here only Malto has a past stem with *-c*.

B. *ʔ* / Ø type

A few denominative verb bases ending in *ʔ* in Kuṛux form the past stem with zero, or by geminating the consonant before *ʔ*, as in *biḍḍ-* in (6c).

(7) a. Kṛx. *mojxʔ- / mojx-* 'create smoke' from *mojxā* 'smoke' vs. Mlt. *moɢje / moɢj-*, *moɢjy-* 'fumigate' from Mlt. *moɢe* 'smoke'
b. Kṛx. *pudgʔ- / pudg-* 'pluck feathers' from *pudgā* 'feather'

C. Ø / *y* type

Although not relevant to our discussion of Kṛx. *ʔ*, there are also denominatives which do not have *ʔ* in the Kuṛux verb bases and form their past stems with *y*, like Kṛx. *īmā* 'termite', *īm- / īmy-* 'be deteriorated or destroyed by termites'.

To sum up, most denominative verb bases are formed by replacing the final vowel with Kṛx. *ʔ* and Mlt. *y*. Kuṛux denominative verb bases containing two consonants before *ʔ* form past stems with zero, while the others form past stems with *-c*. Unlike Kuṛux, Malto has a few zero past stems from denominative verb bases ending in a short vowel and a single consonant (-VC), such as Mlt. *qop- / qop-*, *qopy-* 'heap' from *qope* 'heap' (see §3 below). Kṛx. *-ʔ* and Mlt. *-y* may be traced back to proto-Kṛx.-Mlt. **-i*, but Kṛx. *-ʔ* is used more widely than in Malto, as in the above-mentioned denominative verb Kṛx. *aguwaʔ-*.

2.2 ʔ in Verbs Borrowed from Indo-Aryan

Kṛx. *ʔ* and Mlt. *y* are found when borrowed Indo-Aryan verbs are adapted to the inflectional systems of Kuṛux and Malto.

(8) a. Kṛx. *jitʔ- / jitc-*, Mlt. *jīty- / jītc-* 'win', from Hindi *jītnā*
b. Kṛx. *ṭekʔ- / ṭekc-* 'prop up', from Hindi *ṭeknā* 'support, prop up' (Mlt. *ṭēky- / ṭēkc-* 'to hinder' might be from Hindi *ṭoknā* 'to check')
c. Kṛx. *badlaʔ- / badlāc-*, Mlt. *badley- / badlēc-* 'change', from Hindi *badalnā*

Kṛx. *ʔ* and Mlt. *y* in these verbs can be reconstructed as **-i* for proto-Kuṛux-Malto. Borrowing from Indo-Aryan is relatively recent and it might be anachronistic to reconstruct a proto-Dravidian adapting suffix **-i*, but other Dravidian languages also have such adaptive morphemes traceable to **-i*, e.g., Naiki *uṛay* 'fly' from Indo-Aryan *uṛ-* 'fly', *sikay* 'teach' from *śikh* 'teach' (Bhattacharya 1961, p. 103). Adapting borrowed verbs might, therefore, have been one of the functions of the Proto-Dravidian denominative suffix **-i*.

2.3 Kuṛux ʔ with Transitivizing Function

There are at least six Kuṛux verb pairs in which *ʔ* appears to derive a transitive verb from an intransitive one. In contrast, Malto has no comparable minimal pair with *y* and normally uses the productive causative-transitive suffix *-tr* instead. Mlt. *bat-* in (9i) is a transitive-intransitive pair contrasting in the past stems, and Mlt. *pūɢ-* in (9f) is a labile verb that has both transitive and intransitive meanings.

(9) a. Kṛx. *arg- / argy-* 'climb' vs. *argʔ- / arg-* 'lift up', also *argaʔ- / argāc-* 'lift up'. With epenthesized *a* (DEDR 231; isolated); cf. Mlt. *arg- / argy-* 'climb', *argtr- / argtry-* 'lift'

b. Kṛx. *dolkh- / dolkhy-* vs. *dolkh?- / dolkh-* 'bend'
c. Kṛx. *nind- / nindy-* 'be filled' vs. *nind?- / nind-, nindc-* 'fill' (DEDR 3682); cf. Mlt. *nindɢr- / nindɢr-* 'be filled', *nind- / nind-* 'fill'
d. Kṛx. *padx- / padxy-* 'thicken' vs. *padx?- / padx-* 'render half fluid'; Mlt. *paðɢ- / paðɢ-* 'be congealed'
e. Kṛx. *pard- / pardy-* 'grow' vs. *pard?- / pard-* 'bring up'; Mlt. *paðr- / paðry-* 'grow'
f. Kṛx. *pūx- / pūxy-* 'swell' vs. *pūx?- / pūx-, pūxc-* 'boil'; Mlt. *pūɢ- / pūɢ-* 'swell, boil'
g. Kṛx. *xarx- / xarxy-* 'ring' vs. *xarx?- / xarx-* 'make ring'
h. Kṛx. *turd- / turdy-* 'pass through any narrow aperture' vs. *turd?- / turd-* 'pass (a thread, etc.)'
i. Mlt. *bat- / baty-* 'dry up' vs. *bat-* (from **bat-t-*) / *bat-* 'expose to heat'; cf. Kṛx. *batt- / batty-* 'decrease by evaporation', *batta?- / battāc-* 'dry' (/batt-ta?/-)

Since there is no Malto verb transitivized with *-y*, we cannot reconstruct a transitive suffix **-i* for proto-Kuṛux-Malto. Still, Kṛx. *?* and Mlt. *y* share the functions of deriving verbs from nouns and adapting borrowed verbs; in other words, proto-Kṛx.-Mlt. **-i* is a verbalizing suffix. As far as our data shows, the *?* in examples (9a) to (9h) appears to be the result of a Kuṛux innovation to extend this suffix **-i* to derive a transitive from an intransitive verb.

In other Dravidian languages, Tamil *-vi*, *-ppi*, Telugu *-impu / -incu*, Kannada *-isu* are known as transitivizing or causative suffixes. Of these, the Telugu and Kannada forms are the same as denominative suffixes. Caldwell (1913, pp. 457–462) extracts a causative morpheme **-i*, and we are tempted to connect proto-Kṛx.-Mlt. **-i* with it. But it would be more prudent to reconstruct causative **-pi* and **-vi* for proto-Dravidian, as was done by Krishnamurti (2003, p. 283) and Subrahmanyam (2013, p. 313).[2]

[2] In this connection, it is worth noting that the Malto denominative and adaptive suffix *-y* (*-ey* after a consonant cluster) has a transitive connotation when it makes transitive-intransitive verb pairs with the intransitive suffix *-ar*, e.g., Mlt. *badlar-* 'be changed' vs. *badley-* 'change' (from Hindi *badalnā* 'change'); Mlt. *uglar-* 'remember, recollect' vs. *ugley-* 'think of, wish, care for' (from *ugli* 'mind'); Mlt. *sibṛar-* 'be smeared all over' vs. *sibṛey-* 'smear all over' (no clear base); Mlt. *ṭēkar-* 'be hindered' vs. *ṭēky-* 'hinder, intervene' (from Hindi *ṭeknā* 'support, prop up').

3 Origins of the Kuṛux Base-final *ʔ*

3.1 Etymological *ʔ*

As mentioned in §1, the base-final *ʔ* of the -V*ʔ* : -V*y* verb bases such as Kṛx. *ciʔ- / cicc-*, Mlt. *ciy- / cic-* 'give' and (2a) Kṛx. *hoʔ- / (h)occ-*, Mlt. *oy- / oc-* 'take' is reconstructed as proto-Kṛx.-Mlt. **y*. The *c*(*c*) in the past stems of these verbs might come from the proto-Dravidian past suffix *-*tt* palatalized after **y* as suggested by Krishnamurti (2003, p. 193), e.g., **oy-tt-* > **occ-*.[3]

In (2b) Kṛx. *coʔ- / cōc-* : Mlt. *coy- / cōc-* 'get up', Kṛx. *baʔ- / bāc-* 'say', Kṛx. *cā̃ʔ- / cā̃c-* 'stink' and Kṛx. *lauʔ- / lauc-* 'hit', no front vocoid is reconstructed. *ʔ* : *y* in these cases was most probably a hiatus breaker. On the *-c* in the past stems, see below.

Verb bases of the pattern -VC*ʔ* / -VC*c* in Kuṛux and -VC*y* / -VC*c* in Malto, as in (4) Kṛx. *emʔ- / emc-* : Mlt. *amy- / amc-* 'take a bath' and Kṛx. *nāxʔ- / nāxc-* : Mlt. *nēɢy- / nēɢc-* 'breathe', can be explained by the proto-Dravidian denominative suffix *-*i*. The *c*(*c*) in the past stems can be explained as the proto-Dravidian past suffix *-*tt* palatalized after **i*. The progressive palatalization of *-*tt* after **i* does not occur in base-internal **itt* as in Kṛx. *kitt-* : Mlt. *kit-* 'rot' (DEDR 1606; cf. Kota *kit- / kity-* 'rot'), but this might be a case of blocking in non-derived environments, and we can accept Krishnamurti's hypothesis for now.

3.2 Verb Bases of the Pattern Kuṛux *ʔ / c* vs. Malto ∅ / *c*

In this connection, there is a small group of verbs with the pattern *ʔ / c* in Kuṛux and ∅ / *c* in Malto in contrast with the majority pattern, *ʔ / c* in Kuṛux and *y / c* in Malto.

[3] Even though **y-tt* > **cc* is also found in South Dravidian, there it is an innovation within South Dravidian independent of Kuṛux-Malto. Instead of explaining Kuṛux-Malto -*c*(*c*) from *-*y-tt*, Kobayashi (2022, p. 276) proposes to reconstruct the past suffix *-*cc*, which is a morphological innovation shared by proto-South-Central Dravidian and proto-Kuṛux-Malto. Since Kuṛux-Malto Class 4 verbs such as Mlt. *ōn- / oṇḍ-* 'drink' and *qoy- / qoj-* 'measure' reflect the past suffixes *-*t* and *-*c* anyway (Kobayashi 2022, pp. 266 & 277), I take the position in this essay that -*c*(*c*) in the Kuṛux-Malto past has multiple sources, i.e., palatalization of *-*tt* after **i*/*y* and morphological innovation of the past suffix *-*cc*.

(10) a. Kṛx. *barʔ- / barc-* (but *bar-* in the irregular imperative *bar-ā*) vs. Mlt. *bar- / barc-* 'come' (DEDR 5270; cf. Tamil *varu- / vant-*, Telugu *vaccu / rā*, Kolami *var- / vatt-*, Brahui *banning, bar / bass*)
b. Kṛx. *korʔ- / korc-* vs. Mlt. *kor- / korc-* 'enter' (DEDR 2236; isolated)
c. Kṛx. *nuñjʔ- / nuñjc-* vs. Mlt. *nuñj- / nuñjc-* 'pain' (DEDR 3793; cf. Tamil *nōy- / -tt-* 'be ill', Telugu *noncu* 'pain', Parji *noy- / noñ-* 'be painful')
d. Kṛx. *uṛʔ- / uṛc-* vs. Mlt. *uṛ- / uṛc-* 'be satisfied' (DEDR 598; isolated)
e. Mlt. *tal- / talc-* 'cut' (DEDR 3124; cf. Manḍa *taṛ-* 'strip off (bark)')

Since we cannot explain why only Malto has the distinction of *y / c* and Ø / *c* patterns, we should start from the assumption that the Ø / *c* pattern was original and Kuṛux imposed the more general *ʔ / c* pattern on these verbs. Judging from the irregular Kuṛux imperative *bar-ā* without *ʔ*, it is highly likely that the original verb base of 'come' was **bar-* in Kuṛux, as well, which is preserved in the imperative.

Unlike the verb bases of the pattern Kṛx. -VC*ʔ* / -VC*c* vs. Mlt. -VC*y* / -VC*c*, the verb bases of this group have no reconstructible front vocoid, which would have palatalized the proto-Dravidian past suffix **-tt* to *-c*(*c*). Kobayashi (2022, pp. 275–276) proposes that proto-Kuṛux-Malto and proto-South-Central Dravidian had a past suffix **-c*(*c*), also reflected in Pengo and Gondi converbs. If that was the case, the past stems of proto-Kṛx.-Mlt. **bar-* / **bar-c-* 'come' and proto-Kṛx.-Mlt. **am-i-* / **am-c-* 'take a bath' are of different origins (**bar-cc-* and **am-i-tt*), but Kuṛux generalized the pattern *ʔ / c*. The *-c* in the verbs mentioned above in §3.1, (2b) Kṛx. *coʔ- / cōc-* : Mlt. *coy- / cōc-* 'get up', Kṛx. *baʔ- / bāc-* 'to say', Kṛx. *coʔ- / cōc-*, Mlt. *cuy- / cūc-* 'to put on (a lungee etc.)', and other such underived verbs, where there is no front vowel that would cause palatalization of *-tt, might have the same origin as that of proto-Kṛx.-Mlt. **bar-* / **bar-c-*.

3.3 Kuṛux *ʔ* / Ø by Double Marking

We discussed in §2.3 that Kuṛux innovated by extending the verbalizing suffix **-i* to derive a transitive from an intransitive verb, as in (9a) *argʔ- /*

arg- 'lift up'. Now, Kuṛux and Malto share a few causative verbs with the suffix *-d*, such as Kṛx. *kīdʔ- / kīd-* : Mlt. *kīd- / kīd-* 'lay down', Kṛx. *tindʔ- / tind-* : Mlt. *tind- / tind-* 'feed', which are considered old causatives. Since proto-Dravidian causative **-t* (**-tt* in other branches according to Krishnamurti 2003, p. 280) and **-i* are both transitivizing morphemes, it is strange that the Kuṛux verb bases reflect both (i.e., *-dʔ* < **-t-i*). For this group, the pattern *d / d* as in Malto was probably more original, and the Kuṛux verb bases are doubly marked for transitivity with *-d* and *-ʔ*. As Kuryłowicz's first law of analogy predicts, doubly marked forms seem to have replaced singly marked forms.

Let us now turn to the origin of the past stems with zero. We saw in §2.1 and §2.3 that some of the Kuṛux -C*ʔ* bases form their past stems with *-c*, whereas others form their past stems with zero. The conditioning factor seems to be the skeletal structure of the verb base: past stems with zero are limited to verb bases ending in -VXC*ʔ* (Kobayashi 2022, p. 279). While the older pattern of *ʔ-c* had no prosodic condition and is also found in -VXC*ʔ* verbs, the new pattern of *ʔ-Ø* was prosodically conditioned; this is why only some verb bases ending in *ʔ* form the zero past.

If the *-d* of verbs like Kṛx. *kīdʔ-* vs. Mlt. *kīd-*, and Kṛx. *tindʔ-* vs. Mlt. *tind-*, was a portmanteau suffix signaling both past tense and transitivity in proto-Kuṛux-Malto or proto-Dravidian, like the past transitive suffix **-tt* of South Dravidian (Krishnamurti 2003, pp. 188 & 286–287), the proto-Kuṛux-Malto bases **kīd-*, **tind-*, etc. were already marked for past tense. If that was the case, the zero past probably spread from these *-d* verbs by reanalysis. Another possible source of the zero past, which I propose in Kobayashi (2022, p. 279), is the geminating past. This small group is found both in Kuṛux and Malto, and contains basic verbs like Kṛx. *mōx- / mokkh-* : Mlt. *mōq- / moq-* 'eat' < proto-Kṛx.-Mlt. **mōq- / *moqq-*, Kṛx. *poll- / poll-* : Mlt. *pol- / pol-* 'be unable' < proto-Kṛx.-Mlt. **pol- / *poll-*. If this pattern spread to verb bases ending in a consonant cluster by analogical extension, the gemination would be invisible and would create past stems that appear to be marked with zero. For *-Ø / -Ø* verbs like Kṛx. *urkh- / urkh-* : Mlt. *urq- / urq-* 'come out', this is the only possible explanation.

While the zero past is limited to -VXC(*ʔ*) verbs in Kuṛux, Malto has many zero past stems even in -VC bases. Since Malto underwent widespread degemination, this caused the original gemination of the stem-final consonant as in (9i) *bat-* / *bat-* < **bat-t-* 'expose to heat' to be reanalyzed as zero. Then the zero past became productive and spread to originally non-geminating -VC verb bases, such as Mlt. *bit-* / *bit-* 'cook', *cat-* / *cat-* 'leak', *ceḍ-* / *ceḍ-* 'convey', *nuk-* / *nuk-* 'shake', etc.

3.4 Kuṛux Verbs with *ʔ* and Geminating Past

Another group of Kuṛux verb bases with final *ʔ* whose Malto cognates do not end in *y* are verbs with geminating past stems, e.g., Kṛx. *axʔ-* / *akkh-* vs. Mlt. *āɢ-* / *aq-* 'know', Kṛx. *idʔ-* / *idd-* vs. Mlt. *id-* / *id-* 'plant'. These verb bases are suspected of being remade within Kuṛux by the generalization of the *ʔ* / Ø pattern found in transitive and denominative verbs ending in a consonant cluster such as (9a) *argʔ-* / *arg-*.[4] To take another example, we can reconstruct proto-Kṛx.-Mlt. **qaḷ-* / **qaḷ-t-* from Mlt. *qal-* / *qaḍ-* 'steal' on the grounds of cognates like Tamil *kaḷ-* / *kaṭṭ-* 'steal', etc. (DEDR 1372). While Mlt. *qal-* is a regular reflex of proto-Kṛx.-Mlt. **qaḷ-*, its Kuṛux cognate *xaṛʔ-* / *xaḍḍ-* was probably remodeled from *xaḍḍ-* after the now productive pattern *ʔ* / Ø. Our view that verbs of the type *idʔ-* / *idd-* with geminating pasts are innovations within Kuṛux is further supported by the existence of optional bases with *ʔ* like Kṛx. *xotʔ-* along with *xot-*, which has a geminating past stem *xott-* 'chop'.[5]

As a result of the spread of *ʔ* / -Ø, unlike Malto which has about 170 -VC verb bases, Kuṛux has only 23 such verbs, partly because the base-final consonant is often geminated in Kuṛux, as in Kṛx. *kirr-* / *kirry-* vs. Mlt. *kir-* / *kiry-* 'come back', Kṛx. *ess-* / *issy-* 'weave' vs. Mlt. *es-* / *es-* 'plait', but mainly because many Kuṛux verb bases have secondary *ʔ* by double marking or analogy.

---

[4] To be precise, application of the *ʔ* / Ø pattern would have produced verb bases like **iddʔ-*, etc., but voiced consonants are not geminated before *ʔ* in Kuṛux.

[5] This verb base is also more innovative than Mlt. *qōh-* / *qot-* 'cut down', which is explained from PDrav. **qoṯ-* / **qoṯ-ṯ-*. The expected Kuṛux forms are †*xos-* / *xott-*.

4 Conclusion

To sum up the discussion, the final *ʔ* of Kuṛux verb bases has multiple origins, listed below in (11). Some of these base-final *ʔ* reflect original proto-Dravidian segments, i.e., final **y* which was a part of the verb root such as **ciy-* 'give', and the denominative or verbalizing suffix **-i*. By regular phonological developments, **y* between vowels and **i* before a vowel become *ʔ* in Kuṛux. The past stems of these verb bases have *c*(*c*) in the place of **y* or **i*, whether it comes from PDrav. **-tt* with palatalization or from **-cc*.

(11) a. Kṛx. -V*ʔ* / *-c* vs. Mlt. -V*y* / *-c* type (§1, §3.1): in the verbs of this type, the *ʔ* is a result of regular sound change on a part of the verb root.
b. Kṛx. -VC*ʔ* / *-c* vs. Mlt. -VC*y* / *-c* type (§2, §3.1): the *ʔ* in verbs of this type is a result of regular sound change on the denominative or verbalizing suffix **-i*.
c. Kṛx. -VC*ʔ* / *-c* vs. Mlt. -VC / *-c* type (§3.2): in this type, the *-c* of the past stem has an origin different from (11b). But since the past stems of these types both end in *-c*, the Kuṛux verbs of this type acquired *ʔ* by analogy.
d. Kṛx. -VCC*ʔ* / -Ø vs. Mlt. -VCC / -Ø type (§2.3, §3.3, §3.4): Kuṛux extended the use of the denominative suffix *ʔ* < **-i* to transitivizing intransitive verbs. In Kuṛux, this suffix was added to already transitive verbs, thereby resulting in double marking for transitivity.

In addition, Kuṛux and Malto had a small class of verbs which form the past stem by geminating the final consonant; by analogical extension from these, Kuṛux verbs ending in -VXC*ʔ* form the past stem with zero. The pattern *ʔ* / Ø became productive in Kuṛux. In Malto, the pattern Ø / Ø became productive and is encroaching on the Ø / *y* verbs. Malto might thus be following the path of Dravidian languages like Parji and Brahui, where a majority of verbs form a zero or vowel-past and only a few verbs retain relic past stems with consonantal suffixes.

References

Bhattacharya, S. (1961). Naiki of Chanda. *Indo-Iranian journal, 5*, 85–117.

Caldwell, R. (1913). *A comparative grammar of the Dravidian or South-Indian family of languages*[3]. Kegan Paul, Trench, Trübner (reprint 1974, Oriental Book Reprint).

CDIAL = Turner, R. L. (1962–1966). *A comparative dictionary of the Indo-Aryan languages*. Oxford University Press.

DEDR = Burrow, T., & Emeneau, M. B. (1984). *A Dravidian etymological dictionary*[2]. Clarendon Press.

Droese, E. (1884). *Introduction to the Malto language. The Malto vocabulary*. Secundra Orphanage Press.

Gordon, K. (1976). *A phonology of Dhangar-Kurux*. Summer Institute of Linguistics.

Grignard, A. (1924). *An Oraon-English dictionary in the Roman character*. Catholic Orphan Press / Anthropos.

Kobayashi, M. (2022). Proto-Dravidian origins of the Kuṛux-Malto past stems. *Bhāṣā. Journal of South Asian linguistics, philology and grammatical traditions, 1*, 263–282.

Kobayashi, M., & Tirkey, B. (2017). *The Kurux language. Grammar, texts and lexicon*. Brill.

Krishnamurti, B. (2003). *The Dravidian languages*. Cambridge University Press.

Kumaraswami Raja, N. (1969). *Post-nasal voiceless plosives in Dravidian*. Annamalai University.

Pfeiffer, M. (1972). *Kurux historical phonology*. Brill.

Subrahmanyam, P. S. (2013). *The morphosyntax of the Dravidian languages*. Dravidian Linguistics Association.

7

Very Old Latin

Michael Weiss

1 Introduction

The periodization of Latin—or any language—is always an uncertain enterprise. There are no hard lines to be drawn in what is a continuous process of successive acquisitions. Nevertheless, it is equally obvious that, e.g., Old English and Modern English, are different languages with radically different structures.

In the historical study of Latin it has been the norm to distinguish between Classical Latin and its predecessor, called either Archaic or Old Latin. Ernout's famous collection *Recueil de textes latins archaïques* (^{4}1957) divides the texts into epigraphical and literary, with no discussion of any substantial caesuras within this period. Neither Leumann (1977) nor

I am delighted to have the opportunity to honor Don Ringe, who first introduced me to the fascination of historical linguistics and Indo-European. Don's inspiring teaching and scholarly model lit a fire in me back in 1986 that has yet to go out.

M. Weiss (✉)
Cornell University, Ithaca, NY, USA
e-mail: mlw36@cornell.edu

J. F. Eska et al. (eds.), *The Method Works*,
https://doi.org/10.1007/978-3-031-48959-4_7

Meillet & Vendryes (1979) make any explicit periodization of Latin. Sommer (1914: 17) writes:

> Within the Latin literary language, aside from the scant pre-literary remains (the fragments of the *Carmen Saliare*, the Twelve Tables etc.), it is customary to distinguish the following periods: I. the archaic period from the beginning of literature flowering under the stimulating influence of Greek civilization (first half of the third cent. BC) to the first half of the first cent. BC.... (my translation)

thereby tacitly consigning the oldest remnants of Latin to an unnamed state.[1]

More recent works, however, have drawn a line within the preclassical language. Penney (2011: 220) addresses the various divisions and non-divisions directly:

> The language of the six pre-Classical centuries is sometimes labelled as a whole 'Archaic Latin' or 'Early Latin' or 'Old Latin', and a single term has the advantage of acknowledging that there is a continuum, but a division into periods has also been proposed by some scholars and these same labels (and others) may then be applied in narrower senses, which may unfortunately vary from author to author. For instance, Meiser (1998) 2 distinguishes between Frühlatein ('Early Latin'), from the first attestations down to 240 BCE and the first literary productions, and Altlatein ('Old Latin') from 240 down to the first half of the first century, and is happy to use Archaisches Latein ('Archaic Latin') as an all-embracing term. Weiss (2009) 23 makes a similar division between 'Very Old Latin' (down to the third century and the first literature) and 'Old Latin' (third and second centuries). Clackson & Horrocks (2007 [p. 92 M.W.]) adopt an alternative division between the language of the first inscriptions, down to c. 400, which is labelled 'Archaic Latin', and the language from c. 400 to the first century, which is labelled 'Old Latin'; there is virtually no evidence for Latin in the later fifth and early fourth centuries which makes 400 a convenient dividing point.

[1] Similarly Buck (1933: 26), Sihler (1995: 16). The most extensive discussion of the periodization of Latin is offered by Adamík (2015: 643), who call the period from the seventh century to the last quarter of the fourth century 'Archaic Latin' with whom—modulo the label—I am in basic agreement.

In this chapter, I would like to examine the question of subdividing the periodization of the pre-Classical Latin monuments in four regards:

- Is a division justified? And, assuming the answer to the first question is 'yes',
- What linguistic features distinguish the first from the second period?
- What date should be assigned to the end point of the first period?
- What is the best name for the first period?

Explicit discussion of this topic may seem pointless to anyone who has dealt with the *Carmen Saliare* or the *Duenos* inscription, since the difference between the language of these texts and Plautus is so obvious, but I note that historians (and perhaps classicists more generally) do not, in general, seem to be aware of the problems involved.

2 Is a Division Justified?

It was evident to speakers of Latin that the language of the sixth century and earlier was another kind of Latin based on the criterion of intelligibility. This observation is first recorded in Polybius (3.22.3), who commented that the language of the earliest treaty between Rome and Carthage, which he dated to 508–507 BCE, was partly incomprehensible even after the effort of scholars:

(1) γίνονται τοιγαροῦν συνθῆκαι Ῥωμαίοις καὶ Καρχηδονίοις πρῶται κατὰ Λεύκιον Ἰούνιον Βροῦτον καὶ Μάρκον Ὡράτιον, τοὺς πρώτους κατασταθέντας ὑπάτους μετὰ τὴν τῶν βασιλέων κατάλυσιν, ὑφ' ὧν συνέβη καθιερωθῆναι καὶ τὸ τοῦ Διὸς ἱερὸν τοῦ Καπετωλίου. ταῦταδ ἔστι πρότερα τῆς Ξέρξου διαβάσεως εἰς τὴν Ἑλλάδα τριάκοντ' ἔτεσι λείπουσι δυεῖν. ἃς καθ ὅσον ἦν δυνατὸν ἀκριβέστατα διερμηνεύσαντες ἡμεῖς ὑπογεγράφαμεν. τηλικαύτη γὰρ ἡ διαφορὰ γέγονε τῆς διαλέκτου καὶ παρὰ Ῥωμαίοις τῆς νῦν πρὸς τὴν ἀρχαίαν ὥστε τοὺς συνετωτάτους ἔνια μόλις ἐξ ἐπιστάσεως διευκρινεῖν.

> The first treaty between Rome and Carthage dates from the consulship of Lucius Junius Brutus and Marcus Horatius, the first Consuls after the expulsion of the kings, and the founders of the Temple of Jupiter Capitolinus. This is twenty-eight years before the crossing of Xerxes to Greece. (508–507 BCE) I give below as accurate a rendering as I can of this treaty, but the ancient Roman language differs so much from the modern that it can only be partially made out, and that after much application, by the most intelligent men.[2]

Polybius, writing sometime between 146 and 117 BCE—not long after the end of the Old Latin period—thus found this treaty only partially interpretable with the help of experts. The dating of this treaty has been disputed, but scholars generally agree that Polybius' date is plausible based on the geographical details, which fit the end of the sixth century well.[3] Horace, *Epist.* 2.1.86 commented on the general ignorance of the meaning of the *Carmen Saliare* in early Imperial times:

(2) *iam Saliare Numae carmen qui laudat et illud,*
quod mecum ignorat, solus uolt scire uideri,
ingeniis non ille fauet plauditque sepultis,
nostra sed impugnat, nos nostraque liuidus odit.

> Indeed, whoever cries up Numa's Salian hymn, and would alone seem to understand what he knows as little of as I do, that man does not favor and applaud the genius of the dead, but assails ours to-day, spitefully hating us and everything of ours.

and Quintilian 1.6.40 continued the motif of the obscurity of the Salian hymns:

(3) *Sed opus est modo, ut neque crebra sint haec nec manifesta, quia nihil est odiosius adfectatione, nec utique ab ultimis et iam oblitteratis repetita temporibus, qualia sunt 'topper' et 'antegerio' et 'exanclare' et 'prosapia' et Saliorum carmina uix sacerdotibus suis satis intellecta*

---

[2] Longer translations are from the Loeb Library editions unless otherwise noted.

[3] It is also likely that Polybius' reference to the incomprehensibility is an argument for the correctness of the higher date.

> But moderation is essential; they must not be frequent or obvious (nothing is more tiresome than affectation), and certainly not taken from remote and now forgotten ages, like *topper, antegerio, exanclare, prosapia*, and the hymns of the Salii that their own priests now hardly understand.

Finally,[4] Isidore of Seville (560–636) *Orig.* 9.1.6 offers a stage model of Latin:

(4) *Latinas autem linguas quattuor esse quidam dixerunt, id est Priscam, Latinam, Romanam, mixtam. Prisca est qua uetustissimi Italiae sub Iano et Saturno sunt usi incondita, ut se habent carmina Saliorum. Latina, quam sub Latino et regibus Tusci et ceteri in Latio sunt locuti, ex qua fuerunt duodecim tabulae scriptae. Romana, quae post reges exactos a populo Romano coepta est, qua Naeuius, Plautus, Ennius, Vergilius poetae, et ex oratoribus Gracchus et Cato et Cicero uel ceteri effuderunt. Mixta, quae post imperium latius promotum simul cum moribus et hominibus in Romanam ciuitatem inrupit, integritatem uerbi per soloecismos et barbarismos corrumpent*

> But some have said that there are four Latin languages: the ancient, the Latin, the Roman, and the mixed. Ancient Latin is what the earliest people of Italy used under the reign of Janus and Saturn, disorganized like the *Carmina Saliorum.* Latin Latin is what the Etruscans and others in Latium spoke under the reign of Latinus and the kings, in which the Twelve Tables were written. Roman Latin is the Latin which was begun after the kings were driven out by the Roman people, in which the poets Naevius, Plautus, Ennius, and Vergil and, among the orators, Gracchus, Cato, Cicero, and others expressed themselves. Mixed Latin is the Latin which after the wider spread of the empire invaded the Roman state together with new morals and people, corrupting verbal integrity through solecisms and barbarisms.

Here Isidore, not without some justice, separates the language of the *Carmen Saliare* (*Prisca Latina*) from the Latin of the Twelve Tables (*Latina*). He then groups together what we would call Old Latin and Classical Latin (Plautus + Vergil) as *Romana* and finally calls imperial and later Latin *mixta.*

---

[4] I skip the testimony of Symmachus and Sidonius Apollinaris for reasons of space.

We see that there was a very clear feeling on the part of native speakers of Latin extending through many centuries that the first period of Latin was something different from later periods. There is, thus, solid precedent from ancient authorities for making such a distinction in our scholarship.

3 What Linguistic Features Distinguish the First from the Second Period?[5]

3.1 Rhotacism

The most notable change between the earliest Latin texts and later ones, and certainly the most frequently commented on, was rhotacism. Here we have an abundance of quoted pre-rhotacism examples (see the table below) and even an explicit notice of the graphic realization of the change. The change from [z] to *r* must have happened before the middle of the fourth century BCE,[6] since Cicero reports (*Fam.* 9.21.2) that L. Papirius Crassus, the dictator of 339 BCE, was the first in his gens no longer to be called *Papīsius*. Safarewicz (1932) noted that the XII Tables, which were reconstituted immediately after the Gaulish sack of Rome in 390, never have pre-rhotacized forms and, therefore, preferred an earlier date for rhotacism, the beginning of the fourth century. This earlier date is possible, but the argument is not strong, since the XII Tables, unlike religious texts, rarely preserve phonological archaisms.

Epigraphical attestations of pre-rhotacized forms:

- VETVSIA *Veturia* fem. gentilic (Vetusia)
- NVMASIOI *Numerio* dat. sg. (Manios)
- IOVESAT *iurat* (Duenos)
- VALESIOSIO *Valeriī* (the first *s* only; the second is not intervocalic; Lapis Satricanus)
- ESOM *sum* (Garigliano)
- IOVO[SD]ỊCASE *iudicare* (Corcolle)
- LASES *Lares* (Arval Hymn)

[5] I can cover only the most important phonological changes here.

[6] See Niedermann (1953: 94–96), Leumann (1977: 178–179), and Sommer & Pfister (1977: 146).

The first certain epigraphical evidence for rhotacism in any Italic language is the Faliscan form **carefo** 'I will lack' (Bakkum, 2009: no. 59, early fourth century BCE) < **kasēfō*; cf. Lat. *cas-tus* 'free from'. Ferrandes et al. (2021) date the Latin version of the same text to ca. 370 BCE. Rhotacism appears to have been an areal feature that spread across Latin, Faliscan, and Umbrian during the fourth century BCE. The earliest Latin epigraphical attestation is C(E)RERE 'to Ceres' (ILLRP 64, Veii) from 300–270 BCE, about 50 years after the claim about Papirius.

The pre-rhotacism forms attested in the literary tradition are given below (Tables 7.1 and 7.2).[7]

As can be seen from Tables 1 and 2, most of the forms are known from Verrius Flaccus, with 16 examples in Paulus ex Festo or Festus. The salience of rhotacism is notable in that we have no comparable discussions of the date of other changes distinguishing the very old material from just the old material. It is also notable that the pre-rhotacized forms often have other potential archaisms which pass without comment. For example:

- *astasent statuerunt* 'they set up' (P. ex F. p. 24 L) < **ad-steh₂-sn̥t*; cf. Gk. ἔστησαν? This form could be a unique survival of an *s*-aorist built to a vowel-final stem. It is usually doubly emended to *astasint statuerint.*
- *dasi dari* 'be given' (P. ex F. p. 60 L). At face value, this suggests that the passive infinitive in *-rī* comes from **-sī*, with the long vowel not from monophthongization of a diphthong.
- *Helus et helusa antiqui dicebant, quod nunc holus et holera* 'The ancients used to say *helus* and *helusa* for what we now call *holus* and *holera* "vegetables"' (P. ex F. p. 89 L). This form predates backing before *l* pinguis and medial weakening.
- *iusa iura* 'laws' (ms. *iussa*) (P. ex F. p. 92 L), a double zero-grade thematic derivative of the neuter *s*-stem **i̯eu̯os* 'law' < 'binding', which is also the base for the denominative verb **i̯useh₂-i̯e-*: *dēierāre* 'take an oath' (Plaut. +), *peiierāre* 'swear falsely' (Plaut. +).

[7] VIASIEIS '(people living) along the roads' (CIL I² 585.12; 111 BCE) must be borrowed from a non-rhotacizing dialect or from a variety, like Umbrian, with desyllabified *-ii̯V-* before rhotacism. Similarly *amāsius* 'someone prone to love' (Plaut. +).

Table 7.1 Pre-rhotacism forms in the literary tradition: Non-names

	Verrius Flaccus	Varro	Cicero	Quintilian	Livy	Terentius Scaurus	Velius Longus	Fronto	Pomponius	Macrobius	Pseudo-Placidus	Servius (Danielis)	Dionysius of Halicarnassus
arbosem/ arboses	X												
asa								X		(Var.)	X		
asena		X											
ausum	X												
dasi	X												
esum		X											
astasent	X												
fasena							X						
Fesiae							X						
foedesum		X											
hasena											X		
helusa	X												
iusa	X												
Lases		X		X		X					X		
Loebasium											X	X	
loebeso	X	X											
maiosibus	X												
meliosem	X	X											
pignosa	X												
plisima	X	X											
robosem	X												

Table 7.2 Pre-rhotacism forms in the literary tradition: Names

	Verrius Flaccus	Varro	Cicero	Quintilian	Livy	Terentius Scaurus	Pomponius	Macrobius	Pseudo-Placidus	Servius (Danielis)	Dionynius of Halicarnassus	Plutarch
Auselius	X			X		X						
Fusius	X		X	X	X	X	X	X		X		
Halesus										X		
Papisius	X		X									
Spusius											X	
Valesius	X			X						X		
Οὐελεσος/ *Volesus*		X										X
Vetusius					X							

- *Loebasium* and *Loebesum*
  Servius Dan. ad *Georg.* 1.7: *quamuis Sabini Cererem Pandam appellant Liberum Loebasium dictum autem quia graece* λοιβή *dicitur res diuina* 'Although the Sabines call *Ceres Panda*, they call *Liberum Loebasium*. It is so called because λοιβή means a sacred matter in Greek.'
  CGL v 30.9; v 80.22: *Libassius Liber pater*
  P. ex F. p. 108 L: *loebesum et loebertatem antique liberum et libertatem*
  Varro, *De ling. Lat.* 6.2: *ab libero liberum declinatum*

  The last passage from Varro was emended by K. O. Müller to *loebesum* on the basis of Festus, but in fact it is not necessary to saddle Varro with this form. One could restore *Loeberum*, but *loebesum* is unavoidable in Paulus. Based on these forms with *s*, Benveniste (1936) suggested deriving the divine name *Līber* (the Roman god of wine) from **h₁leu̯dʱesos*, a thematic derivative of an *s*-stem **h₁leu̯dʱos* 'growth' (cf. Ved. *ródhati*, Goth. *liudan* 'grow'; OIr. *lus* 'plant' < **h₁ludʱtu-*). But (1) there is no evidence for this *s*-stem; (2) it is not specified that *Līber* the god is meant. In fact, it is clear from the context that Paulus is referring to the adjective. For these reasons, it is best to take ***loebesum*** as a false archaism or even a corruption for *līberum* 'free'. But the situation is different for *Loebasium*, which *is* explicitly connected with the god *Līber Pater*. In addition, it is not a simple misapplication of the *r* > *s* substitution rule. Instead the suffix is the well attested *-ārius* < *-āsi̯o-* and the introduction of such a morpheme is not obviously motivated. It is possible that *Loebasium* and *Libassius* are separate forms to be connected with *lībum* and *lībāre*, representing a Sabine **loibāsi̯o-* 'of the offering cake' and only secondarily approximated to *Līber*.

- *plisima* (Fest. p. 222 L) < **plei̯sVmo-* < **pleh₁-ism̥o-* (cf. Gk. πλεῖστος 'most', Av. *fraēšta-* < **pleh₁-istos*), preserving the expected superlative of 'many'.

3.2 The Loss of *s* Before a Voiced Consonant with Compensatory Lengthening

Another feature of the earliest epigraphical texts which also receives mention in the literary tradition is the preservation of *s* before a voiced consonant. The epigraphical survivals are:

- COSMIS OLat. *cōmis* 'kind' (Duenos)
- IOVXMENTA OLat. *iūmenta* 'yoked teams' (Forum)
- LOSNA (ILLRP 1200, Praeneste, ca. 330) OLat. *lūna* 'moon'[8]

At a morpheme boundary we have:

- IOVOSḌ (Corcolle) *iūs dīcere/iūdicāre* 'to judge'

The treatment of *s* before a voiced consonant is not completely uniform. Before *u̯* and *g*, it became *r* apparently already in proto-Italic (**menesua* > *Minerua;* **katesu̯ā* > *caterua* 'throng', Umb. *caterahamo* 'gather in throngs!'; **mezgō* > *mergō* 'I sink'); before *r*, it becomes *b* (**fou̯nesri-* > *fūnebris* 'funerary'). So it is not self-evident that all the remaining *s* plus voiced consonant sequences would necessarily be treated in the same way and at the same time. In fact, aside from IOVOSD- which is at a prominent morpheme boundary (cf. *iūs dīcere*), all the other survivals can be grouped in one of two ways. Either they are all cases of *s* before a nasal or they are all cases of *CsC* (COSMIS < **komsmis*; LOSNA < **lou̯ksna*). We have no other instances of either *sD* or *VsD* in the epigraphical record.

The survival of *s* in this environment was known to Roman scholars. Here are all the examples:

[8] Cf. also FASNI (AE 1987, 323) for *fānī* 'shrine' (gen. sg.), dated by EDR to 50 BCE! If correctly read, we must be dealing with an archaizing inscription with apparent access to accurate information from Pescorocchiano (Rieti), the territory of the Aequicoli; or is FASNI perhaps by contamination with Osc. /fe:sno/-?

3.2.1 Probably Genuine

- *cesnas* for *caenas*, i.e., *cēnās* 'meals' (Fest. p. 222 L) is a correct reminiscence of an earlier form, since Umbrian has *śesna* and Osc. has **kerss-naís** (ST Cp 31). The etymon is **kertsneh₂* from the root **kert-* 'cut' (Ved. *kr̥ntáti* 'cuts').
- *dusmo* 'thicketed' (Liv. Andr., P. ex F. p. 59 L; Ps. Plac. gloss. D 18 *dusmum: incultum dumosum uel squalidum,* probably derived from Festus); cf. Class. Lat. *dūmī* 'thickets' (Cic. +, the word is plurale tantum in Classical Latin). Livius Andronicus' *s* before *m* certainly does not reflect contemporary speech, since PRIMOGENIA (Praeneste ILLRP 101, ca. 300–250) has already lost *s*, but *dusmo* is likely to have a correct *s*. It has been compared with OIr. *dos* m. *o*-stem 'bushy tree' < **dusto-* and ME *tō-tūsen* 'pull roughly', OHG *zir-zûsôn* 'pull to pieces'.
- *Desnas* : *denas* (Lib. Gloss. DE 1089). Presumably the antecedent of *dēnī* 'ten at a time' < **deknsoi̯*, an analogical, but probably real, form.

3.2.2 Potentially Genuine

- *cosmittere* for *committere* 'join together' (P. ex F., p. 59 L). *cosmittere* cannot be the direct preform of Class. Lat. *committere*. A preform **kom-smeit-* would have given †*cōmittere*; cf. *cōnubium* 'marriage' < **kom-snou̯bʱi̯io-m*. Similarly, what is evidently an old compound *omittō* < **ommittō* < **obmei̯tō* cannot continue **obsmei̯tō*. It is possible that *committere* had simply been remade from **cōmittere*, but on what model and for what reason? I am inclined to accept the form as genuine, pointing to an *s*-mobile variant of the root **mei̯th₂-*.
- '*pesnis*' *pennis, ut 'casmenas' dicebant pro Camenis et 'cesnas' pro caenis* (Fest. p. 222 L) 'They used to say *pesnis* for *pennis* "feathers" (dat.-abl. pl.) like *casmenas* for *Camenis* and *cesnas* for *caenis,* i.e., *cenis* "meals", dat.-abl. pl.'[9] The Latin word for 'feather' is *penna,*[10] which is

[9] Or is this a confused gloss for *pesnis* : *pēnis* 'penis' as suggested by TLL s.v. *penis*?

[10] The commonly attested form in literature and inscriptions and reflected by the Romance languages is *pinna* (cf. Logudorese Sardinian *pinna*), which was proscribed by Servius ad *Aen.* 2.479: *ueteres pennas dicebant, non pinnas*. The origin of this variant is unknown. Krostenko (2000) suggests that *e* was raised to *i* before *-nn-* in some dialect, and such a change does seem unavoidable.

undoubtedly a derivative of the PIE root **pet(h_2)-* 'fly'. If we knew nothing else, it would be assumed that *penna* was from **pet-na*, but the picture is complicated by the existence of the forms *pesnis* and *pesnas* (Fest. p. 228 L). This has led some scholars, e.g., Meiser (1998: 118), to suppose that *penna* is from **petsna* and that the outcome of **-VtsnV-* was not *-V:nV-*, as one might have expected, but *-VnnV-*. This is not impossible, since *pullus* 'chick' < **putslo-* (cf. *pusillus*) shows that at least one **-VtsRV-* sequence could lead to *-VRRV-*. But I think the Festus passage at p. 228 L suggests a solution other than the one favored by Meiser. The passage reads in Lindsay's edition:

Pennas antiquos fertur appellasse †peenas† ex Graeco quod illi πετηνὰ *quae sunt uolucria, dicant. Item easdem pesnas ut cesnas.*

It is said that the ancients called *pennas †peenas†* from the Greek because they call flying things πετηνὰ. Again (some ancients said) *pesnas* like *cesnas.*

It is evident that what stands between the obels must be emended to *pet(V)nas*, as suggested by Mueller, since only if the form had a *t* in it would the derivation from Gk. πετηνὰ make sense. The second sentence (*item easdem pesnas ut cesnas*) means that Festus' source also knew or created a form with *s*. Thus there may have been two forms floating around, *petna* and *pesna*, just like **putslo-* (Lat. *pullus*) beside **putlo-* (Osc. **pukl(o)**-). Nothing stands in the way of deriving *penna* from **petna*. Whether **petsna* would have given *penna*, too, or **pēna* cannot be answered with certainty.[11] A possible diminutive is *petellium*, the name of a plant, if derived from **petello-* < **petnelo-*.

3.2.3 Probably Pseudo-archaisms

- TRIRESMOS 'triremes' (ILLRP 319, Duilius inscription) vs. PRIMOS from the same inscription < **prīsmos*, but that in itself does not prove that TRIRESMOS is a false archaism. The root in question is **$h_1$reh$_1$-* ~**$h_1$erh$_1$-* 'row' (Ved. *aritā́* 'rower', Gk. ἐρέττω 'I row' < **$h_1$erh$_1$-t̯i̯ō*, etc.) and nowhere but in Greek is there any evidence for a *t*-extension

[11] I am mainly repeating what I wrote in Weiss (2020: 182–183).

of the root; note that the unextended form of the root is still attested in Myc. *e-re-e* /erehen/ 'row'. So *h_1reh_1t-*smos* is not likely. The Latin form points to an *e*-grade preform *h_1reh_1-*mos*, but a *h_1reh_1-*smos* cannot be excluded.

- *osmen* is said to be the earlier form of *ōmen* by Varro (*De ling. lat.* 6.76 & 7.97), but we do not have a convincing etymology of this word. Varro (*De ling. lat.* 7.97) explicitly connects the supposed preform *osmen* with *ōs*, which does not inspire confidence. If it is from *$h_3ek^w s$-*mn̥* 'vision' from *h_3ek^w- 'see', the *s* could be real, but *ōmen* does not often refer to specifically visual phenomena.

3.2.4 Definitely Pseudo-archaisms

- *Casmenae pro Camenae* (P. ex F. p. 59 L). The *s* is attested here not only in the citation from Festus, but also in the so-called *Carmen Priami*, quoted by Varro (*De ling. lat.* 7.28): *ueteres Casmenas cascam rem uolo profari* 'I want the ancient *Casmenae* to speak of an old affair' or 'I want, o ancient *Casmenae*,[12] to speak of an old affair.' The problem is that the *a* is short and hence the syllable *ca-* cannot have lost an ancient *s*. Cf. Lucil. 10.28 *cui sua committunt mortali claustra Camenae* 'To which mortal the Camenae entrust their enclosures' (note the cooccurrence of *committō* and *Camēna*!) and Enn. *Ann.* 487 Sk[13] *Musas quas memorant, nosce*[*s*] *nos esse Camenas* 'You will learn that those whom they call muses are us the Camenae.' The word was remade by folk etymology to *Carmena* after *carmen* 'song', and this was pseudo-archaized on the basis of an overapplication of rhotacism as *Casmēna*. As Varro, *De ling. lat.* 7.27 states: *qua re est Casmena Carmena Carmena carmina* <*et*>*carmen, R extrito Camena factum* 'Therefore from *Casmena Carmena* was made and from *carmen*, with the *r* worn away *Camena* was made.'[14]

[12] Taking *Casmenas* as a nom.-voc. in *-as* with Timpanaro Jr (1947).

[13] This verse has been much emended to produce a scannable hexameter.

[14] On the general phenomenon of 'reconstructed' forms in the Roman grammarians, see Zair (2019).

In comparing the treatment of rhotacism and *s*-loss/insertion, we can make two observations. First, *s*-insertion is more prone to employment as an archaism, real or false, in literary contexts. In addition to Livius Andronicus' *dusmo*, we have *Casmena*, and TRIRESMOS in the consciously archaizing Duilius inscription. Vergil even created a *Casmilla* as the mother of the Volscian *Cămilla* (*Aen.* 11.452–453) *matrisque uocauit/nomine Casmillae mutata parte Camillam*, inspired no doubt by Varro's derivation (*De ling. lat.* 7.34) of *camillus* from Samothracian *Casmilus*. In contrast, pre-rhotacized forms are largely a matter of grammatical discussion.[15] Second, the first epigraphical evidence for *s*-loss is at least 50 years later than the first evidence for rhotacism.

In fact, I believe we can show that the two sound laws must be ordered 1. rhotacism; 2. *s*-loss by a relative chronology which to my knowledge has not been noticed before. It is clear that the syncope of a syllable beginning with a liquid or nasal happened before the loss of *s* before a sonorant, as the derivation of the following diminutives shows:

- *mālae* 'cheeks'< **makslai̯* vs. *maxilla* 'jaw'< **maksl̥*$_2$*la* < **makslela*
- *āla* 'wing' < **aklsa* vs. *axilla* 'armpit' < **aksl̥*$_2$*la* < **akslela*
- *uēlum* 'sail'< **u̯ekslom* vs. *uexillum* 'standard' < **u̯eksl̥*$_2$*lom* < **u̯ekslelom*

But one form is of interest for the question at hand:

- *quālum* 'woven basket' vs. *quăsillum* 'little basket'

The short vowel of *quăsillum* is confirmed by Sulpicia 4.10.3–4, and single *s* is confirmed by Logudorese and Campidanese Sardinian *kaziḍḍu* 'beehive'. One view derives this noun from *quatiō* 'shake' based on the

[15] The one apparent exception to this is Fronto's (100–160 CE) use of *asae* (*Laudes fumi et pulueris* p. 217): *Laudabo igitur deos infrequentes quidem a laudibus, uerum in usu cultuque humano frequentissimos, Fumum et Pulverem, sine quis neque asae neque foci nec uiae, quod uolgo aiunt, nec semitae usurpantur* 'I will therefore praise gods who are indeed not much in evidence in the matter of praises, but are very much in evidence in the experience and life of men, Smoke and Dust, without whom neither altars, nor hearths, nor highways, as people say, nor paths can be used.' This passage survives uniquely in the Ambrosian palimpsest of Fronto and is illegible to me, at least in the digital image which can be viewed at https://ambrosiana.comperio.it/opac/detail/view/ambro:catalog:72845. I am dubious that even a lover of archaisms like Fronto would have ventured such a form.

idea that a *quālum* was originally a kind of sieve that one agitated (so André, 1963: 70–71). But although *quassō* is the vox propria for this kind of action, there is no evidence that *quālum* or *quasillum* ever means 'sieve'. The second and fatal flaw is that we know that the outcome of *-VtslV- is *-VllV-* (*pullus* 'chick' < *putslo-; cf. *pusillus* 'little' < *putsl̥$_2$l̥s < *putslelos). Thus the outcome of *kwatslo- should be †*quallus*, but the form is quite consistently *quālus*.

The alternative is derivation from a root *k^{w}as-, which finds a good semantic and formal match in OCS *koši* 'basket' < *ko/asii̯o- with reflexes in all branches of Slavic. The semantics require no comment. Schulze (1904: 462) derived *quālus* from *k^{w}asslo- and the diminutive from *k^{w}as-slelo-, which became *k^{w}assl̥$_2$lo- > *k^{w}assillo- and finally *quasillus* by the *Mamilla* rule. This works, but the addition of the suffix *-slo- to a root ending in *-s-* is implausible. A simpler solution is as follows:

	*k^{w}aslelo-	*k^{w}aslo-	*makslela	*maksla
Rhoticism	*k^{w}aslelo-	*k^{w}aslo-	*makslela	*maksla
Celo-syncope	*k^{w}asl̥$_2$lo-	*k^{w}aslo-	*maksl̥$_2$la	*maksla
s-loss	*k^{w}asl̥$_2$lo-	*k^{w}ālo-	*maksl̥$_2$la	*māla

The epenthesis producing *quasillus* and *maxilla* cannot be ordered with regard to *s*-loss.

If we order rhotacism before syncope, then the *s in *k^{w}aslelo- will not be intervocalic at the crucial time. *s*-loss obviously must be ordered after the same syncope. *catēlla* 'small chain', the diminutive of *catena*, would have to be analogical. But, as we will see in §3.3, making *Celo*-syncope follow rhotacism will create difficulties for us when we consider the chronology of *l*-backing, so we cannot commit to this definitively just yet. It is true that the syncope seen in *posinō 'I put' famously precedes rhotacism and *s*-loss:

	*posinō
syncope	*posnō
rhotacism	—
s-loss	*pōnō*

On the other hand, syncope in the identical environment just as famously followed rhoticism in *ornus* 'ash tree' < **osinos*.[16] These examples, thus, provide no information on the relative ordering of *s*-loss and rhotacism.

The *s*-loss rule requires a further clarification. Was the loss of *s* before a voiced stop the same rule as the loss of *s* before a nasal and *l*? It is hard to answer definitively, but one point speaks in favor of a slightly earlier loss for *s* before a voiced stop: the Latin grammatical tradition knows many examples, some correct, some incorrect, of *s* before nasals, but to my knowledge none of *s* before a voiced stop.[17]

Assimilations of *-*tn*-, *-*bn*- must also be post-*Celo*-syncope (cf. *vannus* 'fan'< **uatnos* vs. *vatillum* 'shovel' < **u̯atn̥*$_2$*los* < **u̯atnelos* and *scamnum* 'bench'< **skabnom* vs. *scabillum* 'stool' < **skabn̥*$_2$*lom* < **skabnelom*), so we might potentially find unassimilated sequences in post-rhotacism literary or epigraphical remains. I suggest that we may have a possible trace of such a form in the transmitted *amosio annuo* (P. ex. F p. 24 L), which Burroni & Brezigia (2017) have correctly interpreted as a temporal genitive of the word which becomes Class. Lat. *annus*. They propose to restore *annosio*, but given that this must be from quite an ancient source which would presumably not have originally written geminates, and that the reading *annosio* would have been strongly supported by its evident gloss *annuo*, I suggest that the more likely reading was *atnosio*, which could easily have been misread as *amosio*. So, to sum up the relevant chronologies:

proto-forms	**k*^{w}*aslo*-	**k*^{w}*aslelo*-	**u̯atno*-	**u̯atnelo*-
rhotacism	**k*^{w}*aslo*-	**k*^{w}*aslelo*-	**u̯atno*-	**u̯atnelo*-
Ce*lo*-syncope	**k*^{w}*aslo*-	**k*^{w}*asl̥*$_2$*lo*-	–	**u̯atn̥lo*-
s-loss	*quālos*	–	–	–
assimilations, epenthesis, etc.	*quālus*	*quasillus*	*uannus*	*uatillum*

[16] The superlatives *prīmus* < **prīsmo*- and *summus* < **supmo*- must have undergone an irregular early syncope, perhaps already in proto-Italic. Cf. Paelig. *prismu*, which contrasts with Osc. **nessimo**- or may never have had the syllabic variant of -*m̥mo*-.

[17] One possible exception, CGL v 14.16 *caesditum creditum*, CGL v 54.12 *cesditum creditum* [Placidus]), if for **cresditum*, would be at a morpheme boundary.

3.3 *l*-backing

As is well known, Latin had two allophones of *l*, one *exīlis* and one *pinguis*. An **e*, either original or from medial weakening, was changed to *o* before *l pinguis*, and an epenthetic vowel arising in *C* + *l* pinguis clusters was also realized as *o*. The vowel *o* of both origins was ultimately raised to *u* except after *u̯*. We have our first evidence for a back, rounded realization of a vowel before an *l pinguis* in the form FICOLOS = CL *figulus* 'potter' (Rome, ca. 475–440 BCE) (see Colonna, 2016; Rocca, 2020). In this case, the vowel *-o-* is probably epenthetic.[18] A second, less certain example is the name CANOLEIVS (AE 1981, 370, Vulci, ca. 400–350 BCE) = Class. Lat. *Canuleius* if the suffix *-oleius* is from **-elei̯i̯o-*.

Inscriptions from the Very Old Latin period show one possible pre-backing form, HAVELOD from the Forum inscription, if *hau̯elo-* is a diminutive adjective in *-elo-* like **du̯enelo-* > *bellus* 'beautiful'. *hau̯elo-* might point to a thematic **hau̯o-* 'false' < **ĝʰou̯ó-* by Thurneysen-Havet's Law; cf. OIr. *gáu* 'lie' < proto-Celt. **gou̯ā* (following the etymological lead of Eichner, 1995, modified after Zair, 2011: 201). But this analysis

---

[18] Latin has a fair number of agent nouns, adjectives, and instrument nouns formed with the suffix *-ulus*, *-ula*, or *-ulum*. These are typically built to an uncharacterized verbal root. So, for example, from third *-iō* or fourth conjugation presents we have: *capulus* 'hilt, coffin' (Plaut. +) ← *capiō* 'take'; *iaculum* 'throwing spear' (Plaut. +) ← *iaciō* 'throw', and from second conjugation presents we have: *tumulus* 'barrow, mound' (Cic. +) ← *tumeō* 'swell'; *propatulus* 'open' or *propatulum* 'an open space' (Cic. +) ← *pateō* 'be open'. And from thematic presents of various sorts we have: *legulus* 'gatherer' (of fruits etc.) (Cat. +) ← *legō* 'gather'; *gerulus* 'porter' (Plaut. +) ← *gerō* 'carry'; *figulus* 'potter' (Naev. +) ← *fingō* 'fashion'; *bibulus* 'thirsty' (not as name first in Verg. L. Publicius Bibulus; Liv. 22.53.2, 216 BCE) ← *bibō* 'drink'. The suffix *-ulus*, etc. cannot be separated from the suffix **-lo-* with identical function found in Latin and other Indo-European languages, e.g., *rāllum* 'scraper' ← *rādō* 'scrape', *sella* 'seat' ← *sedeō* 'sit', *caelum* 'chisel' ← *caedō* 'smite' (in Latin confined to feminine and neuter forms). The question is, what is the source of the medial vowel? Given that *-ulus*, etc. forms are often deradical, it is unlikely that the *-u-* has been extracted from thematic presents. Instead it must originate in a regular epenthesis after some consonant(s), and subsequently the union vowel was extended by analogy. Epenthesis is regular after labial and velar stops. In the case of the clusters *-kl-* and *-pl-*, both beginning with a voiceless stop, the epenthesis is recent since unepenthesized forms are still attested in Old Latin (*uinclum*, *perīclum*, *poplus*, *maniplus*, etc.). In the case of the voiced velar and labial clusters **-gl-* and **-bl-*, the epenthesis must be older because we do not find unepenthesized variants in Old Latin. A further argument for the epenthetic nature of the union vowel in *-ulus* is the fact that intervocalic **gʰ* should become *h*. A preform **dʰiĝʰlos* might, thus, have the added advantage of explaining the survival of the stop in *figulus*, and similarly in *trāgula* 'javelin' < **dʰrāgʰla*.

of HAVELOD is quite uncertain. Faliscan preserves **arcentelom**, **urnela**, but we do not know if Faliscan ever had *l*-backing.

But incorporating *l*-backing into the chronology we have attempted to establish above is problematic. We now know on absolute grounds that *l*-backing happened before 440 and rhotacism before 350. That much seems indisputable. But we have argued above that *Celo*-syncope follows rhotacism based on *quasillus*. This contradicts the apparent relative chronology of *l*-backing and *Celo*-syncope required to produce forms like *porcellus*. If we order *l*-backing before rhotacism, as absolute data suggest we must, and if we order *Celo*-syncope after rhotacism, then we predict the wrong outcome:

	**porkelelos*
l-backing	**porkololos*
rhotacism	—
Celo-syncope	†*porkollus*

Instead, it seems that we must order *Celo*-syncope even before *l*-backing:

	**porkelelos*
Celo-syncope	**porkellos*
l-backing	**porkellos*

There are several ways to address this contradiction:

- The inference we have drawn from *quasillus* is wrong. The word really was **quass-* at the relevant time.
- There was no backing before short *e* and, therefore, **porkelelos* became *porkellos*, no matter when the syncope operated.
- The reduction of **porkelelos* to **porkellos* was not *Celo*-syncope, but a different, earlier process comparable to the reduction of reduplicated syllables like **redidō* to *reddō* or **repeperai* to *repperī*.

I have explained the reasons to favor my analysis of *quasillus* above, but I admit they are not conclusive. The idea that *l* was *exilis* before a short *e* has recently been brought to the fore in a recent article by Imberciadori

(2023) and does allow a straightforward explanation of *scelus*, *elementum* (from *h_1el- 'scratch'; cf. ON *alr* m. 'awl'). But it is contradicted by a neglected piece of evidence. The founder of the Valerian gens was a certain man referred to variously as Οὐέλεσος (Plut. *Num.* 5.1.4) or Volesus (*de praenomin.* 1). The same form *Velesos* is mentioned by Serv. Dan. ad Aen. 1.24 as the name of the Euganean king who was defeated by Antenor. This name, whether of Etruscan origin (cf. **Veleśial** 'of Veleshi', ET[2] Cl 1.586, etc.) or native Italic (to PIE *$u̯elh_x$- 'be strong'; cf. Toch. B *walo* 'king', OIr. *flaith* 'realm, rule', hence *$\hat{u̯}elh_xos$ 'strength' → *$\hat{u̯}elh_xes$-o- 'strong' → *Velesos* > *Volesus* and *$u̯l̥h_x$-eh_1- 'be powerful' > *valēre*, in turn influencing the vocalism of *Valerius*) is transmitted in both a pre- and a post-backing form, but the *o*-forms can only be explained if *l* was *pinguis* before *e*. So perhaps the third solution is best, but the first option is also possible.

A problem for early *l*-backing are the forms ATELETA /atelenta/, supposedly *Atalanta* (CIL I[2] 566, ca. 340–311), and HERCELE (CIL I[2] 551, ca. 300) by epenthesis from *Hercles*,[19] both from Praeneste, which, in Latin terms, appear to show *e* in medial syllables before *l*, but no backing a century after the first evidence for *l*-backing. We know that *a*-weakening must have preceded *l*-backing because of forms like *insulsus* 'tasteless'< *enselsso- <*ensalsso- and *inculcō* 'trample on' < *enkelkō < *enkalkō. These Praenestine forms are sometimes thought to show Etruscan or Etruscan-influenced epenthesis; cf. **herecele** (ET[2] OI S.91 spec 5:1), **atlenta** (ET[2] OI S.104 spec 4/3). Imberciadori's (2023) model of *l pinguis* before short *e* would account for ATELETA directly and HERCELE on the theory that this form represented a form extracted from the affirmation *meherclĕ* (so Rix, 2004: 444). Alternatively, they might show that *l*-backing did not originally apply in Praenestine Latin, although it does eventually show up in HERCOLE (CIL I[2] 61 & 62, 270–230 BCE).

The literary tradition records the pre-backing forms *helus* and *helusa* (P. ex F. p. 89 L) for *holus* and *holera* 'vegetable(s)'. If they are genuine, we are dealing with a remarkable archaism preserving intact a form which must date back to at least 500 BCE. A preform *$\hat{g}^{h}elh_3u$-s- points to an *s*-stem substantivization of a *u*-stem *$\hat{g}^{h}elh_3u$-; cf. ON *gulr* 'yellow' <

[19] See Poccetti (2012) on the forms of *Hercules* in Italy.

*$\hat{g}^{h}\mathring{l}h_{3}u$-.[20] We have no context for the words, but such an archaism must belong to the religious language. A second example is preserved in the form Οὐέλεσος/ *Velesos* discussed above.

We may put together the following relative chronology A (single arrows mean relative chronology; double means absolute chronology):

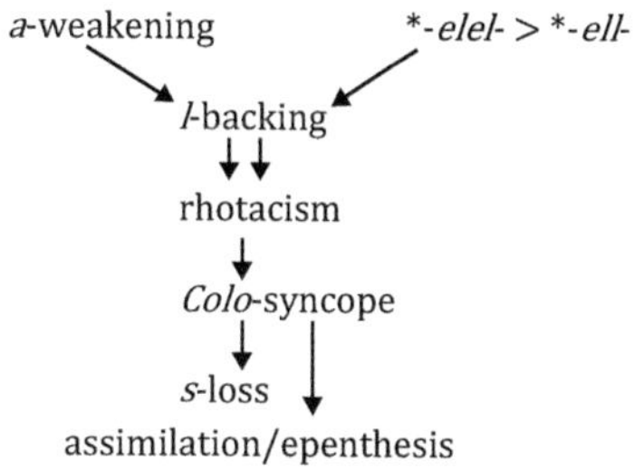

or alternatively relative chronology B:

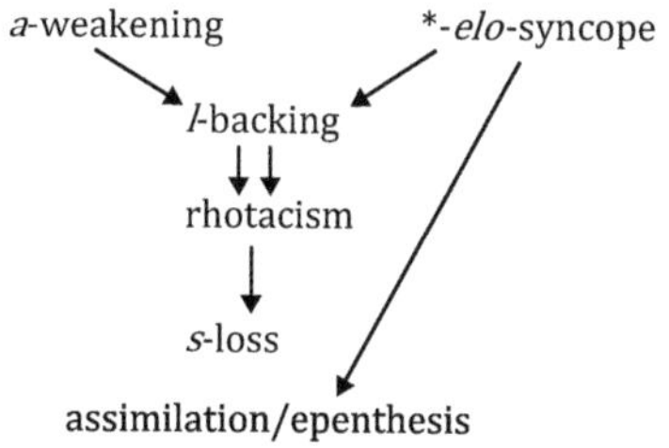

The forms discussed above would then have developed in the following stages.

Chronology A

TAQ	proto-forms	*k^waslo-	*k^waslelo-	*u̯atno-	*u̯atnelo-	*porkelo-	*porkelelo-
500?	*-elel- > -ell-	–	–	–	–	–	*porkello-
450	l-backing		*k^waslolo-			*porkolo-	
370	rhotacism	–	–	–	–		
	Colo-syncope	–	*k^was$\mathring{l}_2$lo-	–	*u̯atn̥lo-		
300	s-loss	*quālo-	–	–	–		
	assimilations /epenthesis		*quasillo-	*uanno-	*uatillo-	–	–
Class. Lat.		quālus	quăsillus	uannus	uatillus	porculus	porcellus

[20] See EDPG 174 and Merritt (2023: 151). *helitor* for *holitor* 'greengrocer' (CGL iv 243 *helitores* : *ortolani*) is not reliable; see Pokrowskij (1908: 128).

Chronology B

TAQ	proto-forms	*k^waslo-	*k^waslelo-	*u̯atno-	*u̯atnelo-	*porkelo-	*porkelelo-
500?	*Celo*-syncope	–	*k^wasl̥$_2$lo-	–	*u̯atn̥lo-	–	*porkello-
450	*l*-backing					*porkolo-	
370	rhotacism	–	–	–	–		
300	*s*-loss	*quālo-	–	–	–		
	assimilations /epenthesis		*quasillo-	*uanno-	*uatillo-	–	–
Class. Lat.		*quālus*	*quăsillus*	*uannus*	*uatillus*	*porculus*	*porcellus*

3.4 *a*-weakening

Another very characteristic feature of Old Latin of the literary period is the weakening of vowels in non-initial syllables. The first step of this process is *a*-weakening. The city of Μασσαλία was founded in 600 BCE and must have been known to Latin speakers before *a*-weakening, since it became *Massilia*.

In fact, it is quite difficult to identify pre-weakened short *a* in the remnants of the earliest Latin inscriptions, as there are just not that many trisyllabic or longer words attested in the early inscriptions. The best examples are:

- MAMARCOM (Satricum, AE 2003, 297; 580–530 BCE), which is probably the genitive plural of *Mamarcos* (Adamík, 2010). The post-weakening *Mamercus* is attested as a praenomen in Rome for the gens Aemilia, and despite Festus' claim (*Mamercus praenomen oscum est ab eo, quod hi Martem Mamertem uocant* [Fest. p. 98 L]), it is probable that the Aemilian praenomen is not Oscan, but the direct descendant of the form now attested at Satricum.
- MAMARTEI of the *Lapis Satricanus* (520–500 BCE).

Since *a*-weakening is ordered before *l*-backing and *l*-backing is attested on an inscription dated between 470–440 BCE (§3.3), we know that *a*-weakening must predate the mid-fifth century BCE. The earliest positive evidence for *a*-weakening is not until quite late, the form ALIXENTROS (CIL I^2 557, Praeneste) sometime around 375 BCE, and even that form has been suspected of Etruscan influence. So *a*-weakening is to be dated around 500 ± 30 years, but we do not see it for over 100 years due to the gap in records in the fifth century.

It will be difficult in principle to identify convincing cases of pre-*a*-weakening forms in later literary citations since most examples of weakening are in compound verbs, which are normally subject to analogical restoration and hence not reliable witnesses. Nevertheless, we find in the Salian hymns *adpatula* 'open up' in contrast to the weakened form *praeceptat* 'often receives in advance' (Fest. p. 222 L). Mancini (2018) argues that there are some pre-weakening forms reliably transmitted in the Twelve Tables, which were composed in 450 BCE. Given what we now know about the date of *a*-weakening, we would not expect to find any pre-*a*-weakening forms in the Twelve Tables, unless they are copying even earlier material. Mancini points to the following forms:

- *concapit* (6.7 Festus p. 502 L)
- *delapidassint* (7.7, Festus p. 508 L)
- *endoiacito* (1.2)
- *excantassit* (8. 8a Pliny *N.H.* 28.17; Seneca *QN* 47)
- *incantassit* (8.1 Pliny *N.H.* 28.17)
- *subuades* (1.10 Aulus Gellius 16.10.8)

But I do not think any of these stand up to scrutiny. The Festus passage which transmits *concapit* is corrupt and has been variously emended. The verbs *dēlapidō*, *incantō*, and *excantō* are always unweakened even in later texts. It is not clear that *endo iacitō* is a compound. This leaves only *subuades*, and Gellius' exact wording *uades et subuades* 'sureties and subsureties' supports the idea that *subuades* has been restored on the basis of the simplex.

4 The End of the First Period of Latin

Drawing a line is going to be arbitrary, but I think the *s*-loss rule makes the best cut-off point.

- It is the latest of the rules that we have examined here (§3).
- The pre-*s*-loss forms were known to later Latin speakers and manipulated in the service of archaizing.
- The loss of *s* was phonologically significant in that it increased the number of long vowels.
- This change can be dated to sometime in the last third of the fourth century.
- I would say that the 400 BCE offered by Penney is too early to conclude the first period since it is pre-rhotacism and pre-*s*-loss.
- Likewise, the date offered by me (2020: 25) of the third century BCE is a little too late.
- So let's say 330 BCE *cum grano salis* (in basic agreement with Adamík, 2015).

5 Naming the First Period

As mentioned above in the quote from Penney (2011), I have advocated the name Very Old Latin for this first period. This term was inspired by Warren Cowgill, who first used Very Old Latin in this sense in his paper 'The source of Latin *vīs*' (Cowgill, 1978: 30). The terminology was taken over by Michiel de Vaan in his etymological dictionary of 2008, but it has attracted a little critical attention on Twitter (now known after a pedestrian rebrand as X) from people complaining that it is awkward. The problem is that Old Latin is already a well-established term for the Latin of Plautus and Cato. It cannot on linguistic grounds be stretched back *ad infinitum* as we continue to learn more about the Latin of earlier centuries. We also cannot reassign Old Latin to the period of the earliest inscriptions and rename the Latin of Plautus and Cato Middle Latin, which would be logical. Using *Frühlatein* and *Altlatein* or their English equivalents Early Latin/Archaic Latin and Old Latin (so Adamík, 2015) is liable to lead to confusion.[21] We should stick to the name first coined by Don Ringe's revered teacher.

[21] After an oral presentation of this essay, Reiner Lipp suggested 'Paleo-Latin' as a name for the earliest period, but, as a native speaker of American English, I, at least, have no intuition about the relative antiquity of *paleo-*, *archaeo-*, or *old*.

References

Adamík, B. (2010). Zu den archaischen lateinischen Inschriftfragmenten auf Bruchstücken eines Tonfasses von Satricum. In P. Anreiter & M. Kienpointer (Eds.), *Latin linguistics today* (pp. 17–30). Institut für Sprachen und Literaturen der Universität Innsbruck.

Adamík, B. (2015). The periodization of Latin. An old question revisited. In G. Haverling (Ed.), *Latin linguistics in the early 21st century* (pp. 640–652). Uppsala Universitet.

AE = *L'année épigraphique.*

Andre, J. (1963). Glanures de lexicologie latine. *Archivio glottologico italiano, 48*, 67–73.

Bakkum, G. C. L. M. (2009). *The Latin dialect of the Ager Faliscus. 150 years of scholarship*. Amsterdam University Press.

Benveniste, É. (1936). *Liber* et *liberi*. *Revue des études latines, 14*, 51–58.

Buck, C. D. (1933). *Comparative grammar of Greek and Latin.* 4th printing. University of Chicago Press.

Burroni, F., & Brezigia, M. (2017). Lat. *amosio*. A previously unnoticed *-osio* genitive in Latin. *Pallas, 103*, 77–86.

CGL = Goetz, G., (Ed.). (1888–1923). *Corpus glossariorum Latinorum.* B. G. Teubner.

CIL = Mommsen, T., et al. (1863–). *Corpus inscriptionum Latinarum.* Georg Reimer.

Clackson, J., & Horrocks, G. (2007). *The Blackwell history of the Latin language.* Blackwell.

Colonna, G. (2016). Iscrizioni arcaiche dal santuario romano delle Curiae Veteres. *Scienze dell'antichità, 22*, 93–109.

Cowgill, W. (1978). The source of Latin *vīs*. *Die Sprache, 24*, 29–44.

de Vaan, M. (2008). *Etymological dictionary of Latin and the other Italic languages*. Brill.

EDPG = Kroonen, G. (2013). *Etymological dictionary of Proto-Germanic*. Brill.

EDR = *Epigraphic database Roma.* https://www.edr-edr.it/default/index.php

Eichner, H. (1995). Zu frühlateinischen Wortformen auf dem Forumscippus CIL I^2.1 (1. HAUELOD, 2. LOIUQUIOD, 3. KAPIA(D) : DOTAUE[RE], 4. Eventuelles Gesamtszenario). In M. Ofitsch & C. Zinko (Eds.), *Studia onomastica et Indogermanica. Festschrift für Fritz Lochner von Hüttenbach zum 65. Geburtstag* (pp. 65–73). Leykam.

Ernout, A. (1957). *Recueil de textes latins archaïques*[4]. Klincksieck.

ET² = Meiser, G. (2014). *Etruskische Texte. Editio minor*². Baar.

Ferrandes, A. F., Nonnis, D., & Pola, A. (2021). Da Falerii a Roma. A proposito di un frammento iscritto di kylix a figure rosse dalle pendici nord-orientali del Palatino. *Scienze dell'antichità, 27*, 89–121.

ILLRP = Degrassi, A. (1965). *Inscriptiones Latinae liberae rei publicae*². «La Nuova Italia».

Imberciadori, G. (2023). Zur Etymologie von lat. *celeber* 'verkehrsreich, belebt; berühmt', lat. *celer* 'schnell' und der Artikulation von frühlat. **-l- / _ ĕ̆. Glotta, 99*, 66–92.

Krostenko, B. (2000). Latin *vinnus, vinnulus. Glotta, 76*, 66–74.

Leumann, M. (1977). *Lateinische Grammatik i, Lateinische Laut- und Formenlehre*. C. H. Beck.

Mancini, M. (2018). Essai de stratigraphie linguistique de la *Lex XII tabularum. Revue de linguistique latine du Centre Alfred Ernout (De Lingua Latina)* 16. https://hal.sorbonne-universite.fr/hal-03365064.

Meillet, A., & Vendryes, J. (1979). *Traité de grammaire comparée des langues classiques*⁵. Champion.

Meiser, G. (1998). *Historische Laut- und Formenlehre der lateinischen Sprache*. Wissenschaftliche Buchgesellschaft.

Merritt, A. (2023). Κάλλος *and* καλός. *Morphology, etymology, and conceptual genealogy*. Ph.D. dissertation, Cornell University.

Niedermann, M. (1953). *Précis de phonétique historique du latin*⁴. Klincksieck.

Penney, J. (2011). Archaic and Old Latin. In J. Clackson & G. Horrocks (Eds.), *A companion to the Latin language* (pp. 220–235). Blackwell.

Poccetti, P. (2012). Reflexes of variations in Latin and Greek through neither Latin nor Greek documentation. Names of Greek religion and mythology in the languages of ancient Italy. In M. Leiwo, H. Halla-aho, & M. Vierros (Eds.), *Variation and change in Greek and Latin* (pp. 71–96). Suomen Ateenan-Instituutin säätiö.

Pokrowskij, M. (1908). Glossae emendatae. *Archiv für lateinische Lexicographie und Grammatik, 15*, 121–128.

Rix, H. (2004). I nomi delle figure dei miti greci nelle lingue dell'Italia arcaica. The first traces of Achilles and Hercules in Latin. In J. H. W. Penney (Ed.), *Indo-European perspectives. Studies in honour of Anna Morpurgo Davies* (pp. 436–446). Oxford University Press.

Rocca, G. (2020). Ficolos feced med. *Annali del Dipartimento di Studi Letterari, Linguistici e Comparati. Sezione linguistica, 9*, 115–124.

Safarewicz, J. (1932). *Le rhotacisme latin*. Towarzystwo Przyjaciól Nauk.

Schulze, W. (1904). *Zur Geschichte lateinischer Eigennamen.* Weidmannsche Buchhandlung.

Sihler, A. L. (1995). *New comparative grammar of Greek and Latin.* Oxford University Press.

Sommer, F. (1914). *Handbuch der lateinischen Laut-und Formenlehre. Eine Einführung in das sprachwissenschaftliche Studium des Lateins*[2]. Winter.

Sommer, F., & Pfister, R. (1977). *Handbuch der lateinischen Laut- und Formenlehre. Eine Einführung in das sprachwissenschaftliche Studium des Lateins i, Einleitung und Lautlehre*[4]. Winter.

ST = Rix, H. (2002). *Sabellische Texte. Die Texte des Oskischen, Umbrischen und Südpikenischen.* Winter.

Timpanaro, S., Jr. (1947). Il «Carmen Priami». *Annali della Scuola Normale Superiore di Pisa. Lettere, storia e filosofia, serie II, 16*, 194–200.

TLL = *Thesaurus linguae Latinae.*

Weiss, M. (2009). *Outline of the historical and comparative grammar of Latin.* Beech Stave Press.

Weiss, M. (2020). *Outline of the historical and comparative grammar of Latin*[2]. Beech Stave Press.

Zair, N. (2011). British **-ā-* and **-āg-*, and the Celtic words for 'sun'. *Die Sprache, 49*, 194–216.

Zair, N. (2019). Reconstructed forms in the Roman writers on language. *Language & History, 62*, 227–246.

Part III

Theoretical Approaches to Language Change

8

Iceberg Phenomena and Synchronic Rules

Olav Hackstein

1 Linguistic Diachrony Is Not Confined to History. Language Acquisition and Long-Term Inheritance

Modern linguistic theories, e.g., the Minimalist Program (Chomsky, 1995) and Distributed Morphology (Halle & Marantz, 1993, 1994), largely converge in regarding the synchrony and the diachrony of a human language as separate entities. On the other hand, it is commonly acknowledged that human languages contain both inherited and innovative elements: inherited elements are usually relegated to purely

I am pleased to offer this article, which scrutinizes the intersection of historical and general linguistic issues, as a sincere tribute to Don Ringe, an eminent Indo-Europeanist, linguist, and teacher, with whom I had the privilege to study back in 1987–1989, when I stayed at Penn first as a visiting student and later as a visiting lecturer. I would like to thank Ryan Sandell, Ron Kim, and Teigo Onishi for valuable feedback which helped me to improve this article. Of course, I alone remain responsible for its contents.

O. Hackstein (✉)
Ludwig-Maximilians-Universität, München, Germany
e-mail: olav.hackstein@lmu.de

J. F. Eska et al. (eds.), *The Method Works*,
https://doi.org/10.1007/978-3-031-48959-4_8

synchronic repositories such as the lexicon under Minimalism, or the encyclopedia or special synchronic rules such as the elsewhere rule (Kiparsky, 1973), blocking effects (Kiparsky, 2005; Embick, 2007), and vowel readjustment rules (Embick & Halle, 2005) under the approach of Distributed Morphology.

It appears, however, that the strict division between synchrony and diachrony should be qualified. While everyone would subscribe to the statement that, say, English- or German-speaking children have no knowledge of Middle English or Middle High German, respectively,[1] it would nonetheless be a fallacy to take this as a justification for viewing diachrony as *a priori* disconnected from the synchronic production of language and for excluding diachrony outright from modern linguistic theory.

The fallacy to be avoided is that lack of awareness of an entity is not evidence for its synchronic absence. The lack of knowledge or awareness of prior linguistic stages does not prevent the speakers of a language from actively employing older, inherited elements. Although native non-linguist speakers are mostly unaware that forms such as Engl. *were* and Germ. *wäre* are inherited from proto-Germanic, both forms are nevertheless synchronically not only not obsolete but actively used. Thus, speakers do not need to have knowledge or awareness of earlier linguistic stages in order to be able to reproduce elements or rules that descend from those stages.[2]

---

[1] In the words of Labov (1989, p. 85), '[o]ne of the strongest arguments for the separation of synchronic and diachronic linguistics is that children do not know the history of the language they are learning. As the grammar of the language must be the rule system that is learned and internalized by the language learner, and the child is ignorant of its history, it follows that historical linguistics is irrelevant for students of synchronic linguistics.' Consequently, as Elly van Gelderen (2015, p. 328) observed, 'generative conferences and journals do not see historical linguistics as a crucial component to their enterprise of understanding the faculty of language.'

[2] The same holds for linguistic synchrony. The lack of awareness among native (non-linguist) speakers of syntactic rules like V-to-T movement in English does not entail the non-existence of these rules.

The crucial phenomenon to be dealt with in this chapter is the following: older linguistic structures may partly or fully survive their obsolescence by inheritance in various ways. The fragmentation of prior structures, rules, and feature sets into defunct features alongside persistent, active features is more common than previously assumed. Exemplification will follow below.

The major gateway for the transmission of inherited parameters and forms is natural language acquisition, aided by usage-based factors such as the conserving effect of high-token frequency (see Meillet, 1937; Zipf, 1949; Bybee, 2006),[3] and cues from contextual embedding (not necessarily dependent on high frequency; see Arnon & Clark, 2011; Hackstein & Sandell, 2023, p. 5). Given the enormous importance of natural language acquisition as a channel for the oral transmission of older structures alongside innovative ones, Labov (1989) rightly proclaimed the child to be 'a linguistic historian' in its own right (i.e., inheritance by language acquisition). In this cutting-edge article, he adduced firm evidence that language acquisition and the language-learning faculty are not isolated from social and historical developments; '[o]n the contrary, children appear to focus sharply on the pattern of social variation, and so reproduce the historically variable patterns' (Labov, 1989, p. 96). Specifically, he demonstrated that phonological variation in the realization of the morpheme {-ing} as [-ɪŋ] ~ [-ɪn] is the 'continuation of a geographic alternation of late Old English, which had become transformed into a social and stylistic variable' (Labov, 1989, p. 87). Labov documented that the variable [-ɪn] ~ [-ɪŋ] tends to be partly morphologically conditioned, as described in Table 8.1.

[3] 'Relics often occur in the most commonly used expressions of a language' (Meillet, 1937, pp. 31–32). '[I]nnovating "Forces" tend to impinge more successfully upon the forms and functions of less frequent acts at the *outer periphery* than those of the more frequent ones which serve as the more conservative core or matrix' (Zipf, 1949, p. 120). '[F]requency strengthens the memory's representation of words and phrases' (Bybee, 2006, p. 715).

Table 8.1 Modern English {ing}: [ɪn] ~ [-ɪŋ]

Velar nasal [ɪŋ]	favored in adjectives and most of all in lexicalized, non-verbal nouns such as *ceiling* and *morning*. 'There is a sharp drop to a set of nominal forms that have no such capacity [i.e. verbal capacity of assigning theta roles]: gerunds incorporated into noun phrases (*swimming pool*), nouns (*ceiling, morning*), and adjectives (*interesting, disgusting*)' (Labov, 2001, p. 88)
apical nasal [ɪn]	favored in most progressives and participles such as *laughing* and *working* (Labov, 1989, p. 87). 'The /in/ form consistently shows higher frequencies for the progressive, lower for participles and adjectives, and lowest for gerunds and nouns' (Labov, 2001, p. 86)

Labov went on to demonstrate that the distribution shown in Table 8.1 ultimately replicates that of Old English (= OE) *-inde* and *-ing* (Labov, 1989, pp. 87–88): -[ɪn] originates in the suffix of the present active participle *-inde* (> *-ində* > *-ind* > *-in*), thus accounting for its preference for the verbal domain; in contrast, -[ɪŋ] descends historically from the nominal abstract suffix OE *-inge*, *-ynge* (> *-ingə* > *-ing*), which explains its preference for nominal abstracts that are not deverbatives.[4]

Such cases of long-term historical continuity as orally transmitted variables are not at all isolated. Further conditioned phonological variables inherited from Middle English include (1) and (2):

(1) Engl. *will* → negated *won't*, where *won't* may be traced back to dialectal (Midlands) Middle English (Mossé, 1952, p. 85).

(2) Engl. *woman* [wʊmən] with labialized onset [wʊ] versus pl. *women* [wɪmɨn], with preserved onset [wi], because the historical *e*-vocalism of the following syllable inhibited the labialization of **wi* > *wu* (Bammesberger, 1984, p. 55). This example illustrates the long-term preservation of historical allophony that persisted purely orally, detached from the notoriously historical graphemic conventions of the language.

[4] Cf. Labov (1989, pp. 87–88, 2001, pp. 86–90, 2006, pp. 254–261), Miller (2012, pp. 130–132).

In short, linguistic diachrony is not confined to history, but remains relevant to the description of synchronic linguistic structures and rules.

2 Linguistic Heterochrony. Fifth-Pocket and Iceberg Phenomena

While the all-pervasive property of synchronic language as a patchwork of retention and innovation has always been acknowledged by diachronic linguistics (split and layering as per Givón, 1984, pp. 32–35 and Hopper, 1991, pp. 22–24), the division between diachrony and synchrony has remained a creed of generativist grammar, since all generative mechanisms are conceived of as purely synchronic. This divide is generally attributed to de Saussure. Yet the separation of synchrony and diachrony in the synchronic generative mechanism calls for multiple qualifications.

To begin with, it is entirely true that de Saussure insisted on drawing a strict line between the diachronic and the synchronic dimensions. Nevertheless, in his *Cours de linguistique générale*, de Saussure conceded that aside from sound laws that have gone to completion, which are purely historical, one must inevitably admit a certain overlap of the diachronic and synchronic dimension of language. De Saussure casts this as a rhetorical question: 'Given that all linguistic synchrony as it occurs on a syntagmatic level has its [linguistic] age, how should it be possible to uphold an absolute divide between diachrony and synchrony? This turns out to be very difficult if one departs from pure sound change and historical phonology[, where this divide can be justified].'[5]

Second, and more importantly, the claimed strict divide between diachrony and synchrony runs afoul of a basic evolutionary property of human language: linguistic elements (parameters, forms, rules) change at differing speeds, with the effect that linguistic change operates unevenly, so that the elements of linguistic utterances will then differ in age

[5] 'Et si tous les faits de synchronie associative et syntagmique ont leur histoire, comment maintenir la distinction absolue entre la diachronie et la synchronie? Cela devient très difficile dès que l'on sort de la phonétique pure' (de Saussure, 1976, p. 194).

(*linguistic heterochrony*). The heterochronic nature of synchronic language and the question of how linguistic heterochrony actively affects the synchronic grammar of human language have not sufficiently been taken into account.

Regarding cultural evolution, the connection between past and present has never been questioned. The fact that not all cultural developments evolve at the same pace has the consequence that synchrony always consists of coexisting entities that differ in age. Knowledge of the past then allows us to distinguish between innovations and retentions, to identify the latter, and to classify variants according to their relative age. Conversely, ignoring the past deprives us of the capacity to account for such anomalies.

In what follows, it is important to differentiate between two categories of inheritance. First, inheritance can be purely historical if a cultural invention outlives its original function. An iconic example is the fifth pocket of the original jeans design, as invented by Levi Strauss. This pocket originally served to accommodate the miniature, onion-shaped personal watches that were popularly worn in the nineteenth century. It lost this original function upon the invention of wristwatches in the twentieth century, but has nonetheless persisted up to the present. Crucially, the existence of the 'fifth pocket' can only be explained in purely historical terms. The original conditioning relationship of purpose and artifact is no longer active. In the following, I will label phenomena of this kind *fifth-pocket phenomena*.

As distinct from purely historical (*fifth-pocket*) explanations, there are cases of historical inheritance involving functional continuity, e.g., the invention of the wheel, which can be traced back at least to 3500 BCE in the area of present-day Iraq and since then has never lost its basic function. Phenomena belonging to the latter category can be referred to as *iceberg phenomena*. This metaphor is suitable, because icebergs exemplify the synchronically unbroken connection between a smaller visible part (the tip of the iceberg above the water standing for the present) and a larger invisible portion underwater, which represents the older aspects that synchronically remain active into the present.

2.1 *Linguistic Fifth-Pocket Phenomena and Elsewhere Rules*

A classic case of a linguistic fifth-pocket phenomenon is the zero-ending of English modals. Present-day English modal verbs (continuing Germanic preterite-presents), such as 3sg. pres. *can* with a null ending, are synchronically anomalous because they deviate from the majority type with 3sg. pres. ind. *-s* (= -/z/). The zero-ending constitutes a minority type that applies only to a lexically defined subset of modal verbs, e.g., to *can* (3sg. pres. *can-Ø*), and *shall* (3sg. pres. *shall-Ø*), but not to *want* (3sg. pres. *want-s*).

Minimalism derives forms like 3sg. pres. *can* from the lexicon. Distributed Morphology uses *elsewhere rules* and *blocking* instead to activate Engl. 3sg. pres. *can* with null termination (*can-Ø*) instead of constructing **can-s* under the general rule of encoding 3sg. present indicative with -/z/. Forms activated by subset rules are usually inherited forms that exhibit the blurring of morpheme boundaries due to sound change, hence an increase in functional load of the resulting fused morphemes. The *elsewhere rule* involves a synchronic ordering principle (recognized already by the ancient Indian grammarian Pāṇini, therefore sometimes also referred to as Pāṇini's Principle) that applies to cases in which we find a choice of competing options of vocabulary insertion. In these cases, the exceptional, specific rules (*viśeṣa, apavāda*) capture their domains from the more general rules (*samānya, utsarga*; cf. Cardona, 1967, 1970, 2009). For example, English has two options for constructing a 3sg. present indicative verb form: either adding -/z/ (R1), which is the majority rule (= default) applying to a nonfinite set of verbs, or adding a null ending (R2), as in a subset of modal verbs like *can*, *shall*, and others which are lexically restricted (3). Thus, rule R2 applies to *can*, *shall*, and a finite set of additional modal verbs, but not to all verbs of modal meaning. The English modal verb *want*, for instance, follows rule 1 (3sg. pres. ind. *wants*).

(3) a. R1: general rule (applicable to an open set of roots):
[pres., 3, sg., ind.] ↔ -/z/ /[X___] (nonfinite set),
with X = *say*, *want*, etc. producing 3sg. pres. *says*, *wants*, etc.

b. R2: subset rule, overriding and blocking R1 (applicable to a restricted set of roots)
[pres., 3, sg., ind.] ↔ -/Ø/ /[Y___] (finite set),
with Y = *can*, *shall*, etc. producing 3sg. pres. *can*, *shall*, etc.

During vocabulary insertion, the subset rule R2 overrides and thereby blocks the application of the general rule R1 due to the elsewhere condition, according to which the more specific takes precedence over the more general ('the most specified entry takes precedence over entries that are less specified'; Halle & Marantz, 1993, p. 120). For X = *can*, R1 would produce the form **can-s*, whose stem would carry the feature set [be able, pres.], whereas R2 produces the form *can* with the richer feature set. This is illustrated in (4).

(4) a. R1general rule:
[pres., 3, sg.] ↔ **can-s* /X__,
with present stem **can-* ↔ [be able, pres.]
(stem *can* with poorer feature set)
b. R2 specific rule, blocking R1:
with pres. 3sg. *can* ↔ [be able, pres., 3, sg.]
(stem *can* with richer feature set)

From a diachronic perspective, the elsewhere condition and the null allomorph found with 3sg. pres. *can*, *shall* is an example of a fifth-pocket phenomenon. The null-ending is clearly inherited, being pan-Germanic (present in Gothic, Old Norse, and West Germanic languages such as English, German, and Frisian) and historically conditioned, morphologically by the underlying proto-Indo-European (= PIE) perfect-stative ending *-*e* and phonologically by the Germanic apocope of non-high short vowels, resulting in a zero-ending. Crucially, the Germanic preterite-presents merged functionally with the inherited proper presents, thereby relegating the zero-ending to a functionless anomaly. The phonologically null allomorph of 3sg. present on modal verbs in English thus constitutes a fifth-pocket phenomenon, in which the synchronic motivation for a special 3sg. pres. *shall* beside *need-s* with default 3sg. pres. -/z/ is no longer apparent. The non-default forms 3sg. pres. *can*, *shall* resulting from the effects of the elsewhere condition involve the compression of functions due to phonological change. The motivation behind the elsewhere condition and especially the compression of functions into fewer morphemes is thus diachronic and involves inheritance. Furthermore, the combination of irregularity in terms of morphological compression and frequency makes sense under a usage-based approach, because it is more economical to employ special morphemes for a combination of functions if these functions are contextually frequent.

With regard to the morphological variable 3sg. pres. -[z] and -[Ø], however, blocking by greater functional complexity need not be the only governing principle to steer the actual selection of either ending. For instance, the modal verb *need* takes either ending, depending on criteria other than morphological complexity. 3sg. pres. -[z] is maintained by *need* if used as a main verb meaning 'require something' (Table 8.2, a. and b.), whereas *need* as a modal auxiliary of deontic meaning 'be obliged to do something' exhibits a divide into -[z] in the affirmative (c.) and -[Ø] in negative sentences (d.), whereby either the verb is negated (*need not*) or a negated constituent has negative scope over the entire proposition (cf., e.g., the notorious slogan *No Irish need apply*, as attested in nineteenth-century America).[6]

The rule ordering according to decreasing complexity, such that the stem variant with more features outranks the stem variant with fewer features, does not apply in contexts (a)–(c). In modal auxiliary use, both the less complex stem *need-s* (c) and the more complex stem *need-Ø* (d.)

Table 8.2 Verbal root {need}, [pres., 3, sg.] ↔ -[z]/-[Ø] as inheritance -[z] (a)–(c) and innovative 'modal 3sg. termination' -[Ø] (d)

a. [main verb, pres., 3, sg.] / [aff]__	↔ -[z]	e.g., *Love needs no excuse.*
b. [main verb, pres., 3, sg.] / [neg]__	↔ [does not need]	e.g., *Love does not need an excuse.*
c. [modal verb, pres., 3, sg.] / [aff]__	↔ -[z]	e.g., *It needs to be said.*
d. [modal verb, pres., 3, sg.] / [neg]__	**↔ -[Ø]**	e.g., *It need not be said.*

[6] Cf. Quirk et al. (1985, p. 138); Huddleston et al. (2002, p. 110).

are licensed. The conditioning factor is not feature complexity of the stem, but the inheritance criterion: in (a)–(c), -/z/ is the ending to be expected for an inherited weak verb,[7] and in (d) the criterion of morphosyntactic attraction of negated modal *need not* 'be not obliged' by the inherited negated modals *can not, may not, must not, should not* applies.[8]

In sum, fifth-pocket phenomenon and elsewhere rules describe the application of the same irregularity from different angles. The fifth-pocket approach typically explains synchronic irregularities as historical inheritance and accounts for its synchronic survival through the correlation established by Meillet, Zipf, and Bybee: 'frequency preserves'[9] and contextual embedding (not necessarily dependent on high frequency; Hackstein & Sandell, 2023, p. 5). By contrast, the elsewhere condition and blocking are confined to the synchronic derivation, leaving the motivation for the synchronic distribution of disjunctive rules arbitrary.

Another well-known case of inheritance of morphological structure with obliteration of function is inherent noun gender in German. I propose here to use the terms M-gender, F-gender, and N-gender instead of masculine, feminine, and neuter to indicate that the grammatical genders of German and many other Indo-European languages continue, to a large extent, to be semantically defined noun classes with a broad array of functions that cannot in any way be reduced to or correlated with biological sex or gender. Examples include *der Hals* 'the neck' (M-gender), *die Tat* 'the deed' (F-gender), and *das Rad* 'the wheel' (N-gender). In these

---

[7] OE *nēodian* and Middle English *nēden* are weak verbs with expected overt 3sg. pres. termination. The variant 3sg. pres. ind. *need-Ø* is attested from the sixteenth century; see Ekwall (1965, p. 141); Hansen and Nielsen (2007, p. 184).

[8] A parallel for the adaptation of weak modal verbs to the morphosyntax of the inherited modal preterite-presents is furnished by Germ. *brauchen* 'require, need', which like Engl. *need* is a weak verb that has begun to adopt morphosyntactic features of deontic modals like *müssen* and *sollen* (3sg. pres. ind. null ending, bare infinitive), giving rise to the 3sg. pres. ind. *brauch-Ø* alongside *braucht*. This analogical attraction and adaptation is attested at least from the nineteenth century, but has remained a vernacular phenomenon. For bibliography, see Maitz and Tronka (2009), to which add Paul (1920a, p. 99). Maitz and Tronka adduce evidence for the phonetic-prosodic deletion of verb-final *-t*. However, final *t*-deletion in *brauch-t* does not conform to any sound law, but is best explained by its analogical adaptation to inherited preterite-present modals (as in the case of Engl. 3sg. pres. *need not*). This does not preclude, of course, that final *t*-deletion may occur as a phonostylistic (allegro) phenomenon with phonological attrition that typically does not comply with regular sound change.

[9] Cf. n. 4.

three cases, the connection of the grammatical gender with its original function is synchronically covert because the stem formants have been eroded by sound change; there is thus no overt cue on the noun itself as to its grammatical gender.

Synchronically, the gender contrast between *der Hals*, *die Tat*, and *das Rad* is unmotivated, which means that its explanation must be purely historical. Originally, the M-gender of *der Hals* 'neck' served an individualizing function; *Hals* goes back to PIE $^{*}k^{w}\acute{o}l(h_1)sos$ 'the single turning (body part)'. The F-gender of *die Tat* 'deed' is historically motivated by the fact that the F-gender comprised abstracts, and *die Tat* descends from the PIE verbal abstract $^{*}d^{h}\acute{e}h_1\text{-}ti\text{-}s$ 'putting, making'. Finally, the N-gender of Germ. *das Rad* 'wheel' is accounted for by the inanimacy of the underlying PIE $^{*}r\acute{o}th_2om$ 'inanimate part being provided with turning'. The functions of the N-gender include the designation of inanimate entities or actions that are not specified for sex. Due to sound change and morphological and semantic decomposition, *Hals*, *Tat*, and *Rat* surface in Modern German as nonsegmentable lexemes that no longer exhibit overt phonological, morphological, or semantic cues as to their membership in an M/F/N-gender class. The inherent gender of these three nouns, and countless others, is thus nothing but a fifth-pocket phenomenon.

2.2 *Linguistic Iceberg Phenomena and Stranded Rules*

Turning now to linguistic *iceberg phenomena*, the fragmentation of feature sets into defunct features and individual persistent features is commonly found. Iceberg phenomena may be selective and appear as non-systematic outliers, as in the case of English volitional *would*, which retains the verb's original semantics. Cf., e.g., (5) *I would rather be anywhere else*, which semantically and etymologically matches its German translational equivalent *Ich wollte lieber woanders sein*.

(5) *I would rather be anywhere else than here today.*
(Oliver Costello, 'Oliver's Army', 1979)

But iceberg phenomena can also be systematic and productive. We have already encountered an example on the phonological level, namely, the tendency for Modern English {ing} to be realized as -[ɪn] when verbal and -[ɪŋ] when nominal (§1 with Table 8.1).

On a morphological level, systematic iceberg phenomena are found in German in the application of gender (noun class) assignment. Alongside the notorious cases of lexically inherent historical gender (§2.1), the three German gender categories may, under certain systematic conditions, serve to encode semantic roles, rather than sex. This is a relic of the situation in (late) PIE, where there is a growing consensus that the grammatical genders were semantically defined noun classes. PIE first used the common gender and then later the M-gender to encode individuatives, the F-gender to encode collectives and abstracts, and the N-gender to encode inanimate entities, as in the examples in (6) and (7); cf. Balles (2004) on PIE, and for German, Köpcke & Zubin (1984) and Weber (2000, pp. 504–505).

(6) a. PIE M-gender individuative **bʱor-s > *bʱōr* ‘someone carrying away, thief’ (Lat. *fūr* m. = f., Gk. φώρ m., iterative-habitual agent noun; Schindler, 1972, p. 36);
b. PIE F-gender deverbal abstract **bʱér-ti-s /*bʰr̥-téi̯-* ‘carriage’ (Germ. *Geburt*, OE *ġebyrd* ‘birth’; cf. Ringe, 2017, p. 305);
c. PIE N-gender aspectually unspecified verbal noun **bʱér-ono-m* ‘carrying’ (infinitive Germ. *(ge)bären*, Engl. *bear*; for the morphological type, cf. Krahe & Meid, 1969, p. 107).

(7) a. PIE M-gender individuative **ĝénh*$_1$*-tōr* ‘creator’ (Gk. γενετήρ, Skt. *janitā́*);
b. PIE F-gender abstract **ĝénh*$_1$*-ti-s* ‘quality of activity of creation’ (Lat. *gēns*, Gk. γένεσις, YAv. *(fra)zaiṇtiš*);
c. PIE N-gender unspecified exemplar **ĝénh*$_1$*tom* ‘created being’ (Germ. *Kind*), unspecified action noun **ĝénh*$_1$*os* ‘creation, descendance, kind’ (Lat. *genus*, Gk. γένος, Ved. *jánas*)

These three functions are continued in German for deverbative inanimate nouns and certain suffix-types which continue to actively cue inherited gender selection synchronically. Examples include the following:

(8) Individuative M-gender Germ. *-er* (e.g., *der Lacher* 'single incident of laughing, single laughter'), abstract F-gender Germ. *-erei* (e.g., *die Lacherei* 'the [negative] quality of laughing'), neutral N-gender Germ. *-en* (*das Lachen* '[the] laughing'); cf. Weber (2000, pp. 504–505).

Other systematic iceberg phenomena illustrate *the fragmentation of feature sets*, such that some features have become inactive while other features have been left intact. Agreement features of head nouns that outlive the freezing of these same head nouns constitute a model case, where one may speak of *stranded rules*.

A handbook example of the persistence of grammatical parameters is offered by New High German (= NHG) adverbs in *-maßen* and *-falls*. Germ. *-maßen* is an adverb-forming suffix, which requires its adjectival base to be suffixed with the feminine termination *-er*; cf., e.g., *zugegeben-er-maßen* 'admittedly'. In contrast, Germ. *-falls* is conditional and requires its adjectival base to be suffixed with the masculine termination *-en*; cf., e.g., *gegeben-en-falls* 'conditionally; if it is the case'. Both *-maßen* and *-falls* are frozen nominal forms. The former descends from the Middle High German (= MHG) feminine noun *die maße*, gen. sg. *der maßen* 'appropriate, apposite measure' (weak *n*-stem-inflection; Paul, 1917, p. 119), whereas the latter descends from the masc. gen. sg. form (*des) Falls* to masc. nom. sg. *der Fall* 'case'. Both adverb types exemplify a network of iceberg phenomena.

a. Regarding wordhood versus phrasehood, the adverbial formations in -*maßen* are synchronically gradient, occupying an intermediate position between a single-word adverb and a multiword phrase form; cf., e.g., the exemplar in (9) with the adjective phrase *erwähnter* modified by a sister adverbial phrase *oben*.

(9) *oben erwähnter maßen* 'as mentioned above'. (Ludovici, Carl Günther: Eröffnete Akademie der Kaufleute, oder vollständiges Kaufmanns-Lexicon. Bd. 5. Leipzig, 1756. S. 500, DTA, accessed 8 April 2023)

Prosodically, the adverbs in *-maßen* comply with the accentuation of noun phrases too, the default pattern being secondary accent on the adjectival base and more prominent, right-edge noun phrase accent falling on the adverbial head *-mäßen*; cf., e.g., *èiniger-mäßen* 'to some extent, fairly, reasonably'. As with noun phrases, other marked patterns are possible, e.g., focus accent on the adjectival modifier producing *eíniger-màßen*, if the speaker wishes to stress the adjectival modifier.

b. Both *-maßen* and *-falls* show internal inflection and possible gapping as morphosyntactic lags. Despite their frozen status, both morphemes continue to check the gender feature of their respective adjectival bases, thereby contrasting with one other: *-maßen* demands fem. *-er*, *-falls* demands masc. *-en*. NHG *-maßen* exhibits rule fragmentation in that it has blurred its case and number features (oblique, SG = PL), but kept its gender feature [F] intact. In contrast, NHG *-falls* fully checks its case [GEN], number [SG], and [M] gender features.
c. That these synchronic phenomena constitute iceberg phenomena and are due to persistence is proven by two facts: (i) diachronically, some adjective + *maßen*/*falls* combinations (seen in Table 8.3) are continued to the present day; (ii) synchronically, the adjective slot remains lexically open, as can be seen from results of a corpus search at the *Digitales Wörterbuch der Deutschen Sprache* (DWDS) under the search string '**maßen*', seen in (10).

Table 8.3 German adverbs in *-maßen*, diachronic lexical continuation

New High German (20th-21st centuries CE)	*dermaßen*	*gleichermaßen*	*solchermaßen*
New High German (17th-19th centuries CE) Early New High German (16th century CE)	*der maszen, dermaszen,der masze,in der masze*	*gleichermaszen,gleicher maszen,gleicher masze in gleicher maß* (von Tepl Ackermann, 10)	*solchermaszen,auf solche masze,in solcher masze,mit sulher mâzen*
Middle High German (11th-14th centuries CE)	*der mâze*	*in gelîcher mâze, gelîcher mâze*	*in solher mâze*

(10) *erwiesenermaßen*, *geduldetermaßen*, *nachgewiesenermaßen*, *eingestandenermaßen*, *konsequentermaßen*, *unverdientermaßen*, *verlangtermaßen*, etc.; see https://www.dwds.de (search string: '*maßen'); *genehmigter- oder geduldetermaßen*, see Wolf-Dietrich Deckert in Urteilskommentierung aus *Deutsches Anwalt Office Premium*.[10]

The combination of internal inflection and the licitness of gapping suggests that the hybrid status of the *maßen*-adverb type occupies an intermediate position between an NP and a single-word adverb. An example such as (11) looks like an instance of gapping:

(11) *erwiesener- und anerkanntermaßen* 'in a proven and acknowledged manner'

Gapping alone, however, is not sufficient to prove a multiword origin for this formation because gapping can also be due to suspended affixation as, for instance, in Germ. *ess- und trinkbar*, literally 'eat- and drinkable'. More probative is that the frozen status of the head noun *maßen* impairs neither the lexical selection of the NP's modifier nor the possibility for the modifier of the NP to be inflected. The adjective is gradable, as, e.g., in (12).

(12) positive *bekannter-maßen* → comparative *bekannterer-maßen*

The same phenomenon, namely, rule fragmentation, recurs with Western Romance adverbs in *-mente* (Italian, Spanish, Portuguese) or *-ment* (French). This suffix descends from the Lat. abl. sg. *mente* of the feminine noun *mēns* 'mind'. The case and number features [ABL, SG] have long since gone defunct, and the noun has turned into an adverbial suffix (cf. Karlsson, 1981, pp. 35–50; Wolf & Hupka, 1981, pp. 107–109; Ringe & Eska, 2013, pp. 174–175) and its semantics changed from attitude to manner (Karlsson, 1981). Crucially, however, selectional requirements for an adjectival base inflected in the feminine singular outlive the freezing as stranded rules.

---

[10] https://www.haufe.de/recht/deutsches-anwalt-office-premium/veraenderung-von-gruenflaechen_idesk_PI17574_HI554649.html (accessed 15 April 2023).

(13) [AP NP]$_{DP}$ > [Adj *-ment*]$_{Adv}$
Lat. *férā ménte* 'with a wild mind' > OFren. *fierement* > Fren. *fièrement* 'high-spirited, arrogantly, proudly' (Rheinfelder, 1976a, p. 61)
Lat. *bona mente* 'with good intention' (Quint. *Inst.* 7.4.25) > Fren. *bonnement*, Span. *buenamente*

Like the German adverbs in *-maßen* and *-falls*, the Western Romance adverbs in *-ment*(*e*) exemplify a network of iceberg phenomena:

a. Regarding their status as a word or a phrase, the *-ment*(*e*) formations behave as hybrids, showing the accentual pattern of a two-word syntagm as a prosodic lag, and group inflection on a morphosyntactic level in Spanish, e.g., *clara y efectivamente* 'clearly and effectively'.
b. The internal inflection of the adjectival base is an inherited and persistent rule, documented diachronically from Latin through Vulgar Latin and Early Romance down to the present day. The adjectival base takes the feminine form by default (Detges, 2015, pp. 1824–1825), as in the examples in (14).

(14) Ital. *chiar-a-mente 'clearly'* ← *chiaro*, *-a* 'clear'
Fren. *lent-e-ment* 'slowly' ← *lent*, *-e* 'slow'
Span. *generos-a-mente* 'generously' ← *generoso, -a* 'generous' (Detges, 2015, p. 1825)

This template continues to be productive for the former *o*-stems. This fact strongly suggests that the termination of the adjectival base, Ital., Span. *-a-* and Fren. *-e-*, should not be regarded as a Theme suffix (without syntactic or semantic role; cf., e.g., Halle & Marantz, 1993, p. 135), but rather as the inflectional ending of the feminine. The internal feminine ending is a long-term inheritance, with persistence of the F-gender feature of *-ment(e)*, which has outlived its delexicalization and morphological freezing. The historical vitality of the gender feature is also hinted at by the restoration of feminine form; cf. Rheinfelder (1976b, pp. 72–73); Lausberg (1972, p. 102); Wolf and Hupka (1981, p. 109).

(15) Lat. **grandi mente* > OFren. *granment* → analogically renewed (M)Fren. *grandement* (since the fourteenth century)

The vitality of the feminine gender feature is not contradicted by cases that do not overtly show a feminine base (Fren. *absolument*, *vraiment*, *joliment*), in which the feminine ending had been lost by sound change. Nor is it contradicted by occasional lexicalizations, e.g., Fren. *bonnement* 'simply'. Long-term productive patterns typically present sedimentation alongside productive exemplars.

c. That (a) and (b) constitute iceberg phenomena and, thus, cases of long-term historical continuity are proven by *diachronic lexical continuation* at a significant level. Several Western Romance languages exhibit agreement across a huge lexical network of etymologically matching combinations of adjectival base and adverbial head in Ital., Span. *-mente* and Fren. *-ment*. See Table 8.4, compiled from McCartney (1920, p. 217) and Karlsson (1981, pp. 135–148).[11]

Table 8.4 Diachronic lexical continuation of adverbs in Ital., Span. *-mente* and Fren. *-ment*

Latin	Italian	Spanish	French
High frequency			
tota mente	*totalmente*	*totalmente*	*totalement*
sola mente atque animo	*solamente*	*solamente*	*seulement*
tali mente	*talmente*	*talmente*	*tellement*
Middle and low frequency			
divina mente	*divinamente*	*divinamente*	*divinement*
mente dura	*duramente*	*duramente*	*durement*
fera mente	*fieramente*	*fieramente*	*fièrement*
firma mente	*fermamente*	*firmemente*	*fermement*
forti mente	*fortemente*	*fuertemente*	*fortement*
generosa mente	*generosamente*	*generosamente*	*généreusement*
honesta mente	*onestamente*	*honestamente*	*honnêtement*
pia mente	*piamente*	*piadosamente*	*pieusement*
pura mente	*puramente*	*puramente*	*purement*
sana mente	*sanamente* (literary)	*sanamente*	*sainement*
secura mente	*sicuramente*	*seguramente*	*sûrement*
mente sincera	*sinceramente*	*sinceramente*	*sincèrement*
tacita mente	*tacitamente*	*tácitamente*	*tacitement*
tranquilla mente	*tranquillamente*	*tranquilamente*	*tranquillement*

[11] It is true that Latin attests the adjective plus *mente* phrase type in poetic registers (cf. Bauer, 2010), but Vulgar Latin attests a great productivity of this type (as evidenced, e.g., by the corpus of Justinian's writings from the fifth century CE), so that *mente*-phrase formulas can be assumed to have been productive in vernacular registers of Latin.

Table 8.5 Lexicalization and semantic specialization of *mente* adverbs in French

Latin	French
bona mente 'with good intention'	*bonnement* 'simply', only in the collocation *tout bonnement* (Detges, 2015, p. 1826)
fera mente 'fiercely'	*fièrement* 'proudly'
forti mente 'bravely'	*fortement* 'firmly'

Due to its long-term inheritance, this adverb type also shows lexicalization and semantic specialization, as illustrated in Table 8.5.

At the same time, however, this adverb type has always remained productive, allowing any adjectival base to enter the slot and check the inherited feminine feature (Fren. *-e-*, Ital., Span. *-a-*); cf. Table 8.4 and (16). It is, moreover, the only synthetic adverb type in these languages (cf. Detges, 2015, pp. 1825–1826).

(16) Span. *concisamente, cupidiosamente*

The combination of internal inflection and gapping points toward the hybrid status of the *-ment(e)* adverbs, which mirrors the phrasal status of the inflected adjectival bases:

(17) Span. *clara y concisamente* 'clearly and precisely' (Lausberg, 1972, p. 101), *rápida y cuidadosamente* 'quickly and carefully'

Prosodically, Span. *-mente* bears secondary stress like a compound member and, unlike suffixes, it shows no clitic prosody (Norde, 2009, pp. 44–45). The non-affixal prosody of Span. *-mente* is easily accounted for by its persistent underlying prosodic independence (Norde, 2009, pp. 41–46).

Morphologically, the adjectival base shows online internal inflection not only by taking the feminine form of the adjective, but also by being gradable.

(18) Ital. *costantissimamente*, providing a match of Lat. *constantissima mente* (Cicero, *De domo sua* 139.5–6).
Ital. *chiarissimamente*. (Ringe & Eska, 2013, p. 174)

Under a Distributed Morphology approach, the feminine terminations of the adjectival bases would be accounted for as Theme vowels devoid of syntactic and semantic content that are generated by special syntactic rules (cf. Halle & Marantz, 1993, p. 135). This approach, however, would create arbitrariness in the motivation of the presumed Theme vowel (putative readjustment instead of diachronically documented inheritance). In contrast, viewing the internal feminine endings as iceberg phenomena is a simpler and more straightforward explanation. The diachronically attested transmission (and occasional analogical renewal) of the feminine terminations (cf. [15]) speaks in favor of a diachronically persistent fragmented rule.

To summarize, the two case studies considered here demonstrate that linguistic inheritance need not be purely historical and that morphosyntactic rules may over time undergo fragmentation into defunct and persistent parameters. With regard to the lexically open adjectival slots and their inflection, the above cases are iceberg phenomena, exhibiting stranded rules that have outlived the freezing of superordinate controlling constituents.

3 Gradience and Stranded Rules as Iceberg Phenomena

Iceberg phenomena must also be acknowledged as a potential cause of synchronic gradience. Linguistic gradience has so far been regarded as a purely synchronic phenomenon, and to my knowledge, no attempt has been made to test its diachronic properties. According to the standard concept of gradience as laid out by Aarts (2007), gradience is the synchronic vagueness of the boundaries between morphosyntactic categories.

3.1 *Synchronic Gradience Effects as Iceberg Phenomena:* Thin, Utter, *and* Away

A type of gradience that may be interpreted diachronically is the gradient behavior of exemplars of the same morphosyntactic category (subsective gradience). Aarts (2007, pp. 105–107, 143–144, 208–210) treats the case of adjectives which check the features to be expected of adjectives to varying degrees, comparing Engl. *happy*, *thin*, *alive*, *utter*, and pseudoadjectives of the type *alive*. Interestingly, with regard to adjectives such as *thin*, *utter*, and *away*, their gradient adjectival behavior is not confined to English alone, but also shared by their German cognates *dünn*, *äußerer*, and *weg*. Germ. *dünn*/Engl. *thin*, Germ. *äußerer*/Engl. *utter*, and Germ. *weg*/Engl. *away* converge as to their availability for inflection, gradation, attributive and predicative use, and intensification; cf. the matrix in Table 8.6. Engl. *thin* and Germ. *dünn* satisfy all five adjectival parameters: full case, number, and gender inflection in German; gradation, attributive use, predicative use, and intensification in German and English. Others, like Engl. *utter* and Germ. *äußerer*, satisfy only two to three parameters: inflection in German; no clear semantic distinction between positive and comparative; restricted suppletive gradation with superlative *utmost* in English; attributive use in English and German, but barred predicative use; and intensification in both English and German. Yet other adjectives, like Engl. *alive* and *away*, check only a single parameter (predicative use).

The matrix in Table 8.6 shows that Germ. *dünn* 'thin' behaves most adjective-like with a score of 5, Germ. *äußerer* occupies a middle range with a score of 2–3, and Germ. *weg*, with a score of 1, is least adjective-like. The following gradient emerges:

Table 8.6 Shared gradience of Germ. *dünn*, Engl. *thin*, Germ. *äußerer*, Engl. *utter*, Germ. *weg*, Engl. *away*

	dünn, thin	*äußerer, utter*	*weg, away*	
INFLECTION (Germ.)	+	+	–	
GRADATION (Germ., Engl.)	+	(+)	–	
ATTRIBUTIVE (Germ., Engl.)	+	+	–	
PREDICATIVE (Germ., Engl.)	+	–	+[a]	
INTENSIFICATION (Germ., Engl.)	+	–	–	
Score	**5**	**2–3**	**1**	
Adjectival	>	>	>	**Less adjectival**

[a]Germ. *weg* and Engl. *away* share the restriction on predicative use. Unlike Germ. *weg*, however, Engl. predicative *away* needs to be further specified such that *He is away on business*/*away for two weeks* or *far away* appears to be well-formed, whereas the acceptability of *He is away* seems dubious to native speakers. In the latter case, acceptability hinges on the possible situational inference of the specification of *away* (*away*: *from where?*, p.c., Ryan Sandell and Ron Kim)

(19) [Adjective] Germ. *dünn*, Engl. *thin* > Germ. *äußerer*, Engl. *utter* > Germ. *weg*, Engl. *away* [less adjectival]

The discussion of gradience has so far been mostly confined to its synchronic dimension, and indeed, some of the limitations (especially as concerns semantics) are synchronic, as is, for instance, blocking due to semantic incompatibility (e.g., Engl. **a married bachelor* [Cruse, 1986, p. 12], Germ. **ich versammle mich* 'I gather myself') or pragmatic infelicities, e.g., *un*-prefixation for negative adjectives, Engl. **unthin*, Germ. **undünn*.[12] But as the English-German convergence by itself suggests, the phenomenon also has an important diachronic dimension. In fact, upon closer inspection, both rule inheritance and rule fragmentation turn out to play an important role. To begin, Germ. *dünn* and Engl. *thin* are property concept adjectives inherited from PIE (**tn̥*h_2*-eu̯/u-* > PWGmc. **þunw-ija-* > OE *þynne*, OHG *dunni*; cf. Lat. *tenuis*, Ved. *tanú-*, and see Ringe, 2017, p. 164). Unsurprisingly, they have retained all adjectival parameters intact.

In contrast, Germ. *äußerer* and Engl. *utter* are derived from the local particle and adverb PIE **ud/ūd* with the locatival-contrastive suffix **-(t)er-o-*, yielding PIE **udero-/*ūdero-/*ud-tero-* 'being located more in the outer/latter sphere'.[13] The semantics intersect between comparative and positive-contrastive, which explains why the reflexes of PIE **udero-/*ūdero-/*ud-tero-* lack a clear semantic distinction between positive and comparative. Traditionally, PIE **udero-/*ūdero-/*ud-tero-* is considered to be defective in the positive (cf. LSJ s.v. ὕστερος 'latter'). But, in reality, PIE **udero-/*ūdero-/*ud-tero-* is employed as an attributive positive adjective in complementary syntactic distribution with the local adverb PIE **ud-en-eh*$_1$*/ūd-en-eh*$_1$ in predicative use. On the syntactic level, the adverb PIE **ud-en-eh*$_1$*/ūd-en-eh*$_1$ supplied the predicative form of attributive PIE **ū́d-ero-*, **ud-tero-*. This scheme is projected via OE *ūtera*, OHG *ûȥero* into present-day English and German (cf. Pilch, 1970,

[12] Core property adjectives like Engl. *thin*, Germ. *dünn* usually express their antonyms lexically; cf. Cruse (1986, pp. 197–198).

[13] Continued by Gk. ὕστερος 'coming after, behind, latter, last', Ved. *úttara* 'higher, later'; see Dunkel (2014, p. 827). On PIE locatival **-er-* and contrastive-comparative *-(*t*)*ero-*, see respectively Lundquist (2014) with references and Lundquist and Yates (2018, p. 2117).

pp. 116–117; Euler, 2022, pp. 115–117).[14] In English, *utter* is confined to attributive use, being replaced by the adverb *out*/*outside* for predicative use. The same holds for German attributive *äußerer* with predicative adverbial *außen*; likewise, Swedish attributive *yttre* is supplied by the adverbs *ute*, *utanför* in predicative function.

		Engl.	Germ.	Swed.
(20)	attributive adjective:	*an utter disgrace*	*ein äußerer Schaden*	*en yttre skada*
	*predicative adjective barred:	**the disgrace is utter*	**der Schaden ist außer/ äußer*	**skadan är yttre*
	predicative adverb:	*He is out(side)*	*der Schaden ist außen*	*skadan är utanför*

Likewise, Gk. ὕστερος 'latter' < PIE **ud-ter-o-* is also primarily used attributively; other adjectives supply the predicative use. In sum, the synchronic limitations on the morphology and syntax of Engl. *utter* and Germ. *äußerer* are continuations of inherited rules and parameters.

Finally, Germ. *weg* and Engl. *away* show the fewest adjectival properties simply because they are of *non*-adjectival origin, having evolved from a prepositional phrase meaning 'on the way':

(21) MHG *ën-wëc* [ɛnˈvɛk], by apheresis > *wëc* [ˈvɛk] > NHG *weg* [ˈvɛk] 'away' with prosodic conservation of [ɛ] (contrast the NHG noun *Weg* [ˈveːk] 'way' and cf. Yid. *avek*, *vek*, Swed. *iväg* 'away'); see generally OED s.v. *away*, DWB s.v. *weg*.

To sum up, the synchronic scale of defectivity exhibited by the adjectives Engl. *thin* > *utter* > *away* (subsective gradience) and their cognates can be accommodated if we acknowledge the synchronic projection of fragmented diachronic sets of parameters. Precisely the same applies to the other type of gradience, namely, gradience between different categories and word order types, i.e., intersective gradience. A handbook case is the Engl. *ing*-formation, already mentioned in §1. The gradient behavior of *-ing* between noun and verb is dealt with purely synchronically by Aarts (2007, pp. 143–145, 223–225). In reality, it is a case of diachronic-synchronic projection and an iceberg phenomenon, as demonstrated by

[14] PGmc. **ūtera* > OE *ūtera* > *ūttra* (syncope, gemination of [t] before [r]) > *uttra* (vowel shortening before *ttr*) > Engl. *utter*.

the comparison of Engl. *-ing* and its German cognate *-ung* (dialectal *-ing*). In contrast to German, Engl. *-ing* carries an optional verbal feature due to its merger in Middle English with participial *-nd-*. Germ. *-ung* lacks this verbal feature since it has always remained distinct from participial *-nd-*.

3.2 *More Linguistic Iceberg Phenomena and Stranded Rules. German Predicative* Voll *'Full (of)' and* Voller *'Full of, Fraught With'*

The failure to take into account iceberg phenomena has occasionally led to major problems in the synchronic description of languages. The grammatical description of predicative Germ. *voll* 'full (of)' and *voller* 'full of, fraught with' is an excellent case.

The German predicative form *voll* 'full (of)' has a variant with roughly the same meaning, namely, *voller* 'full of, fraught with'.

(22) a. ***voll** reifer Äpfel* 'full of ripe apples'.
b. *Der Baum ist **voller** reifer Äpfel* 'The tree is full of ripe apples.'

Predicative *voller* carries non-comparative semantics meaning 'full of' and exhibits the following irregularities. Morphologically, predicative *voller* is an uninflected form that can agree with all cases and genders.

(23) [nom. sg. masc.]: *ein Baum voller reifer Äpfel* 'a tree full of ripe apples'.
[nom. sg. fem.]: *eine Wiese voller schöner Blumen* 'a meadow full of beautiful flowers'.
[nom. sg. neut.]: *ein Meer voller verschiedener Lebewesen* 'an ocean full of different animals'.
[gen. sg. masc.]: *Ich stand am Fuße eines Baumes voller reifer Äpfel* 'I stood at the foot of a tree full of ripe apples.'
[dat. sg. masc.]: *Ich stand an einem Baum voller reifer Äpfel* 'I stood at a tree full of ripe apples.'
[acc. sg. masc.]: *Ich sah einen Baum voller reifer Äpfel* 'I saw a tree full of ripe apples.'
[acc. pl. masc.]: *Ich sah viele Bäume voller reifer Äpfel* 'I saw many trees full of ripe apples.'

Syntactically, *voller* is restricted to predicative use, as a predicate noun after the copula 'be' or as a predicative adjective phrase immediately following a DP. Furthermore, *voller* requires a complement in the guise of either marked genitive forms or forms that are not specified for case.

On the whole, *voller* 'full of, fraught with' exhibits many more morphological and syntactic restrictions than *voll* 'full (of)'. Table 8.7 lists six limitations on the morphosyntactic use of *voller*.

The limitations listed in Table 8.7 square with the fact that Germ. *voller* is a frozen form, datable to Old High German. More morphosyntactic limitations typically indicate greater linguistic age (Hackstein & Sandell, 2023, pp. 67–68). In accordance with this pattern, the syntactic freezing of the nominative ending *-er* in predicative use matches the freezing of the inherited government of genitive complements.

Table 8.7 Overview of anomalies of predicative Germ. *voller* 'full of, fraught with'

	Germ. *voll* 'full (of)'	Germ. *voller* 'full of, fraught with'
INFLECTION (CASE, NUMBER, GENDER)	fully inflected	uninflected
GRADATION	(*voll, voller, vollsten*)	defective
COMPLEMENTATION	non-obligatory	obligatory
COMPLEMENT TYPE	no complement, genitive complement (restricted to idioms, otherwise obsolete) or prepositional complement	genitive complement or underspecified oblique complement, prepositional complements ungrammatical
ATTRIBUTIVE/PREDICATIVE USAGE	attributive and predicative	predicative only
POSITION	pre- or post-complement position, prepositional complements pre- or postposed (*der mit vielen Fahrgästen sehr volle Zug; der Zug war voll mit Ausflüglern*)	pre-complement position only (*voller guter Absichten*; ungrammatical **guter Absichten voller*)

3.2.1 Synchronic Analysis. Adjective or Preposition?

The synchronic analysis of German predicative *voller* has been controversial. Two approaches have been pursued: taking *voller* to be either an inherited frozen adjective (§3.2.1.1) or a preposition (§3.2.1.2).

3.2.1.1 German *Voller* as Indeclinable Predicative Adjective

Until recently, German predicative *voller* has been regarded as a frozen form of the German adjective *voll*. Cf. the following standard works, listed in reverse chronological order:

(24) Duden 9[8] (2016, p. 997).
Engel (2009, pp. 390–391) ('Adj. mit präpositionalartiger Funktion').
Duden 9[4] (1997, pp. 795–796 s.v. *voll*) ('Nach *voll* wird ein von dem Adjektiv abhängendes Substantiv (Pronomen) entweder in den Genitiv gesetzt oder mit der Präposition *voll* angeschlossen'), 796 ('Gelegentlich wird auch noch die erstarrte gebeugte Form *voller* gebraucht …').
Duden, Deutsches Universalwörterbuch (2001, p. 1744 s.v. *voller*) ('indekl. Adj.').
Duden 4[3] (1973, p. 226, §514) 'unflektiertes Adjektiv', 'Nach dem Substantiv (veraltet) ... mit einem Kopf *voll* Sorgen (oder mit der erstarrten gebeugten Form *voller*: mit einem Kopf *voller* Sorgen)'.
Behaghel, *Deutsche Syntax* I (1923, p. 555).
Paul, *Prinzipien* (1920b, pp. 261–262).
Paul, *Deutsche Grammatik* III (1919, p. 95, §78 & p. 330, §243).
Wilmanns (1906, pp. 574–575, §272 & p. 739, §344[2]).

3.2.1.2 Germ. *Voller* as Preposition

A turn in the synchronic classification of German predicative *voller* has recently occurred (roughly after 2000), under which *voller* plus complement is claimed to be a prepositional phrase. Cf., again in reverse chronological order:

(25) Duden 4[10] (2022, p. 446, §734 & p. 817, §1447).
Duden 4[8] (2009, p. 612, §917) ('*voll* und *voller* [Präpositionen mit dem Genitiv]').

Viewing *voller* as a preposition seems overtly convincing, since syntactically it bears similarities to a preposition in that it requires a complement, and it must be preposed to that obligatory complement. It is furthermore possible for adjectives to turn into prepositions; cf. Aarts (2007, pp. 156–158). Despite these formal similarities to a preposition, however, *voller* does not fully pattern like a preposition and shows more adjectival properties, thus recommending its synchronic classification as a frozen adjective.

3.2.1.3 Synchronic Arguments for *Voller* as Adjective

There are a host of indications that New High German predicative *voller* still functions synchronically as a frozen adjective form:

a. In predicative function, *voll* and *voller* overlap semantically and can be used interchangeably.

(26) a. *ein Platz voll Menschen*
= *ein Platz voller Menschen*
'a square full of people'
b. *Der Platz war voll Menschen.*
= *Der Platz war voller Menschen.*
'the square was full of people'

b. Prepositions indicate primarily spatial or temporal relations, e.g., Germ. *hinter dem Sofa* 'behind the sofa', *nach der Arbeit* 'after work'. The alleged preposition *voller* 'full of, fraught with' is neither spatial nor temporal.
c. *Voller* occurs interchangeably with *voll* postnominally or with the copula *sein* or other copula-like verbs such as *bleiben* 'remain', *hängen* 'hang', *stecken* 'stick'. This would support the adjectival status of Germ. *voller*.

(27) *Der Baum ist/hängt voller/voll reifer Äpfel.*
'The tree is/hangs full of ripe apples.'
Sie war/blieb voller/voll Misstrauen.
'She was/remained full of mistrust.'
Er war/steckte voller/voll Hoffnung.
'He was/*stuck full of hope.'

d. *Voller* occurs interchangeably with the undisputed adjective *voll* in predicative constructions like (28).

(28) *Er kam voller/voll guter Absichten.*
'He came full of good intentions.'

e. The fact that predicative *voller* allows coordination with predicative adjectives might argue for regarding *voller* as an adjective, in accordance with the tendency of identical elements to coordinate.

(29) *eine herrliche Landschaft blühend und voller Leben*
'a beautiful landscape flourishing and full of life'
die Landschaft ist blühend und voller Leben
'the landscape is flourishing and full of life'
jung und voller Ideen
'young and full of ideas'

f. The historical trajectory of Germ. *voller* as continuing a frozen adjectival form of *voll* is well documented; see Wilmanns (1906, pp. 574–575, §272 & p. 739, §344[2]), Paul (1919, p. 95, §78 & p. 330, §243; 1920a, pp. 261–262), and Behaghel (1923, p. 555). In contrast with the Modern German form, OHG *foll* is still fully inflected in predicative use, agreeing in case, gender, and number with its referents; see (30). Besides fully inflected predicative *foll*, Old High German licenses the uninflected use of predicative *foll* in some instances with genitive (31) and with a prepositional phrase *fona* + dative as its complement (32), thus foreshadowing the morphosyntactic use of Modern German predicative *voll*. Cf. the following attestations, found in Ahd. Wb. 3, Sp. 1025–1026.

(30) Old High German predicative *fol*, inflected:

so ist etelicher allero tugede foller[15]
thus is some.NOM.SG.M all.GEN.PL.F virtue.GEN.PL.F full.NOM.SG.M
'thus many are full of virtues' (Nb 285.19 [308.20])

gat siu in eina gruba uolla uuazzeres[16]
go.3.SG.PRES she in a:ACC.SG.F pit.ACC.SG.F full.ACC.SG water.GEN.SG.N
'she steps into a pit full of water' (S 129.83)

(31) Old High German predicative *fol*, uninflected + genitive:

char uol milichi[17]
bowl.ACC.SG.N full.ACC.SG.N milk.GEN.SG
'a bowl full of milk' (Gl 2.683.51)

innan sintun auuar fol totero kapeinnono enti allera unhreinida[18]
inside are in_turn full dead.GEN.PL bone.GEN.PL and all.GEN.SG impurity.GEN.SG
'but inside (they, the graves) are full of dead bones and of all impurity' (z. gl. St. T 141.22)

(32) Old High German predicative *fol*, uninflected with PP *fona* + dative:

thu findist fol then salmon fon thesen selben thingon
you find.2.SG.PRES full.ACC.SG the.ACC.SG salmon.ACC.SG of these.DAT.PL same.DAT.PL thing.DAT.PL
'you find the salmon full of the same things.' (Otfrid 4.28.23)

In sum, the cumulative evidence (a–f) strongly suggests that German predicative *voller* is a frozen adjective form. It may thus be roughly compared with, e.g., Germ. *bar* 'free, devoid of' (= Engl. *bare*, from PIE **bʰosó-* 'naked') in predicative use, which has inflected forms preserved in idioms like *bares Geld* 'cash money'.

---

15 Glossing *est alius cunctis virtutibus absolutus.*

16 Glossing *pergit ad lacum magnum et ingreditur.*

17 Glossing *sinum lactis* (Verg., Ecl. VII.33).

18 Glossing *intus vero plena sunt ossibus mortuorum et omni spurcitia* (F 18.2).

3.2.2 *Germ.* Voller *as an Iceberg Phenomenon*

It emerges from the preceding section that Germ. *voller* continues to function synchronically as an adjective, albeit a frozen one that is restricted to predicative use. The syntax of German can derive the following three sentences:

(33) a. *Der Garten ist voller schöner Blumen.*
b. *Der Garten ist voll schöner Blumen.*
c. *Der Garten ist voll von schönen Blumen.*
'The garden is full of beautiful flowers.'

Germ. *voller*, as in (33a), occurs as a frozen predicative form, agreeing with all cases, numbers, and genders. It can be traced back to OHG *foller*, which is specifically the nominative singular masculine form; cf. (34a) and (34b), (35a) and (35b):

(34) a. OHG *foller spahida* 'full of wisdom'[19] (Gl 1.736.5, Ahd. Wb. 3, Sp. 1026)
b. NHG *er ist voller Weisheit* 'he is full of wisdom'

(35) a. OHG *tes munt foller ist ubelo sprechennis*[20] (NpNpw 9, Diaps. 7 = Npw 9.30, Ahd. Wb. 3, Sp. 1026)
b. NHG *wessen Mund voller übler Rede ist* 'whose mouth is full of malediction'

Furthermore, Germ. *voller* demands an obligatory complement in the genitive. The government of a genitive complement after *voller* is likewise inherited from Old High German and proto-Indo-European; cf., for Old High German, Ahd. Wb. 3, Sp. 1025–1026 (article *fol*), and, for proto-Indo-European, the comparanda in (36).

[19] Predicatively referring to the Christ Child and glossing (*Puer autem crescebat et confortabatur*) *plenus sapientia* (Luke 2.40).

[20] Glossing *cuius maledictione os plenum est.*

(36) NHG *voll* + genitive, OHG *fol*, Engl. *full*, Goth. *fulls* + genitive 'full (of)', Lat. *plēnus* + genitive/ablative 'id.', OIr. *lán* + genitive 'full (of), filled with', Lith. *pìlnas* + genitive 'full, complete', Russ. *pólnyi* + genitive 'full (of), filled with', Ved. *pūrṇá-* + instrumental/genitive 'filled, full, complete', all < PIE *$*p\mathring{l}h_1$-nó-*, resulative verbal adjective 'filled (with)' to *$*pleh_1$-* 'fill' (EWA 3.446, EWAia 2.156).

In contrast, German predicative *voll* in (33b) and (33c) represents the younger form of the predicative adjective, reflexes of which are already recognizable in Old High German; cf. (31) and (32) above. Crucially, (33a–c) are now free variants, with no blocking or elsewhere rules involved. Remarkably, the morphosyntactically inherited form in (33a) *voller*, despite its frozen status, continues to cue the inherited genitive-complement construction. The phenomenon is parallel to that found with the frozen adverbial heads that continue to actively project gender features to be checked by their adjectival bases (§2). We once again encounter the fragmentation of parameters into defunct and active. The inflection of predicative *voller* is defunct, but it continues to cue and actively check its inherited syntactic features in the guise of non-prepositional, genitive complements.

The vitality of predicative *voller* is underscored by the descriptive fact that German predicative *voll* and *voller* do not diverge substantially in their token frequencies. In the *Deutsches Nachrichten-Korpus*, based on texts from 2020 and comprising 35,021,957 sentences, predicative *voll* is grouped in frequency class 8,[21] just above predicative *voller*, which is located in frequency class 9.[22]

4 Conclusion and Prospects

The case studies above underscore the possibility of diachronic continuity in natural language acquisition and illustrate the fragmentation of feature sets, as well as the synchronic vitality of select inherited morphosyntactic

[21] Occupying rank 997; see https://corpora.uni-leipzig.de/de/res?corpusId=deu_news_2020&word=voll (accessed 24 April 2023).

[22] Occupying rank 1848; see https://corpora.uni-leipzig.de/de/res?corpusId=deu_news_2020&word=voller (accessed 24 April 2023).

features. It is a pitfall to reduce linguistic change to obsolescence and complete replacement of older by younger elements. In reality, linguistic splits very often lead to the coexistence of older and younger elements or features, sometimes over long periods of time. This phenomenon is often encountered locally with single lexemes and forms which either are differentiated in meaning, like German inherited strong (irregular) preterite *hieb* 'hit, hewed' alongside innovative weak (regular) *haute* 'hit', or are synonymous, as in the case of English-inherited *dreamt* and *lept* and their innovative counterparts *dreamed* and *leaped*.

Aside from such local inheritances, systematic inheritance of selected grammatical features may also occur. Following the principle that not all linguistic elements change at the same rate, sets of grammatical features may come to be fragmented into defunct and persistently active features. The latter will then surface synchronically as stranded rules and cue effects. Despite differing degrees of deactivation and freezing, frozen constituents may retain fragments of their inherited structural scope. Examples include the German adverbs in *-maßen* and the Western Romance adverbs in *-ment(e)* (§2). In these adverb types, the feminine gender feature of the frozen adverbial heads has outlived their freezing into pseudosuffixes and must be checked by the preceding adjectival bases. In light of the documented transmission of the feminine termination of the adjectival bases, the assumption of stranded rules is less arbitrary and circular than reckoning with ad hoc readjustment rules or acategorial Theme suffixes. We have also seen that German predicative *voller* 'full of, fraught with'—despite its freezing—retains its inherited construction requiring a genitive complement and excluding the innovative PP complement type headed by Germ. *von*. Germ. *voller* 'full of, fraught with' and the competing synonymous *voll* are vacuous with respect to mutual blocking and elsewhere conditions. Since stranded rules as described in this chapter need not involve an elsewhere condition nor blocking or readjustment rules, they must be recognized as a phenomenon in their own right, which should be added to the spell-out mechanisms of Minimalism and Distributed Morphology.

In the case of disjunctive options like English 3sg. pres. with termination -/z/ or -/Ø/, reduction to the synchronic level creates arbitrariness in the morphosyntactic derivation on a synchronic level (why modal verb

3sg. pres. *want-s*, but *can* with null ending?) and circularity on the explanatory level, e.g., 'null ending in 3sg. pres. *can* is preferred over -/z/ in *need-s* because it is an exception.' Why is the same exception not found with the modal verb *want* producing 3sg. pres. **want*?

Such examples argue for the inclusion of more disjunctive heterochrony in synchronic generative modules. The acknowledgment of disjunctive special rules with fragmented persistence of single features (and hence the inclusion of heterochrony in synchronic syntax and morphology) reduces the arbitrariness of the morphosyntactic derivation and replaces circularity on the explanatory level with persistent rule fragments that are not just posited, but in many cases documented in earlier stages of a language. As the abovementioned cases have shown, fragments of inherited rules are transmitted by natural language transmission and, thus, continue to play an active role in the way learners construct their synchronic grammar. On the whole, the results of this chapter accord with the assessment of Kiparsky (2015, pp. 81–86), according to which '[t]he Saussurian firewall between synchrony and diachrony has effectively been breached in research practice, and it would be time to recognise the fact in the academic structure of the field as well.'

References

Aarts, B. (2007). *Syntactic gradience*. Oxford University Press.

Ahd. Wb. 3 = *Althochdeutsches Wörterbuch*. Band 3 (E–F). (1985). (Rudolf Große). Akademie Verlag. https://awb.saw-leipzig.de

Arnon, I., & Clark, E. V. (2011). Why *brush your teeth* is better than *teeth* – Children's word production is facilitated in familiar sentence-frames. *Language Learning and Development, 7*, 107–129.

Balles, I. (2004). Zur Rekonstruktion des früh-urindogermanischen Nominalklassensystems. In A. Hyllested, A. R. Jørgensen, J. H. Larsson, & T. Olander (Eds.), *Per aspera ad asteriscos. Studia Indogermanica in honorem Jens Elmegård Rasmussen* (pp. 43–57). Institut für Sprachen und Literaturen der Universität Innsbruck Innsbrucker.

Bammesberger, A. (1984). *English etymology*. Carl Winter.

Bauer, B. (2010). Forerunners of Romance *-mente* adverbs in Latin prose and poetry. In E. Dickey & A. Chahoud (Eds.), *Colloquial and literary Latin* (pp. 339–353). Cambridge University Press.
Behaghel, O. (1923). *Deutsche Syntax. Eine geschichtliche Darstellung, Band I, Die Wortklassen und Wortformen. A. Nomen. Pronomen.* Carl Winter.
Bybee, J. (2006). From usage to grammar. The mind's response to repetition. *Language, 82*, 711–733.
Cardona, G. (1967). Negations in Pāṇinian rules. *Language, 43*, 34–56.
Cardona, G. (1970). Some principles of Pāṇini's grammar. *Journal of Indian Philosophy, 1*, 40–74.
Cardona, G. (2009). On the structure of Pāṇini's system. In G. Huet, A. Kulkarni, & P. Scharf (Eds.), *Sanskrit computational linguistics. First and Second International Symposia, Rocquencourt, France, October 2007* (pp. 1–32). Springer.
Chomsky, N. (1995). *The Minimalist Program.* MIT Press.
Cruse, D. A. (1986). *Lexical semantics.* Cambridge University Press.
De Saussure, F. (1976). *Cours de linguistique générale.* Édition critique préparée par Tullio de Mauro. Payot.
Detges, U. (2015). The Romance adverbs in *-mente.* A case-study in grammaticalization. In P. O. Müller, I. Ohnheiser, S. Olsen, & F. Rainer (Eds.), *Word formation. An international handbook of the languages of Europe, Band III* (pp. 1824–1842). de Gruyter.
DTA = *Deutsches Textarchiv.* https://www.deutschestextarchiv.de/
Duden 4^{10} = *Duden. Die Grammatik. Struktur und Verwendung der deutschen Sprache. Satz – Wortgruppe – Wort.* (2022). herausgegeben von Angelika Wöllstein und der Dudenredaktion. Cornelsen Verlag.
Duden 4^{3} = *Duden. Grammatik der deutschen Gegenwartssprache.* (1973). bearbeitet von Paul Grebe unter Mitwirkung von Helmut Gipper, Max Mangold, Wolfgang Mentrup, & Christian Winkler. Dudenverlag.
Duden 4^{8} = *Duden. Die Grammatik. Unentbehrlich für richtiges Deutsch.* (2009). herausgegeben von der Dudenredaktion. Dudenverlag.
Duden 9^{4} = *Duden. Richtiges und gutes Deutsch. Wörterbuch der sprachlichen Zweifelsfälle.* (1997). Dudenverlag.
Duden 9^{8} = *Duden. Richtiges und gutes Deutsch. Wörterbuch der sprachlichen Zweifelsfälle^{8}*. (2016). Dudenverlag.
Duden. Deutsches Universalwörterbuch = *Duden. Deutsches Universalwörterbuch^{4}*. (2001). Dudenverlag.
Dunkel, George. (2014). *Lexikon der indogermanischen Partikeln und Pronominalstämme*, Band 2: Lexikon. Carl Winter.

DWB = *Deutsches Wörterbuch von Jacob und Wilhelm Grimm*. https://woerterbuchnetz.de
DWDS = *Digitales Wörterbuch der deutschen Sprache*. https://www.dwds.de/
Ekwall, E. (1965). *Historische neuenglische Laut- und Formenlehre*[4]. de Gruyter.
Embick, D. (2007). Blocking effects and analytic/synthetic relations. *Natural Language & Linguistic Theory, 25*, 1–37.
Embick, D., & Halle, M. (2005). On the status of *stems* in morphological theory. In T. Geerts, I. van Ginneken, & H. Jacobs (Eds.), *Proceedings of going Romance 2003* (pp. 37–62). John Benjamins.
Engel, U. (2009). *Deutsche Grammatik. Eine Neubearbeitung*[2]. Iudicium Verlag.
Euler, W. (2022). *Das Westgermanische. Seine Rekonstruktion von der Herausbildung im 3. Jahrhundert bis zur Aufgliederung im 7. Jahrhundert*. Verlag Inspiration Unlimited.
EWA 3 = Albert L. Lloyd & Rosemarie Lühr, *Etymologisches Wörterbuch des Althochdeutschen*, Band 3: *fadum–fûstslag* (2003). Vandenhoeck & Ruprecht.
EWAia 2 = Manfred Mayrhofer, *Etymologisches Wörterbuch des Altindoarischen*. II. Band (1996). Carl Winter.
Givón, T. (1984). *Syntax. An introduction 1*. John Benjamins.
Hackstein, O., & Sandell, R. (2023). The rise of colligations. E. *can't stand*, G. *nicht ausstehen können*. *International Journal of Corpus Linguistics, 28*, 60–90.
Halle, M., & Marantz, A. (1993). Distributed morphology and the pieces of inflection. In K. Hale & S. J. Keyser (Eds.), *The view from building 20. Essays in linguistics in honor of Sylvain Bromberger* (pp. 111–176). MIT Press.
Halle, M., & Marantz, A. (1994). Some key features of distributed morphology. *MIT Working Papers in Linguistics, 21*, 275–288.
Hansen, E., & Nielsen, H. F. (2007). *Irregularities in modern English*[2]. Rev. by E. Hansen. John Benjamins.
Hopper, P. J. (1991). On some principles of grammaticization. In E. C. Traugott & B. Heine (Eds.), *Approaches to grammaticalization* (Vol. I, pp. 17–36). John Benjamins.
Huddleston, R., Pullum, G. K., et al. (2002). *The Cambridge grammar of the English language*. Cambridge University Press.
Karlsson, K. E. (1981). *Syntax and affixation. The evolution of MENTE in Latin and Romance*. Max Niemeyer.
Kiparsky, P. (1973). 'Elsewhere' in phonology. In S. R. Anderson & P. Kiparsky (Eds.), *A festschrift for Morris Halle* (pp. 93–106). Holt, Reinhart, and Winston.

Kiparsky, P. (2005). Blocking and periphrasis in inflectional paradigms. In G. Booij & J. van Marle (Eds.), *Yearbook of morphology 2004* (pp. 113–135). Springer.
Kiparsky, P. (2015). New perspectives on historical linguistics. In C. Bowern & B. Evans (Eds.), *The Routledge handbook of historical linguistics* (pp. 64–102). Routledge.
Köpcke, K.-M., & Zubin, D. A. (1984). Sechs Prinzipien für die Genuszuweisung im Deutschen. *Linguistische Berichte, 93*, 26–50.
Krahe, H., & Meid, W. (1969). *Germanische Sprachwissenschaft III, Wortbildungslehre*. Walter de Gruyter.
Labov, W. (1989). The child as linguistic historian. *Language Variation and Change, 1*, 85–97.
Labov, W. (2001). *Principles of linguistic change 2, Social factors*. Blackwell.
Labov, W. (2006). *The Social Stratification of English in New York City*.[2] Cambridge University Press.
Lausberg, H. (1972). *Romanische Sprachwissenschaft, Band III, Formenlehre*. Walter de Gruyter.
LSJ = *A Greek-English lexicon*, compiled by Henry George Liddell & Robert Scott, revised and augmented by Sir Henry Stuart Jones. With a supplement 1968. Clarendon Press.
Lundquist, J. (2014). Rigvedic *uṣar* and the Indo-European locatival **-er*. In S. W. Jamison, H. Craig Melchert, & B. Vine (Eds.), *Proceedings of the 25th Annual UCLA Indo-European Conference* (pp. 87–103). Hempen.
Lundquist, J., & Yates, A. D. (2018). The morphology of proto-Indo-European. In J. Klein, B. Joseph, & M. Fritz (Eds.), *Handbook of historical and Indo-European linguistics* (pp. 2056–2195). De Guyter Mouton.
Maitz, P., & Tronka, K. (2009). *Brauchen*–Phonologische Aspekte der Auxiliarisierung. *Zeitschrift für Dialektologie und Linguistik, 76*, 189–202.
McCartney, E. S. (1920). Forerunners of the Romance adverbial suffix. *Classical Philology, 15*, 213–229.
Meillet, A. (1937). *Introduction à l'étude comparative des langues indo-européennes*[8]. Hachette.
Miller, D. G. (2012). *External influences on English. From its beginnings to its Renaissance*. Oxford University Press.
Mossé, F. (1952). *Handbook of Middle English* (James A. Walker, Trans.). The Johns Hopkins Press.
Norde, M. (2009). *Degrammaticalization*. Oxford University Press.
OED = *Oxford English dictionary*. https://www.oed.com

Paul, H. (1917). *Deutsche Grammatik*. Band II. Teil III: *Flexionslehre*. Max Niemeyer.
Paul, H. (1919). *Deutsche Grammatik*. Band III. Teil IV: *Syntax* (Erste Hälfte). Max Niemeyer.
Paul, H. (1920a). *Deutsche Grammatik*. Band IV. Teil IV: *Syntax* (Zweite Hälfte). Max Niemeyer Verlag.
Paul, H. (1920b). *Prinzipien der Sprachgeschichte*[5]. M. Niemeyer.
Pilch, H. (1970). *Altenglische Grammatik*. Max Hueber.
Quirk, R., Greenbaum, S., Leech, G., & Svartvik, J. (1985). *A comprehensive grammar of the English language*. Longman.
Rheinfelder, H. (1976a). *Alfranzösische Grammatik*. 2. Teil: *Formenlehre und Syntax*[2]. Max Hueber Verlag.
Rheinfelder, H. (1976b). *Alfranzösische Grammatik*. 1. Teil: *Lautlehre*[5]. Max Hueber Verlag.
Ringe, D. (2017). *From proto-Indo-European to proto-Germanic*[2]. Oxford University Press.
Ringe, D., & Eska, J. F. (2013). *Historical linguistics. Toward a twenty-first century reintegration*. Cambridge University Press.
Schindler, J. (1972). L'apophonie des noms-racines indo-européens. *Bulletin de la Société de Linguistique, 67*, 31–38.
van Gelderen, E. (2015). Generative syntax and language change. In C. Bowern & B. Evans (Eds.), *The Routledge handbook of historical linguistics* (pp. 326–342). Routledge.
Weber, D. (2000). On the function of gender. In B. Unterbeck, M. Rissanen, T. Nevlainen, & M. Saari (Eds.), *Gender in grammar and cognition* (pp. 495–509). Mouton de Gruyter.
Wilmanns, W. (1906). *Deutsche Grammatik*. Dritte Abteilung: *Flexion*. 1. Hälfte: *Verbum*. Erste und zweite Auflage. Karl J. Trübner.
Wolf, L., & Hupka, W. (1981). *Altfranzösisch, Entstehung und Charakteristik*. Wissenschaftliche Buchgesellschaft.
Zipf, G. K. (1949). *Human behavior and the principle of least effort. An Introduction to human ecology*. Addison-Wesley Press.

9

Forced to Force? Remarks on the Architecture of the Left Periphery of Early Irish and Absolute/Conjunct Morphology

Jean-François Mondon and Joseph F. Eska

1 What's Going on in the Left Periphery of Early Irish?[1]

The VSO word order of Irish is generally presumed to be the result of verb movement to the beginning of the clause for special marking, and then that special value having become semantically bleached so that the initial position of the verb became unmarked (going back to Watkins, 1963; so also Newton, 2006).

[1] It is our pleasure to offer this piece to Don Ringe, who introduced the first author to Old Irish 20 years ago.

J.-F. Mondon (✉)
Muskingum University, New Concord, OH, USA
e-mail: jmondon@muskingum.edu

J. F. Eska
Virginia Polytechnic Institute & State University, Blacksburg, VA, USA
e-mail: eska@vt.edu

J. F. Eska et al. (eds.), *The Method Works*,
https://doi.org/10.1007/978-3-031-48959-4_9

In contemporary terms, we would say that a verb that had been fronted to a TOPIC (e.g., [1a]) or FOCUS position (1b) in the left periphery of the clause was reanalysed by a new generation of language learners as occurring in the FINITE head (1c) once it became pragmatically neutral.

(1) a. $[_{\text{FrameP}}$ $[_{\text{ForceP}}$ $[_{\text{AbTopP}}$ $[_{\text{AbTop}}$ **V**] $[_{\text{ContrTopP}}$ $[_{\text{FocP}}$ $[_{\text{Foc}}$ $[_{\text{FamTopP}}$ $[_{\text{FinP}}$ $[_{\text{TP}}$ **S** $[_{\text{T}}$ ~~**V**~~] $[_{\text{vP}}$ $[_{\text{v}}$ ~~**V**~~] **O**]]]]]]]]]
b. $[_{\text{FrameP}}$ $[_{\text{ForceP}}$ $[_{\text{AbTopP}}$ $[_{\text{ContrTopP}}$ $[_{\text{FocP}}$ $[_{\text{Foc}}$ **V**] $[_{\text{FamTopP}}$ $[_{\text{FinP}}$ $[_{\text{TP}}$ **S** $[_{\text{T}}$ ~~**V**~~] $[_{\text{vP}}$ $[_{\text{v}}$ ~~**V**~~] **O**]]]]]]]]]
c. $[_{\text{FrameP}}$ $[_{\text{ForceP}}$ $[_{\text{AbTopP}}$ $[_{\text{ContrTopP}}$ $[_{\text{FocP}}$ $[_{\text{FamTopP}}$ $[_{\text{FinP}}$ $[_{\text{Fin}}$ **V**] $[_{\text{TP}}$ **S** $[_{\text{T}}$ ~~**V**~~] $[_{\text{vP}}$ $[_{\text{v}}$ ~~**V**~~] **O**]]]]]]]]]

This looks straightforward enough. Since we need FRAMEP for hanging topics (nominativi pendentes) and FORCEP for complementisers in embedded clauses, it looks like the left periphery for Early Irish should be:

(2) $[_{\text{FrameP}}$ $[_{\text{ForceP}}$ $[_{\text{FinP}}$ $[_{\text{TP}}$ …]]]]

The situation is not so simple, however. Lash (2014) has shown that, in fact, there are multiple subject positions in Early Irish. Cf.:

(3) a. MT §38.14–15:

Ma	*do·airli*	*[sale]*	***danō***	*ind*	*lāim*	*oc*	*praind*
if	PV·fall.3.SG.PRES	spittle.NOM.SG	ADV	into	hand.ACC.SG	at	meal.DAT.SG

'Now, if spittle falls into the hand at a meal …'

b. WMS 316.17–18:

Do·ber	***danō***	*[rí*	*Locha Léin]*	*a*	*gīall*	*do*
PV·give.3.SG.PRES	ADV	king.NOM.SG	L.L.GEN.SG	3.SG.M.POSS	hostage.ACC.SG	to
ríg	*Cīarraige*	*fri*	*a*	*folta*	*tēcti*	
king.DAT.SG	C.GEN.SG	against	3.SG.M.POSS	obligation.ACC.PL	proper.ACC.PL	

'The king of L. L. gives his hostage to the king of C. in accord with his proper obligations.'

Lash demonstrates that the pre-adverbial position correlates with old information, while the post-adverbial position correlates with new information. He, furthermore, shows that the pre-adverbial position is not specialised for subjects alone, while the post-adverbial position is (2014, p. 305, 2020), e.g.:

(4) a. Ml. 128[a]4:

Ní·cinni	*[aimsir]*	[donec]	*hi*	*sunt*
NEG·define.3.SG.PRES	time.ACC.SG	*donec*	in	here

'(The word) *donec* does not define time here.'

b. TBC[1] 55.1788:

At·bail	*[fo*	*chétóir]*	*[Fer Báeth]*	*isinn*	*glind*
PV.3.SG.N·throw.3.SG.PRES	under	first-hour.DAT.SG	F. B.NOM.SG	in.DEF	glen.DAT.SG

'F. B. falls dead at once in the glen.'

Since SpecTP is a position that is known to be specified for (active) subjects, we presume that the adverb adjoins to TP and that the pre-adverbial position, obviously, is higher.

(5) $[_{\text{FrameP}}\ [_{\text{ForceP}}\ [_{\text{AbTopP}}\ [_{\text{ContrTopP}}\ [_{\text{FocP}}\ [_{\text{FamTopP}}\ [_{\text{FinP}}\ [_{\text{Fin}}\ \mathbf{V}]\ [_{\text{TP}}\ \mathbf{Adv}\ [_{\text{TP}}\ \mathbf{S}\ \ldots]]]]]]]]]$

But where does the pre-adverbial XP land? Since Lash shows that there are at least two positions to the left of the adverb, e.g.:

(6) AMC 2.53:

Do·romel	*[Cathal]*	*[na*	*hubla]*	***īarum***
PV·PERF.consume.3.SG.PRET	C.NOM.SG	DEF	apple.ACC.PL	ADV

'C. thereupon ate the apples.'

the verb evidently must be higher in the left periphery. The best candidate appears to be Force; cf. the existence of Force V2 languages as originally posited by Poletto (2002), e.g., Modern Dutch and Modern German:

(7) $[_{\text{FrameP}}\ [_{\text{ForceP}}\ \mathbf{XP}\ [_{\text{Force}}\ \mathbf{V}]\ [_{\text{AbTopP}}\ [_{\text{ContrTopP}}\ [_{\text{FocP}}\ [_{\text{FamTopP}}\ [_{\text{FinP}}$ ~~**XP**~~ $[_{\text{Fin}}$ ~~**V**~~ $]\ \ldots]]]]]]$

This creates a dilemma, however, because it is usually assumed either that the absolute versus conjunct flexional opposition in simplex verbs in Early Irish is triggered by the verb being in different positions in the syntactic tree or that the verb raises no higher than the T node.

Any synchronic theory, therefore, must account for the following facts:

(8) a. The distribution of absolute versus conjunct flexion
b. The location of stress in the verbal complex
c. The verb's position relative to adverbs

2 Previous Accounts

To date there have been three proposals for the synchronic analysis of Early Irish verbal inflexion:

(9) a. Carnie et al. (1994, 2000; hereafter CHP)
b. Adger (2006) (with a minor modification by Arregi & Nevins, 2012, pp. 246–250)
c. Newton (2006, 2008, 2009)

Since these theories predate Lash's work, they do not address (8c). In light of his work, Adger's and Newton's theories both falter, since they assume that the verb never moves beyond T.

CHP's proposal, on the other hand, does allow for verb movement. It follows the Germanic V2-literature by assuming that Old Irish has a filled-C requirement. When a simplex verb raises to C, it receives absolute endings; when it remains in T, it bears conjunct endings. In forms such as compound *do·beir*, to prevent the verb from moving to C and, hence, receiving absolute endings, CHP maintain that the preverb *do-* excorporates from the verbal complex and it alone moves. The attractive simplicity of their model is compromised by their recourse to excorporation, a process largely rejected by syntacticians (e.g., Dékány, 2018).

3 Distribution of Absolute Versus Conjunct

We limit ourselves here primarily to addressing (8a), the absolute versus conjunct opposition, though we return briefly to (8b) at the end of this chapter. It is straightforward to describe the parameters under which the two sets of endings occur. Absolute endings appear on verbs which are preceded neither by a conjunct particle (a variety of conjunctions, negators, and complementisers) nor by a preverb. Conjunct endings occur in all other contexts. This distribution is illustrated in (10) with present forms of simplex *biru* 'I bring' and compound *do·biur* 'I give' with and without the INTERROG. PTCL. *in·*.

(10)

	Simplex verb	Simplex verb with conjunct particle	Compound verb with preverb	Compound verb with preverb and conjunct particle
1. sg.	*biru*	*in·biur*	*do·biur*	*in·tabur*
2.	*biri*	*in·bir*	*do·bir*	*in·tabair*
3.	*beirid*	*in·beir*	*do·beir*	*in·tabair*
1. pl.	*bermai*	*in·beram*	*do·beram*	*in·taibrem*
2.	*beirthe*	*in·beirid*	*do·beirid*	*in·taibrid*
3.	*berait*	*in·berat*	*do·berat*	*in·taibret*

Translating this clear partition into a synchronic analysis is not a straightforward task, however, owing to the limitations imposed by the theoretical model which is adopted.

4 Distributed Morphology and Locality

We follow Adger (2006), Newton (2006), and Arregi & Nevins (2012) in employing the framework of Distributed Morphology (Halle & Marantz, 1993). The main innovation of this framework is the rejection of a lexical component, wholly independent of the syntax, in which words are created and stored. It proposes, instead, that the structure of words and the structure of sentences are both built from the same blueprint. Strong evidence for this proposal comes from the observation that the order of morphemes within words seems to mirror the order of syntactic elements in a clause (Baker, 1985, 1988). Observe the interplay between reciprocal (RECIP) and causative (CAUS) morphemes in Quechua (Muysken, 1981):

(11) a. *maqa- naku- ya- chi- -n*
beat RECIP DUR CAUS 3.SG
'He is causing them to beat each other.'

b. *maqa- chi- naku- rka- -n*
beat CAUS RECIP PL 3.SG
'They let someone beat each other.'

The difference in interpretation between (11a) and (11b) is the result of the different order of morphemes, i.e., 'scope'. Scope differences also arise within sentences from the interplay of individual words.

(12) a. Mary did *not* say that it would snow.
b. Mary said that it would *not* snow.

One major constraint imposed upon Distributed Morphology is a locality condition (Embick, 2010): a morpheme can only interact with another morpheme with which it is local. This poses an obvious problem for Early Irish. In order to insert the 2. PL. PRES. INDIC. conjunct ending *-id* after the root *beir-*, for example, the ending must see beyond the root and determine whether anything precedes the verbal root itself, whether preverb or conjunct particle. The ending, therefore, needs to look to something which is not immediately local to it. The same is true in the case of absolute flexion. 2. PL. PRES. INDIC. absolute *-the* must look for the absence of a preverb or conjunct particle on the other side of the root, likewise a non-local environment.

5 The Old Irish Verb Complex

In order to frame the selection of absolute/conjunct endings to local conditions only, it is necessary to treat preverbs and conjunct particles separately, since we take them to be located in different positions in the syntactic structure. Preverbs are structurally closer to verbs than are conjunct particles (contra Newton). This proximity allows preverbs to alter the fundamental lexical semantics of verbal roots, e.g. (adapted after Schumacher, 2004, pp. 538–539):

(13) a. *reith-* 'rennen, laufen' ('run')
b. (**ad-*): *ad·reith* 'zulaufen auf, angreifen, überholen, fassen' ('run up to', 'attack', overtake', 'grasp')
c. (**ambi-*): *imm·reith* '(um etwas) herumlaufen' ('run around [something]')

d. (**ari-*): *ar·reith* 'angreifen, einholen, fassen' ('attack', 'obtain', 'grasp')
e. (**dī-uss-*): *do·fúarat* '(übrig)bleiben' ('be left over')
f. (**en-uss-*): *in·úarat* 'angreifen' ('attack')
g. (**ēr-u̯o-uss-*): *íarmi·forat* '(ver)folgen' ('pursue')
h. (**kom-to-enter-*): *con·tetarrat* 'erfassen, einschließen' ('seize', 'include')
i. (**to-*): *do·reith* 'eilen (zu), durchqueren' ('rush [to]', 'traverse')
j. (**to-ari-ande-*): *do·airndret* 'durcheinanderlaufen' ('clutter')
k. (**to-ambi-dī-*): *do·immthiret* 'dienen' ('serve')
l. **to-ēr-u̯o-uss-*): *do·íarmórat* 'folgen' ('follow')
m. (**u̯o-to-ambi-dī-*): *fo·timmdiret* 'suffire' ('suffice')
n. (**u̯or-de-uss-*): *for·dúarat* 'superesse' ('remain')

The complex head resulting from the verb's movement to Force, therefore, is (14).

(14) Old Irish verbal complex

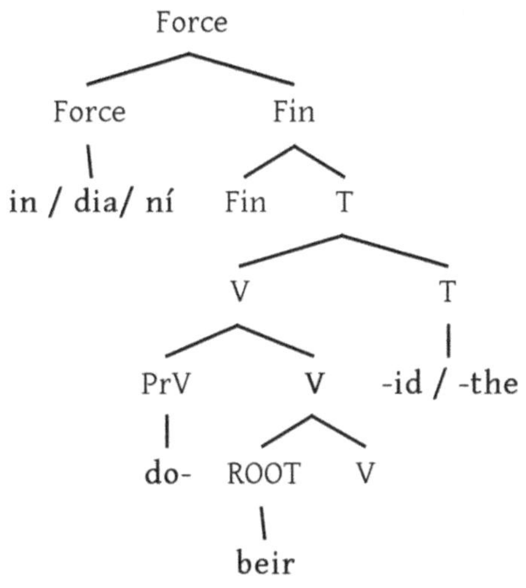

6 Conditioning of Absolute/Conjunct Endings. Preverbs

It is clear where each morpheme is located, but not how to locally condition the endings in T. It is well known that certain affixes can affect the phonology of the stem to which they are attached, whereas others cannot. English, for example, has long been known to possess two types of affixes, termed 'Class 1' and 'Class 2'. The former, among other things, can affect the location of stress on the root to which they attach, whereas the latter cannot:

(15) a. Class 1 affix: ˈautumn → auˈtumn-al
b. Class 2 affix: ˈautumn → ˈautumn-ness

A Class 2 affix is unable to affect the location of the stress not only of the root to which it attaches, but also of the stem to which it attaches, as when it follows a Class 1 affix:

(16) auˈtumn-al-ness

Class 2 affixes, thus, seem to be blind to the phonetics of the root/stem to which they attach. This insight has been incorporated into various instantiations of the idea of cycles in phonology. There is a clear similarity between the idea of a phonological cycle and a syntactic phase. Specifically, it has been proposed that a morpheme in one phase is incapable of seeing a particular morpheme in an earlier phase, even if they are linearly adjacent (Embick, 2010, 2014).

Following research on preverbs in a variety of languages (cf. especially Šereikaitė, 2018 on Lithuanian), we propose that Old Irish preverbs instantiate their own phase. When a preverb is present, it is attached to the root first, making the root invisible to subsequent phases. In such a situation, then, when the verbal ending is attached, it cannot see the root, since the root had appeared in an earlier phase. This (in)visibility of the root is what conditions the appearance of absolute endings.

(17) Conditioning of absolute versus conjunct endings

Absolute: ending occurs in the same phase as the root
Conjunct: elsewhere

The derivation of the 2. PL. PRES. INDIC. conjunct *do·beirid*, which has two phases, thus runs as follows. The preverb is added in Phase 1; as a result, the ending cannot see the root in Phase 2 and so selects the conjunct form *-id*.

(18) a. Phase 1: *do – beir*
b. Phase 2: *-id*
c. Output: *do·beirid*

The derivation of the 2. PL. PRES. INDIC. absolute *beirthe*, which has only one phase, runs as follows. Since the ending is added in the same phase as the root, the absolute form *-the* is selected.

(19) a. Phase 1: *beir – the*
b. Output: *beirthe*

7 Conditioning of Absolute/Conjunct Endings. Conjunct Particles

With preverbs addressed, we turn now to conjunct particles. As it currently stands, the conditioning environment in (17) predicts that absolute endings should be added to a simplex verb when a conjunct particle is present, since the verbal ending is attached in the same phase as the verbal root (cf. 19a). This, however, cannot be correct, since we do not get 2. PL. PRES. INDIC. ***in·beirthe* (cf. correct *in·beirid*). How, then, can the endings be conditioned by a conjunct particle to which they are not local?

It has been proposed that a morpheme can be conditioned by the presence of a semantic or morphosyntactic feature which occurs above it in a syntactic tree. Bobaljik (2000, p. 15) illustrates this with the Bulgarian preterite suffix. The suffix has two allomorphs, *-x-* and *-∅-*:

(20) Allomorphy in the Bulgarian preterite

	Singular	*Plural*
1.	*pék-o-**x***	*pék-o-**x**-me*
2.	*pék-e*	*pék-o-**x**-te*
3.	*pék-e*	*pék-o-**x**-a*

The allomorph selection is conditioned by the person/number of the subject affix, which is outside of the tense suffix (and hence higher in the syntactic tree). The preterite allomorph is *not* conditioned, however, by the specific individual subject morphemes.

(21) Bulgarian verbal complex[2]

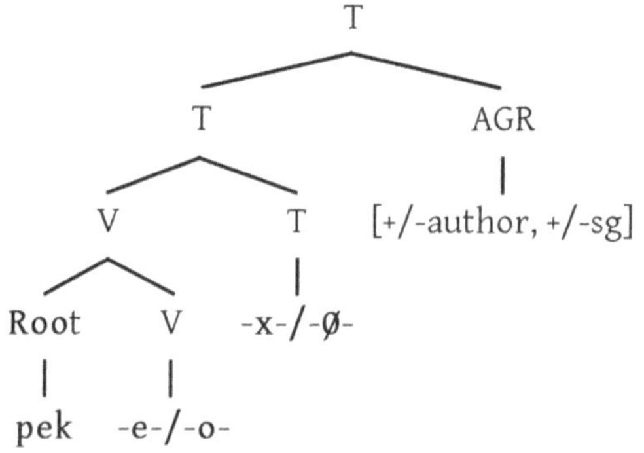

(22) Bulgarian preterite suffix

-Ø-: when followed by [–author, +sg]
-x-: elsewhere

Applying this to the Early Irish absolute/conjunct distinction, we propose the added conditioning environment for absolute endings: there must be no syntactico-semantic feature hierarchically above T in the verbal complex. Representing the lack of features by [ ], we rewrite the conditioning environments for absolute and conjunct as in (23):

[2] We adopt the feature [author] from Halle (1997) and Nevins (2007), the latter of whom defines [+author] as 'the reference set contain[ing] the speaker'.

(23) Conditioning of absolute versus conjunct endings

Absolute: when the ending is in the same phase as the root and immediately dominated by [ ]
Conjunct: elsewhere[3]

The derivations of 2. PL. PRES. INDIC. (a) *in·beirid*, (b) *do·beirid*, (c) *in·taibrid*, and (d) *beirthe* run as follows. [Q] represents an interrogative feature.

(24)

	(a)	(b)	(c)	(d)
Phase1	[Q] *beir – id*	[ ] *do – beir*	[Q] *do – beir*	[ ] *beir – the*
Phase 2	*in-beir – id*	*do-beir – id*	[Q] *do·beir – id*	—
Phase 3	—	—	*in-do·beir – id*	—
Input to phonology	*in·beirid*	*do·beirid*	*in-do·beirid*	*beirthe*
Output	*in·beirid*	*do·beirid*	*in·taibrid*	*beirthe*

8 Morphosyntactic Reflex of the Cowgill Particle

It has been the communis opinio for some time now that the absolute versus conjunct dichotomy has its origin in the eponymous particle proposed by Cowgill (1975). The Cowgill Particle—one common reconstruction of which is **eti* (Schrijver, 1994; Schumacher, 2004, pp. 97–103)—followed the initial element of the verbal complex. It appeared after the initial conjunct particle or preverb of the verbal complex; absent either, it occurred after the inflectional ending. The conditioning environment for the absolute endings in (23) is a direct morphosyntactic reflection of the original conditions in which the Cowgill Particle found itself following a verb, viz., when the verb lacked a preverb and was in clause initial position.

[3] It is possible to avoid a conditionless default via the following vocabulary entries:
Absolute: when the ending is in the same phase as the root
Conjunct: when the ending is immediately dominated by some feature [x]
This analysis requires ordering, however, with the conjunct vocabulary entry taking priority over the absolute vocabulary entry, otherwise non-prefixed negative verbs would occur with absolute endings. In order to avoid rule-ordering, we prefer the conditioning environments presented in the main text.

9 Morphophonological Reflex of the Cowgill Particle

It is still possible, however, to see a morphophonological reflex of the Cowgill Particle when one considers (8b): the location of stress in the verbal complex. In Old Irish, stress falls on the initial syllable of a verbal root when no preverb or conjunct particle is present. Stress otherwise falls on the initial syllable of the second syntactic head in the verbal complex.

(25) a. No preverb or conjunct particle: *ˈbeirid*
b. Preverb: *do·ˈbeir*
c. Conjunct particle: *in·ˈbeir*
d. Conjunct particle and preverb: *in·ˈtabair*

These synchronic forms can be straightforwardly rendered into a Bracket and Erasure formulation (Idsardi & Halle, 1995).[4] The correct location of stress is predicted by assuming:

(26) a. Every Old Irish verb contains at least one foot—indicated by a right round bracket inserted at the end of the word.
b. All preverbs and conjunct particles are marked as forming the left boundary of a following foot—indicated by a left round bracket placed immediately after each preverb and conjunct particle.
c. The leftmost syllable of the leftmost foot bears the stress.

The underlying accentual specification of the relevant morphemes would thus have been:

[4] In this model, feet may be determined by a single bracket, whose head is determined by a language's setting for the binary parameter HEAD. This parameter, whose possible settings are R(ight) and L(eft), determines which syllable in a foot is projected onto the following line. In Early Irish, HEAD is set to L, resulting in the leftmost syllable of each foot being projected to the following line. When there is more than one foot initially, the head of each projects to the second line, and the leftmost syllable of those projected syllables alone is projected to the next line. This process is iterative until only one syllable is projected, which bears the word's stress. These are the Basic Accentuation Principle(s) inherited from proto-Indo-European (Kiparsky & Halle, 1977).

(27)

x	x(	x(
beir	in	do

The forms in (25) were thus specified as:

(28)

x x	x(x	x(x	x(x(x
ˈbeir – id	do ˈbeir	in ˈbeir	in ˈta bair

Insertion of right round bracket:

(29)

x x)	x(x)	x(x)	x(x(x)
ˈbeir – id	do ˈbeir	in ˈbeir	in ˈta bair

Projection of leftmost syllable of each foot:

(30)

x	x	x	x x
x x)	x(x)	x(x)	x(x(x)
ˈbeir – id	do ˈbeir	in ˈbeir	in ˈta bair

Insertion of right round bracket and projection of leftmost syllable:

			x
x	x	x	x x)
x x)	x(x)	x(x)	x(x(x)
ˈbeir – id	do ˈbeir	in ˈbeir	in ˈta bair

We propose that the underlying left round bracket which follows preverbs and conjunct particles is the phonological detritus of the original Cowgill Particle.[5]

[5] This approach also accounts for deuterotonic forms following certain particles, such as *ma* 'if', e.g., *ma·dugnether* 'if it should be done' (Wb. 5c23). This particle does not have a left round bracket underlying. How this came about historically, however, is another question.

This particle is also unique in that a following simplex verb takes absolute endings rather than conjunct endings. One way to account for this oddity synchronically is to assume that it is base-generated in the Spec of ForceP and not in Force itself, as are other particles, such as the semantically close *día* 'if'. As such, *ma* does not form part of the verb's morphosyntactic head, and its syntactico-semantic features are, thus, irrelevant to the selection of absolute endings. How this morphosyntactic situation arose diachronically, however, is, likewise, an open question.

10 Conclusion

This approach is wholly compatible with Lash's result, thereby accounting for (8a) and (8c), and it does not present any issue in accounting for the stress placement (8b). It has the added advantage of treating conjunct endings as the default forms, which seems to be the case, since they occur in a disparate range of syntactico-semantic environments, even when a preverb or conjunct particle is not present, as in responses to direct questions or in imperatives. Much work remains, however. Among other questions, it would be ideal to have the appearance of the default preverb *no-* fall out naturally from our analysis.

References

Adger, D. (2006). Post-syntactic movement and the Old Irish verb. *Natural Language & Linguistic Theory, 24*, 605–654.

AMC = Jackson, K. H. (ed.). (1990). *Aislinge meic Con Glinne*. Dublin Institute for Advanced Studies.

Arregi, K., & Nevins, A. (2012). *Morphotactics. Basque auxiliaries and the structure of spellout*. Springer.

Baker, M. (1985). The mirror principle and morphosyntactic explanation. *Linguistic Inquiry, 16*, 373–416.

Baker, M. (1988). *Incorporation. A theory of grammatical function changing*. University of Chicago Press.

Bobaljik, J. (2000). The ins and outs of contextual allomorphy. *University of Maryland Working Papers in Linguistics, 10*, 35–71.

Carnie, A., Harley, H., & Pyatt, E. (1994). The resurrection. Raising to Comp. Evidence from Old Irish. *Studies in the Linguistic Sciences, 24*, 85–100.

Carnie, A., Harley, H., & Pyatt, E. (2000). VSO order as raising out of IP? In A. Carnie & E. Guilfoyle (Eds.), *The syntax of verb initial languages* (pp. 39–59). Oxford University Press.

Cowgill, W. (1975). The origins of the Insular Celtic conjunct and absolute verbal endings. In H. Rix (Ed.), *Flexion und Wortbildung, Akten der V. Fachtagung der Indogermanischen Gesellschaft, Regensburg, 9.-14. September 1973* (pp. 40–70). Dr. Ludwig Reichert.

Dékány, É. (2018). Approaches to head movement. A critical assessment. *Glossa. A Journal of General Linguistics, 3: 65*, 1–43.

Embick, D. (2010). *Localism versus globalism in morphology and phonology.* MIT Press.

Embick, D. (2014). Phase cycles, φ-cycles, and phonological (in)activity. In S. Bendjaballah, N. Faust, M. Lahrouchi, & N. Lampitelli (Eds.), *The form of structure, the structure of forms. Essays in honor of Jean Lowenstamm* (pp. 270–286). John Benjamins.

Halle, M. (1997). Impoverishment and fission. In B. Bruening, Y. Kang, & M. McGinnis (Eds.), *PF. Papers at the interface* (pp. 425–450). MITWPL.

Halle, M., & Marantz, A. (1993). Distributed morphology and the pieces of inflection. In K. Hale & S. J. Keyser (Eds.), *The view from building 20. Essays in linguistics in honor of Sylvain Bromberger* (pp. 111–176). MIT Press.

Idsardi, W., & Halle, M. (1995). General properties of stress and metrical structure. In J. Goldsmith (Ed.), *The handbook of phonological theory* (pp. 403–443). Blackwell.

Kiparsky, P., & Halle, M. (1977). Towards a reconstruction of the Indo-European accent. In L. M. Hyman (Ed.), *Studies in stress and accent* (pp. 209–238). Department of Linguistics, University of Southern California.

Lash, E. (2014). Subject positions in Old and Middle Irish. *Lingua, 148*, 278–308.

Lash, E. (2020). Transitivity and subject positions in Old Irish. *Transactions of the Philological Society, 118*, 94–140.

Ml. = The Milan glosses and scholia on the psalms. In Whitley Stokes & John Strachan (Eds. & Trs.). (1903–1905). *Thesaurus Palaeohibernicus. A collection of Old-Irish glosses, scholia, prose, and verse* (Vol. i, pp. 7–483). Cambridge University Press.

MT = Gwynn, E. J., & Purton, W. J. (Eds. & Trs.). (1911/1912). The monastery of Tallaght. *Proceedings of the Royal Irish Academy, 29C*, 115–179.

Muysken, P. C. (1981). Quechua causatives and logical form. A case study in markedness. In A. Belletti, L. Brandi, & L. Rizzi (Eds.), *Theory of markedness in generative grammar* (pp. 445–473). Scuola Normale Superiore.

Nevins, A. (2007). The representation of third person and its consequences for person-case effects. *Natural language & linguistic theory, 25*, 273–313.

Newton, G. (2006). *The development and loss of the Old Irish double system of inflection*. Unpublished Ph.D. dissertation. University of Cambridge.

Newton, G. (2008). Exploring the nature of the syntax-phonology interface. A post-syntactic account of the Old Irish verbal system. Ms. University of Cambridge.

Newton, G. (2009). Accounting for *do*-support post-syntactically. Evidence from Old Irish. *UPenn Working Papers in Linguistics, 15*(1), 163–172.

Poletto, C. (2002). The left periphery of V2-Rhaetoromance dialects. A new view on V2 and V3. In S. Barbiers, L. Cornips, & S. van der Kleij (Eds.), *Syntactic microvariation* (pp. 214–242). Meertens Instituut.

Schrijver, P. (1994). The Celtic adverbs for 'against' and 'with' and the early apocope of **-i*. *Ériu, 44*, 33–52.

Schumacher, S. (2004). *Die keltischen Primärverben. Ein vergleichendes, etymologisches und morphologisches Lexikon*. Institut für Sprachwissenschaft der Universität.

Šereikaitė, M. (2018). Lexical vs. nominal prefixes and their meaning domains. *UPenn Working Papers in Linguistics, 24*(1), 190–198.

TBC[1] = O'Rahilly, C. (Ed. & Tr.). (1976). *Táin bó Cúailnge. Recension I*. Dublin Institute for Advanced Studies.

Watkins, C. (1963). Preliminaries to a historical and comparative analysis of the syntax of the Old Irish verb. *Celtica, 6*, 1–49.

Wb. = The Würzburg glosses and scholia on the Pauline epistles. In Whitley Stokes & John Strachan (Eds. & Trs.). (1903–1905). *Thesaurus Palaeohibernicus. A collection of Old-Irish glosses, scholia, prose, and verse* (Vol. i, pp. 499–712). Cambridge University Press.

WMS = Meyer, K. (Ed.). (1912). The West Munster synod. The Laud genealogies and tribal histories. *Zeitschrift für celtische Philologie, 8*, 315–317.

10

On the Functional Superstructure of the Noun Phrase in Indo-European

Augustin Speyer

1 Introduction

Many old Indo-European languages feature noun phrases (hereafter NP; all generative phrase labels are written out at the first mention. For the other levels of generative structure holds the following: If X be any label, then XP stands for: X-phrase, X' for: intermediate projection of X, and X or X° for: head of the XP) that look as if they are devoid of any functional superstructure (1). The definite article is an exponent of such a superstructure; in the examples in (1), the interpretation of the noun phrases is definite (as can be seen from the use of the definite article in the English translations), yet there is no sign of anything marking definiteness in the language samples from Sanskrit, Latin, or Gothic themselves.

A. Speyer (✉)
University of Saarland, Saarbrücken, Germany
e-mail: a.speyer@mx.uni-saarland.de

J. F. Eska et al. (eds.), *The Method Works*,
https://doi.org/10.1007/978-3-031-48959-4_10

(1) a. pathor devayānasya pitr̥yāṇasya ca
'of *the* two roads leading respectively to *the* gods and to *the* fathers'
(Sanskrit, cited from Whitney, 1889, p. 88)

b. a cultu atque humanitate provinciae
'from *the* way of life and *the* civilization of *the* province'
(Latin, Caesar (1987), *BG* 1.1)

c. us garda fadreinais Daveidis
'from *the* house, *the* kinship of David'
(Gothic, Lk. 2.4)

The term 'functional superstructure' is meant to denote functional projections that embed the noun phrase in the relevant linguistic and extralinguistic context. In a generative grammar model, to which this chapter adheres (e.g., Chomsky, 1986; cf., e.g., Gallmann & Lindauer, 1994, pp. 5–8), there is a distinction between lexical projections and functional projections. Lexical projections are projections (phrases) that are headed by a lexeme (usually a word), which is taken from the mental lexicon. The mental lexicon is by necessity context-neutral. Functional projections are projections (phrases) that are headed by a 'feature', to be thought of more abstractly as a piece of information by which the lexeme heading the lexical phrase is enriched. In a clause like 'I walked', the lexeme 'walk' is taken from the mental lexicon in order to denote the concept of walking, but the information about the concrete usage of the verb in this situation (referring to a past event, referring to an event that is real) cannot come from the lexicon, but has to be enriched from the context. This enrichment is the job of functional projections. In the present example, the verb phrase headed by 'walk' would be taken as a complement by a mood phrase (MP), which adds the information 'referring to an event that is real', which in turn is taken as a complement by a tense phrase (TP) that adds the information 'referring to a past event' (I-split account, following Pollock, 1989). The exponents of these functional heads (shorthand: 'functional exponents' in the following) are inflectional morphemes in a language that makes use of inflection (or agglutination), and in this case the verb undergoes trolleying (cyclic head movement) through the functional projections forming the superstructure (2a; AspP = aspect phrase; VP = verb phrase; t = trace). Such functional exponents also can be function words in a language that belongs to the isolating type (2b).

(2) a. Donaldum lauda-v-eri-s
'you might have praised Donald' (Latin)

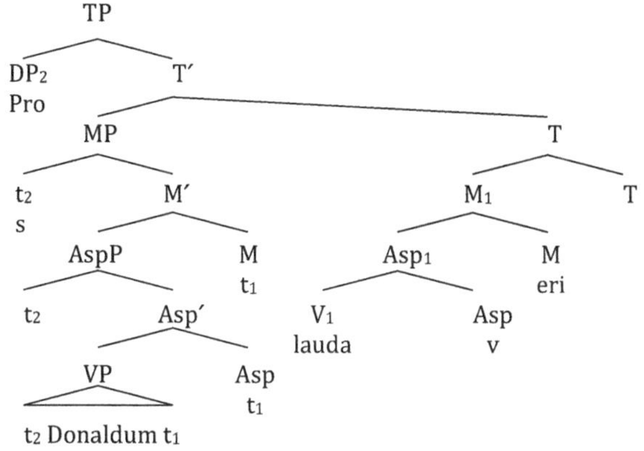

b. tā zhōngfàn chī le
s/he lunch eat **PFV**
's/he has eaten lunch' (Mandarin)

As is the case with verbs, nouns also are enriched by non-lexical situational information. This information could be:

(3) a. definiteness (i.e., whether the noun is referring to a unique referent that belongs to the extension expressed by the noun, or not)
b. deixis (i.e., whether only one referent out of the extension is singled out, but also pointed to, or not),
c. number (it is dependent on the context whether reference is made to one or more members of the extension), and
d. case (case is not inherent to a noun, but assigned by means of 'Rektion' by some other linguistic element—i.e., case is also information that is context-sensitive).

Abney (1987) first identified the functional superstructure of nouns in English and dubbed it 'determiner phrase' (DP), as the relevant piece of information (definiteness) is expressed by a functional word, the determiner; see (4; AP = adjective phrase; NP = noun phrase).

(4)

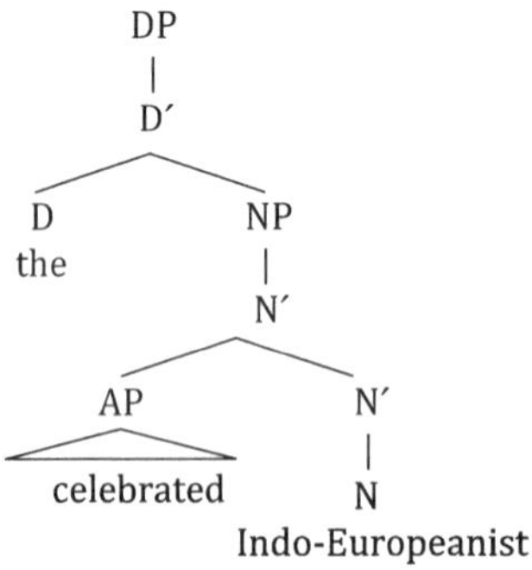

Further research showed that actually not only definiteness is encoded in a functional projection on its own, but also the other context-induced enrichments like number and case. This led to the assumption of a richly articulated functional superstructure above NP, comparable to the richly articulated IP-structure (following Pollock, 1989; IP = inflection phrase) and CP-structure (following Rizzi, 1997; CP = complementizer phrase, the highest projection forming a clause). The articulated functional overlay of an NP in an inflected Indo-European language would approximately look like in (5; IndP = index phrase; NumP = number phrase; KP = case phrase).[1]

(5)

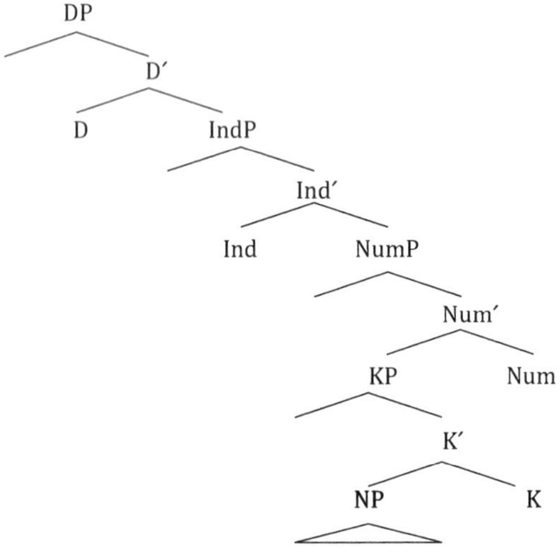

[1] The categories have been proposed by Ritter (1991): NumP (number phrase); Bittner & Hale (1996): KP (case phrase); Roehrs (2010): IndP (index phrase).

Ritter (1991) proposes a structure quite parallel to the functional overlay of the verb phrase. NumP and KP form the 'inner functional shell', being the 'nominal' equivalents of (a split) IP, hosting grammatical information that stems partly from the situational context and partly from syntactic constraints like 'Rektion' and congruence. In an inflected language, these categories are expressed by inflectional morphology on the lexemes.[2] DP and IndP constitute the 'outer functional shell' and anchor the nominal lexeme in a broader context, just as CP does with the verb. These exponents are not part of inflectional morphology, neither with CP nor with DP/IndP, at least not in the Indo-European languages.

As for KP and NumP, it is quite obvious that even the Indo-European languages of the type presented in (1) probably have this superstructure, as this is responsible for the inflectional morphology. For the outer functional shell, the evidence is missing in the languages in (1). Yet there are classical Indo-European languages that show a DP from very early on, such as Ancient Greek. Most branches of the Indo-European language family have developed DP structures in a rather similar fashion:[3] the determiner, a function word that has been grammaticalized out of a weak demonstrative, is at the left periphery of the noun phrase. Number and (potentially) case are regularly expressed on the head noun. The determiner may show no agreement (6a), but there can be an agreement in either number and gender (6b) or number, gender, and case (6c) with the head noun.[4]

---

[2] In contrast to the original proposal of case phrase as the most peripheral projection the functional superstructure of the noun phrase (Bittner & Hale, 1996, p. 4), it is assumed here to be in the inner shell below number, as the exponent of case is closest to the noun in instances where number and case exponents can be distinguished, as, e.g., in the accusative plural of the thematic stems: ROOT-o-n.ACC–s.PL (e.g., Anc. Gk. φίλους < *p^hilons, Lat. *amicōs* < **amicons*). Moreover, the original motivation for positing KP as the outermost shell was to explain the variation between marking a thematic role by either case or a preposition in, e.g., English (*Don's* versus *of Don*), but in languages in which prepositions themselves govern case, this consideration cannot hold.

[3] See Nakleh et al. (2005) on the branching of the Indo-European languages.

[4] Of course, there are exceptions such as the enclitic determiners in the Scandinavian languages, Rumanian, and Bulgarian, or the proto-Germanic marking of definiteness by a morpheme. The point is that, in almost all branches of Indo-European, some languages developed a system as outlined here.

(6) a. [$_{DP}$ the [$_{NP}$ celebrated Indo-Europeanist]](English)
b. [$_{DP}$ il [$_{NP}$ linguista celebrato]](Italian)
the.M.SG linguist.M.SG celebrated.M.SG
c. [$_{DP}$ den [$_{NP}$ gefeierten Indoeuropäisten]](German)
the.M.SG.ACC celebrated.M.SG.ACC Indoeuropeanist.M.SG.ACC

This chapter addresses the question of whether the outer functional shell, especially the DP structure, was non-existent in proto-Indo-European or whether it was present, but not visible, since it lacked an overt exponent.

2 The DP in Ancient Greek

If we look at Ancient Greek, it is obvious that this language developed an articulated determiner system. The weak demonstrative ὁ/ἡ/τό is recruited first as a means to denote familiarity of the referent in Homeric Greek (Brugmann, 1913, p. 484) and is already, at this stage, on its way to grammaticalization toward a determiner (Humbert, 1954, p. 43). In later Attic, it has developed to a fully grammaticalized determiner (Humbert, 1954, p. 44). Analyzing this determiner by means of a DP analysis readily suggests itself. As a matter of fact, the Attic determiner can be couched quite easily in terms of a DP analysis.

The noun phrase in Ancient Greek is stably right-headed. This can be seen from the fact that all kinds of attributes, be they nominal (7a), prepositional (7b), or adjectival (7c), usually precede the noun. The analysis in generative terms is outlined in (7d).

A word about the positions of the attributes is in order. In languages in which there is a special case used for NP-internal noun phrases (most Indo-European languages belong to this type, and the unmarked case here is the genitive), these nominal attributes tend to be assigned a theta-role by the head noun. They either receive this role by the noun's valency (agent, patient, etc.) as *genitivus subiectivus/obiectivus*—this holds for (7a), 'the stronger ones' being the agent of 'slavery' (slavery is a bivalent concept that has to be exercised by someone on someone else in order to be slavery)—or simply assume a possessor role (*genitivus possessivus*). Therefore, they are usually analyzed in the complement position. Adjectival adjuncts, on the other hand, never are valency-bound and do not receive a theta-role by the head noun. The same holds true for prepositional attributes. Therefore, they are usually analyzed as adjuncts.

(7) a. τὴν τῶν κρεισσόνον δουλείαν
'the slavery of the stronger ones' (Thucydides (1942), 1.8.3, ll. 18–19)
b. τῶν ἐν τῇ κεφαλῇ τριχῶν
'of the hairs on the head' (Thucydides (1942), 1.6.3, ll. 14–15)
c. τῷ παλαιῷ τρόπῳ
'in the old manner' (Thucydides (1942), 1.5.3, l. 1)
d.

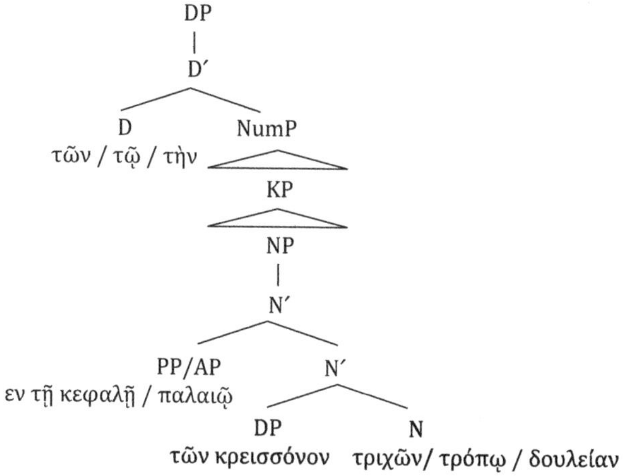

An index phrase is missing in (7d), simply because the Ancient Greek evidence does not support this projection below DP. Demonstrative pronouns (in adjectival usage) rather seem to be phrasal and positioned in the specifier of DP (8a). As opposed to, e.gg., Modern German or English, they do not occupy the D^0 position. In German or English, demonstrative pronouns and the article are in complementary distribution, suggesting that they, indeed, compete for the same position (8b–d). This does not hold for Ancient Greek: here they usually co-occur with the article in a strict order 'demonstrative > article' (8e–f), which suggests the analysis in (8a).

(8) a.

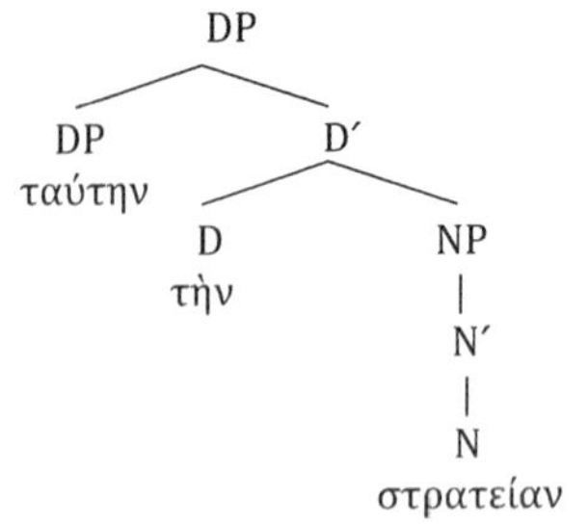

b. Dieser Wissenschaftler
this scientist
'this scientist'

c. ^{X}Der dieser Wissenschaftler[5]
^{X}the this scientist

d. ^{X}Dieser der Wissenschaftler
^{X}this the scientist

e. ταύτην τὴν στρατείαν (Thucydides (1942), 1.3.4, l.10)
this the campaign
'this army'

e. ^{X}τὴν ταύτην στρατείαν
the this campaign

Cases of postposed nominal attributes (9a) are best seen as extraposition within the DP. The extraposition character is suggested by the fact that often the determiner of the head noun is repeated before the nominal (9b), adjectival (9c), or prepositional attribute (9d). I will return to the question of extraposition in §3.

(9) a. οἱ παλαιοὶ τῶν ποιητῶν
the old the.GEN.PL poet-GEN.PL
'the old ones among the poets' (Thucydides (1942), 1.5.2 ll. 27–28)

b. τήν τε γοῦν στρατείαν τὴν Ξέρξου
the.ACC.SG and thus campaign.ACC.SG the.ACC.SG Xerxes.GEN.SG
'and, thus, the campaign of Xerxes' (Philostratus, *Heroicus* 667, from Perseus)

---

[5] The superscript X indicates ungrammaticality. Because the asterisk is reserved for reconstructed forms in language historic treatises, the marking of ungrammatical forms by means of an asterisk, as usual in synchronic linguistic literature, forbids itself.

c. ταῖς στρατείαις ταῖς κοιναῖς
the.DAT.PL campaign.DAT.PL the.DAT.PL common.DAT.PL
'the joint campaigns' (Aristides, *Orationes* 47.325), from Perseus

d. τῆς στρατείας τῆς ἐπὶ τοὺς Φωκέας
the.GEN.SG campaign.GEN.SG the.GEN.SG against the.ACC.PL Phocean.ACC.PL
'of the campaign against the Phoceans' (Demosth.enes18.32, from Perseus)

Why can we be confident that the analysis with an articulated DP is the right one, as opposed to, say, an analysis with the article being adjoined somehow to the outer edge of NP? To answer this question, it might be worthwhile to look at typical properties of functional heads, the D-head in particular, and to check whether the Greek determiner fulfills these criteria.

In his study on the DP in German, Fortmann (1996, p. 31) lists properties to which functional heads typically conform. His aim is to show that the determiner in German is the exponent of a functional projection. We can play the same game for Ancient Greek.

Functional exponents of a given functional category usually form a closed lexical class. In Modern German, for instance, the class of determiners (= D^0-elements) consists of the definite and the indefinite articles, interrogative pronouns, demonstrative pronouns, and possessive pronouns. The same criterion certainly holds for Ancient Greek, as the D^0 position hosts either the definite article, the interrogative pronoun (if the DP is introducing a *wh*-question), or a zero element (in the case of indefinite reference). We have already seen that demonstrative pronouns do not belong to the potential D^0-elements in Ancient Greek. Likewise, possessive pronouns are not possible as D^0 in Ancient Greek. They are treated as 'normal' adjectives, standing before the other adjectives, because their scope potentially contains other adjectives in the NP.

Functional exponents are usually dependent phonologically and/or morphologically on the lexical category enriched by them. The criterion of morphological dependency is certainly met, as the article agrees on gender (which comes from the noun). Phonologically, at least the non-neuter nominative forms of the definite article are dependent, as they are proclitics.

The relationship between functional exponents and their complement is such that they are specialized for one type of complement, and they cannot be separated from their complement. The DP in Ancient Greek has an NP as typical complement, and it cannot be separated from the noun phrase, not even in poetry.

Functional heads encode grammatical features (which is, after all, their primary task). This criterion depends on the definition of 'grammatical feature'. If we define this term as context-sensitive information that is not part of the lexical entry of the lexeme which is in the scope of the functional head, definiteness certainly belongs to this class. The lexical entry of a noun cannot be specified with respect to definiteness, as it then could not be used sometimes definite, sometimes indefinite. Whether reference is made to a unique member of the extension denoted by the noun or to some unspecified member of the extension depends on the utterance context. So, the determiner fulfills this criterion, as well.

Functional heads are usually compulsory. This holds certainly for the article in Attic Greek and onward, for a noun phrase without an article is automatically interpreted as indefinite (the null article being the marking for indefiniteness).

We have seen that there are indications favoring an analysis of the definite article in Ancient Greek as a D^0-head. The article fulfills the functional and distributional criteria for functional heads, and its structural configuration with the noun phrase is strictly determined.

The article was not present from the beginning, of course. One would not expect that, however, as the Indo-European languages contemporary to Ancient Greek lack an overt determiner. This indicates that proto-Indo-European did not have an overt determiner either. Determiners in Indo-European languages are always the product of grammaticalization (see, e.gg., Roberts & Roussou, 2003 and van Gelderen, 2009 for the concept in a more formal manner): a weak demonstrative, forming a DP on its own and being adjoined to the NP, loses some semantic features, such as [deixis], by reason of inflationary usage ('semantic bleaching'), until only the feature [unique reference] is left. At the same time, a reanalysis takes place of this phrasal adjunct into the specifier of a functional projection to the head of this functional projection, to wit, DP. The functional category is not created in the moment of reanalysis, but it is already present, lacking, however, an overt exponent. What happens is that the grammaticalized element is reanalyzed as the overt exponent of this otherwise mute head position. This is the general grammaticalization pathway of determiners in Indo-European. Ancient Greek was the first to tread this path in the first millennium BCE, other languages following later along the same lines.

3 Extraposition Out of DP

Let us now turn to DP-internal extraposition. In Ancient Greek, which has an articulated DP, we can study the structural properties of this construction more closely. As already seen in (9), it is possible to extrapose nominal and prepositional attributes, to some extent also adjectival ones. The extraposition of adjectival attributes is rare, however. A potential explanation for this asymmetry could come from extraposition in clauses. Here, it has been found for modern languages like German or English that the complexity of the extraposed material plays a role: the more lengthy or complex a phrase is, the more easily it can be extraposed (on German, e.g., Hoberg, 1997; on English, e.g., Wasow, 1997). In Modern German, for example, clausal constituents are the perfect candidates for extraposition, prepositional phrases are common, too, less so noun phrases, but almost impossible is the extraposition of adjectival or adverbial phrases (Hoberg, 1997). If we apply this explanation to DP-internal extraposition, other nominal phrases and prepositional phrases are better candidates for extraposition simply because they have an articulated functional superstructure and, thus, come with higher structural complexity than adjectival phrases. Thus, adjectival phrases are only infrequently extraposed in Ancient Greek.

A question that needs to be addressed, in general, is what the syntactic structure of such extrapositions is. Clausal extrapositions are usually analyzed as adjuncts to some position in the lower functional shells of the clause, such as vP (that is, the 'little vP' which embeds a state or activity predicate under a causation predicate and adds an agent) or TP (see, e.g.,

Büring & Hartmann, 1997 and Frey, 2015, p. 55). This would then correspond to some projection like NumP or KP as adjunction site. However, the fact that the article often is repeated in Greek, as seen earlier, suggests two things that lead to a different analysis:

(10) a. It is not so much extraposition of a phrase which is part of the NP to the right periphery of the NP, but a copying of the entire DP. The exponent of D^0 is present, as well, with subsequent (incomplete) deletion of material in the copy.

b. The adjunction site must be outside DP (as the DP as a whole is moved), but yet in the DP domain (as the extraposed/copied DP is in the unmarked case not separated from its host DP).

The most suitable analysis would be the 'Big-DP' analysis, which was proposed originally to deal with resumptive clitics in the Romance languages (e.gg., Belletti, 1999; Cardinaletti, 2019). In this analysis, a DP gets another DP as superstructure. For the clitics that are co-indexed with the DP, it has been suggested they represent the higher D head ([11a]; see, e.g., Belletti, 1999). Within the higher DP, agreement takes place and, subsequently, the (original) DP can move and occupy some other position in the clause, e.g., in Left Dislocation (11b). The clitic pronoun functions then as a kind of an overt trace, so to speak.

(11) a.

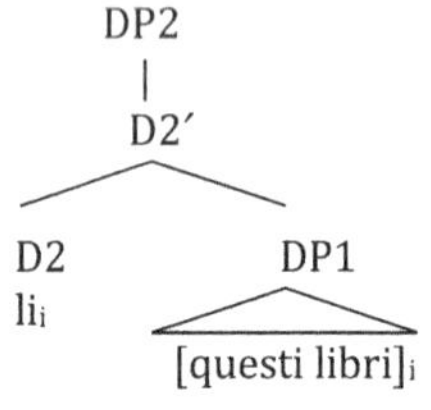

b. [$_{DP1}$ Questi libri]$_{i1}$, Gianni [$_{DP2}$ li$_i$ t$_1$] a letti
'as for these books, Gianni read them'

We can utilize this structure now for the Greek extraposition cases; a copy of the DP is merged in the specifier of the outer DP (12a). As the DP is phrasal, it must be merged in a phrasal position. In spelling out the structure, 'distributed deletion' takes place (see Fanselow & Ćavar, 2002), which means that parts of one copy and parts of the other copy are spelled out (12b). Which parts are spelled out where is an outcome of conflicting features within the copies, such as a [+focus]-feature in one part (the 'extraposed' one) and a [–focus]-feature in the other part, or vice versa. In Greek, sometimes incomplete distributed deletion takes place, resulting in the D head being spelled out on both copies (12c).

(12) a. (see [9a])

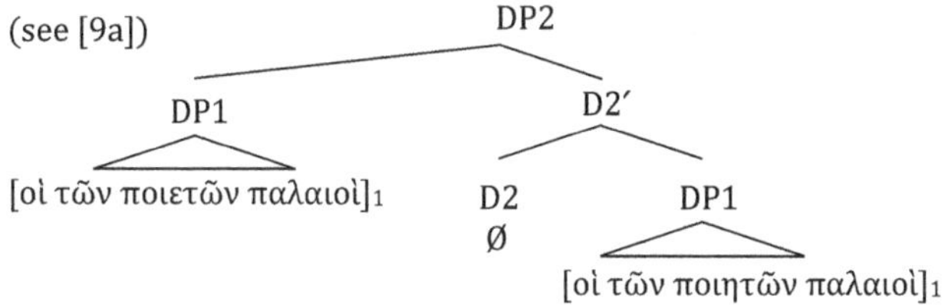

b. (see [9a])

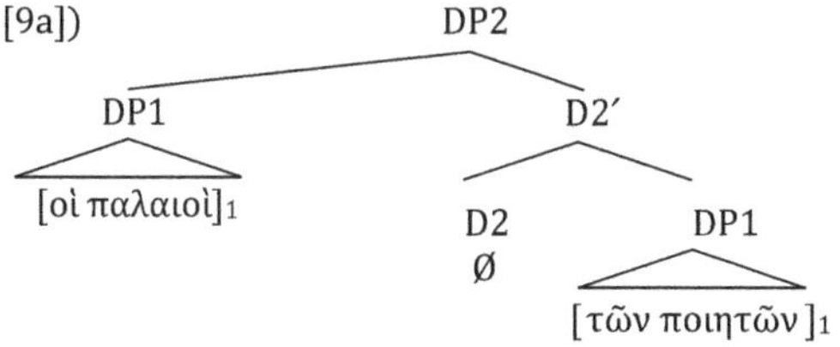

c. (see [9d])

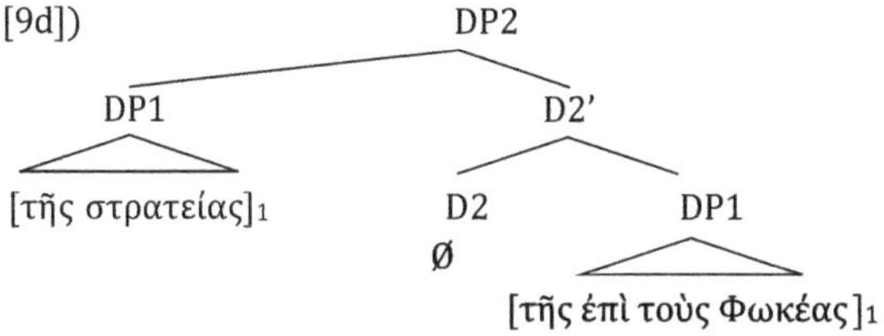

This can be interpreted in a fashion comparable to the 'original' Big-DP-hypothesis. Here, the clitic (or any other resumptive pronoun) serves to indicate the place (and case/number) from which the subsequent movement of the associated DP takes place. It serves as an overt trace. In this case, the function is not to indicate the starting site of movement, but rather to indicate that the 'extraposed' phrase is part of the DP, functions as an attribute, and is not to be interpreted as an independent constituent of the clause, be it predicatively, as an adverbial or even as an object. In ([9d] / [12c]), the phrase ἐπὶ τοὺς Φωκέας 'against / to / onto the Phoceans' could easily receive an adverbial function in its clause, and similar ambiguities hold for basically all sorts of possible attribute types (including genitive attributes, as the genitive can principally serve as an object case in Ancient Greek).

Cases in which an analysis following the 'Big-DP-hypothesis' is suggested are found throughout modern and ancient Indo-European languages. In many languages (such as the Germanic languages and Old Irish), there is a relative regular pattern of clausal extraposition with a correlate in the host clause (13a–b). Such cases can be analyzed as a DP headed by the clitic and taking the lexical noun phrase as a complement; subsequently, the complement is moved (13c). Even closer to the Greek case is 'extraposition' to the right periphery of the constituent containing the DP (usually a PP [= preposition phrase]). A clitic, usually governed by a preposition, stands in the noun phrase indicating the starting site, and the lexical material of the attribute is attached to the right of the PP (13d–e). A secondary process of Local Dislocation takes place that swaps the head noun and the clitic pronoun representing the attribute, so that the clitic subsequently can fuse to the preposition (see Embick & Noyer, 2001).

(13) a. Diesen Wissenschaftler, den findet jeder hervorragend
this scientist him finds everybody excellent
'Everybody thinks this scientist to be excellent' (German)

b. conid de ata Morand mac main ***fair*** .i. **mac**
therefore=is from=it is Morand mac Main on=him, viz. son
Cairpri Cindchait.
Carpre.GEN.SG Cennchait.GEN.SG
'therefore it is that <the name> Morand mac Main is on him, the son of Carpre Cennchait.' (Old Irish, *Fir Flatha* (1891) 14)

c.

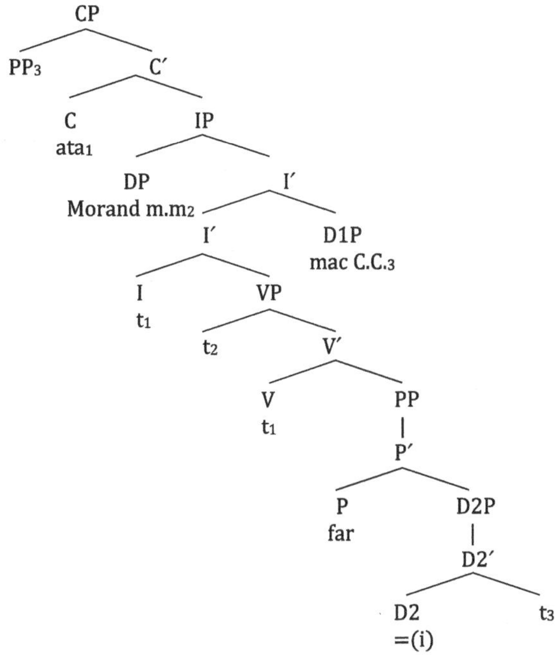

d. Ailbe ainm in chon, ocus ba lán Hériu ***dia*** airdircus
Ailbe name the.GEN.SG dog.GEN.SG and was full Ireland of=his fame
in chon.
the.GEN.SG dog.GEN.SG
'Ailbe was the name of the dog, and Ireland was full ***of* his** fame, the fame **of the dog.**' (Old Irish, *Meic Dathó* (1935) 1)

e.

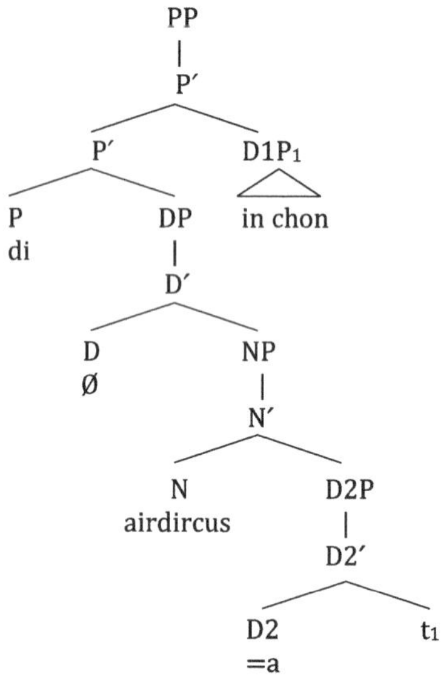

In sum, we can find evidence of an extraposition process in several Indo-European languages, which have an overtly expressed DP and in which the boundaries of the noun phrase plus functional superstructure are, therefore, visible, that starts with the merging of a 'Big DP', either featuring a pronoun in the head position of the 'Big DP' (which allows for extraposition out of the phrase to, e.g., the clausal peripheries in, e.gg., Germanic languages, Old Irish, or the modern Romance languages) or, if the head is empty, copying the associate DP in the specifier position and spelling the copies out under Distributed Deletion. The second option is what we see in Ancient Greek, in which movement out of the DP seems to be banned. If noun phrases in other Indo-European languages, such as Latin, show massive extraposition out of noun phrases, it could be debated whether a similar 'Big DP' structure serves as a starting point of the extraposition.

4 Does DP Go Back to Proto-Indo-European? On the Search for DP in Latin

We have seen that Ancient Greek has a full-fledged DP-architecture. It is, however, the only 'old' Indo-European language with this property (if we count under this heading all languages that are attested before the end of the first millennium BCE). The other languages in this exclusive club, viz., Hittite (and the other Anatolian languages), Latin (and the other Italic languages), Vedic Sanskrit and Avestan (with Old Persian), and Continental Celtic all lack overt exponents of DP. In what ways could we feel justified to assume that proto-Indo-European already had this functional DP layer?

First, the interpretative content of DP is present nevertheless. Even in a language like Latin, which lacks marking of a noun phrase as definite or indefinite, any noun phrase is interpreted as referring to a uniquely identifiable, i.e., definite entity, or to an entity that is not uniquely identifiable, i.e., indefinite. If we believe that semantic distinctions are mirrored in syntax, we must assume that there is something like a DP as the locus for this distinction. The interpretation as a definite or indefinite noun phrase would then be a phenomenon of the 'Logical Form' interface.

But even leaving such considerations aside, there are two pieces of evidence that suggest an affirmative answer to the question of whether proto-Indo-European possessed a DP layer or not. One is simply that virtually all successors of these 'old' Indo-European languages developed a determiner system which looks rather similar in all cases and can be analyzed along the same lines. Let us look at Latin as an exemplary case. The Romance languages as successors of Latin all developed a compulsory DP, continuing the demonstrative pronoun *ille* / *illa* / *illud* as exponent of the D head. They all share the same development (the postposition of the Romanian determiner is a separate problem), which indicates that, at least, the seed out of which this development would grow was already planted, so to speak, at a time when these languages were not yet separated from one another. This points to the era before the fall of the Roman Empire, i.e., a period in which the extant literature is composed in 'Classical' Latin. We know that 'Classical' Latin is a kind of an artificial language to begin with, picking up archaisms in morphology and presumably also in syntax. Spoken Latin was probably closer to the later Romance languages than Classical Latin would suggest. Celtic also developed a determiner system in the course of its history, which is apparent in Old Irish. Furthermore, one of the Indo-European language subfamilies, whose date of first attestation is later, viz., the Germanic languages, acquired a determiner system early in their history.[6] It is hard to imagine that all of these languages should develop a similar determiner system out of the blue. The assumption that all of these languages made use of an already prefigured structure that only lacked a lexical exponent in the early forms of this language is much more plausible. Thus, it seems reasonable to assume a DP-structure already in proto-Indo-European.

The second piece of evidence comes just from languages like Latin, which show no determiner system. The crucial question is the syntactic status of adjectivally used demonstrative pronouns such as *is / ea / id* or *ille / illa / illud* that develop to determiners in the successor languages of Latin. If we assume that there is no DP layer, such demonstrative pronouns should behave like 'normal' adjectives. For instance, they should show the same or, at least, similar serialization restrictions as adjectives. In cases in which an adjectival attribute is adjacent to its head noun, the relative order of these two elements is variable, either adjective-noun or noun-adjective. If there were no DP layer, adjectivally used demonstratives should occupy the same slot in the noun phrase as normal adjectives. If this slot could stand before or after the head noun, demonstrative pronouns should show the same variation.

I tested this with two texts that are arguably relatively close to spoken Latin. One text from the earlier period of Classical Latin is Cicero's *Letters to Atticus*. While they are stylized to a certain degree, they belong to a less formal text type and, therefore, offer a better glimpse into what was spoken at that time than, say, contemporary speeches or historiography. A smaller sample was taken from a text of late Latinity, the report of the pilgrimage of the nun Egeria. The Ciceronian text is available via *Perseus*. Here the strategy was to search for certain forms (accusative and ablative) of the demonstratives *is / ea / id*, *hic / haec / hoc*, and *ille / illa / illud* and to categorize the hits as to whether the demonstrative stands before or after the head noun. Likewise, the same was done for a random selection

[6]Tocharian shows no determiner system and we cannot but speculate whether it would have developed one before dying out. Most Balto-Slavic languages did not develop a determiner system either. Germanic seems to have experimented with a determiner system early on: the so-called weak declension of adjectives seems to have been an early attempt to express definite reference, as can be seen from the distribution of weak and strong adjectives in the earliest attested Germanic languages. Here, the D^0-head was not filled with an overt exponent, but rather head movement of the adjective to D^0 took place, which is marked by morphological means.

Table 10.1 Combinations of noun and adjective/demonstrative: Cicero, epistulae ad Atticum

	A/D > *N*	*N* > A/D
Adjective and noun	122	62
Demonstrative and noun	239	13

$\chi^2 = 60.8066$, $p < 0.00001$ (χ^2-test calculated using https://www.socscistatistics.com/tests/chisquare/default2.aspx)

Table 10.2 Combinations of noun and adjective/demonstrative: Egeria

	A/D > *N*	*N* > A/D
Adjective and noun	24	25
Demonstrative and noun	51	20

$\chi^2 = 6.4593$, $p = 0.019$

of adjectives. The Egeria text is not available via *Perseus*; here, Chaps. 1, 2, 3, and 4 of the text were read and the demonstrative-noun or adjective-noun combinations were collected by hand.

The results are reported in Tables 10.1 and 10.2.

In both texts, there are statistically significant differences in the distribution of the two positions. Weak demonstratives are significantly more often positioned before the head noun than adjectives. This can be interpreted in such a way that demonstratives and adjectives do not occupy the same slot. As some demonstratives develop into determiners later on, it is not too far-fetched to assume that their position is already in the DP layer, probably already as exponents of D^0.

A problem for assigning the demonstratives to the D^0-position is, of course, that the order should be categorical if this is true. There are a few cases of demonstratives following the head noun, however. A closer look at the Ciceronian data shows, however, that the 13 cases of a demonstrative after a noun are cases in which a relative clause follows, as in (14a).

(14) a. medicamentis iis quae parantur
medicines.ABL.PL this.ABL.PL which.PL prepare.3PL.PRES.PASS
'these medicines which are prepared' (Cicero, epist. ad Att. 9.5, cited from *Perseus*)
b. Medikamente, und zwar die, die vorbereitet sind.
medicine.PL and however this.PL which.PL prepare.PST-PTCP be.3PL.PRES
'medicines, to wit those that have been prepared'

This is not incompatible with the DP analysis proposed here. It can be analyzed as extraposition out of DP much in the same way as was described in §3. The trigger of the extraposition is the relative clause. A similar construction occurs in Modern German (14b).

The distribution is not as clear in the Egeria text. Prenominal position is categorical with *is / ea / id*, however. This can be interpreted such that, in the vulgar Latin variant Egeria was speaking, it was *is / ea / id* that was utilized as determiner. This is interesting because it is in contrast to the Romance languages, in which it is *ille / illa / illud* that develops into the determiner.

So we can say that Latin probably had a DP-layer that manifests itself not in an overt determiner, but in a position that is occupied by weak demonstratives. Weak determiners are interpreted as definite, so they are apt to serve as overt exponents of the definiteness feature in D^0.

5 Conclusions

While proto-Indo-European most probably did not possess a determiner system as an overt exponent of DP, the DP as functional superstructure of the noun phrase certainly was already present in this language. This can be seen from the fact that later Indo-European languages developed determiner systems much in the same manner, with Ancient Greek as forerunner. This suggests that the functional superstructure was already present in the parent language, and the later daughter languages did not do much else than develop overt exponents of this structure by grammaticalization of weak demonstratives. Even in languages that presumably reflect the proto-Indo-European state of affairs, such as Latin, the distribution of weak demonstratives in comparison to 'normal' adjectives suggests that demonstratives and adjectives occupy a different structural position. As weak demonstratives are almost categorically before the head noun, we may assume that they are exponents of a left-headed functional category that forms the outermost shell of the functional superstructure of noun phrases—to wit, the DP.

References

Primary Sources

Caesar, C. Iulius (1987). *C. Iulii Caesaris Commentarii rerum gestarum vol.i, Bellum Gallicum*, ed. W. Hering. Teubner.

Fir Flatha (1891). Scél na Fir Flatha, Echtra Cormaic i Tir Tairngiri ocus Ceart Claidib Cormaic. In *Irische Texte* 3. Serie, ed. W. Stokes & E. Windisch, 185–229. S. Hirzel.

Meic Dathó (1935). *Scéla mucce Meic Dathó*, ed. Rudolf Thurneysen. Dublin Institue for Advanced Studies

Perseus. Retrieved February 27, 2023, from https://perseus.tufts.edu

Thucydides (1942). *Thucydidis historiae* vol.1, ed. H.S. Jones. Oxford University Press.

Grammars

Brugmann, K. (1913). *Griechische Grammatik[4]. 4. vermehrte Auflage bearbeitet von Dr. Albert Thumb*. C. H. Beck.

Humbert, J. (1954). *Syntaxe grecque[2]*. C. Klincksieck.

Whitney, W. D. (1889). *Sanskrit grammar; Including both the classical language, and the older dialects, of Veda and Brahmana[2]*. Breitkopf & Härtel / Boston, Ginn & Company.

Research Literature

Abney, S. (1987). *The English Noun Phrase in its sentential aspect*. Ph.D. dissertation, MIT.

Belletti, A. (1999). Italian/Romance clitics. Structure and derivation. In H. van Riemsdijk (Ed.), *Clitics in the languages of Europe* (pp. 543–579). Mouton de Gruyter.

Bittner, M., & Hale, K. (1996). The structural determination of case and agreement. *Linguistic Inquiry, 27*, 1–68.

Büring, D., & Hartmann, K. (1997). Doing the right thing. *The Linguistic Review, 14*, 1–42.

Cardinaletti, A. (2019). Cliticization as extraction. The Big DP hypothesis revisited. *Revista da Associação Portuguesa de Linguística, 5*, 1–16.
Chomsky, N. (1986). *Barriers*. MIT Press.
Embick, D., & Noyer, R. (2001). Movement operations after Syntax. *Linguistic Inquiry, 32*, 555–595.
Fanselow, G., & Ćavar, D. (2002). Distributed deletion. In A. Alexiadou (Ed.), *Theoretical approaches to universals* (pp. 65–107). John Benjamins.
Fortmann, C. (1996). *Konstituentenbewegung in der DP-Struktur. Zur funktionalen Analyse der Nominalphrase im Deutschen*. Max Niemeyer.
Frey, W. (2015). Zur Struktur des Nachfelds im Deutschen. In H. Vinckel-Roisin (Ed.), *Das Nachfeld im Deutschen. Theorie und Empirie* (pp. 53–76). De Gruyter.
Gallmann, P., & Lindauer, T. (1994). Funktionale Kategorien in Nominalphrasen. *Beiträge zur Geschichte der Deutsche Sprache und Literatur, 116*, 1–27.
Hoberg, U. (1997). Die Linearstruktur des Satzes. In G. Zifonun, L. Hoffmann, & B. Strecker (Eds.), *Grammatik der deutschen Sprache* (Vol. ii, pp. 1496–1680). De Gruyter.
Nakleh, L., Ringe, D., & Warnow, T. (2005). Perfect phylogenetic networks. A new methodology for reconstructing the evolutionary history of natural languages. *Language, 81*, 382–420.
Pollock, J.-Y. (1989). Verb movement, Universal Grammar, and the structure of IP. *Linguistic Inquiry, 20*, 365–424.
Ritter, E. (1991). Two functional categories in noun phrases. Evidence from Modern Hebrew. In S. Rothstein (Ed.), *Syntax & semantics 26, Syntax and the lexicon* (pp. 37–62). Academic Press.
Rizzi, L. (1997). The fine structure of the left periphery. In L. Haegeman (Ed.), *Elements of grammar* (pp. 281–337). Reidel.
Roberts, I., & Roussou, A. (2003). *Syntactic change. A minimalist approach to grammaticalization*. Cambridge University Press.
Roehrs, D. (2010). Demonstrative-reinforcer constructions. *Journal of Comparative Germanic Linguistics, 13*, 225–268.
van Gelderen, E. (2009). Features in reanalysis and grammaticalization. In E. Traugott & G. Trousdale (Eds.), *Gradience, gradualness, and grammaticalization* (pp. 129–147). John Benjamins.
Wasow, T. (1997). Remarks on grammatical weight. *Language Variation and Change, 9*, 81–105.

11

Understanding Translation Effects: Lessons from the Old English Heptateuch

Ann Taylor

1 Introduction

Many of our surviving Old English (OE) texts are translations from Latin originals. Given that the syntax of Latin and Old English differ in a number of ways, it is natural to ask: what kind of effect, if any, does translation from Latin have on OE syntax? Answering this question will serve to increase both our understanding of native Old English syntax and how and to what extent it can be influenced by external effects.

This question is particularly important for studies of Old English syntax because, first of all, translated texts are not evenly distributed across the OE period. In the early period (< 950), there are a number of very extensive translated texts and very little non-translated material, while post-950 there are many more non-translated texts to work with. Secondly, previous work has suggested that biblical translations are significantly different in the type of effect they show than non-biblical

A. Taylor (✉)
University of York, Heslington, UK
e-mail: ann.taylor@york.ac.uk

J. F. Eska et al. (eds.), *The Method Works*,
https://doi.org/10.1007/978-3-031-48959-4_11

translations (Taylor, 2008). Given that both the biblical translations (Old and New Testaments) are located in the late period where there is very little non-biblical translation, we have another potential source of difficulty. This uneven distribution of texts means that any influence from translation will not be evenly distributed either, potentially creating a distorted view of OE syntax in any one period, as well as of change over time.

Increasing our understanding of the effect of translation on OE texts, therefore, has the potential to (1) increase our understanding of syntactic variation across synchronic texts and (2) determine whether translation effects distort our understanding of change over time. This chapter is intended as a small contribution to moving towards that goal.

Much previous work on translation effects on OE has focussed on particular constructions, such as the dative absolute (Timofeeva, 2006), or the accusative and infinitive construction with verbs of declaring/knowing/thinking (Fischer, 1989, 1992, 1994, a.o.), whose native status is dubious at best.[1] Another way to approach this question is to focus on the effect of translation on indisputably native constructions. In this case, therefore, it is not so much a question of a temporary or permanent effect on the structure of the language through some kind of transfer; rather the effect is on usage, in particular, the frequency of use of different variants in constructions which allow more than one surface manifestation. Such constructions are extremely common in OE, for instance: verb-medial versus verb-final; verb-object versus object-verb order, genitive-noun versus noun-genitive order; adjective-noun versus noun-adjective order, etc. Translators do not generally produce ungrammatical sentences. However, if the target language is variable with respect to a certain construction, the frequency of the variants might be affected by the source, if the source is either non-variant or variant, but with different frequencies.[2] The approach is quantitative, therefore, the aim being to uncover and explain general trends across categories of texts, not to explain the genesis of individual examples or particular constructions.

[1] But see Haeberli (2018), who applies the same methodology used here to object pronouns in Middle English texts translated from French.

[2] Glosses are a special case, where ungrammatical constructions may arise because glossators generally follow the word order of the source. No glosses are included in the data here.

Due to the anonymous nature of the majority of OE texts, we often have little information about the translator.[3] In the case of the Heptateuch (seven books of the Old Testament), however, we know the identity of one of the translators, Ælfric of Eynsham, a skilled writer and Latinist, who also produced a large portion of the extant non-translated Old English prose. The remainder of the text is translated by one or more unknowns, usually referred to as 'the anonymous translator(s)' (hereafter AT). The Heptateuch is a compilation; in particular, Judges was not originally part of the book. Unlike the rest of the books, it appears to have been originally produced as a homily and, at some point, was added to an already existing version of the first six books of the Old Testament (the Hexateuch). While it contains straightforward translation, it also contains some exposition (Marsden, 2008, pp. lxx–lxxi).

Ælfric's contribution to the Heptateuch consists of the following: Gen 1–24:26 (with the exception of a few verses, which are not excluded here), Numbers 13–end, Joshua, and Judges. The attribution of Genesis 1–24:26, as well as Judges, to Ælfric is based on his own claim to have translated it; for the remainder, the attribution is based on linguistic evidence, particularly style (Marsden, 2000, p. 45). The remainder was contributed by one or more unknown translators. The Heptateuch, therefore, contains sections of four books attributed to Ælfric, with parts of Genesis and Numbers also attributed to the AT. The AT also contributed Exodus, Deuteronomy, and Leviticus, while Ælfric contributed Joshua and Judges. Literary scholars claim that Ælfric's translations in the Heptateuch are most literal in Genesis (Marsden, 1991) and we would expect it to be least literal in Judges, as it contains some exposition, as well as translation (Langeslag, 2016). Ælfric is considered a skilled translator, while the AT generally is not. The Heptateuch, thus, offers a unique opportunity to look in more detail at two different translators (or possibly more than two) in the form of Ælfric and the AT, but also, since Ælfric also wrote original OE works, we can compare his translations to his non-translated works.

[3] Many of the large early translations are associated with King Alfred, although there is a great deal of contention over which of them, if any, he translated himself (see Bately, 2009, for instance). Beyond these works and the work by Ælfric discussed in this chapter, translators are anonymous.

In this chapter, I look at two constructions that I have previously examined in a wider context, prepositional phrases (PPs) with a pronominal complement (PPRO) (Taylor, 2008) and object pronouns (OP) (Taylor, 2015). The study is largely exploratory, but based on previous work and hypotheses, we can make a number of predictions.

1. Sections considered more 'literal' by literary scholars will show a greater influence of the source, and particularly, more of an 'indirect effect' (see Sect. 3.3.2).
2. The AT, as a less skilled translator, will show more influence from the source.
3. Ælfric's translations, in particular his Genesis, will show more Latin order than his non-translated texts.

2 Methodology and Data

2.1 Data

The study is based on the complete text of the Heptateuch as included in the York-Helsinki Parsed Corpus of Old English Prose, filename *cootest.o3.psd*. (Taylor et al., 2003). The exact Latin source of the Heptateuch is not known, but according to Marsden (1994, p. 209), it is based on 'good Vulgate exemplars'; this study, therefore, uses the Vulgate (as found on the website: http://www.latinvulgate.com/) as the closest source available.

2.1.1 PP Data

The PP data includes all PPs in the OE text with a personal pronoun complement, apart from PPs matching a Latin PP with cliticized *cum* (*et erit Deus* ***tecum*** 'and the Lord will be with you'), which are always head-final in Latin. Latin demonstratives of all types except *iste* 'that (of yours)' (i.e., *is* 'this/that', *hic* 'this', *ille* 'that', *ipse* 'self': examples [1] and [2]) are included as a match for an OE pronoun since they are commonly used as third person pronouns. Finally, *wh*-complements of P in Latin also count as matches for an OE personal pronoun, because, again, these are commonly used in Latin with pronominal force (example [3]).

(1) OE: & Drihten wæs **mid him**:
and Lord was with him
Latin: fuitque Dominus **cum eo**
was.and Lord with this/that.one
'and the Lord was with him' (cootest,Gen:39.2.1550)

(2) OE: & min nama is **on him**
and my name is in him
Latin: et est nomen meum **in illo**
and is name my in that.one
'and my name is in him' (cootest,Exod:23.21.3331)

(3) OE: & Faraones dohtor cwæþ **to hyre**
and Pharoah daughter said to her
Latin: **Ad quam** locuta filia Pharaonis
to whom spoke daughter Pharoah
'and Pharoah's daughter said to her' (cootest,Exod:2.9.2280)

2.1.2 OP Data

For the purposes of this study, the OP data are limited to matrix clauses:

1. with a finite main verb
2. with or without an initial conjunction
3. with an initial full NP or pronoun subject, OR an elided subject

The following examples illustrate the possibilities:

(4) Full NP subject:
a. God **lædde hyne** þa ut
God led him then out
'Then God led him out' (cootest,Gen:15.5.564)
b. & God **hyne gehirde**
and God him heard
'and God heard him' (cootest,Gen:46.2.1985)

(5) Pronoun subject:

a. ic **bletsige** **eow**
I bless you
'I bless you' (cootest,Exod:23.25.3337)

b. & he **genam** **hi** in to ðam arce
and he took them in to the ark
'and he took them into the ark' (cootest,Gen:8.9.343)

(6) Elided subject:[4]

a. **behelode** **hine** eft
covered him again
'[she] covered him again' (cootest,Judg:4.19.5641)

b. & **bletsode** **hyne**
and blessed him
'and [he] blessed him' (cootest,Gen:28.1.1148)

Embedded clauses are excluded because, although the same alternation is possible, the high pre-verbal position is much more frequent than in matrix clauses (> 95% in non-translated text). In addition, so-called CP-V2 clauses, where the verb has raised to a very high position, have been excluded because, in these clauses, pronouns categorically follow the verb.

2.2 Methodology

2.2.1 PP Data

This study is an extension of work reported in Taylor (2008). In that paper, I investigated a very simple case of potential Latin influence on Old English prose, namely the position of pronominal complements of prepositions, in which the underlying Latin construction is invariably head-initial,[5] i.e., the pronoun always follows the preposition (7a), while in OE the position of the pronoun varies, either preceding or following the preposition (7b–c).

[4] The type with an elided subject and no conjunction is rare (3 examples) and are all in V-PRO order.

[5] With the exception of the preposition *cum*, which is omitted from the study, as discussed in Sect. 2.2.1.

(7) a. Dixitque Dominus **ad** **eum**
said.and Lord to him
'and the Lord said to him' (cootest,Genesis 7:1)
b. & ic adrife hæþene **fram** **ðe**
and I drive heathen from you
'and I shall drive the heathen from you' (cootest,Exod:34.24.3600)
c. þa cwædon hi **him** **to**:
then said they him to
'then they said to him' (cootest,Gen:18.9.697)

The methodology of the PP study is fairly simple. The Latin source of each relevant OE example is located, and the OE example is categorized in one of four ways:

1. matching the Latin text, i.e., both PPs are head-initial (P-PRO), as in (8)
2. not matching the Latin text, i.e., the Latin PP is head-initial (P-PRO), but the OE PP is not (PRO-P or PRO … P), as in (9)
3. the OE PP has no source in Latin and is head-initial (P-PRO), as in (10)
4. the OE PP has no source and is not head-initial (PRO-P or PRO … P), as in (11)

The examples in (8)–(11) illustrate the different possibilities. In (8), we see matching head-initial PPs, while (9) illustrates the non-matching case, where the Latin is P-PRO, but the OE is PRO-P. In (10a), there is no Latin source and the OE PP is head-initial; in (10b), the Latin has a pronoun which is reproduced by a head-initial PP in the Old English. Both these cases are counted as P-PRO order with no source. Finally, (11) illustrates three types that are categorized as PRO-P order with no source. (11a) is the case with no Latin source at all; that is, the translator added the whole sentence. (11b) is similar to (10b) in that there is a PP in the OE where the Latin has only a pronoun. And, finally, in (11c), the pronoun appears before the preposition, but is separated from it; this type is counted as PRO-P the same as non-separated cases.[6]

[6] See Taylor (2008) for justification.

(8) Type 1:
OE: & þonne hi ut farað **to us**
and when they out go to us
Latin: cumque exierint **contra nos**
when.and they.out.go against us
'and when they go out against us' (cootest,Josh:8.3.5378)

(9) Type 2:
OE: & eode **him togeanes**
and went them against
Latin: et ivit **obviam eis**
and went against them
'and [he] went against them' (cootest,Gen:19.1.754)

(10) Type 3:
a. OE: & hi brohton ða heora gold **to me**
and they brought then their gold to me
Latin: —
'and then they brought their gold to me' (cootest,Exod:32.24.3478)
b. OE: & cwæð **to me**
and said to me
Latin: sed dixit **mihi**
but he.said to.me
'and/but he said to me' (cootest,Deut:3.26.4517)

(11) Type 4:
a. OE: Þa eode Sodomitiscra cyning sona **him togeanes**
then went Sodomitish king immediately him against
Latin: —
'then the king of Sodom immediately went against him' (cootest,Gen:14.17.544)
b. OE: gyf ic hine **þe ongean** ne bringe
if I him you against not bring
Latin: si non reduxero illum **tibi**
if not I.bring him to.you
'if I do not bring him before you' (cootest,Gen:42.37.1799)
c. OE: … þæt hyt **me** swa hrædlice **ongean** com þæt ic wolde
… that it me so quickly against came what I wanted
Latin: … ut cito **mihi** occurreret quod volebam
… that quickly to.me came what I.wanted
'… that what I wanted came to me so quickly' (cootest,Gen:27.20.1079)

2.2.2 OP Data

The OP case is theoretically more complicated. First of all, unlike PPs, where the Latin is essentially invariant and only the OE varies, in this case both languages vary, allowing both pre- and post-verbal OPs. Secondly, the PP construction is very well circumscribed and its translation is in most cases word for word; i.e., a preposition + pronoun, when translated, is normally translated as a preposition + pronoun, even if the order differs. By contrast, an object pronoun is embedded in a larger and more variable structure, essentially a VP or clause. Within this unit, there are potentially many more units that may vary, making the match/no match dichotomy rather more difficult to apply. To simplify, the OPs are coded simply as pre- or post-verbal, according to where they appear in the surface string in respect to the lexical verb, regardless of how closely the clauses themselves match. Thus, for example, the examples in (12) are both coded as pre-verbal (OP-V); post-verbal pronouns always follow the verb immediately in OE, so all post-verbal examples are as in (13).[7]

(12) a. Ic **hi** **gebletsige**
I her bless
'I will bless her' (cootest,Gen:17.16.656)
b. & hi **hi** yfele **geswencað**
and they them evilly afflict
'and they will evilly afflict them' (cootest,Gen:15.13.580)

(13) & **gelædde** **hi** to Adame
and led her to Adam
'and [he] led her to Adam' (cootest,Gen:2.22.112)

As it happens, however, the Latin of the Heptateuch is overwhelmingly V-OP, to the extent that including the Latin pre-verbal cases is not really viable due to low numbers (total Latin pre-verbal cases = 19/300 tokens with a Latin source).[8] The OP data is, therefore, only based on the Latin

[7] Post-verbal Latin OPs are almost invariably immediately post-verbal, as well.

[8] It is possible that this high rate of V-OP order in the Vulgate is itself a translation effect from Hebrew, in which object pronouns or suffixes routinely appear after the verb.

V-OP data, making it more similar to the PP case, as the Latin source is then invariantly head-initial in both cases.[9]

The possible OP cases, therefore, fall into one of four categories, in the same way as the PPs: Types (3) and (4) also include cases in which the translator has added the whole sentence, not just the pronoun, as discussed above in relation to the PP cases.

1. matching the Latin text, i.e., both Latin and OE are head-initial (V-OP), as in (14)
2. not matching the Latin text, i.e., the Latin is head-initial (V-OP), but the OE is head-final (O-VP), as in (15)
3. the OE has no source in the Latin and is head-initial (V-OP), as in (16)
4. the OE has no source and is head-final (OP-V), as in (17)

(14) Type 1:
OE: & **bletsode** **hi** ðus cweðende:
and blessed them thus saying ...
Latin: **benedixitque** **eis** dicens ...
blessed.and them saying
'and [he] blessed them, saying thus ...' (cootest,Gen:1.22.44)

(15) Type 2:
OE: & God **hi** **bletsode**
and God them blessed
Latin: **benedixitque** **illis** Deus
blessed.and them God
'and God blessed them' (cootest,Gen:1.28.59)

(16) Type 3:
OE: Hi **sædon** **him**
they said him
Latin: atque **dixerunt**
and they.said
'and they said to him' (cootest,Josh:2.24.5225)

[9] This more complicated case is discussed in Taylor (2015). The results show the same kind of effects as found with the PPs: a Latin V-OP source raises the rate of OE V-OP order and a Latin OP-V order decreases it.

(17) Type 4:

OE:	&	se	stan	**eow**	**sylþ**	wæter
	and	the	stone	you	gives	water
Latin:	et	illa	**dabit**	aquas		
	and	it	will.give	water		

'and the stone will give you water' (cootest,Num:20.7.4265)

The translations are then compared to non-translations to see how the frequencies behave. The expectation is that, if there is, indeed, influence from Latin, the translations will have higher rates of head-initial constructions than the non-translations.

The results of the 2008 and 2015 studies essentially confirm this, although the pattern is actually rather more complicated in an interesting way. In particular, there is a striking difference in the behaviour of the biblical and non-biblical translations. In the non-biblical translations, Latin orders are only more likely to occur in Old English when there is a source construction in the Latin; when there is not (i.e., the translator has supplied the PP or OP himself), the probability of Latin order is about the same as in non-translations. In the biblical translations, on the other hand, the frequency of Latin order is higher than in non-translated texts whether there is a Latin source or not. I refer to these two types of effects as direct and indirect effects, respectively, as discussed further in Sect. 3.3.

3 Results and Discussion

3.1 Reproduction of Latin Source Construction

The first question of interest is how closely Ælfric follows his source in his translations in comparison to the AT. It is generally accepted that his translation of Genesis is his most literal, although exactly how literal is disputed (see Minkoff, 1976 for a claim to extreme literalness, discussed in, and refuted by, Marsden, 1991). Marsden produces statistics on how many passages of various parts of Genesis are faithful to the Latin versus those that more freely paraphrase the source material, arguing that while often faithful to the Latin, Ælfric did not seem at all adverse to paraphrasing. In this section, I discuss two potentially objective measures of how closely a translator is attending to the source text.

The first measure is how often the translator, Ælfric or the AT, reproduces the two constructions of interest from his source, regardless of whether the order matches or not. The idea is that the closer the translation, the more likely that individual instances of the constructions will be transferred. In addition to a source for the OE clause not being present in the Latin at all, the clause may be represented, but the OE translator has added either the PP or the preposition to represent a Latin case. See examples (8)–(11) in Sect. 2.1.1.

3.1.1 Object Pronouns (OPs)

As shown in Table 11.1, this prediction is born out for OPs; the AT reproduces a Latin source OP (63.5%) more often than Ælfric does (52.1%). Moreover, if we separate out the different sections of Ælfric's contributions, we can see that, in fact, his part of Genesis (ÆGen) is quite similar to the contributions of the AT ($\chi^2 = 0.95, p = 0.33$),[10] while his other sections (ÆOther) have a significantly lower rate of reproduction[11] ($\chi^2 = 5.57, p = 0.02$), as shown in Table 11.2.

Table 11.1 Percentage of OE object pronouns with a Latin source: Ælfric versus the AT

Translator	Source	No source	Total	%source
AT	214	123	337	63.5%
Ælfric	87	80	167	52.1%

Table 11.2 Percentage of OE object pronouns with a Latin source: Ælfric Genesis (ÆGen) separated from Ælfric's other books (ÆOther)

Translator/section	Source	No source	Total	%source
AT	214	123	337	63.5%
ÆGen	50	21	71	70.4%
ÆOther	37	59	96	38.5%

[10] All chi-square statistics include Yates correction.

[11] The other three sections attributed to Ælfric do not differ significantly from one another ($\chi^2 = 0.69$, df = 2, $p = 0.71$).

Table 11.3 Percentage of OE PPs with a Latin source: ÆGen and ÆOther separated

Translator/section	Source	No source	Total	%source
AT	218	254	472	46.2%
ÆGen	50	47	97	51.5%
ÆOther	34	75	109	31.2%

3.1.2 PPs

The pattern in the PP data is very similar to that seen with the OPs. As shown in Table 11.3, again the AT and ÆGen reproduce the source construction at about the same rate (difference is not significant: $\chi^2 = 0.73$, $p = 0.39$), while ÆOther reproduces a source PP at a significantly lower rate than ÆGen ($\chi^2 = 7.98$, $p = 0.005$).

3.1.3 Discussion

Both the reproduction of OPs and PPs correspond to the prediction that the AT is a more literal (or closer) translator than Ælfric, at least in his non-Genesis books. The lack of a difference between ÆGen and the AT, appears to show, by this measure at least, that at his closest or most literal, Ælfric translated in a similar manner to the AT, and that his translation of the other books was less close.

3.2 Frequency of Latin Order

If the Latin source is influencing the frequency of Latin order in V-OP and P-PRO sequences, we expect a higher rate of the Latin order in the more closely translated sections of the text: the prediction is, therefore, that the highest rates will manifest in AT, followed by ÆGen and then ÆOther.

Table 11.4 shows the overall rate of V-OP order in the sections of the Heptateuch. Here we see a cline from the most V-OP (Latin) order in the AT section with progressively less in ÆGen and ÆOther, as predicted.

Table 11.4 Overall percentage of V-OP order

	V-OP	OV-P	Total	%V-OP
AT	219	118	337	65.0%
ÆGen	34	37	71	47.9%
ÆOther	32	64	96	33.3%

Table 11.5 Overall percentage of P-PRO order

	P-PRO	PRO-P	Total	%P-PRO
AT	445	27	472	97.1%
ÆGen	59	38	97	60.8%
ÆOther	71	38	109	65.1%
Total Ælfric	130	76	206	63.1%

Table 11.5 gives the results for the PPs. As with the OPs, AT produces a very high rate of the Latin order. The Ælfric sections, however, have similar frequencies (the difference is not significant $\chi^2 = 0.25$, $p = 0.62$).

3.2.1 Discussion

By this measure, the OP data shows a clear separation between the three sections (AT, ÆGen, and ÆOther), as we also saw in Sect. 3.1.1, again suggesting that ÆGen differs in closeness of translation from ÆOther.

However, while the PP data agrees with the OP data in suggesting that AT is the most literal part of the translation, Table 11.5 does not support a difference for the two parts of Ælfric's translation.

3.3 Direct and Indirect Effects

A direct effect is when the translator produces a higher rate of the Latin order when reproducing a construction from the source, in comparison to the rate of the Latin order in non-translated text. To test for direct effects, therefore, we need a baseline of non-translated texts. Ælfric's contributions to the Heptateuch are partly written in his metrical style (Numbers and Judges) and partly in straight prose (Genesis and Joshua), and, thus, Ælfric's four large non-translated texts, *Supplemental homilies*, *Lives of saints*, and *Catholic Homilies I and II*, which contain both metrical and non-metrical writing, would appear to make an appropriate baseline. A direct effect would manifest as a difference between the rate of Latin order in Ælfric's non-translated texts (ÆNonTrans) and the translated sections. The prediction is direct effects in all sections, strongest in the AT and weakest in ÆOther.

An indirect effect is a kind of priming that results in a higher rate of Latin orders, even when the translator is not reproducing a construction from the source. To detect indirect effects, we compare the rate of Latin order when there is a source to the cases with no source, as well as to the baseline of non-translated text. An indirect effect would be manifested by similar rates of Latin order with or without a source, both higher than the baseline, while different rates (higher when there is a source) and no difference from the non-translated baseline would indicate a lack of such an effect.

3.3.1 Direct Effects

3.3.1.1 OP Data

Table 11.6 separates the rate of Latin order when there is a source in the Latin (right side) and when there is not (left side). The last row gives the data for ÆNonTrans for comparison.

When there is a source, Ælfric produces a slightly higher rate of the Latin order in ÆOther than in ÆNonTrans (35.3% and 33.4%,

Table 11.6 Percentage of OE V-OP order with and without a Latin source in comparison to non-translated Ælfric texts (ÆNonTrans)

	Latin source				No Latin source			
	V-OP	OP-V	Total	%V-OP	V-OP	OP-V	Total	%V-OP
AT	126	72	198	63.6%	85	38	124	69.1%
ÆGen	23	26	49	46.9%	11	10	21	52.4%
ÆOther	21	22	34	35.3%	19	40	59	32.2%
ÆNonTrans	548	1091	1639	33.4%	548	1091	1639	33.4%

respectively), possibly indicating a small direct effect (on the verge of significance: $\chi^2 = 3.78$, $p = 0.052$). ÆGen and AT show progressively stronger direct effects.

3.3.1.2 PP Data

We saw in Sect. 3.2 Table 11.5 that, as far as the frequency of P-PRO order is concerned, there is no difference between ÆGen and ÆOther. Table 11.7 shows that this similarity persists when direct and indirect effects are separated; in neither case is the difference significant (direct effect: $\chi^2 = 1.19$, $p = 0.28$; indirect effect: $\chi^2 = 0$, $p = 1$). ÆGen and ÆOther are, therefore, combined for comparison with the non-translated texts (ÆNonTrans). Table 11.7 shows a clear direct effect for Ælfric (ÆGen + ÆOther) and the AT, stronger as predicted in the AT.

3.3.2 Indirect Effects

3.3.2.1 OP Data

We have seen in Sect. 3.3.1.1 that the OPs show direct effects. To detect indirect effects, we compare the rates without a source against the baseline, as well as across the table against the cases with a source. Looking back at Table 11.6, ÆOther shows no indirect effect, as it does not differ from the baseline ($\chi^2 = 0$, $p = 1$). ÆGen has a higher percentage of Latin

Table 11.7 Percentage of OE P-PRO order with and without a Latin source in comparison to non-translated Ælfric texts (ÆNonTrans)

	Latin source				No Latin source			
	P-PRO	PRO-P	Total	P-PRO	P-PRO	PRO-P	Total	P-PRO
AT	212	6	218	97.2%	233	21	254	91.7%
ÆGen	35	15	50	70.0%	24	23	47	51.1%
ÆOther	30	4	34	88.2%	41	34	75	54.7%
Total Ælfric	65	19	84	77.4%	65	57	122	53.3%
ÆNonTrans	1406	852	2258	62.3%	1406	852	2258	62.3%

order (52.4%) compared to the baseline, quite similar to the rate of Latin order with a source (46.9%), suggesting an indirect effect, but the difference is not significant (ÆGen $\chi^2 = 2.54$, $p = 0.11$). The AT definitely shows indirect effects in comparison with the baseline ($\chi^2 = 61.7$, $p < 0.0001$). Again the rate is not significantly different from when there is a source ($\chi^2 = 0.78$, $p = 0.38$).

3.3.2.2 PP Data

Looking at the right side of Table 11.7, the PP data does not show quite the same pattern. The rate of Latin order in the non-translated baseline is actually higher than the rate in ÆOther; however, the difference is technically not significant ($\chi^2 = 3.59$, $p = 0.058$), but it is very close, making it difficult to interpret. The baseline is not significantly different from ÆOther and ÆGen separately, so it is perhaps safer to interpret this as no indirect effect in Ælfric. In addition, here we see that the difference between the cases with and without a source is quite large and highly significant (total Ælfric source vs no source: $\chi^2 = 11.4$, $p = 0.0007$[12]), again suggesting that for PPs, there are no (or small) indirect effects in Ælfric.

The AT, unlike Ælfric, shows a clear difference from the baseline ($\chi^2 = 86.12$, $p < 0.0001$); there is also a difference between the source and non-source cases ($\chi^2 = 5.63$, $p = 0.02$), suggesting although there is a clear indirect effect, the direct effect is stronger.

3.3.3 Discussion

For the position of OPs with respect to the finite verb, all the texts, with the possible exception of ÆOther, show direct effects, differing from the baseline non-translated text. The difference between ÆNonTrans and ÆOther is on the border of significance, so it either shows no direct effect or a very small one. In any case, the strength of the direct effect is as

[12] Individually, the difference with ÆOther is significant ($\chi^2 = 10.18$, $p = 0.001$), but that with ÆGen is not ($\chi^2 = 2.89$, $p = 0.89$).

predicted: the AT shows the greatest effect, followed by ÆGen and then ÆOther. As for indirect effects, ÆOther, as the least close translation, does not differ from the baseline with respect to the rate of Latin order, showing no indirect effect at all ($\chi^2 = 0.04$, $p = 0.84$). The AT and ÆGen, on the other hand, show progressively stronger indirect effects.[13]

In the P-PRO data, on the other hand, while the AT acts as expected, showing both direct and indirect effects, we see no difference between ÆGen and ÆOther on any measure. Most surprisingly, unless the baseline is, in fact, to be taken as not significantly different from total Ælfric, the baseline appears to make no sense, since it is actually higher than Ælfric's rate in his translations.

Overall, the AT shows the strongest effects, both direct and indirect for both OP and P-PRO. For the OP data, there is a cline from closest translation (AT) to least close (ÆOther), with ÆGen falling in between as expected. The PP data shows the same relation between the AT and Ælfric, but does not support a difference between the two parts of Ælfric.

It is not entirely clear why the PP data differs from the OP data, in particular, what is triggering a **lower** rate of Latin order in Ælfric's translations than in his native prose. A sample of other non-translated texts (with more than 50 tokens) from the late period have P-PRO rates ranging from 44.9% in Chronicle D to 86.6% in Eustace, with an average of 61.4%, which is not very different from the Ælfric rate of 62.3%. In Taylor (2008), I discussed a number of other factors that affected P-PRO positioning in OE, including the preposition, the verb, case, and pronoun person, and it is possible that something similar is going on here, but it will have to await further research.

4 Conclusions

Due to its composite nature, the OE Heptateuch offers a unique opportunity to explore how different translators are affected by their source. One of the translators, Ælfric, is considered a skilled translator, while the other contributors to this work generally are not. In addition, since Ælfric

[13] However, recall that the difference is not significant in the case of ÆGen.

also wrote original OE works, we can compare his translations to his non-translated works.

The study tested a number of predictions, based on the hypothesized skill of the translators and previous work on the two constructions (PPRO and OP) under consideration.

1. Sections considered more 'literal' by literary scholars will show a greater influence of the source, and particularly, more of an 'indirect effect'.
2. The AT, as a less skilled translator, will show more influence from the source.
3. Ælfric's translations, in particular his Genesis, will show more Latin order than his non-translated texts.

The OP data behaves entirely as predicted. The sections of the texts—AT, ÆGen, ÆOther, and Ælfric's non-translations (ÆNonTrans)—are distinguishable from one another in the expected direction, based on the rate of the Latin (V-OP) order.

The PP data, on the other hand, while distinguishing the AT from the other sections of the text and the non-translations in the way predicted, did not distinguish Ælfric's contributions. In addition, the rate of Latin (P-PRO) order in Ælfric's non-translations is much higher than in his translations, a completely unexpected result. More work is needed to understand this result and its implications for the translated texts.

References

Bately, J. (2009). Did King Alfred actually translate anything? The integrity of the Alfredian canon revisited. *Medium Ævum, 78*, 189–215.

Fischer, O. (1989). The origin and spread of the accusative and infinitive construction in English. *Folia Linguistica Historica, 8*, 143–217.

Fischer, O. (1992). Syntactic change and borrowing. The case of the accusative-and-infinitive construction in English. In M. Gerritsen & D. Stein (Eds.), *Internal and external factors in syntactic change* (pp. 17–89). Mouton de Gruyter.

Fischer, O. (1994). The development of quasi-auxiliaries in English and changes in word order. *Neophilologus, 78*, 137–164.

Haeberli, E. (2018). Syntactic effects of contact in translations. Evidence from object pronoun placement in Middle English. *English Language and Linguistics, 22*, 301–321.

Langeslag, P. S. (2016). Reverse-engineering the Old English Book of Judges. *Neophilologus, 100*, 303–314.

Marsden, R. (1991). Ælfric as translator. The Old English prose Genesis. *Anglia. Zeitschrift für englische Philologie, 109*, 319–358.

Marsden, R. (1994). Old Latin intervention in the Old English Heptateuch. *Anglo-Saxon England, 23*, 229–264.

Marsden, R. (2000). Translation by committee? The 'anonymous' text of the Old English Hexateuch. In R. Barnhouse & B. C. Withers (Eds.), *The Old English Hexateuch. Aspects and approaches* (pp. 41–90). Medieval Institute Publications.

Marsden, R. (Ed.). (2008). *The Old English Heptateuch and Ælfric's Libellus de Veteri Testamento et Novo*. Oxford University Press.

Minkoff, H. (1976). Some stylistic consequences of Ælfric's theory of translation. *Studies in Philology, 73*, 29–41.

Taylor, A. (2015). The effect of translation on the syntax of Old English pronouns. *Societas Linguistica Europaea*, Workshop: Latin influence on the syntax of the languages of Europe.

Taylor, A., Warner, A., Pintzuk, S., & Beths, F. (2003). The York-Toronto-Helsinki parsed corpus of Old English prose. Electronic texts and manuals available from the Oxford Text Archive. https://ota.bodleian.ox.ac.uk/repository/xmlui/handle/20.500.12024/2462

Taylor, A. (2008). Contact effects of translation. Distinguishing two kinds of influence in Old English. *Language Variation and Change, 20*, 341–365.

Timofeeva, O. (2006). Word be worde – andgit of andgit. A study of the medieval rhetorical formula. In R. W. McConchie, O. Timofeeva, H. Tissari, & T. Saily (Eds.), *Selected proceedings of the 2005 Symposium on New Approaches in English Historical Lexis (HEL-LEX)* (pp. 135–142). Cascadilla Proceedings Project.

12

Phonological Regularity and Breakdown. An Account of Vowel Length Leveling in Middle English

Charles Yang

In Middle English, vowels in stressed syllables had length alternation under certain conditions that has been lost in Modern English. For example, the singular–plural pair *whal–whāles* 'whale–whales' had a short–long alternation and *crădel–cradeles* 'cradle–cradles' had a long–short alternation in Middle English, but there is no difference in their vowel length in Modern English. Building on traditional analyses (e.g., Prokosch, 1939), Lahiri and Dresher (1999) argue that the vowel length alternation in Middle English predictably follows from the interactions of several phonological processes, some shared across the West Germanic family and others unique to English. However, independent phonological changes

It is with pleasure and gratitude to dedicate the present paper to Don Ringe for his tutelage, support, and friendship. This work stems from some loose ideas about a decade ago: I would like to thank Aaron Ecay for his help with the historical corpus search at the time. Carola Trips and Jordan Kodner and the editors of the present volume also provided helpful comments and suggestions on an early draft.

C. Yang (✉)
University of Pennsylvania, Philadelphia, PA, USA
e-mail: charles.yang@ling.upenn.edu

J. F. Eska et al. (eds.), *The Method Works*,
https://doi.org/10.1007/978-3-031-48959-4_12

in the late Middle English period obscured the phonological condition on vowel length, which became sufficiently obscure for the learner to uncover. Subsequently, the vowel length was leveled: there is no alternation in Modern English except for a few archaic remnants such as *staff–staves*. Curiously, words that belong to the same historical classes leveled differently. For example, in Middle English, *path–pāthes* 'path–paths' patterned like *whal–whāles*, and *sādel–sadeles* 'saddle–saddles' patterned like *crādel–cradeles*. In Modern English, however, *path* has a short vowel and *whale* has a long vowel, whereas *cradle* has a long vowel and *saddle* has a short vowel.

In this note, I follow Lahiri and Dresher's approach, but supplement it with a learning model known as the Tolerance Principle (TP; Yang, 2005, 2016). The TP is a mathematical measure that formalizes exactly what it means for a phonological process to be systematic and predictable, and when it collapses. I show that the quantitative composition of the learning data in late Middle English, indeed, could not support vowel length alternation across the board, thereby providing a more precise causal explanation for its demise. I also make some suggestions on the directionality of leveling which may appear quite arbitrary at first glance as in the example of *path–whale* and *cradle–saddle* examples above. But first, let us review some of the essential facts and Lahiri and Dresher's proposal.

1 The Leveling of Vowel Length in Middle English

The Open Syllable Lengthening (OSL) rule, which lengthens vowels in stressed open syllables, was a general property of West Germanic languages including Middle English (Prokosch, 1939). From the late Old English period through at least some stages of Middle English, the language also developed the Trisyllabic Shortening (TSS) rule (Lass, 1992; Wright & Wright, 1928). TSS shortens the longer vowel if it is followed by two or more syllables, at least one of which was unstressed. It is productively applied to all vowels in Middle English and retains some productivity even in Modern English (Chomsky & Halle, 1968). The relevant patterns in Table 12.1 are taken from Lahiri and Dresher's paper, which also presents arguments that TSS followed the application of OSL.

Table 12.1 Expected effects of Open Syllable Lengthening (OSL) and Trisyllabic Shorting (TSS) in Middle English (from Lahiri & Dresher, 1999, p. 680)

	SG	PL	SG	PL	SG	PL	SG	PL
Old English	hǣring	hǣringas	hamor	hamoras	stȳpel	stȳpelas	beofor	beoferas
OSL	—	—	hāmor	hāmores	—	—	bēver	bēveres
TSS	—	hæringes	—	hamores	—	stypeles	—	beveres
Expected	hǣring	hǣrings	hāmor	hamors	stȳpel	stypels	bēver	bevers
Modern English	herring	herrings	hammer	hammers	steeple	steeple	beaver	beavers

These rules facilitate a systematic mapping from the underlying representation of the words to their surface inflections. Consider *hǣring* 'herring', which has an underlying long vowel, and *hamor* 'hammer', which has an underlying short vowel. Their surface realizations, however, have the same vowel length, thanks to the vowel length alternation regulated by OSL and TSS: long in the singular and short in the plural. The alternation was lost in later periods of English. In Modern English, almost all nouns have the same vowel (length) in both singular and plural, and their underlying representations—not a particularly useful notion now, unlike in Old English—are largely identical to the surface forms.

Clearly, some kind of leveling had taken place in the intervening centuries from Old English to Modern English. Note further that the leveling went both ways. In Table 12.1, words such as *herring* and *hammer* have preserved the vowel length (short) in the plural, whereas *steeple* and *beaver* have preserved the vowel length (long) in the singular. The aim of this chapter is to understand why and how leveling took place and to predict, when possible, which vowel length (in singular or plural) was retained.

To do so, we need to examine the major phonological classes of nouns and how they are affected by OSL and TSS. Consider the examples in Table 12.2 (Lahiri & Elan Dresher, 1999, p. 690).

A list of example words from these four classes can be found in Sects. 3.1 and 3.2, when I discuss what turns out to be quite different leveling processes for them. For the moment, let us review the basic facts about the way they changed.

The class with vocalic endings in both singular and plural (Table 12.2a) are the neuter nouns that make up about 25% of the Old English vocabulary (Hogg, 1992, p. 126). These were subject to OSL, but not TSS, due

Table 12.2 Expected effects of OSL and TSS in Middle English on the vowel length of Old English nouns

	Old English paradigm				Expected surface length	
	Stem vowel length	Endings	SG	PL	OSL/TSS	Gloss
(a)	short	V-V	talu	tala	L-L	'tale'
(b)	short	Ø-V	hwæl	hwalas	S-L	'whale'
(c)	short	Ø-V	beofor	beoferas	L-S	'beaver'
(d)	long	Ø-V	hǣring	hǣringas	L-S	'herring'

to their bisyllabic nature, and, therefore, surface as L-L (long-long) in both singular and plural. By Middle English, the plural suffix *-es* had already become dominant irrespective of the historical classes (Lass, 1992, p. 109) so *talu–tala*, therefore, would become *tāle–tāles* with a pronounced schwa. These nouns generally retained the long vowel, including those from the major *a-*, *e-*, and *o*-stem classes such as *nāma* 'name', *bēdu* 'bead', and *clōca* 'cloak'. An important characteristic of these nouns is that their singular form had a vocalic ending and, in particular, a schwa by the Middle English period as in *tale*, *name*, *bede*, and *cloke*.[1] This characteristic will prove critical to the relative orderliness of their vowel length change as I discuss in Sect. 3.1.

By contrast, the other three classes in Table 12.2 leveled to both long and short vowels in a seemingly chaotic fashion, the focus of my discussion in Sect. 3.2. The old monosyllabic *a*-stem nouns (Table 12.2b) have an underlying short vowel. They have a closed syllable in the singular and an open syllable in the plural, resulting in an S–L (short–long) alternation due to OSL. Again, TSS does not apply. These nouns lost the length alternation with some leveling to short, e.g., *back*, while others to long, e.g., *blade*. The disyllabic nouns with an underlying short vowel (Table 12.2c) are bisyllabic in the singular, but trisyllabic in the plural, due to the addition of the inflectional suffix. These are, thus, subject to OSL in the singular and both OSL and TSS in the plural, resulting in an L–S alternation. Some of these nouns leveled to short, e.g., *botm* 'bottom', while others leveled to long, e.g., *æcer* 'acre'. Similarly, the disyllabic

[1] Their orthography in Modern English follows the so-called silent-e rule: word-final *e* is silent, which reflects the loss of schwa by the mid-fifteenth century, and the preceding vowel is long.

nouns with an underlying long vowel (Table 12.2d) are subject to TSS in the plural, resulting in L–S alternation. Again, leveling to both lengths can be observed: *bēacon* 'beacon' to long and *bōsm* 'bosom' to short.

What led to the breakdown of vowel length alternation and subsequent leveling? According to Lahiri & Dresher (1999), the state of confusion arose due to the loss of the inflectional vowel in late Middle English (e.g., Lass, 1992; Minkova, 1982). The schwa in plurals was dropped after vowel-final stems, as well as in polysyllabic words, eventually leading to the loss of schwa generally (except following sibilants): the suffix became just *-s*, which was assimilated for voicing to the final segment. Importantly, the loss of the inflectional vowel resulted in the loss of a syllable so that TSS would not be applicable to words such as those in Tables 12.2c and d. As I illustrate with some examples in Sect. 3, this independent change of schwa loss made it impossible to make consistent inference about vowel length. Lahiri and Dresher (1999) suggest that the unpredictability of length alternation led the learner to postulate a uniform length of the vowels in the singular and plural: 'On our account, language learners despair of a rule, and opt instead to choose a consistent vowel quantity on a word-by-word basis' (698).

In what follows, I review the Tolerance Principle (TP; Yang, 2005, 2016), a mathematical principle that governs how language learner detects regularities in linguistic data (Sect. 2). I then apply the TP to the present case to provide a quantitative argument as to why leveling took place. I agree with Lahiri and Dresher (1999): leveling resulted from the unpredictability of vowel length following the loss of the inflectional schwa. The TP provides a concrete measure of what exactly it means to be unpredictable, a notion only alluded to in their analysis. The nouns in one of the phonological classes did in fact behave predictably (Sect. 3.1). For the rest, which genuinely had no regularities for the learner to detect, there still seems to be an interesting pattern in their directionality of leveling (Sect. 3.2), which on first look appears quite arbitrary, with some nouns retaining the length in the singular and others retaining the length in the plural.

2 Quantifying Regularity: The Tolerance Principle

As young children vividly illustrate in the classic Wug test (Berko, 1958), the ability to extend rules to novel items is a key feature of language.[2] But rule formation in language acquisition takes time. Children need to acquire a vocabulary from which rules can be established: word learning takes place very slowly in the early stages, peaking at just over 1000 at age three (Bornstein et al., 2004; Fenson et al., 1994). Additionally, since rules are almost always laden with exceptions, they can only become productive when the exceptions are overcome.

It has long been recognized, and from a broad range of theoretical perspectives (e.g., Aronoff, 1976; Bybee, 1995; Nida, 1949; Plunkett & Marchman, 1993), that the productivity of rules must overcome the exceptions. The Tolerance Principle is a precise theory of how much supporting evidence is necessary for a rule to become productive and generalized.

(1) The Tolerance Principle (TP):
Let a rule R be defined over a set of N items. R generalizes if and only if e, the number of items not supporting R, does not exceed θ_N:

$$e \leq \theta_N = \frac{N}{\ln N}$$

If e exceeds θ_N, then the learner will simply memorize the input that follows R and does not generalize beyond: i.e., R is unproductive. In that case, when the speaker encounters a new item for which R is in principle eligible, they would be at a loss, resulting in gaps and ineffability (Björnsdóttir, 2023; Gorman & Yang, 2019; Halle, 1973; Yang, 2017).

Because of its simplicity, the TP has been effectively applied to a wide range of learning problems in phonology, morphology, and syntax. Recent work includes gender assignment and inflection in Icelandic (Björnsdóttir, 2021), noun diminutives in Dutch (van Tuijl & Coopmans,

[2] It is convenient to think of 'rules' as classical rewrite processes in linguistics, but the term is used here in a pre-theoretic sense to denote any mapping or pattern defined over a set of items.

2021), argument structure mappings in English (Pearl & Sprouse, 2021), verbal inflection variation in Frisian (Merkuur, 2021), possessive suffix in Northern East Cree (Henke 2023), and others. One of the key properties of the TP is its recursive application. If a set of words fails to yield a productive generalization, i.e., if no single rule covers a sufficiently large number of words as defined by θ_N, the learner may subdivide the words into distinct sets and seek productive generalizations recursively within. Recursive application of the TP enables the learner to detect 'nested' regularities such as the German noun plural system, where the selection of the suffix is conditioned on the subsets of nouns defined by phonological properties as well as grammatical gender (Wiese, 1996; Yang, 2016). Furthermore, the experimental finding that infants follow the TP in implicit learning tasks (Emond & Shi, 2021; see also Schuler et al., 2016) suggests that the TP is likely a formal principle of learning and generalization, one that is not restricted to rule formation in language.

A theory of productivity in language acquisition has immediate consequences for language change. A new linguistic form regardless of its origin—contact, innovation, or innate biological capacity—must be transmitted by generations of child learners in order to take hold (Halle, 1962; Lightfoot, 1979; Paul, 1920). When a rule is acquired as productive, its openness may assimilate new eligible members. When a rule is acquired as unproductive, the only connection between it and the words that follow it would be experience, i.e., rote learning. Reduced exposure would result in words drifting to other (productive) rules, akin to overregularization errors in child language. Under this view, the traditional notion of analogical change (e.g., leveling and extension) can be understood as words responding to changes in the productivity of rules they fall under (Yang, 2016, pp. 139–170).

Since the calibration of productivity under the TP depends on only two values, N and e, it is possible to develop *predictive* accounts of language change. Or more precisely, since we are dealing with the past, accounts that aim to show that certain attested changes in history were, in fact, inevitable. Successful case studies can be found in the inflection of past participles in Latin (Kodner, 2023), the reorganization of the English metrical stress system due to the influx of Latinate vocabulary (Dresher & Lahiri, 2022), contact-induced phonological change in the city of Philadelphia (Sneller et al., 2019), the rise and fall of English past tense inflection (Ringe & Yang, 2022), and the development of psych-experiencer verbs in English in contact with French (Trips & Rainsford, 2022), among others.

Quite critical to any TP-based analysis is to obtain accurate measures of *N* and *e* such that productivity calculation can be made. These values can be precisely manipulated in artificial language learning studies even at the individual level (e.g., Schuler, 2017) and can also be reliably obtained when the relevant vocabulary set is small and their linguistic history is well understood. For example, Ringe and Yang (2022) studied the productivity of a strong verb class that has/had no more than 20 items. Their dates of attestation and usage patterns can be found in the OED and the historical databases such as the Penn-Helsinki Parsed Corpus of Early Modern English (Kroch et al., 2004) and the Parsed Corpus of Early English Correspondence (Taylor et al., 2006), allowing for fine-grained TP calculations and predictions. But the general problem remains: it is hard enough to obtain realistic acquisition data for living languages, what is to do with dead languages with perhaps only a few hundred thousand words of surviving text?

It turns out that the psychological condition on child language acquisition greatly mitigates the problem of data poverty. Recall that children learn the core of their grammar very early: major properties such as inflections, case marking, word order, and transformations are all in place by age three, a stage where the vocabulary size can reach just north of 1000 words and often even lower for many children. Furthermore, these vocabulary items are all among the most frequent items in the language, so children have a realistic chance of acquiring them (Goodman et al., 2008): high-frequency items are, of course, also those that are more likely to be preserved in historical documents. In an important contribution, Kodner (2019) demonstrates the methodological soundness of using historical data as an approximation of child input data at the time. Specifically, when we restrict the words to the most frequent ones—e.g., the top 1000—in child-directed corpora, as well as adult language materials including historical corpora, we obviously obtain very different words, but the *rules* that these words support are very similar. Under the TP, the productivity of rules may be the same even if they are derived from very different words, as long as the ratio of exceptions (i.e., e/N) falls on the same side of the TP threshold (i.e., $1/\ln N$).

With these methodological considerations in mind, let us proceed to the vowel length leveling problem from the perspective of the Tolerance Principle.

3 What Leveled, Why, and Where To?

The phenomenon of vowel length alternation and its leveling can be framed in terms of productivity. What Lahiri & Dresher (1999) refer to as 'predictable' vowel lengths is interpreted as native speakers having learned the phonological rules at the time, as described in Tables 12.1 and 12.2, and, therefore, did not have to memorize the vowel length in surface forms (singular/plural) by rote learning. This is formally equivalent to what we mean by a productive rule. For example, Modern English past tense is predictable because the rule (add *-ed*) is productive, and children learn so, presumably by following the TP, when the number of irregular verbs they know falls below the threshold. In this section, I will apply the TP to show that, following the loss of the inflectional vowel, the predictability of vowel length alternation was, indeed, undermined.

To carry out such an analysis requires concrete lexical statistics. To do so, I again turn to Lahiri & Dresher (1999), who provide a list of words of 186 nouns to adduce quantitative support for their analysis. These authors are quite explicit that their data are not a full description of the language at the time. Nevertheless, their decision to select only the most common words may just prove appropriate for our learning-theoretic approach to change. Of course, it is impossible to directly study the acquisition of historical languages. But there are reasons to believe that vowel length alternation would be among the first phonological properties that children learn. For example, Icelandic is a language that has a similar vowel-lengthening process in stressed open syllables (Árnason, 1998). Icelandic-learning children learn vowel length (Masdottir, 2008) and associated inflection (Thordardottir et al., 2002) very accurately by two and one-half—and they must have done so on a very modest, but high frequency, vocabulary that probably contains little more than 186 nouns. Unless the proportion of exceptions in Lahiri and Dresher's word list were very different from that in late Middle English child learner's vocabulary—the *only* condition that invalidates the application of the TP—we can be content with using their data as a surrogate.

3.1 What Leveled and Why

Let us now examine how the loss of the inflected vowel in the plural suffix could lead to the breakdown of vowel length alternation. Consider the representative examples below from Lahiri & Dresher (1999, p. 698):

(2) a. Before the loss of inflected vowel:

SG	PL	SG	PL	SG	PL	SG	PL
stōn	stōnes	god	gōdes	bōdi	bodies	bēver	beveres

b. After the loss of inflected vowel:

SG	PL	SG	PL	SG	PL	SG	PL
stōn	stōns	god	gōds	bōdi	bodis	bēver	bevers

(2a) reflects the grammar of Middle English speakers before the loss of inflectional vowel. As noted before, the vowel length alternation was predictable. (2b) would be the output of speakers after the loss of the inflectional vowel, which took place in late Middle English, a change that affected not only the plural suffix but also the past tense suffix (Lass, 1992). These forms would result from removing the schwa from (2a), which can be viewed as schwa deletion taking place after the application of OSL and TSS.

For the monosyllabic word *stōn* 'stone' in (2b), which has an underlying long vowel, the loss of the inflectional schwa affects nothing as the vowel surfaces as long for both singular and plural. But the other three examples in (2b) become problematic.

Take the monosyllabic noun *god*, which had an underlying short vowel. Before the loss of the inflectional schwa, the vowel is short in the singular and is lengthened in the plural as the *-es* suffix attracts /d/ as its onset, leaving the vowel open and, thus, eligible for OSL. Both surface forms are consistent with the underlying stem vowel being short. After the loss of the inflectional schwa, /ds/ becomes the coda of the vowel.

Being in a closed syllable, the vowel should not be eligible for OSL and, thus, should be short. However, the learner would hear *gōds* as having a long vowel, presumably produced by adults who had added schwa loss to their grammar. The learner would have to conclude that the underlying vowel is long. However, when the learner heard the singular *god* with a short vowel, with no relevant phonological rule at play, they would have to conclude that the underlying vowel is short. A clear incongruence.

The situation for the bisyllabic *bōdi* 'bodi' and *bēver* 'beaver' is similarly problematic. Before the loss of the inflectional schwa, their length alternation is predictable. The vowel is lengthened by OSL in the singular and shortened by TSS (after OSL) in the plural. Afterward, the plural becomes bisyllabic and is, thus, not subject to TSS, but should surface as long via OSL. But the input data in (2b) shows that the vowel in the plural is short. Again, an incongruence.

Taken together, the language learner would not be in a position to discover a systematic correspondence that regulates vowel length, even though this does not affect all words. It is worth noting that by this stage of late Middle English, other aspects of noun inflection (e.g., gender and case) had completely eroded away (Allen, 1999; Lass, 1992), leaving singular and plural marking the sole source for learning alternations.

The TP offers a quantitative measure of the conundrum the language learner would face when presented with data such as (2b). To take a trivial example, Modern English nouns clearly have no vowel alternation of any sort. This is so despite the fact that a small minority of nouns actually have different vowels in the singular and plural, a matter of historical residue: *child–children*, *tooth–teeth*, *index–indices*, *locus–loci*, *man–men*, etc. But these constitute only a very small proportion of nouns. Based on a standard word frequency norm (Brysbaert & New, 2009), only 15 such plurals appear more than once per million: *bases*, *children*, *criteria*, *data* (*datum*), *feet*, *geese*, *graffiti* (*graffito*), *men*, *media* (*medium*), *mice*, *opera* (*opus*), *phenomena*, *teeth*, *vertebrae*, and *women*. These are nowhere near enough to disrupt the generalization that Modern English has no vowel alternation.

Let us now consider the lexical statistics of vowel length alternation adapted from Lahiri and Dresher (1999, pp. 691–692) and summarized in Table 12.3.

Table 12.3 Four groups of nouns classified by their inflectional ending in Old English (OE), their expected length alternation, and their vowel length in Modern English (Modern)

OE ending		Example	Expected length	Total	Modern short	Modern long
V-V	a-stem	talu 'tale'	L-L	46	3 (6.5%)	43 (93.5%)
	e-stem	bedu 'bead'	L-L	27	9 (33.3%)	18 (66.7%)
	o-stem	nosu 'nose'	L-L	24	3 (12.5%)	21 (87.5%)
	Ø-V	hwæl 'whale'	S-L	36	19 (53%)	17 (47%)
	Ø-V	beofor 'beaver'	L-S	33	19 (58%)	14 (42%)
	Ø-V	hæring 'herring'	L-S	19	10 (53%)	9 (47%)

The situation is clearly very different from Modern English. There are 186 words: any generalization over them cannot have more than $186/\ln 186$ or 35 exceptions. While the slight majority of them in the top half of Table 12.3 have the same vowel length in both singular and plural (L–L), this does not hold for the other three classes in the bottom half, 88 in all, far exceeding the TP threshold. Therefore, the learner confronted with the data represented in Table 12.3 could not reach any coherent conclusion about vowel length: it certainly is not Modern English, which has no vowel alternation.

But there is another route forward. Recall the recursive use of the TP on subdivided vocabulary sets when no 'global' productivity emerges out of the full set. The nouns with vocal endings in Old English, e.g., *talu–tala*, and with a schwa ending in the singular in Middle English, e.g., *tale–tales*, do have a consistent vowel length (L–L) in the singular and plural, as shown in the top half of Table 12.3. Examples of these words, which appear in the *a*-, *e*-, and *u*-stem classes, are given in (3):

(3) Examples of disyllable nouns with vocalic endings in Old English and with a schwa ending in the singular in Middle English (Lahiri and Dresher 1999, p. 690):

a. Stem vowel /a/: *apa* 'ape', *blæse* 'blaze', *bracu* 'brake', *nama* 'name', *snaca* 'snake', *spada* 'spade', *staca* 'stake', stalu 'stale', *talu* 'tale'
b. Stem vowel /e/: *bedu* 'bead', *peru* 'bear', *cwene* 'queen', *slege* 'slay', *smeoru* 'smear', *spere* 'spear', *stæpe/stepe* 'step', *tere/teoru* 'tar'
c. Stem vowel /o/: *cloca* 'cloak', *fola* 'foal', *nosu* 'nose', *smoca* 'smoke', *stole* 'stole', *stoful-a* 'stove', *sopa* 'sup', *þrotal-u* 'throat'

These words are sharply contrasted with the nouns in the bottom half of Table 12.3, which end with a consonant in the singular, as well as problematic words such as *bōdi* 'body' discussed in (2b), whose singular ends in a full vowel. Therefore, the learner should be able to carve out a formal class ('singular schwa ending') and conclude that, for this subset, the vowel should be consistently long. As illustrated in Table 12.3, this is, indeed, what happened. The vast majority of the 97 nouns in this class have long vowel in Modern English, with a small number (15) of exceptions. Lahiri & Dresher (1999) suggest that some of the exceptions are only apparent, with several showing long/short variation before settling on short. The TP offers a more reassuring answer. Even if all 15 exceptions are genuine and have always appeared in the input data with a short vowel, they still fall under the TP threshold as $\theta_{97} = 21$ and, thus, would not undermine the conclusion that the vowel in this class is long.

However, the rest of the 88 nouns in the bottom half of Table 12.3 remain a mess. These nouns have a formal characterization in opposition to those in the top half: their singular ending in Middle English is not a schwa. Even though a majority of these (33 + 19 = 52) have a long vowel in the singular which shortens in the plural, they fail to clear the TP threshold as $\theta_{88} = 19$. As Table 12.3 shows, there is no clear pattern in the direction of leveling, approximately half to long and half to short. This state of affairs accords with Lahiri & Dresher's (1999) perspective, and our reinterpretation, that the learner fails to detect any systematic correspondence in vowel length and must resort to rote memorization on a word-by-word basis. In their discussion, Lahiri and Dresher observe that when language learners make decisions on the assignment of new words into declensional classes, the nominative singular may be given prominence (Lahiri & Dresher 1983), a familiar notion from the theory of markedness (Greenberg, 1966; Jakobson, 1932, 1971). For the three classes of nouns here, the privileged status of the singular would predict more instances of leveling to short for the *whale* class and to long for the *beaver* and *herring* class. But Table 12.3 shows that that is not the case: there is no clear pattern favoring the length in the singular.

While the absence of systematicity does take the learner into the realm of uncertainty, there may still be some discernible patterns to uncover.

3.2 Directionality of Leveling

In general, the singular as an inflection is used far more frequently than the plural. In the one-million-word Brown Corpus (Kučera & Francis 1967), the total frequency of singular nouns outnumbers that of plural nouns by a ratio of 2.5:1. In the 15 million words of child-directed English extracted from the CHILDES database (MacWhinney, 2000), singulars hold an even larger advantage, outnumbering plurals more than five times. The statistical dominance of the singular over the plural can be seen in historical data, as well: the average ratio of singular versus plural frequency in the Penn-Helsinki Parsed Corpus of Middle English (PPCME2; Kroch & Taylor, 2000) is 1.68:1. These statistics do lend support for the privileged status of the singular in leveling and other processes of historical change. The learner hears the singular more often: in the absence of systematic correspondences, they would assume the singular form to be the base.

Except when they do not, as in the Middle English noun classes that do not have a schwa singular ending, which shows no preference for the singular (Table 12.3, bottom half). Previous research has identified similar cases where words leveled to the plural rather than the singular. For example, Tiersma (1982) aims to characterize the nature of the privileged status when the plural trumps the singular in several attested changes: nouns that typically come in pairs or groups (e.g., body parts such as *arm*), those that are more frequently used in the plural (e.g., shells on the beach, citing Berman, 1981), those that are otherwise favored by cultural conventions (e.g., *bacteria*), etc. These considerations are clearly relevant for the understanding of language use and change more generally, but they are of limited value in the present case. It is conceivable that *god* is more prominent than *gods* in a monotheistic culture, leading to the vowel length to level in the direction of the singular (short) over the plural (long). But it is difficult to see how *gates* (long) would have an advantage over *gate* (short), or how *acres* (long) would win over *acre* (short), etc.

I put forward the following conjecture. For leveling of the type considered here, where the paradigm becomes incoherent, the learner fails to find productive generalizations for length alternation and is, thus, compelled to select a length in one of the forms as the base. The directionality does not reflect the inherent privilege of certain inflectional class, but the frequency of usage—but with an important twist.

Let us examine the three problematic classes in turn. Consider first the monosyllabic *a*-stem nouns in (4).

(4) Old English monosyllable *a*-stems with short vowels (Lahiri & Dresher 1999, p. 691):

a. Short in NE: back, bath, black, brass, broth, chaff, glass, god, grass, lock, lot, path, sap, shot, staff, swath, thatch, vat, wer [wolf]
b. Long in NE: bead, blade, coal, crate, dale, day, door, fare, gate, grave, hole, hope 'recess', meet, sole 'mud', way, whale, yoke

Of the 36 nouns in (4), 19 are leveled to short (i.e., singular) and 17 are leveled to long (i.e., plural). In the Brown Corpus, the words that leveled to short/singular (4a) have an average singular frequency of 49.6 and an average plural frequency of 13.3. In comparison, by contrast, the words that leveled to long/plural (4b) have an average singular frequency of 138.8 and an average plural frequency is 44.1. In both cases, the singular is considerably more frequent than the plural: no surprise. But a striking pattern emerges. Those that leveled to the plural are just more frequent across the board: their *plural* forms are almost as frequent as the *singular* forms of the short vowel words (**44.1** vs. **49.6**), and they are over three times more frequent than the plural frequency of those that leveled to the short vowel (44.1 vs. 13.3).

These patterns are also observed in the Middle English corpus (Kroch & Taylor, 2000). The nouns that leveled to short/singular (4a) have an average singular frequency of 14.3 (out of 1.1 million words) and an average plural frequency of 3.4. Those that leveled to long/plural (4b) have an average singular frequency of 74.1 and an average plural frequency of 14.8. Again, as in the Brown Corpus, the *plural* frequency of those leveled to the plural length is comparable to the *singular* frequency of those leveled to the singular length (**14.8** vs. **14.3**). Once again, as is the case more generally, the singular is almost always more frequent than the plural. If leveling were to favor to more frequent, one would expect most nouns to level to the singular by preserving the short vowel, contrary to the facts in Table 12.3. Rather, the observed change would be accounted for if the target of leveling must meet some kind of frequency threshold: that only forms above certain frequency—be they singular or plural—are eligible to serve as the target of leveling.

A frequency threshold may be a somewhat alien proposal in the study of language change, but it is rooted in the study of language acquisition and more specifically lexical learning. Children learn words very slowly. On the one hand, the world in which words are embedded is messy and complex: finding the meanings of words can be very challenging (Gleitman & Trueswell, 2020). On the other, learning a word requires repeated exposure as some kind of rote memorization is always involved (Goodman et al., 2008). But lexical memory has a ceiling: if the exposure to a word is sufficiently high, then the learner will successfully acquire it. A case in point is the acquisition of irregular verbs. After the productive '-ed' rule is acquired, over-regularization errors will ensue: more frequent irregular verbs (e.g., *think–thinked* as opposed to *thought*) tend to have lower error rates than less frequent ones (e.g., *draw–drawed* instead of *drew*); see Marcus et al. (1992), Maratsos (2000), Yang (2002) for discussion. But eventually, everyone learns the irregular verbs correctly, despite the fact that *thought* is more frequent than *drew* at every stage of language acquisition. A similar notion is the finding that words occurring at least once per million are generally known to all high school graduates (Nagy & Anderson, 1984): more frequent than that does not make a word 'more' known. A frequency threshold boils down to this: if you know a word, you know a word. And if you know a word—by hearing it enough—you know the length of the vowel in it.

The proposal of a frequency threshold is also consistent with the two disyllabic noun classes.

(5) Old English disyllabic nouns with short open syllables (Lahiri & Dresher 1999, p. 691):

a. Long in NE: æcer 'acre', bydel 'beadle', beofor 'beaver', cradol 'cradle', efes 'eaves', efen 'even', hæfen 'haven', hæsel 'hazel', hlædel 'ladle', mapul- 'maple', nacod 'naked', hræfn 'raven', stapol 'staple', tapor 'taper'
b. Short in NE: botm 'bottom', camel 'camel', canon 'canon', copor 'copper', fæder 'father', fæþm 'fathom', feþer 'feather', fetel 'fettle', hamor 'hammer', heofon 'heaven', hofel 'hovel', lator 'latter', ofen 'oven', oter 'otter', sadol 'saddle', seofen 'seven', sc(e)ofl 'shovel', wæter 'water', weder 'weather'

(6) Old English disyllabic nouns with long vowels (Lahiri and Dresher 1999, p. 692):

a. Long in NE: bēacon 'beacon', bītel, bīetel 'beetle', ǣfenn 'even(ing)', hūsl 'housel, Eucharist', stȳpl 'steeple', tācn 'token', brīdels 'bridle', fēfor 'fever', hæþen 'heathen'
b. Short in NE: bōsm 'bosom', brōþor 'brother', dēofol 'devil', fōdor 'fodder', hæring 'herring', mōdor 'mother', rædels 'riddle', spātl 'spattle, saliva', þȳmel 'thimble', wæpen 'weapon'

As discussed earlier, both classes would show L–S alternation in Middle English, and the loss of the inflectional vowel in late Middle English led to the breakdown of predictable vowel length alternation. In the Brown Corpus, the nouns that leveled to long/singular (i.e., 5a and 6a) have an average singular frequency of 12.5 and an average plural frequency of 7.8.[3] The nouns that leveled to short/plural (i.e., 5b and 6b) have an average singular frequency of 46.6 and an average plural frequency of 12.9. Again, we see that the words that leveled to the plural length are on average much more frequent than those that leveled to the singular length. And again, the plural frequency of (5b) and (6b) is comparable to the singular frequency of (5a) and (6a): **12.9** versus **12.5**. Results from PPCME2 are similar. The nouns that leveled to the singular are quite infrequent: the singulars average 1.8 occurrences and the plurals 1.1. By contrast, those that leveled to the plural length have an average singular frequency of 16.7 and plural frequency of **2.7**, which is a bit higher than the *singular* frequency (**1.8**) of those that leveled to long, although the data is quite sparse.

For both the monosyllabic *a*-stem nouns (4) and the disyllabic nouns (5–6), those that leveled to the plural length are generally high frequency across the board. Even when their singular frequencies are still higher, their plural frequencies are high enough so the plural forms become eligible as target of leveling. The privileged status of the singular in leveling and change reflects the typical situation where the singular is more

[3] It is not surprising that bisyllabic words are less frequent than monosyllabic words reviewed earlier: longer words are less frequent than shorter ones (Caplan et al., 2020; Zipf, 1949).

frequent than the plural. But if the plural is already in the upper echelon of frequency, it can effectively neutralize the singular's advantage and become a target for leveling, even though the singular may be more frequent still.

4 Conclusion and Prospects

This has been a thought experiment. We imagined ourselves as child learners in the late period of Middle English. Armed with independently motivated mechanisms of language acquisition, we wondered what kind of grammar could have been acquired, one which would differ from our parents as the learning data had changed. The thought experiment is also enabled by the uniformitarian assumption. The psychological mechanism for language acquisition has not changed in the past few hundred years, nor has the ecological condition of language acquisition: children, then as now, learn their grammar from a fairly small set of highly frequent words. These considerations collectively allow us to build on previous scholarship (Lahiri & Dresher 1999) and develop precise hypotheses about change, which can then be verified on the available historical data. The methods are general and can be extended to other empirical studies. For example, we have assumed that if the child learner fails to detect any systematic pattern in the vowel alternations, they would simply take the surface representations as the underlying representation, as is in the case of Modern English. This is a traditional idea, tracing back at least to Kiparsky's Alternation Condition (1968), but now supplemented with a quantitative learning principle that specifies just how systematic an alternation needs to be to justify the postulation of abstract representations. We could also apply the method to, say, Old English, to see what would motivate a child learner to postulate an underlying representation (e.g., vowel length) that is distinct from its surface realizations. To do so, they must also acquire the morpho-phonological processes that manipulate and relate these (potential) representations. The reader is directed to Richter (2021) and Belth (2023) for interesting research pursuing these lines.

Our thought experiment has yielded some new insights and refined understanding of previous efforts. For one class of Middle English nouns, i.e., those that have a schwa ending in the singular, they are mechanistically predicted to retain the long vowel with a tolerable number of exceptions according to the TP. The other nouns were predicted not to reach the requisite level of regularity for vowel length alternation, also according to the TP. For these, it seems that usage frequency has played an important but hardly deterministic role, as the threshold hypothesis reigns in the exaggerated effect of frequency in previous work (e.g., Bybee, 2010).

It is perhaps worth pointing out that all historical studies of languages are thought experiments. The language is dead and there are no native speakers around to consult. Nevertheless, linguists have been able to reconstruct the properties of numerous dead languages and their historical trajectories with astonishing detail and accuracy, based on the distributional properties of often fragmentary data. The same can be said about children. The linguistic experience for every child is a somewhat arbitrary sample of the language, which is, in turn, a somewhat arbitrary product of history. Yet children in the same speech community are able to acquire a largely uniform grammar (Labov, 2012). There must be a mechanism that reliably projects a grammar from children's messy data. Understanding this mechanism may help historical linguists understand their own messy data.

References

Allen, C. L. (1999). *Case marking and reanalysis. Grammatical relations from Old to Early Modern English*. Clarendon Press.

Árnason, K. (1998). Vowel shortness in Icelandic. In W. Kehrein & R. Wiese (Eds.), *Phonology and morphology of the Germanic languages* (pp. 3–25). De Gruyter Mouton.

Aronoff, M. (1976). *Word formation in generative grammar*. MIT Press.

Belth, C. (2023). Toward an algorithmic account of phonological rules and representations. Ph.D. dissertation. University of Michigan, Ann Arbor, MI.

Berko, J. (1958). The child's learning of English morphology. *Word, 14*, 150–177.

Berman, R. A. (1981). Regularity vs anomaly. The acquisition of Hebrew inflectional morphology. *Journal of Child Language, 8*, 265–282.

Björnsdóttir, S. M. (2023). Predicting ineffability. Grammatical gender and noun pluralization in Icelandic. *Glossa. A Journal of General Linguistics,* 8. https://doi.org/10.16995/glossa.5823

Björnsdóttir, S. M. (2021). Productivity and the acquisition of gender. *Journal of Child Language, 48,* 1209–1234.

Bornstein, M. H., Cote, L. R., Maital, S., Painter, K., Park, S.-Y., Pascual, L., Pêcheux, M.-G., Ruel, J., Venuti, P., & Vyt, A. (2004). Cross-linguistic analysis of vocabulary in young children. Spanish, Dutch, French, Hebrew, Italian, Korean, and American English. *Child Development, 75,* 1115–1139.

Brysbaert, M., & New, B. (2009). Moving beyond Kučera and Francis. A critical evaluation of current word frequency norms and the introduction of a new and improved word frequency measure for American English. *Behavior Research Methods, 41,* 977–990.

Bybee, J. L. (1995). Regular morphology and the lexicon. *Language and Cognitive Processes, 10,* 425–455.

Bybee, J. L. (2010). *Language, usage and cognition.* Cambridge University Press.

Caplan, S., Kodner, J., & Yang, C. (2020). Miller's monkey updated. Communicative efficiency and the statistics of words in natural language. *Cognition, 205,* 1044–1066.

Chomsky, N., & Halle, M. (1968). *The sound pattern of English.* MIT Press.

Dresher, B. E., & Lahiri, A. (2022). The foot in the history of English. Challenges to metrical coherence. In Los et al. 2022: 42–59.

Emond, E., & Shi, R. (2021). Infants' rule generalization is governed by the Tolerance Principle. In D. Dionne & L.-A. V. Covas (Eds.), *Proceedings of the 45th annual Boston University Conference on Language Development* (pp. 191–204). Cascadilla Press.

Fenson, L., Dale, P. S., Steven Reznick, J., Bates, E., Thal, D. J., Pethick, S. J., Tomasello, M., Mervis, C. B., & Stiles, J. (1994). *Variability in early communicative development.* Society for Research in Child Development.

Gleitman, L. R., & Trueswell, J. C. (2020). Easy words. Reference resolution in a malevolent referent world. *Topics in Cognitive Science, 12,* 22–47.

Goodman, J. C., Dale, P. S., & Li, P. (2008). Does frequency count? Parental input and the acquisition of vocabulary. *Journal of Child Language, 35,* 515–531.

Gorman, K., & Yang, C. (2019). When nobody wins. In F. Rainer, F. Gardani, H. C. Luschützky, & W. U. Dressler (Eds.), *Competition in inflection and word formation* (pp. 169–193). Springer.

Greenberg, J. H. (1966). *Language universals.* Mouton.

Halle, M. (1962). Phonology in generative grammar. *Word, 18,* 54–72.

Halle, M. (1973). Prolegomena to a theory of word formation. *Linguistic Inquiry, 4*, 3–16.
Henke, R. E. (2023). Rules and exceptions; A Tolerance Principle account of the possessive suffix in Northern East Cree. *Journal of Child Language, 50*(5), 1119–1154. https://doi.org/10.1017/S0305000922000277
Hogg, R. M. (1992). Phonology and morphology. In R. M. Hogg (Ed.), *The Cambridge history of the English language i, The beginnings to 1066* (pp. 67–167). Cambridge University Press.
Jakobson, R. (1932). Zur Struktur des russischen Verbums. In V. Mathesius (Ed.), *Charisteria mathesio oblata quinquagenario a discipulis et circuli linguistici pragensis sodalibus oblata* (pp. 74–83). Pražský Linguistický Kroužek.
Jakobson, R. (1971). *Selected writings i, Word and language*. Mouton.
Kiparsky, P. (1968). *How abstract is phonology?* Indiana University Linguistics Club.
Kodner, J. (2019). Estimating child linguistic experience from historical corpora. *Glossa, 4*, 122. https://doi.org/10.5334/gjgl.926
Kodner, J. (2023). What Latin verbal morphology tells us about morphological theory. *Natural Language and Linguistic Theory, 41*, 733–792.
Kroch, A., Santorini, B., & Delfs, L. (2004). *Penn-Helsinki Parsed Corpus of Early Modern English.*
Kroch, A., & Taylor, A. (2000). *Penn-Helsinki parsed corpus of Middle English*[2].
Kučera, H., & Nelson Francis, W. (1967). *Computational analysis of present-day American English*. Brown University Press.
Labov, W. (2012). What is to be learned. *Review of Cognitive Linguistics, 10*, 265–293.
Lahiri, A., & Elan Dresher, B. (1983). Diachronic and synchronic implications of declension shifts. *The Linguistic Review, 3*, 141–163.
Lahiri, A., & Elan Dresher, B. (1999). Open syllable lengthening in West Germanic. *Language, 75*, 678–719.
Lass, R. (1992). Phonology and morphology. In N. Blake (Ed.), *The Cambridge history of the English language ii, 1066–1476* (pp. 23–155). Cambridge University Press.
Lightfoot, D. W. (1979). *Principles of diachronic syntax*. Cambridge University Press.
MacWhinney, B. (2000). *The CHILDES project. Tools for analyzing talk*[3]. Lawrence Erlbaum.
Maratsos, M. (2000). More overregularizations after all. New data and discussion on Marcus, Pinker, Ullman, Hollander, Rosen and Xu. *Journal of Child Language, 27*, 183–212.

Marcus, G., Pinker, S., Ullman, M. T., Hollander, M., Rosen, J., & Fei, X. (1992). *Overregularization in language acquisition*. University of Chicago Press.
Masdottir, T. (2008). Phonological development and disorders in Icelandic-speaking children. Ph.D. dissertation, University of Newcastle upon Tyne.
Merkuur, A. (2021). Changes in modern Frisian verbal inflection. Ph.D. dissertation, University of Amsterdam.
Minkova, D. (1982). The environment for open syllable lengthening in Middle English. *Folia linguistica historica, 16*, 29–58.
Nagy, W. E., & Anderson, R. C. (1984). How many words are there in printed school English? *Reading Research Quarterly, 19*, 304–330.
Nida, E. A. (1949). *Morphology. The descriptive analysis of words*[2]. University of Michigan Press.
Paul, H. (1920). *Prinzipien der Sprachgeschichte*. Max Niemeye.
Pearl, L., & Sprouse, J. (2021). The acquisition of linking theories. A tolerance and sufficiency principle approach to deriving UTAH and rUTAH. *Language Acquisition, 28*, 294–325.
Plunkett, K., & Marchman, V. A. (1993). From rote learning to system building. Acquiring verb morphology in children and connectionist nets. *Cognition, 48*, 21–69.
Prokosch, E. (1939). *A comparative Germanic grammar*. Linguistic Society of America.
Richter, C. (2021). *Alternation-sensitive phoneme learning. Implications for children's development and language change*. Ph.D. dissertation, University of Pennsylvania.
Ringe, D., & Yang, C. (2022). The threshold of productivity and the irregularization of verbs in Early Modern English. In Los, B. et al. (Eds.), *English historical linguistics: Change in structure and meaning* (pp. 91–111). Amsterdam: John Benjamins.
Schuler, K. (2017). *The acquisition of productive rules in child and adult language learners*. Ph.D. dissertation, Georgetown University.
Schuler, K., Yang, C., & Newport, E. (2016). Testing the Tolerance Principle. Children form productive rules when it is more computationally efficient to do so. In A. Papafragou, D. Grodner, D. Mirman, & J. Trueswell (Eds.), *Proceedings of the 38th annual meeting of the cognitive science society* (pp. 2321–2326). Lawrence Erlbaum Associates.
Sneller, B., Fruehwald, J., & Yang, C. (2019). Using the tolerance principle to predict phonological change. *Language Variation and Change, 31*, 1–20.

Taylor, A., Warner, A., Pintzuk, S., Arja, N., & Nevalainen, T. (2006). *The parsed corpus of Early English correspondence*. University of York and University of Helsinki.

Thordardottir, E. T., Weismer, S. E., & Evans, J. L. (2002). Continuity in lexical and morphological development in Icelandic and English-speaking 2-year-olds. *First Language, 22*, 3–28.

Tiersma, P. (1982). Local and general markedness. *Language, 58*, 832–849.

Trips, C., & Rainsford, T. (2022). Tolerating subject-experiencers? Yang's tolerance principle applied to psych verbs under contact in Middle English. *Journal of Historical Syntax, 6*, 1–43.

van Tuijl, R., & Coopmans, P. (2021). The productivity of Dutch diminutives. *Linguistics in the Netherlands, 38*, 128–143.

Wiese, R. (1996). *The phonology of German*. Oxford: Clarendon Press. *Proceedings of the 45th annual Boston University Conference on Language Development*, ed.

Wright, J., & Wright, E. (1928). *An elementary Middle English grammar*. Oxford University Press.

Yang, C. (2002). *Knowledge and learning in natural language*. Oxford University Press.

Yang, C. (2005). On productivity. *Linguistic Variation Yearbook, 5*, 333–370.

Yang, C. (2016). *The price of linguistic productivity. How children learn to break rules of language*. MIT Press.

Yang, C. (2017). How to wake irregular (and speechless). In C. Bowern, L. Horn, & R. Zanuttini (Eds.), *On looking into words (and beyond). Structures, relations, analyses* (pp. 211–232). Language Science Press.

Zipf, G. K. (1949). *Human behavior and the principle of least effort. An introduction to human ecology*. Addison-Wesley.

Part IV

Indo-European Philology and Etymology

13

Guests. Welcome or not

Sara Kimball

Yakubovich (2005, pp. 118–119[40]) interprets Palaic nom. pl. *mārhas* (KUB 32.18 I 6MS) as 'guests' connecting the Palaic verbs *marha-*, which he translates as 'present oneself, come as a guest' and *marhina-* translated as 'treat as a guest'.[1] He also connects a Luwian verb that appears in the *Apology of Hattusili III* with a Glossenkeil, ˋˋ*marha-*, which he interprets as 'present oneself' (see also Melchert, 2016, pp. 203–204). These words do not have a secure etymology.

The first part of KUB 32.18 is a version of the Anatolian myth of the disappearing god (Carruba, 1970, p. 7 with references). While the translation of the Palaic noun as 'guests' is not compelled by the context, it is not impossible either, and it fits as well as 'gods', the gloss supplied by Carruba (1970, p. 63 with references). The relevant two lines, I 6–7, are:

[1] On the value of the Palaic suffix *-ina-*, see Sasseville (2021, pp. 529–541).

S. Kimball (✉)
University of Texas, Austin, TX, USA

J. F. Eska et al. (eds.), *The Method Works*,
https://doi.org/10.1007/978-3-031-48959-4_13

(1) … āntienta mārhas
atānti ni=ppa=si musānti ahuwanti ni=pp=as hasanti

The *m*. enter.
(They) eat, (but) do not satiate themselves. They drink (but) do not satiate themselves.

Yakubovich renders the first line as: 'The guests enter. (They) eat, (but) do not satiate themselves.'

The Palaic passage closely parallels KUB.17 10 I 19–20 from the Hittite myth of the disappearing god Telepinus, in which gods invited to a feast eat and drink but remain unsatiated, suggesting that the guests of the Palaic version belong to the supernatural realm:

(2) GAL-is=za ᴰUTU-us EZEN-an iēt nu=za 1 *LIM* DINGIR^MEŠ^ halzaīs eter ne *ŪL* ispiēr ekuiēr=ma (sic) ne=za *ŪL* hass[i]ker

The Great Sun God made a feast and invited the Thousand Gods. They ate but couldn't get enough. They drank but couldn't quench their thirst.[2]

Pal. *marhīna-* occurs beside a participle *marhānt-* in KUB 35.165 Rs. 22–24, (= Carruba 2.A), a text in OS or MS. The passage in which it occurs is part of a chant in a bread-offering ritual:

(3) KUB 35.165 Rs. 22–24 (Carruba, 1970, p. 19):

… ᴰZaparwāi ahūna hussīnta
[a=a]n marhīnanta mān=as marhanza ānnī wasū(=)ha
tabarbna ti=kuar [ ] sūna a=du pīsa

Sasseville (2021, pp. 536–537) glosses *marhīna-* as transitive 'invite as a guest' and *marhānt-* as 'having come as a guest', translating this passage as follows:

[2] Hoffner (1998, p. 15); see also the parallel version on p. 18.

(4) They poured Ziparwa to drink. They invited him as a guest. If he has come as a guest. (sic) Tabarna, be good as well to that one![3] Fill yourself (the cups) and give (them) to him.

The participle also shows up in Vs. 5–9, a passage concerning the ritual breaking and offering of stuffed bread. Sasseville (2019, p. 27) provides a new transcription and translation:

(5) KUB 35.165 Vs. 5–9:

[lu]kīt=ku tabarnas ^{MUNUS}tawanannas pulāsin[a]
[su]nnuttila sarkut=a=at pathinat sapāman hā[ntan]
^{D}Zaparwās=an=pa=ti takuwāti mān=ti marhānza mān=t[i iy]anza
a=apa arie a=anta wu$_{\text{ú}}$lāsina sunnuttila
[s]uwānta tāzzunta[4]

The Tabarna and Tawananna have broken the stuffed bread into pieces, lifted them (and) spread them out as a warm meal. Ziparwa looks at it: 'Whether you have come as a guest or you have wandered by, pick them up!' Then they (*scil.* gods) have taken the stuffed and filled bread.

The Luwian verb occurs once in the *Apology of Hattusilis III*, and three duplicates have different spellings.[5]

(6) KUB 1.1 IV 1–6:

[nu]=ssi GIM-an kē INIM^{MEŠ} w[atarnahhun]
ēhu=wa apās=ma=kan ^{URU}Marassa[ntiyaza arha parsta]
n=as *INA* KUR UTU^{TI} wet ^{M}Sipa-L[Ú-s]a=ssi DUMU $^{\text{M.D}}$30-DU
GAM-an ēsta n=an=kan *AN*[*A* ERIN^{M}]^{EŠ} KUR UGU^{TI} weriyat
^{M}Sipa-LÚ-is=ma ammuk IGI-an-[da] idalus kuit ēsta
ŪL-as=mu IGI-anda ˵marhta

[3] Sasseville (2021, p. 536^{7,8}) takes *ānnī* as sentence particle *a*= + enclitic dem. pron. dat. sg. =*anni* and *wasūha* as *wasuwahh*- 'be good' + =(*y*)*a* 'and' with contraction of *uwa* to *ū*, but he does not explain the single *h*. Alternatively, it is *wasū*(=)*ha* 'and good (things)', direct object of *sūna*- 'pour', and *ānnī* is the dative singular of the tonic demonstrative pronoun. For other interpretations, see the references that he provides.

[4] For the restorations and references for previous translations, see Sasseville (2021, p. 27)$^{27–35}$.

[5] ˵*mar-ha-ta* KUB 1.1 IV 6 with duplicates ˵*ma-ar-ah-da* KUB 1.4 III 50 + Bo 69/256 III 51, and *ma-ar-ha-ta* (no Glossenkeil) KUB 1.10 II 23.

Yakubovich does not provide a translation for the passage, just glossing *marh-* as 'present oneself'. Sasseville (2021, pp. 268–269), who follows Yakubovich on the basic meaning of the verb, translates:

(7) As I (*scil.* Hattušili) o[rdered] him (*scil.* Urhitešup) these words: Come! He fled from Maraššantiya and came to the Upper Land. Šipapešna, son of Armatarhunta, was with him. He called to the troops of the Upper Land. Because Šipapešna was malevolent toward me, he did not present himself before me.

HED vi 64–65 views the Luwian verb as implying confrontation, translating: 'While S. was evil against me, he was no match for me.' Again, the meaning is plausible.[6] It suggests that the verb might be from *(*s*)*mer-*, also in Gk. μείρομαι 'have a share in' and Lat. *mereor* 'get one's (due) share, deserve, be a match for', claiming that *marh-* and the Greek perfect ἔμμορε both reflect an Indo-European perfect. However, since the Luwian verb is a hapax and only found in the third person singular preterite, it cannot be confirmed that it is *hi*-conjugation. IE **smer-* 'divide up, distribute, have a share in' also shows no trace of a root-final laryngeal and is more likely to be the source for Lyc. *mar-* 'authorize' and Mil. *mara-* 'law' (Kimball, 2017).[7]

Mechanically, the Palaic and Luwian words can be derived from an IE *$merh_{2/3}$-. The retention of the laryngeal points to a zero-grade *$m̥rh_{2/3}$-, since a prevocalic full-grade *$me/orh_{2/3}$- would have become ***marr-* with gemination, while *$me/orh_{2/3}$-$C°$ would have resulted in ***mar-C°-*. A source for the Palaic words, at least, might be found in the entry for a root that IEW 735–737 reconstructs under 5. **mer-*, **merə-* (in more modern terms *$merh_x$-) 'aufreiben, reiben' und 'packen, rauben'. This entry surely subsumes more than one homophonous or partially homophonous root. IEW's reconstruction of a seṭ root **merə-* is based on Gk. μάρναμαι 'fight, battle', and Skt. impv. *mr̥ṇīhí*, 3. sg. pres. *mr̥ṇáti* 'robs, seizes, crushes, grabs', which point to an Indo-European nasal present *$m̥rh_2$-*né*-,

---

[6] Neither Otten (1970, p. 23) nor CHD (L–N 182) translates *marh-* in this passage.

[7] The similar-looking Hier. Luw. *marat(a)-* 'word' and *maratam(i)-* 'statement' or 'retainer' are perhaps related or alternatively to be derived from *(*s*)*mer-* 'think of, remember' in, e.g., Ved. *smárati* 'thinks of'. Sheveroshkin (1979, p. 180) connects Luw. ˶*marh-* with Lyc. *mara-* and Mil. *mara-*.

**m̥rh₂-n-* with a meaning denoting violent action. LIV^2 440 reconstructs **merh₂-* 'gewaltsam packen, zerdrücken', and Beekes (2010, p. 907) suggests that the original idea was 'crush (an opponent), grab (as in wrestling)'.

IEW and LIV^2 also connect Hitt. *marri-* (or *marre-*), *marra-*, *marriya-* 'melt down, dissolve, stew until tender', which IEW cites as *marriattari* 'wird zerschmettert' and which LIV^2 derives from a thematic **mérh₂e-*.[8] But this etymology does not work well semantically, since the Hittite verb means 'stew, melt (down), dissolve, liquify' (CHD [L–N] 180–181; HED vi 62–64). Within Anatolian, the Hittite verb belongs with the Hitt.-Luw. noun *marhā-* 'stew' < proto-Anat. **m̥rh$_{2/3}$ó-* 'stew' (something that has been melted down, dissolved, stewed) (Kimball, 2015/2016, p. 60[16, 17]) and with Cun. Luw. *marhuwa-* (in ptcp. *marhanuwamman-*) 'brew, stew, dissolve'. Sasseville (2021, p. 474) understands Cun. Luw. *marhuwa-* as a denominative in *-nuwa-* from the noun.

The idea behind IEW and LIV^2's etymology seems to be that dissolution is the result of fragmentation by violent means. Yet there is no hint of the violence of grabbing or crushing in passages with *marri-* (or *marre-*), *marra-, marriya-*. Instead, they describe the melting of fat, the dissolution of salt in water, the ritual dissolution of tears and pus, meat stewing, and a process that beer undergoes. HED vi 62–64 provides an etymology that captures this sense and is, therefore, a semantically more satisfying alternative. Although HED takes Hitt.-Luw. *marhā-* as 'dish, bowl' and does not connect it, it does plausibly connect *marri-* (or *marre-*), *marra-, marriya-* to **(s)mer-* in OE *smorian* 'smother, steep' (in Scottish and northern dial. *smore*), Mod. Engl. *smoor* (possibly a loanword from MLG or MDu. *smōren*), Germ. *schmoren* (loanword from LG) 'smother, braise, stew', and, more remotely, Engl. *smother* (ME *smorðer*), words that otherwise lack obvious Indo-European cognates (Seebold, 2002, p. 816; OED s.vv. *smore, smoor, smother*). If HED is correct, then we have a distinct root **(s)merh$_{2/3}$-* 'smother, braise, stew', essentially 'soften, liquify with the application of heat' from which the Anatolian and Germanic words can be derived. The sense 'dissolve' of salt and other substances in Hittite can be an extension of this meaning. HED suggests that the Germanic verbs

[8] Oettinger (1979, p. 281) also reconstructs a simple thematic. See the references provided by Tischler (1990, pp. 129–130).

can continue a causative, which would be *$smorh_{2/3}$-*é̯ie/o*-. The stem of the Hittite verb varies between *marri-* (or *marre-*) and *marra-* in texts in OS and MS (OH 3. sg. pres. mid. *mar-ri-it-ta*, or *mar-re-et-ta*, MH nom. pl. ptcp. *mar-ra-an-te-es*; see CHD [L–N] 180–181 for examples) with *mar-ri-ya-* occurring in NH copies of OH and MH texts. This pattern parallels that shown by Hitt. *wasse-*, *wassa-*, *wassiya-* 'clothe' (e.g., OH 3. sg. pres. *wa-as-se-ez-zi*, MH *wa-as-si-ez-zi*, MH 1. pl. pres. *wa-as-sa-u-e-ni*, MH 3. pl. pres. *wa-as-sa-an-zi*, MH ptcp. *wa-as-sa-an-t°*, but *wa-as-si-ya-* in later texts and copies) (see EDHIL 1004–1006 for examples). *Wasse-*, *wassa-*, *wassiya-* is plausibly derived from an old causative **u̯os-é̯ie/o-* as in Gmc. **wasjanan*, **wazjanan* (in, e.g., Goth. *wasjan* 'clothe' and OE *werian*) (Melchert, 1984a, pp. 31–32 with references), which suggests that Hitt. *marre-*, *marra-*, *marriya-* can also continue a causative *$morh_{2/3}$-*é̯ie/o*- lacking the initial **s* of the Germanic verb.[9]

The Palaic noun is reminiscent of the feminine noun **morā* that IEW also places under 5. **mer-*, **merə-*, glossing it as 'Alp'. If this is a derivative of *$merh_2$- 'grab, crush', then it would have been *$morh_2eh_2$ > *$morah_2$ with loss of the laryngeal in an *o*-grade formation via de Sausssure's Law within Indo-European. Descendants occurring in Celtic, Germanic, and Slavic refer to supernatural creatures, often, but not exclusively, female and, at least in Germanic and Slavic, causes of nightmares and sleep disturbances. Indeed, Nikolaev (2020, pp. 890–893[31]) considers a connection between Pal. *marha-* and the descendants of *$morah_2$, as well as the Greek demi-goddess Μαῖρα, companion of Artemis. Nikolaev posits an Indo-European source that refers to a 'supernatural, shape-shifting creature hostile to men and often attacking them in their sleep' and reconstructs a root *$merh_x$-.

IE *$morah_2$ shows up in Celt. **morā* 'supernatural being' in OIr. *morrígan* 'female demon, *lamia*, name of the war goddess'. The word is a

[9] It is not clear that the Palaic iterative *mariss-* is related, since it has single *r* rather than geminate *rr*. It takes as direct objects *lāla-* 'tongue' and *tarta-* 'curse'. Melchert (1984b, pp. 34–35) translates the passage in which it is best preserved KUB 35.165 Rs. 9: *lālan=ta kuis tartan marissi mas=pa=si mūsi* 'You who smash/crush the (evil) tongue and curse, enjoy yourself.' Sasseville (2021, p. 510) translates *mariss-* as 'destroy' here. Yakubovich (2005, p. 119) translates it as 'crush' and cf. Carruba (1970, p. 64) with references, and Oettinger (1979, p. 282)[44], who render *mariss-* as 'zerstückeln'. A meaning along the lines of 'dissolve' would also fit.

compound of a descendant of *$morah_2$* plus *rigan* 'queen'; occasional spellings of the first element as *mórr-* result from a folk-etymological connection to *mór* 'great'.[10] Gmc. **marōn-* (HGE 262) is found in ON *mara* 'nightmare, ogress', OE *mere* 'nightmare' (retained in Mod. Engl. *nightmare)*, MLG *mare,* and OHG *mara*. The second element of Fren. *cauchemar* 'nightmare' is borrowed from Germanic. There are numerous descendants of Slav. **morā*, for example: SCr. *mora* 'sorceress', Russ. *móra* (dial.) masc./fem. 'mythological female creature, ghost, darkness', Ukr. (dial.) *móra* 'nightmare, house-spirit-', Pol. *mora*, *zmora* 'shape-shifting demon that disturbs sleep and torments animals', Cz. *můra* 'nightmare, mythological creature that suffocates people in their sleep, moth', Slov. *mora*, *mura* 'demon that torments people in their sleep', SCr. *mòra* 'nightmare, owl', and Bulg. *morá* 'nightmare' (EDSIL 324–325).

The assumption behind deriving *$morah_2$* from *$merh_2$-* 'grab, crush' is that the demon sits on her victim, crushing their chest, a form of torture amply attested in the Germanic and Slavic folk traditions, which is likely a description of sleep paralysis.[11] But this assumption is problematic. Although OE *mære* glosses *incuba*, a feminine form of *incubus*, and *incubi* in later medieval and early modern traditions do cause terrors for sleepers, clear examples of descendants of *$morah_2$* tormenting sleepers from Germanic languages first turn up relatively late.

ON *mara* first shows up in the thirteenth-century *Ynglingatal* (Raudvere, 2020, pp. 7 & 272) and is found in folk legends from the medieval period through the twentieth century in first person accounts, legends, and ritual advice, where she is a threatening presence who presses, squeezes, and paralyzes her victims and is a source of illness in horses, cattle, and humans. Raudvere, who provides a detailed study of the *mara* in the medieval and early modern Scandinavian tradition, notes

[10] See eDIL s.v. *Morrígan, morrígu* and Clark (1987, pp. 223–224). *Fomoire*, which refers to a group of pirate-like demonic beings with whom the Morrígan contends (Epstein, 1998, pp. 19 & 40–51; Nikolaev, 2020, p. 891) may be related. The derivation of EDPC 278 from **mer-* 'die' is unlikely if Pal. *marha-* is connected, since it requires a seṭ root.

[11] Sleep paralysis, which occurs upon falling asleep (hypnogogic) or waking up (hynopompic) involves a feeling of intense pressure on the chest, a choking sensation, as well as hallucinations, often of a presence in the room (Cox, 2015). See Koski (2020) for its eroticization in early modern Europe and Davies (2003) and Millar (2018) for the role of nightmare and sleep paralysis in early modern European and North American witchcraft accusations.

her ability to shape-shift, appearing as a human, an animal, or a shapeless entity belonging to both the human and supernatural spheres (2020, pp. 8, 9, 14, 16, 28–30, 74–77, 182–183, 189–191, & 277). She is usually a female who forces herself on men, and Raudvere translates ON *mara* as 'nightmare hag', though not all of the examples she presents are ugly old women, and not all are even women. The Old Norse *mara* is sometimes said to ride her animal victims to exhaustion (Raudvere, 2020, pp. 8–9, 65, & 169–173). She might also plait and tangle the manes and tails of horses until they cannot be untangled (Raudvere, 2020, pp. 82–83). Batten (2021) portrays the Old English *mære* and Old Norse *mara* as female sexual predators who commit erotic and eroticized violence, mostly against male victims. Batten argues that the Old English word appears in glosses of medical texts, suggesting OE *mære* should be understood as a disease agent, while *mara* appears in Old Norse narrative prose and poetry, indicating a conjoining of sex and violence.

As a medical term, OE *mære* denotes an agent of disease said to 'ride' its victim in the table of contents of the ninth-century *Bald's leechbook*: *gif sio adl wyrde ođđe mare ride … wyrde* 'if a disease injures a person or a *mære* rides and injures [a person]' (Batten, 2021, p. 361). This is the clearest example of the *mære* in the glosses behaving like the Scandinavian *mara*. In an addendum to this text, *Leechbook III*, *mære* appears in a list of maladies, including *feondes costunga* 'temptations of a demon', *nihtgengan* 'night walkers', and *malscra* 'the evil eye' that can be cured using stones from a young swallow's stomach (Batten, 2021, p. 361). The Old English *Metrical charm 11* (Batten, 2021, p. 362) explicitly wards off the *mære*. Batten (2021, p. 363) describes the *mære* in these medical contexts as 'both a relatively specific being and the incarnation of anxieties over bodily invasion and the vulnerability inherent in physical and sexual submission.'

But the Old English *mære* of the glosses seems more a wild spirit who dwells in wild places. Although *mære* glosses *incubus*, *incuba*, the sense of the latter word seems not to be 'demon that suffocates victims', but, instead, it is something more along the lines of 'wild creature who inhabits desolate places and is apt to be sexually dangerous'. In the *Épinal glossary*, *mære* is provided an alternative, *satyrus* 'satyr', and the whole gloss reads: *incuba.mera uel satyrus*. According to van den Lugt (2001, pp. 178–179), the *incubus* originally shows up in Late Latin as a popular name that refers to 'sylvan figures and fauns of Pagan Graeco-Roman mythology: half gods who had a reputation for seducing and harassing women.'[12]

This is the sense in which *incubi* occurs in the *Leiden glossary* (late seventh century), which has: *Pilosi: incubi, monstri idest menae* (mistake for *mærae*) 'Hairy ones, *incubi*, monsters, that is, *mærae*.' According to Hall (2007, pp. 302–306 with references), this gloss is derived from an entry in Isidore of Seville's *Etymologiae* discussing *pilosi* 'hairy beings' in Isaiah 13:21, describing the desolate aftermath of the destruction of Babylon. The idea of pressing is specifically associated with rape in the passage from Isidore from which the Old English gloss derives, but the passage also includes discussion of various demigods such as Pans and Fauns, beings associated with wild places.[13]

(8) Pilosi, qui Graece Panitae, Latine Incubi appellantur, sive Inui ab ineundo passim cum animalibus. Vnde et Incubi dicuntur ab incumbendo, hoc est stuprando. Saepe enim inprobi existunt etiam mulieribus, ut earu, peragun concubitum; quos daemones Galli Dusios vocant, quia assidue hanc peragunt immunditiam. Quem autem vulgo Incubonem vocant, hunc Romani ficarium dicunt.

Pilosi, who in Greek are named *Panitae*, in Latin *incubi*, or *Inui* from mating [*inire*] here and there with animals—from which *Incubi* are also called, from their pressing down [*incumbendus*], that is from raping. For often evil ones even appear to women, so that they succeed in lying with them which Gauls call *Dusii*, because they perpetuate this impurity continually [*assidue*]. But that which they call *Incubo* in everyday language, the Romans say to be Fauns of the Fig.

In the ninth-century Corpus glossary and the tenth-century Cleopatra glossary, *mære* glosses the obscure word *faece*, *fecce*, which may be an ancestor of *fetch*, a word meaning 'apparition, double, or wraith of a living person', first attested in the late eighteenth century and probably

[12] Van den Lugt (2001) argues that many medieval physicians distinguished between *incubus* as a natural disease that caused sleep paralysis and SIDS in infants and folk beliefs about the *incubus* as a female figure pressing down on sleeping victims.

[13] For the text and translation, see Hall (2007, p. 303 with references).

Irish-English (OED s.v. *fetch,* n. 2; Hall, 2007, p. 301). Possibly reinforcing a connection with the wild, *mere* is conjoined with *wudu* 'wood, forest' in a compound *wudumær* glossing *Echo* in several glossaries (e.g., *Echo uuydumer* [*Erfurt glossary*]; *Echo wudumer* [*Corpus glossary*]). Hall (2007, pp. 308–311) argues that this gloss indicates the supernatural creature Echo, who was associated with woods and possibly sexual aggression, and not the echo as a natural phenomenon. He thinks it likely that *wudumær* is a gloss-coinage, suggesting that the connection with woods was not 'usual in the tradition [of *mere*],' but concedes the uncertainty of this conclusion. The English word *mare* does, of course, eventually show up in the 'nightmare, sleep paralysis' sense, but not unambiguously until the fourteenth and fifteenth centuries.[14]

The Irish Morrígan does not cause sleep terrors, but she is terrifying enough. Epstein, whose dissertation is a thorough, nuanced study of the Morrígan in Irish literature, describes her (1998, p. 7) as a 'war goddess who does not fight', though she is wife of Neit, god of battle (Epstein, 1998, p. 31). She manifests herself in triple aspect.[15] She is the equivalent of Badb (from *badb* 'hooded crow') and of Macha 'fate'. Although she incites cattle raids, the Irish version of war (Epstein, 1998, p. 14), she does not crush anyone, nor is she associated with nightmares. She employs insult, frightening noise, and poetic performance to incite warriors, in particular Cú Chulainn, with whom she has a fraught, ambiguous relationship. The Morrígan (as Badb) creates a terrifying din before battles that keeps the enemy from sleep (Epstein, 1998, p. 44). There may be some connection between the Morrigan and fertility (Clark, 1987, pp. 228–230; Epstein, 1998, p. 81), but Epstein concludes that any special association between the Morrigan and cattle occurs not because the Morrigan was a fertility goddess, but because cattle were what the Irish fought over.

Epstein emphasizes instances where the word *morrígan* is used without the definite article as a generic and describes a *morrígan* as one of a class of monstrous supernatural females with 'an appreciation of the spoils of

[14] OED s.vv. *mare*, n. 2 and *nightmare*, n. & adj. Germ. *Mahr* in this sense is similarly late; see DW s.v. *Mahr*.

[15] Epstein (1998, p. 37) notes that the M*orrígan*, *Macha*, *Badb*, and *Anu*/*Danu* are virtually interchangeable names, but reflect different nuances.

slaughter' (1998, p. 28). Used as a generic, *morrígan* occurs in Old Irish glosses (for a discussion, see Epstein, 1998, pp. 25–38). In a gloss on Isaiah 34:14, it glosses *lamia*. *Lamia*, a female monster in Greek mythology who devours children, is itself an attempt in the Vulgate at a translation of *Lilith*, a female, child-devouring night demon (Epstein, 1998, pp. 25–26). In *Cormac's glossary*, the word appears glossing *gúdeman* 'specter': *Gúdeman .i. úatha 7 morrígna* 'Gúdeman, that is, horrors and morrígna' (Epstein, 1998, p. 25 and eDIL s.v. *gudemain*).

The Slavic cognates include shape-shifters who can turn into animals or insects. They are also associated with sleep disturbance and a sensation of crushing or asphyxiation among victims. Russ. *kikimora*, however, is a household demon who spins yarn left unspun by the woman of the house at night (Beletich & Loma, 2013, pp. 56, 64, & 67–69).

To sum up the evidence for the nature of **morah*$_2$: the nightmare hag tradition is confined to Germanic and Slavic, but absent from Celtic, and unequivocal examples occur only in the Middle Ages. One wonders how much of it is the result of cultural contact between Germanic and Slavic speakers.[16] Certainly the idea of the nightmare hag seems to have been elaborated in the medieval and early modern periods in Germanic and Slavic folk traditions and is bound up with the misogyny of the witchcraft hysteria of the early modern period. An earlier sense of the **morah*$_2$ as an uncanny creature associated with the wild is still discernible in the earliest English attestations and is surely congruent with the Irish *Morrígan*, who is dangerous, terrifying even, but not a cause of nightmares or a crusher of sleeping victims.

Pócs (2018, p. 270) characterizes the descendants of **morah*$_2$ in medieval European folklore as 'small gods', marginal deities akin to fairies, 'double beings' who are humans who have become spirits or spirits who take human shape and engage with humans in communication with the dead and the world beyond. Over the course of the medieval and especially early modern periods, the descendants of **morah*$_2$ were absorbed into Christian belief systems becoming re-imagined as demons and witches.

[16] Dekiert (2004, pp. 59–61) describes a fog, known in Polish as *mara*, that could enter the human blood stream through the air finding its way to the heart and killing its victim or, regionally, press down upon sleepers causing breathing problems, as well as plaiting horses' manes, pointing out that the spelling with ⟨a⟩ points to a Germanic origin (cf. Pol. *mora, zmora*).

In the absence of more evidence, one thing seems clear: the Palaic *mārhas* are supernatural or divine beings of some sort. If the Palaic word and its derivatives are related to non-Anat. **morah*$_2$, it is unlikely they are derived from **merh*$_2$- 'crush, grab', given that the unequivocal attestations of the latter as crusher of sleeping victims are so late. Two other possibilities suggest themself.

1. The Palaic noun and IE **morah*$_2$ are derived from a root **merh*$_{2/3}$- meaning something like 'appear' and come from a root noun **morh*$_{2/3}$- : **mr̥h*$_{2/3}$- meaning something on the order of 'apparition'. Non-Anat. **morah*$_2$ is an innovation, formed after the breakup of Indo-Hittite. If related, Cun. Luw. *marh-* would mean 'appear, show up'. 'Apparition, sprite' or 'demon', that is, 'small god of the wild' would be the original meaning of the Germanic, Slavic, and Celtic derivatives. As support, note the use of *mære* in the *Corpus glossary* and the first *Cleopatra glossary* to gloss *faece, fecce*, a possible ancestor of *fetch* 'apparition, double, or wraith of a living person', and perhaps the Irish use of pl. *morrígna* to gloss *gúdemain* 'specters'. The sense 'nightmare hag' of Germanic and Slavic would be a result of later specialization and perhaps cross-cultural contact.
2. There is no underlying verb, or at least such a verb has not been preserved. Pal. *marha-* and **morah*$_2$ in Germanic, Slavic, and Celtic are from a root noun **morh*$_{2/3}$- : **mr̥h*$_{2/3}$- with the original meaning 'small god'. Again, non-Anat. **morah*$_2$ would be a post-Indo-Hittite innovation, and the meaning 'nightmare hag' in Germanic and Slavic would be a fairly late development.

If this essay has done nothing else, I hope it has helped clear some faint paths through the tangles of material under 5. **mer-*, **merə-* in IEW. Hitt. *marri-* (or *marre-*), *marra-*, *marriya-* 'melt down, dissolve, stew until tender' does not belong here. Instead, along with Hitt.-Luv. *marha-* 'stew' and Cun. Luw. *marhuwa-* 'brew, stew, dissolve', it goes with OE *smorian* 'smother, steep', Germ. *schmoren* 'smother, braise, stew', and ME *smorðer* under a root *(*s*)*mer-* 'brew, stew, smother, steep, dissolve'.[17] The Palaic

[17] The lack of initial *s* in Hittite points to *s*-mobilé.

nouns do not belong with this root and neither does Cun. Luw. *marh-*, whatever it means.

The feminine nouns *$m\mathring{r}h_{2/3}(o)$- and *$morh_{2/3}eh_2$ > *$morah_2$ probably deserve their own, separate entry or a sub-entry under a verbal root. This should include: Pal. nom. pl. *mārhas* 'divine guests' (or similar), *marha-* 'present oneself as a divine guest, come as a divine guest', and *marhina-* 'treat (someone) as a divine guest, invite as a divine guest', Celt. **morā* in Ir. *morrígan*, Gmc. **marōn-*, and Slav. **morā*. Gk. Μαῖρα < *$m\mathring{r}h_{2/3}ih_2$ probably also belongs here. This might be a purely nominal root based on a root noun *$morh_{2/3}$- : *$m\mathring{r}h_{2/3}$- with a meaning along the lines of '(female) demon, divine wild woman' or perhaps 'apparition'.[18] We do not know whether the Palaic *mārhas* were welcomed as guests at the feast to which they were invited, but given the nature of their potential cognates, their presence may have been at least somewhat unsettling.

References

Batten, C. R. (2021). Dark riders. Disease, sexual violence, and gender performance in the Old English m*ære* and Old Norse m*ara*. *Journal of English and Germanic philology, 120*, 352–380.

Beekes, R. (2010). *Etymological dictionary of Greek*. Brill.

Beletich, M., & Loma, A. (2013). *Son, smert', sud'ba* (nabljudenija nad praslav. **mora*, *mara) [Dream, death, fate. Observations on proto-Slav. **mora*, **mara*]. In *Slavica Svetlanica. Jazyk i kartina mira. Kjubileju Svetlany Mikhajlovny Tostoj* (pp. 56–75). Indrik.

Carruba, O. (1970). *Das Palaische. Texte, Grammatik, Lexikon*. Harrassowitz.

CHD (L–N) = Güterbock, H., & Hoffner, H. (Eds.). (1989). *The Hittite dictionary of the Oriental Institute of the University of Chicago*. The Oriental Institute of the University of Chicago.

[18] Descendants of Slav. **mora-* are found beside forms of a Slav. **mara-* with the meaning 'ghost, apparition' (e.g., Russ. and ChSlav. *mara* 'ecstasy', Russ. *mára, mará* 'apparition, mirage', as well as dialectal 'house-sprite, evil spirit', Bel. Russ. *mará, mára* 'dream, apparition nightmare', Slov. *mara* 'ghost, apparatiion', pl. 'dream, illusion, ghost' and dialectal 'nightly spirit that attacks people and horses in their sleep' (EDSIL 301–302). EDSIL suggests that originally there were separate nouns **mara* 'illusion, apparition' beside **mora* 'female demon that tortures people with nightmares' that eventually were confused. EDSIL and Beletich & Loma (2013) rightly insist on the blurring of traditions via the homophony of descendants of various roots within the various Slavic languages.

Clark, R. (1987). Aspects of the Morrígan in early Irish literature. *Irish University Review, 17*, 223–236.

Cox, A. (2015). Sleep paralysis and folklore. *Journal of the Royal Society of Medicine Open*. Retrieved February 15, 2023, from https://www.ncbi.nlm.nih.gov/pmc/articles/PMC5167075/

Davies, O. (2003). The nightmare experience, sleep paralysis, and witchcraft accusations. *Folklore, 114*, 181–203.

Dekiert, D. (2004). The unknown Slavic glosses in 'Sefer Hasidim'. *Zagadnienia rodzajów literackich, 17*, 39–66.

DW = *Deutsches Wörterbuch von Jacob Grimm und Wilhelm Grimm*. Retrieved February 15, 2023, from http://dwb.uni-trier.de/de/

EDHIL = Kloekhorst, A. (2008). *Etymological dictionary of the Hittite inherited lexicon*. Brill.

eDIL = *Electronic dictionary of the Irish language*. Retrieved February 15, 2023, from https://dil.ie

EDPC = Matasović, R. (2009). *Etymological dictionary of proto-Celtic*. Brill.

EDSIL = Derksen, R. (2008). *Etymological dictionary of the Slavic inherited lexicon*. Brill.

Epstein, A. G. (1998). *War goddess. The Morrígan and her Germano-Celtic counterparts*. Ph.D. dissertation, University of California—Los Angeles. Retrieved February 15, 2023., from https://archive.org/details/WarGoddessTheMorriganAndHerGermanoCelticCounterparts

Hall, A. (2007). The evidence for *MARAN*, the Anglo-Saxon 'nightmares'. *Neophilogus, 91*, 299–307.

HED vi = Puhvel, J. (2004). *Hittite etymological dictionary vi, Words beginning with M*. Mouton de Gruyter.

HGE = Orel, Vladimir. (2003). *A handbook of Germanic etymology*. Brill.

Hoffner, H. A. (1998). *Hittite myths*[2]. Society of Biblical Literature.

IEW = Pokorny, J. P. (1959). *Indogermanisches etymologisches Wörterbuch*. Francke.

Kimball, S. (2015/2016). Oxytone simple thematic nouns in Anatolian. *Historische Sprachforschung, 128*, 59–71.

Kimball, S. (2017). Luwic *mar-*. *Indogermanische Forschungen, 122*, 208–217.

Koski, K. (2020). Nightmares—from demonic attacks to self-knowledge. *Sömn och hälsa, 4*, 64–75.

LIV2 = Rix, H., Kümmel, M., Zehnder, T., Lipp, R., & Schirmer, B. (Eds.). (2001). *Lexikon der indogermanischen Verben. Die Wurzeln und ihre Primärstammbildunguen*[2]. Dr. Ludwig Reichert.

Melchert, H. C. (1984a). *Studies in Hittite historical phonology*. Vandenhoeck & Ruprecht.

Melchert, H. C. (1984b). Notes on Palaic. *Zeitschrift für vergleichende Sprachforschung, 97*, 22–43.

Melchert, H. C. (2016). New Luwian verb etymologies. In H. Marquardt, S. Reichmuth, & J.-V. G. Trabazo (Eds.), *Anatolica et Indogermanica. Studia linguistica in honorem Johannis Tischler septuagenarii dedicata* (pp. 203–212). Institut für Sprachen und Literaturen der Universität Innsbruck.

Millar, C.-R. (2018). Dangers of the night. The witch, the devil, and the 'nightmare' in early modern England. *Preternaturae. Critical and Historical Studies on the Preternatural, 7*, 154–181.

Nikolaev, A. (2020). Μαῖρα and other dangerous women. *Indo-European Linguistics and Classical Philology, 24*, 885–893.

OED = *Oxford English dictionary.* Retrieved February 15, 2023., from https://www.oed.com

Oettinger, N. (1979). *Die Stammbildung des hethitischen Verbums.* Hans Carl.

Otten, H. (1970). *Die Apologie Hattusilis III.* Harrassowitz.

Pócs, É. (2018). Small gods, small demons. Remnants of an archaic fairly cult in central and south-eastern Europe. In M. Ostling (Ed.), *Fairies, demons, and nature spirits. 'Small gods' at the margins of Christendom* (pp. 255–276). Palgrave Macmillan.

Raudvere, C. (2020). *Narratives and rituals of the nightmare hag in Scandinavian folk belief.* Palgrave Macmillan.

Sasseville, D. (2019). 'To show' in Hittite and Palaic rituals. *Altorientalische Forschungen, 46*, 22–32.

Sasseville, D. (2021). *Anatolian verbal stem formation. Luwian, Lycian and Lydian*. Brill.

Seebold, E. (2002). *Etymologisches Wörterbuch der deutschen Sprache*^{24}. De Gruyter.

Sheveroshkin, V. (1979). On the Hittite-Luwian numerals. *Journal of Indo-European Studies, 7*, 177–204.

Tischler, J. (1990). *Hethitisches etymologisches Glossar*, Teil II/1, Lieferung 5 und 6. Institut für Sprachwissenschaft der Universität Innsbruck.

van der Lugt, M. (2001). The *incubus* in scholastic debate. Medicine, theology and popular belief. In P. Biller & J. Ziegler (Eds.), *Religion and medicine in the Middle Ages* (pp. 175–200). York Medieval Press.

Yakubovich, I. (2005). Were Hittite kings divinely anointed? A Palaic invocation to the sun-god and its significance for Hittite religion. *Journal of Ancient Near Eastern Religions, 5*, 107–137.

14

Asyndetic Verbal Pairs in the Classical Armenian Gospels and Their Treatment in the Other Five First Millennium CE Indo-European Versions

Jared S. Klein

§1. The casual reader of Classical Armenian texts cannot help but be surprised at the occurrence, to a significant degree, of asyndetic verbal pairs signaling either the same or separate, but closely related, actions forming a unified whole. These constructions give the impression of

Kudos to Don Ringe for having had a highly successful career at the University of Pennsylvania and, more particularly, for his studies of Tocharian, Indo-European Cladistics, and Germanic, especially the early history of English, which already have and will continue to exercise a lasting impact on these fields.

J. S. Klein (✉)
University of Georgia, Athens, GA, USA
e-mail: jklein@uga.edu

J. F. Eska et al. (eds.), *The Method Works*,
https://doi.org/10.1007/978-3-031-48959-4_14

representing at least the rudiments of a serial verb construction in the language.[1] Some examples are the following:

(1) a. *ar̄nowin kotorēin* zamenayn bnakičʻsn ver̄nagawar̄acʻn Hayocʻ
'*They took destroyed* all the inhabitants of the upper districts of Armenia.' (Pʻawstos Biwzandacʻi IV, 23 [Thomson, 1989, p. 154])
b. *ar̄now acē* zna satanay i lear̄n mi barjr yoyž
'Satan *took led* (lit. takes leads) him onto a very high mountain.' (Mt. 4.8)
c. ew na *ar̄ ənkalaw* zna i girks iwr
'And he *took received* him into his arms.' (Lk. 2.28)

I have specifically selected examples involving the verb 'take', because this verb is cross-linguistically prominent in serial verb constructions, particularly in African languages, as in (2), taken from Twi, a Kwa language of West Africa:

(2) kofi de pono no baae
Kofi take.PST table the come.PST
'Kofi brought the table.' (Sebba, 1987)

It is also found in English in the closest thing that we have to a serial verb construction, although such instances always involve a conjunction. As a child, I heard many times sentences like that in (3) uttered by my parents and laced with Yiddish words:

(3) I'll take and give you a good *patch* on the *tochus*. ('smack on the rear')

More frequently, however, the initial verb of Armenian asyndetic verb pairs is a verb of motion. This, of course, can be found in many

[1] In this paper, which should be viewed as a contribution to the comparative syntax of the first millennium CE Gospel versions in the older Indo-European languages, I will not address the theoretical status of serial verb constructions (hence my referring to them as 'asyndetic verbal pairs'), their possible existence in proto-Indo-European, or their diachronic development in the various Indo-European languages which may be said, in one way or another, to possess them. For a treatment of these problems with which I am in general agreement, cf. Yates (2014). Moreover, I will not address the likelihood that these structures may be, in part, the result of linguistic contact with Syriac (cf. Kölligan, 2021), the language from which the Classical Armenian Gospels were most likely first translated, and which, like Biblical Hebrew, shows this phenomenon to a significant degree.

languages, including, once again, English, where the idiomaticity of the construction inheres in the fact that there need not be actual motion:

(4) He went and called the cops on me.

Here, of course, the person doing the calling need not have gone anywhere, but simply taken the cell phone out of his pocket. It is apparent that *went* is simply signaling an event, as is proved by the fact that this construction cannot normally be used with stative verbs. Cf. (5), where we understand *went* as a serial verb, not an independent verb of motion:

(5) *He went and knew what had happened.[2] (but *He went and stood there*)

In the parenthesized sentence, the verb *went* can be understood as independent of the eventive verb *stood.*

§2. In this paper, I would like to discuss asyndetic verbal pairs in the Classical Armenian Gospels[3,4] and to compare them with their equivalents in the other five first millennium CE Indo-European Gospel versions, including the Greek exemplar. In order to qualify, such constructions must contain two verbs that represent a single action signaled by the second verb and 'modified' in some sense by the first. In 94% of the cases, the verbs are adjacent; and the few cases that are not contain an adverb (6a–b), a vocative phrase (6c), a subject, including a subject relative clause (6d–e), or a fronted object belonging to V_2 between the two verbs (6f–g):

---

[2] I do not know what to make of such English constructions as 'Go know that he would do such a thing'. Without having studied the literature (if there is one) on this structure, my sense is that it is a Yiddishism, probably generalized from the common *gey shlofen, gey esen* 'go to sleep, go eat'. In my own experience, I have only heard it uttered by people whose family background is culturally Yiddish.

[3] In their corresponding treatment of the parallel phenomenon in Hellenistic Greek, Logozzo & Tronci (2022) include both conjoined and asyndetic structures, considering both to fall under the rubric 'Pseudo-Coordinated Construction', whose subtypes are 'serial verbs' and 'pseudo-coordination' (2022, p. 84).

[4] Jungmann (1967), who canvassed only Matthew and Mark among the Gospels, found a small number of asyndetic participles in these texts. We will not be concerned with these here.

(6) a. *ert'* aysawr *gorcea* yaygwoǰ[M:-n]
'*Go work* today in the vineyard' (Mt. 21.28)
b. *gnac'ēk'* aysowhetew *ašakertec'ēk'*
'*Go*, therefore, *teach*' (Mt. 28.19)
c. *ekayk'* awhrnealk' hawr imoy. *žaṙangec'ēk'* zpatrasteal jez ark'ayowt'iwn
'*Come*, (ye) blessed ones of my father, *inherit* the kingdom prepared for you' (Mt. 25.34)
d. *ekn* YS *egit* zna
'Jesus *came*, *found* him' (Jh. 11.17)
e. *č'ogaw* vaɫvaɫaki or aṙ zhingn. *gorceac'* nok'awk'
'The one who had received the five *went* immediately, *negotiated* with them' (Mt. 25.16)
f. *acēk'* zezn pararak *zenēk'*
'*Lead slaughter* the battened calf' (Lk. 15.23)
g. *ert'*. or inč' ownis *vačarēa*
'*Go*, whatever you have *sell*' (Mk. 10.21)

It is critical that V_1 not take an argument(-like) structure independently of V_2. Otherwise, we are dealing with two separate asyndetic clauses. The following passages do not satisfy this criterion and, therefore, are not considered here to belong to the phenomenon under discussion:

(7) a. zi *ert'ic'en* šowrǰ i šēnsn *gnesc'en* [M: ew gnesc'en] iwreanc' kerakowrs
'That *they go* around into the villages *buy* [M: and buy] food for themselves' (Mt. 14.15)
b. ew *gayin* aṙ na [M: ew] *berein* andamaloyc mi barjeal i č'oric'
'And *they came* to him, [M: and] *they were carrying* a paralytic borne by four' (Mk. 2.3)
c. *ekin* aṙ Yovhannēs *asen* c'na
'*They came* to John, *they said* to him' (Jh. 3.26)

In each of these passages, the initial verb takes an argument-like directional adjunct in the form of a goal following a verb of motion, and, therefore, is best understood as a full clause independent of that in which V_2 occurs. In (7a–b), the M manuscript certainly understands the structure this way, treating the sentence as containing two separate conjoined clauses. In (7b) and (7c), evidence for this analysis is supported by the (rare) unanimous testimony of the other five versions that we will be tracking. In (7b), all of them show the order verb-participle, the only such instance in the entirety of our data. Where a participle and verb are to be found in these versions beside an Armenian asyndetic verbal pair, the participle invariably precedes the verb. Finally, in (7c), all five versions agree in showing the structure V_1 conj V_2.

Conversely, adjacency is not a sufficient condition for a Classical Armenian verb pair to belong to the phenomenon we are studying. In Mt. 21.2, *lowcēkʻ acēkʻ inj* 'Untie, lead to me', the first verb appears to have a full semantic value of its own, indicating an action very much distinct from the second.

In this paper, we will show that while the asyndetic verb pair with unified, monoclausal semantics is not unique to Classical Armenian, its frequency of employment in this language is of a completely different degree of magnitude from that found in any of the other first millennium CE Indo-European versions.

Before we examine the data, it is also important to distinguish these verbal pairs from sequences of three verbs representing separate actions, the first two of which are adjacent and asyndetic and the third conjoined with these (the type of English *X, Y, and Z*), as in the following examples:

(8) a. *ari ar̄* zmahičs kʻo *ew ertʻ* i town kʻo
'*Arise, take* your bed, *and go* to your house.' (Mk. 2.9)
b. ew ar̄eal hacʻ. *gohacʻaw ebek. ew et* nocʻa
'And taking bread, he made a blessing, broke (it), and gave (it) to them.' (Lk. 22.19)

In the first of these passages, the paralytic cannot move, so that the first thing he needs to do is to arise, whereupon he can take his bed and go to his house. Hence, these may be thought of as three different specific actions. This is even clearer in (8b), where the acts of taking the bread, offering a blessing, and distributing it are manifestly distinct.[5]

[5] These cases must be distinguished from those of the same external structure where, however, the first and second verb do form an asyndetic pair, e.g., Mt. 25.25 *erkeay gnacʻi* [M: Ø] *ew tʻakʻucʻi* 'I was afraid, I went, and I hid' = Gk. φοβηθεὶς ἀπελθὼν ἔκρυψα 'fearing, I went off and hid'. Here the Classical Armenian is likely to have a slightly different nuance than the Greek, where our translation treats the (conjunctive) participle ἀπελθών as forming a unit with ἔκρυψα, whereas the Armenian *erkeay gnacʻi* of ms. E appears to represent the type of asyndetic verbal pair of the sort (see below) where the first verb adverbially modifies the second.

Table 14.1 Initial verbs involved in asyndetic verbal constructions in the Classical Armenian Gospels

ert'am 'go': 31×
eki 'come': 19×
č'ogay 'go': 9×
yar̄nem 'arise': 7×
ar̄nowm 'take': 5×
gam 'come': 2×
gnam 'go': 3×
ar̄ak'em 'send': 3×
taray 'draw, lead': 3×
acem 'lead': 2×
nstim 'sit': 2×
t'ołowm 'let, leave, allow': 2×
hanem 'draw, lead': 1×
meknim 'depart': 1×
anc'anem 'pass': 1×
elanem 'go out': 1×
dar̄nam '(re)turn': 1×
p'owt'am 'hasten': 1×
hamarjakim 'dare': 1×
tar̄apim 'be pained with worry': 1×

Once we remove instances of this sort,[6] I have located 96 reasonably certain examples of asyndetic double verb constructions in the Armenian Gospels, involving 20 different initial verbs. These are listed in Table 14.1, where the verbs are entered by their first person singular present or aorist indicative form.

As can be seen, these are overwhelmingly verbs of motion. The only verbs that do not indicate significant motion across a spatial interval are *ar̄nowm* 'take', *nstim* 'sit', *t'ołowm* 'let, leave, allow', and the last three verbs on the list, *hamarjakim* 'dare, make bold', *p'owt'am* 'hasten', and *tar̄apim* 'be pained with worry'. This latter group modifies their V_2 's adverbially, as may be seen in the following examples:

[6] There are certain other instances I have removed, as well. Thus, as Kölligan (2021) points out, because preverbation is not a productive process in Classical Armenian, it may employ asyndetic verb pairs to calque Greek verbal lexemes involving a preverb, such as Lk. 8.26 *nawec'in ijin* 'they sailed, they went down' = κατέπλευσαν 'they sailed down' (with semantic inversion of the Greek preverb + verb), Jh. 20.4 *yar̄ajeac' ənt'ac'aw* 'he went in advance, he ran' = προέδραμεν 'he ran ahead'.

(9) a. *hamarjakec'aw emowt* ar̄ Piłatos
'*He boldly went in* to Pilate' (Mk. 15.43)
b. Zakk'ē. *p'owt'a ēǰ* ayti
'Zacchaeus, *quickly come down* from there' (Lk. 19.5)
c. *tar̄apeak'* [M: tar̄apealk'] *xndreak'* zk'ez
'*We were worried sick* [M: Worrying sick], *we were looking for you.*' (Lk. 2.48)

In all three of these instances, Greek shows a participle + verb construction, where the participle functions like an adverb, and this is matched in nearly every case by a participle or an adverb in the other four versions. In (9c), the E ms. of Classical Armenian[7] is the only instance in all six languages that we are tracking where the first verb is not a participle (Gk. ὀδυνώμενοι). This makes the aorist of E the lectio difficilior, putting this passage in the same category as (9a) and (9b) and indicating that here, as well, the first verb adverbially modifies the second (as it does in ms. M). What may be taken as proof of this is the fact that the corresponding Syriac passage, from which the Armenian was most likely originally translated, employs the very same lexical item which Armenian has borrowed and denominalized within an adverbial prepositional phrase beside a periphrastic perfect construction, which serves as the main verb:

(10) bə-ṭūrāp̱ā saggīā bā'ēn həwayn lāḵ
with-anxiety great search.PTCP be.1PL.PFCT 2SG.ACC
'We were searching for you with great anxiety' (example taken from Kölligan, 2021)

Regarding the first group of non-motion verbs, we have already seen that 'take' is widely represented cross-linguistically in serial verb structures. *t'oł* 'allow, let' stands on the borderline between a full verb and a hortatory particle, especially when it appears with hortatory first person subjunctives (much like English *let's* in *let's go*), as it does in both of its occurrences in our data (cf. Mt. 27.49 *t'oł tesc'owk'* 'let us see', Lk. 6.42 *t'oł hanic' zšiwłd yakanē k'owmmē* 'Let me take out the splinter from your

[7] Following the methodology of Künzle (1984), all citations from the Classical Armenian text are taken from ms. E, with variant readings from M given in brackets, where relevant. Although E is a century younger than M (989 vs. 887), the latter was copied 'avec négligence' (1984, p. 52) and is in much worse condition than E.

eye'). Nevertheless, because it has not become grammaticalized in this usage to the point of English *let*, I still consider these passages to represent asyndetic verbal pairs. Finally, the two occurrences of *nstim* 'sit' appear in adjacent stanzas in Luke in the same collocation, *nist grea* 'sit write' (Lk. 16.6.7). In only the first of these does Greek show the verb 'sit' in the participle + verb construction καθίσας γράψον. The second occurrence must be a carry-over from this, because the Greek text reads only γράψον, and this is matched in the four other versions we are tracking by their single verb 'write'.

Collocations involving a verb of motion followed by a second verb with or without a conjunction are, of course, common in many languages, including English, both with an imperative or hortatory subjunctive and an indicative verb, as seen in (11):

(11) a. *Come live* with me, and be my love (John Donne, 'The Bait')
b. *Venite adoremus* Dominum
'Come let us adore the Lord' ('Adeste Fideles', Christmas carol)
c. *He went and called* the cops on me. (cf. discussion following [4] above)

The Classical Armenian constructions are, therefore, not, after all, surprising. However, they become significant, as a characteristic feature of the language, when they are compared with their treatment in the other five first millennium CE Indo-European versions: the Greek original, Gothic, the Latin Vulgate, Old Church Slavic, and Old English. For what we find is that the Classical Armenian asyndetic verb structure is unique in 64 of its 96 occurrences (66.7%),[8] while being matched in one or more of the other versions only 32× (33.3%). Moreover, all such matching instances involve either two asyndetic imperatives (1× exhortatives in *-ǰir*) (type *come live with me*) or an imperative followed by a first person exhortative subjunctive (type *venite adoremus*); and in nine of these instances, it is only the Vulgate that shows the Classical Armenian construction. Remarkably, the Old English version follows the Armenian on only four occasions, a point to which we shall return later. In fact, there are only four passages in which as many as four of the other five versions follow

[8] Treating the aorist of (7c) as the lectio difficilior and therefore the original form.

the Armenian. In two of these, the Gothic text is not preserved, in a third, Old Church Slavic shows a participle + verb, and, in the final instance, Old English shows a single verb:[9]

(12) a. *arik‘ ert‘ic‘owk‘* asti ‘*Arise, let us go* from here’ (Mt. 26.46)
Gk. *ἐγείρεσθε ἄγωμεν*
Goth. —
Vulg. *surgite eamus*
OCS *vŭstaněte iděmŭ*
OE *árísaþ uton faran*
b. *ert‘ koč‘ea* zayr k‘o ‘*Go call* your husband (Jh. 4.16)
Gk. ὕπαγε φώνησον τὸν ἄνδρα σου
Goth. —
Vulg. *vade voca* virum tuum
OCS *idi prizovi* mǫžĭ tvoi
OE *gá clypa* đinne ceorl
c. *ert‘ c‘oyc‘* zanjn k‘o k‘ahanayin ‘*Go show* yourself to the priest’ (Mt. 8.4)
Gk. ὕπαγε σεαυτὸν δεῖξον τῷ ἱερεῖ
Goth. *gagg*, þuk silban *ataugei* gudjin
Vulg. *vade ostende* te sacerdoti
(OCS *šědŭ pokaži* sę arxiereovi)
OE *gang, æteowe* ðé sacerde
d. *ert‘* zor inč‘ ownis *vačarēa* ‘Go sell whatever you have’ (Mk. 10.21)
Gk. ὕπαγε, ὅσα ἔχεις πώλησον
Goth. *gagg*, swa filu swe habais *frabugei*
Vulg. *vade* quaecumque habes *vende*
OCS *idi* eliko imaši *prodaždŭ*
(OE *gesyle* eall đæt đú áge)

Having introduced the notion that the Armenian text is *sui generis* in the degree to which it employs asyndetic verbal pairs, let us now discuss the data in greater detail. The Armenian verbal pairs fall into eight

[9] The sources for the citations in this paper are: for Classical Armenian (unless otherwise noted), Künzle (1984); for Greek, Nestle & Aland (1979); for Gothic, Streitberg (1919); for the Vulgate, Weber (1994); for Old Church Slavic, Jagić (1883); and for Old English, Bosworth & Waring (1907).

groups based on the grammatical categories of the individual verbs, as indicated in (13):

(13) I. Imperative + imperative (2sg. or pl.): 44×
II. Pret. ind. + pret. ind. (almost always 3sg. or pl.): 29×
III. Imperative (2sg. or pl.) + subj. (1sg. or pl.): 11×
IV. Pres. ind. + pres. ind. (3sg. or pl.): 4×
V. Subj. + subj. (3sg. or pl.): 3×
VI. Subj. + subj. (1pl.): 3×
VII. Pres. ind. + pres. ind. (1sg.): 1×
VIII. Exhortative + exhortative (2sg.): 1×

These pairs may be matched in the other languages by any one of eight possible constructions, as indicated in (14):

(14) a. participle + verb
b. single verb
c. verb_1 + conjunction + verb_2
d. asyndetic verbal pair
e. participle alone
f. verb + infinitive
g. verb + complement clause
h. adverb + verb

(14e–h) are rare.

Instances of categories I and III have already been provided in (12). Examples of other possibilities and matches are seen in (15), where the translation follows the Armenian as literally as possible:

(15) a. kapec‘in zna ew *ar̄in gnac‘in*: Ew etown i jer̄s Pontac‘woy Piłatosi
‘They bound him and *took went*; and they gave (him) into the hands of Pontius Pilate’ (Mt. 27.2)
Gk. καὶ δήσαντες αὐτὸν *ἀπήγαγον* καὶ παρέδωκαν αὐτὸν Ποντίῳ Πιλάτῳ(V)
Goth. jah gabindandans ina *gatauhun* jah anafulhun ina Pauntiau Peilatau (V)
Vulg. et vinctum *adduxerunt* eum et tradiderunt Pontio Pilato (V)

OCS i sŭvězavŭše i *vęsę*. i prědašę i Pontĭskumu Pilatu (V)
OE and hig *lǽddon* hyne gebúndenne, and sealdon hyne ðam Pontiscean Pilate (V)

b. *ekn ankaw* aṙaǰi nora
'*She came fell* before him' (Mk. 5.33)
Gk. *ἦλθεν καὶ προσέπεσεν* αὐτῷ (V_1 conj V_2)
Goth. *qam jah draus* du imma (V_1 conj V_2)
Vulg. *venit et procidit* ante eum (V_1 conj V_2)
OCS *pride i pripade* kŭ nemu (V_1 conj V_2)
OE *com, and ástrehte* hi befóran him (V_1 conj V_2)

c. owr? kamis *ertʻicʻowkʻ patrastescʻowkʻ* zi kericʻes zzatikn
'Where do you wish *we should go we should prepare* that you eat the paschal lamb?' (Mk. 14.12)
Gk. ποῦ θέλεις ἀπελθόντες ἑτοιμάσωμεν ἵνα φάγῃς τὸ πάσχα; (ppl V_{subj})
Goth. ƕar wileis ei *galeiþandans manwjaima*, ei matjais paska? (ppl V_{subj})
Vulg. quo vis *eamus et paremus* tibi ut manduces pascha (V_{subj} conj V_{subj})
OCS kŭde xošteši *šedŭše ugotovimŭ* da ěsi pasxǫ. (ppl V)
OE hwyder wylt ðú ðæt *we faron, and gegearwian* ðé, ðæt ðú eastron ete? (V_1 conj V_2)

d. *hamarjakecʻaw emowt* aṙ Piłatos
'*He dared/made bold he went in* to Pilate' (Mk. 15.43)
Gk. τολμήσας εἰσῆλθεν πρὸς τὸν Πιλᾶτον (ppl V)
Goth. *anananþjands galaiþ inn* du Peilatau (ppl V)
Vulg. *audacter introiit* ad Pilatum (adv V)
OCS *drŭznǫvŭ vŭnide* kŭ Pilatu (ppl V)
OE *he dyrstiglice in* to Pilate *eode* (adv V)

e. *čʻogaw tʻakʻeaw* i nocʻanē '*He went he hid himself* from them' (Jh. 12.36)
Gk. ἀπελθὼν ἐκρύβη ἀπ' αὐτῶν (ppl V)
Goth. *galaiþ jah gafalh sik* faura im (V_1 conj V_2)
Vulg. *abiit et abscondit se* ab eis (V_1 conj V_2)
OCS *ošedŭ sŭkry sę* otŭ nixŭ (ppl V)
OE *eode, and bediglode hine* fram him (V_1 conj V_2)

f. *ertʻam patrastem* jez teli
'*I am going I am preparing* a place for you' (Jh. 14.2)
Gk. πορεύομαι ἑτοιμάσαι τόπον ὑμῖν (V inf)
Goth. *gagga manwjan* stad izwis (V inf)
Vulg. *vado parare* vobis locum (V inf)

OCS *idǫ ogotovati* město vamŭ (V inf)
OE *ic fare and wylle* eow eardung-stowe *gegearwian* (V_1 conj V_2 inf)

g. *ert'ijir bazmesjir* i yetin tełwoǰ
'*Go sit down* in the last place' (Lk. 14.10)
Gk. *πορευθεὶς ἀνάπεσε* εἰς τὸν ἔσχατον τόπον (ppl V)
Goth. *atgaggands anakumbei* ana þamma aftumistin stada (ppl V)
Vulg. *vade recumbe* in novissimo loco (V_1 V_2)
OCS *šĭdŭ sędi* na poslědĭniimĭ městě (ppl V)
OE *gá, and site* on ðam ýtemestan setle (V_1 conj V_2)

h. darjeal *ar̄now acē* zna satanay i lear̄n mi barjr yoyž
'Again Satan *took led* him onto a very high mountain' (Mt. 4.8)
Gk. πάλιν *παραλαμβάνει* αὐτὸν ὁ διάβολος εἰς ὄρος ὑψηλὸν λίαν (V)
Goth.—
Vulg. iterum *adsumit* eum diabolus in montem excelsum valde (V)
OCS paky *poętŭ* i dijavolŭ na gorǫ vysokǫ dzělo (V)
OE eft se deofol hine *genam and lǽdde* hine on swíðe heahne múnt (V_1 conj V_2)

i. *ekn ekac'* Zakk'ēos ew asē c'TR
'Zacchaeus *came stood* and said to the Lord' (Lk 19.8)
Gk. *σταθεὶς* δὲ Ζακχαῖος εἶπεν πρὸς τὸν κύριον (ppl)
Goth. *standands* þan Zakkaius qaþ du fraujin (ppl)
Vulg. *stans* autem Zaccheus dixit ad Dominum (ppl)
OCS *stavŭ* že Zakĭxei reče kŭ gospodi (ppl)
OE ðá *stód* Zacheus and cwæþ to Drihtne (V)

j. *t'oł tesc'owk'* et'e gay Ēłia p'rkel zna
'*Let us see* if Elijah comes to save him' (Mt. 27.49)
Gk. *ἄφες ἴδωμεν* εἰ ἔρχεται Ἠλίας σώσων αὐτόν (V_1 V_{subj})
Goth. *let, ei saihvam* qimaiu Helias nasjan ina (V_1 comp V_{subj})
Vulg. *sine videamus* an veniat Helias liberans eum (V_1 V_{subj})
OCS *ostani da vidimŭ*. ašte pridetŭ Iliě sŭpastŭ ego (V_1 comp V_2)
OE *lǽt; uton geseon* hwæðer Helias cume, and wylle hyne álýsan (V_1 V_2 inf)

k. *t'oł hanic'* zšiwłd yakanē k'owmmē
'*Allow I shall take out* the mote from thine eye' (Lk. 6.42)
Gk. *ἄφες ἐκβάλω* τὸ κάρφος ἐκ τοῦ ὀφθαλμοῦ σου (V_1 V_{fut})
Goth. *let, ik uswairpa* gramsta þamma in augin þeinamma (V_1 V_{fut})
Vulg. *sine eiciam* festucam de oculo tuo (V_1 $V_{subj/fut}$)
OCS *ostavi da izŭmǫ* sǫčecŭ iže estŭ vŭ očě tvoemĭ (V_1 comp V_{fut})
OE *lǽt, ðæt ic áteo* ða egle of ðinum eagan (V_1 comp V_2)

Combining (15a–k) with (12a–d), I have endeavored to present the entire range of data relative to both Classical Armenian and the other versions treated in this paper. All the Armenian types presented in (13) are included, as well as the totality of corresponding structures encapsulated in (14), at least in one or more language. Thus, we have already seen exact matches for the Armenian pattern imperative + imperative in all versions but Old English in (12d) and in all versions but Old Church Slavic in (12c) and for the pattern imperative + first person plural subjunctive in all versions but Gothic (where the passage is not preserved) in (12a). (15a) shows the Armenian sequence preterite + preterite matched by a single verb in all the other versions, while (15b) shows V_1 conj. V_2 in all other versions. More typical is the situation seen in (15c–k), where the other five languages are not unanimous in the structures that they present. Thus, in (15c), the sequence of two first person plural subjunctives is matched by participle + finite verb in Greek, Gothic, and Old Church Slavic, and by V_1 conj. V_2 in Latin and Old English. In (15d), the asyndetic preterites are matched once again by participle + finite verb in Greek, Gothic, and Old Church Slavic, but by a single verb preceded by an adverb in Latin and Old English. (15e) shows participle + finite verb in Greek and Old Church Slavic and V_1 conj. V_2 in Gothic, Latin, and Old English. (15f) shows a rare case of two asyndetic present indicative verbs in Armenian, and these are matched by finite verb + infinitive in Greek, Gothic, Latin, and Old Church Slavic, whereas Old English is alone in showing two conjoined finite verbs, the second of which is a modal verb followed by an infinitive. Three different structures parallel the asyndetic Armenian exhortatives in (15g), including participle + imperative (Greek, Gothic, Old Church Slavic), asyndetic verbs (Latin), and imperative + *and* + imperative (Old English). In (15h), where the two present tense verbs should be interpreted as historical presents, a single verb is seen everywhere but Old English, which shows V_1 *and* V_2. (15i) is unique in showing a simple participle in lieu of the Armenian asyndetic preterite verbs everywhere but Old English, which shows a finite verb *stód*. In each instance here, the participle or verb matches semantically the Armenian second verb *ekac'* 'stood'. The final two passages, (15j–k), both show the common Armenian collocation *t'oł* (lit. 'let') + first person subjunctive, where *t'oł* functions as a hortatory particle; however, the two constructions are different. In (15j), the subjunctive is a first person plural with exhortative/imperative value, whereas in (15k) it is a first person singular subjunctive, which must be parsed as a future, despite the fact that Greek shows the identical structure ἄφες + subjunctive in both passages. In the first instance, Gothic and Old Church Slavic show complementizers *ei* and *da*, respectively, whereas in the second it is Old Church Slavic and Old English which show such forms (*da* and *ðæt*, respectively). Latin is consistent with *sine* + subjunctive in each case (in [15k] *eiciam* may be parsed as a future), whereas in Gothic, *ik uswairpa* of (15k) is contextually to be understood unambiguously as a future. In Old English, the collocation *uton geseon* (subj. + inf.) of (15j) is exhortative ('let us see'), translating the Latin first person plural subjunctive, whereas *lǽt* translates Lat. *sine*. Cf. (12a), where *árísaþ uton faran* translates Lat. *surgite eamus*.

Having canvassed the full range of data in all five languages, we turn now to the more general question of how the Armenian verbal pairs are treated across the board in the other versions. The combined data of the individual treatment of the Armenian asyndetic verb pairs in all five of the other first millennium CE Indo-European versions is tabulated in Table 14.2.

Table 14.2 Renditions by language of instances where Classical Armenian shows asyndetic verbal pairs

Greek	participle + verb	43×
	single verb	24×
	two asyndetic verbs	22×[a]
	$verb_1$ καὶ $verb_2$	5×
	participle alone	1×
	verb + infinitive	1×
Gothic	single verb	20×
	participle + verb	18×
	$verb_1$ *jah/-uh* $verb_2$	9×
	two asyndetic verbs	6×
	verb + infinitive	3×
	participle alone	1×
	verb + complementizer clause	1×

(continued)

Table 14.2 (continued)

Vulgate	two asyndetic verbs	27×
	single verb	26×
	$verb_1$ *et/ac* $verb_2$	25×
	participle + verb	14×
	verb + infinitive	2×
	adverb + verb	1×
	participle alone	1×
OCS	participle + verb	46×
	single verb	24×
	two asyndetic verbs	15×
	$verb_1$ *i* $verb_2$	7×
	verb + complementizer clause	2×
	verb + infinitive	1×
	participle alone	1×
OE	$verb_1$ *and* $verb_2$	59×
	single verb	24×
	verb + infinitive	6×[b]
	two asyndetic verbs	4×
	participle + verb	1×
	verb + comp. clause	1×
	adverb + verb	1×

[a]Logozzo & Tronci (2022) find 17 asyndetic PCC's (pseudo coordination constructions) in the Greek Gospels, involving only the verbs ἐγείρω 'arise' (2×), λαμβάνω 'take' (1×), and ὑπάγω 'go' (14×). However, in several instances involving the last of these, the verbs are not adjacent, and such passages would not be picked up in my data, which looks only at contiguous asyndetic verbal pairs in Classical Armenian. Moreover, they do not include forms such as δεῦτε, δεῦρο, and ἄφες, which are swept into my data because they match the first verb of the Armenian pair in the passages where they occur and are, at least, quasi-verbal. If one were to reclassify them as adverbial, then the number of Greek asyndetic verb pairs would decline by over a third, whereas if one were to take away the Armenian asyndetic pairs involving *t'oł* (the one form that might be considered a hortatory particle), the number would decline by just over 2%. Despite the fact that it is the Armenian verbal form matched by Gk. δεῦτε/δεῦρο in the few instances where these occur in our data set, there is nothing in the facts of Armenian to suggest that *ek'/ekayk'* 'come', even though it is by far the most frequently occurring V_1 in the structures that we have studied, is a hortatory particle

[b]All involve the original first person plural subjunctive form *uton* (lit. 'let's go') + infinitive. Where this construction is found together with a second verb, either in the 'V_1 and V_2' construction or in the asyndetic verb construction, I have not accorded it any special status

The analysis of this data yields a number of interesting facts. The most obvious of these is that the Old English of the Gospels has very nearly banished asyndeton, which correlates with a massive total of 59 instances of conjoined V_1 *and* V_2 (over 61% of the cases). The only language even remotely close to this is Latin, which shows 25 such instances (26%), while Gothic shows nine (out of 58 preserved instances) (15.5%), Old Church Slavic seven (7%), and Greek just five (5%). The only instances where Old English shows asyndeton (cf. 12a–c & 15j) are those in which two or three of the other languages do so, as well; and to these may be added (15k), where Old English, together with Old Church Slavic, shows a complementizer, but otherwise, once again, all the other languages show asyndetic verbs. The other thing of note in Old English is the virtual absence of the collocation participle + verb,[10] which is the single largest category in Greek and Old Church Slavic (respectively, 45% and 48%), is second in frequency in Gothic (31%), and shows 14 appearances in Latin (just under 15%). The last of these figures clearly shows the participle + verb construction to be on the wane in the Vulgate. The super frequency of the conjoined type, the rarity of asyndeton, and the near absence of participle + verb in Old English are particularly surprising in view of the fact that the Old English text was translated from the Vulgate, which shows significant, but not predominant, occurrence of the conjoined type and an employment of asyndeton that is tied for the highest frequency with that of single verbs.

The other important fact emerging from this data is, once again, the frequency of asyndetic verbal pairs in the Classical Armenian text relative to every other version we are considering: Latin (28%), Greek (23%), Old Church Slavic (15.6%), Gothic (10.3%), and Old English (4%). It

[10] Only Lk. 2.48 (7c), where it is matched by every other language (including the M manuscript of Classical Armenian, where we have treated it as the lectio facilior). Here the participle *sárigende* is quasi-adverbial: *đin fæder and ic sárigende đé sóhton* 'Your father and I were looking for you with great anxiety'. Recall that this is one of the passages where the initial verb in Classical Armenian, *tar̄apeakʻ*, adverbially modifies V_2.

is, therefore, certain that such pairs are a characteristic and unique feature of Classical Armenian and should be identified as such in future grammars of the language.[11]

References

Bosworth, J., assisted by Waring, G. (1907). *The Gospels Gothic, Anglo-Saxon, Wycliffe and Tyndale versions*[4]. Gibbings and Company.

Garsoian, N. G. (1989). *The epic histories attributed to P'awstos Buzand. (Buzandaran patmut'iwnk')*. Harvard University Press.

Jagić, V. (1883). *Mariinskoe četveroevangelie s primečanijami i priloženijami* [The Marianus gospels with notes and appendices]. Imperatorskaja akademija nauk.

Jungmann, P. (1967). Zweigliedrige asyndetische Verbalgruppen im Armenischen und die neuarmenische Partikel ku/ke/k'. *Münchener Studien zur Sprachwissenschaft, 21*, 33–43.

Kölligan, D. (2021). Multiverb constructions in Classical Armenian. In M. Lucia Aliffi, A. Bartolotta, & C. Nigrelli (Eds.), *Perspectives on language and linguistics. Essays in honour of Lucio Melazzo* (pp. 235–260). Palermo University Press.

Künzle, B. (1984). *Das altarmenische Evangelium / L'Evangile arménien ancien. Teil I/I*[ère] *partie: Edition, Teil II/II*[e] *partie: Lexikon/lexique*. P. Lang.

Logozzo, F., & Tronci, L. (2022). Pseudo-coordination and serial verbs in Hellenistic Greek? Some insights from the New Testament and the Septuagint. *Journal of Greek Linguistics, 22*, 72–144.

Meillet, A. (1910/1911). Emplois des forms personnelles des verbes. *Mémoires de la Société de Linguistique de Paris, 16*, 92–131.

Nestle, E., & Aland, K. (Eds.). (1979). *Novum testamentum Graece*[26]. Deutsche Bibelgesellschaft.

Sebba, M. (1987). *The syntax of serial verbs. An investigation into serialization in Sranan and other languages*. John Benjamins.

[11] Asyndetic verbal pairs are not limited to the Bible in the Classical Armenian corpus but play an important and characteristic role within narrative discourse throughout the history of the language, as noted by Meillet (1910/1911). An example from the histories is provided in (1a) above. Different in nature, however, is the manneristic heaping up of large numbers of synonyms in prose narrative, as in the passage cited by Kölligan (2021) from the epic histories of P'awstos Buzand (Garsoian, 1989): 3.20 *zayrac'oyc' grgr̄eac' yowzeac' drdeac' srtmtec'oyc' barkac'oyc' zt'agaworn*, where six third person singular aorists, all hovering semantically around the senses 'anger, irritate, disturb', precede the direct object 'the king' (*z-t'agawor-n*).

Streitberg, W. (Ed.). (1919). *Die Gotische Bibel.* Winter.
Thomson, R. W. (1989). *An introduction to Classical Armenian*[2]. Caravan Books.
Weber, R. (Ed.). (1994). *Biblia sacra iuxta vulgatam versionem*[4]. Deutsche Bibelgesellschaft.
Yates, A. D. (2014). On the PIE 'quasi-serial verb' construction. Origin and development. In S. W. Jamison, H. Craig Melchert, & B. Vine (Eds.), *Proceedings of the 25th Annual UCLA Indo-European Conference* (pp. 237–255). Hempen.

15

Celt. *meh_2-ró- 'large, great' versus Gmc. *meh_1-ró- 'made known, spoken of'

H. Craig Melchert

It is a singular pleasure to be invited to contribute to this well-deserved tribute to Don Ringe, a friend and colleague of 40 years' standing. We learned together in the early East Coast Conferences how to become historical linguists and Indo-Europeanists. Germanic has remained an enduring focus of Don's research and teaching, while I left Germanic for the green pastures of Ancient Anatolia. By a stroke of good luck I am able to offer Don a paper whose core lies in Germanic, but no one will be

I am indebted to José Luis García Ramón for advice on the Greek compounds in -μωρος, to Harald Bichlmeier for the reference to the study by Wenzel, to Norbert Oettinger for reading a draft and sparing me from one glaring error, and to Joe Eska for help with the Old English citations. Responsibility for remaining infelicities is mine.

H. C. Melchert (✉)
University of California, Los Angeles, CA, USA
e-mail: melchert@humnet.ucla.edu

J. F. Eska et al. (eds.), *The Method Works*,
https://doi.org/10.1007/978-3-031-48959-4_15

surprised that it began with a Celto-Hittite etymology and will end with a Germano-Hittite one.[1]

1 Celtic **māro-* 'large, great'

Yakubovich (2010) adduces evidence from Iranian, Hittite, and Latin for a root **mā-* = **meh₂-* 'grow': first, Iranian reflexes with the sense 'become' from a proto-Iranian root **maH(i)-* (2010: 479–483); second, Hitt. *mai-* ~ *mi-*^{hhi} 'grow' and derivatives.[2] As he indicates, these two sources cannot establish the identity of the laryngeal, but he argues convincingly that Lat. *mātūrus* in its predominant sense 'ripe, full-grown', once separated from false cognates, certainly reflects **meh₂-* 'grow'. Slavic cognates reflecting a **matorŭ* 'full-grown, old' suggest that the vocalism of the Latin suffix *-tūrus* has been altered by association with the future active participle, which the secondary sense 'precocious, early' testifies is real.[3] Kloekhorst (2008: 541) had already justifiably criticized the standard etymology of Hitt. *mai-* ~ *mi-* 'grow' < **meiH-* 'soft' on semantic grounds and suggested that the verb is cognate rather with Celt. **māro-*. Yakubovich (2010: 484) rejects this solely on the basis of the received opinion that Celt. **māro-* and Gmc. **mēro-* must be cognate, though he concedes (2010: 484[8]) that the latter is morphologically problematic. It is, in fact,

---

[1] New evidence shows that the sense of Hitt. ^{UZU}*muḫr(a)i-* is 'ham, flesh of the thigh', thus confirming, with due revision, the etymology of Weitenberg (1979: 303): see Melchert, forthcoming. Confirmation that it is derived from **meh₂-* 'grow (large)' is found in Hitt. ^{GIŠ}*māḫla-*, which has nothing to do with any word for 'apple', but means '(branch, slip of a) grapevine' (Puhvel, 2004: 4–5). See already for its tentative derivation < **móh₂-lo-* 'growth' Kloekhorst (2008: 539–540). Inter alia, these together finally answer the long-debated question of the fate of **-Vh₂l/rV-* in Hittite.

[2] He cites (2010: 484) as parallels for the semantic change 'grow' > 'become' the common use of English 'grow tired, irritated, more beautiful', etc. and the various reflexes of PIE **bhuh₂-*, including Gk. φύομαι 'grow; become'.

[3] For Lat. *māne* 'early, in the morning', *Mātūta* 'goddess of the dawn', and *mātūtīnus* 'of early morning' as all related to Lat. *mānus* 'good' and Celt. **māti-* 'good', see Yakubovich (2010: 485). I reject only his dismissal of the derivation of Hitt. *mēḫur* 'time' from the same root (2010: 485–486). Since the latter clearly means in some contexts inherently 'the right, proper time', it also reflects the root **meh₂-* 'good, proper'. One need only adjust the sense of the root versus Eichner (1973: 65) by deleting any original restriction to 'time'.

patently impossible, based on facts conceded in every Germanic handbook.

Schmidt (1957), in a magisterial two-part paper on Gaulish personal names, demonstrates beyond all doubt that the basic sense of the Celtic adjective **māro-* is 'large, great'. He shows that Gaulish personal names with a second member *-maro-* are in origin determinative compounds: *Nerto-maro-* 'great in strength', *Sego-maro-* 'great in victories', etc. (1957: 69–73). However, he strongly agrees with Vendryes (1950/1951: 238), that *-maro-* had very early been reduced to a suffix meaning 'having the quality of', as it surely has in OIr. *nert-mar* and W *nerth-mawr* 'strong'. Schmidt cites in support of this the unique productivity of *-maro-* in personal names and hybrid examples with a foreign first member: *Aucto-marus*, *Iulio-marus*, etc. Also noteworthy is the number of pairs where *-maro-* and *-rix* share the same first member (1957: 77). Nevertheless, after this indisputable analysis of Celtic *-*māro-*, where there is no basis whatsoever for a sense 'famous', Schmidt eventually repeats the communis opinio of the handbooks that Gmc. *-*mēro-*, Slav. *-měr*, and Gk. -μωρος are all cognate, declaring that the Celtic and Greek show that the original sense was 'great, large', and that '[i]m Germanischen allein hat sich eine andere Bedeutung "berühmt" entwickelt' (1957: 78–79). How the latter is supposed to have happened he does not explain. In principle, this is not excluded: cf. colloquial English 'in Wall Street circles she is big in derivatives'. The real problem with the received Celto-Germanic equation lies in Germanic.

2 Gmc. **mēro-*

2.1 Personal Names in *-*mēro-*

Despite its universal acceptance, a closer look at the alleged match between Celt. **māro-* 'large, great' and Gmc. **mēro-* 'famous' in male personal names shows that it rests on very little beyond the (quite imperfect) formal resemblance. Schmidt (1957: 238–239[2]) lists more than 60 Gaulish names with *-maro-* as second member (all but a handful determinative compounds). Schönfeld (1911) lists more than 25 Germanic names with *-mēro-* as second member (also in all clear cases determinative compounds). In view of the respective productivity, it is remarkable (and highly disturbing for their alleged cognacy) that there is precisely one word equation. As per Schmidt (1957: 143), Βαλλο-μάριος is Celtic (contra Schönfeld, 1911: 43),[4] while *Catu-meres* in Tacitus (Schönfeld, 1911: 61–62) is manifestly not a cognate, but a half-Celticized variant of the Germanic name seen in OHG *Hadubrand* (Schmidt, 1957: 168). The one genuine match is *Sego-maro-* and *Sigi-meris* (OHG *Sigmar*), but, in view of the productivity of 'victory' in personal names in both traditions, it is hardly a surprise that it appears with the respective very productive **-māro-* and **-mēro-*. They may easily be entirely independent creations. In sum, evidence that the two adjectives appearing as the second members of determinative compound personal names are cognate is far from compelling.[5] The problem with the standard view is the evidence of Germanic appellatives reflecting **mēro-*, to which we now turn.

2.2 Gothic Appellatives

All Germanic evidence from appellatives (duly cited in every handbook!) shows the received opinion that the primary sense of **mēro-* is 'famous, illustrious' to be a *Märchen*. We may begin the deconstruction of this fable with Gothic. Here there is no direct evidence for **mēro-*, only derivatives of proto-Gmc. **mēri-* 'news, report' (see below): a verb *merjan* 'announce, proclaim' (= κηρύσσειν), a noun *meriþa* 'news, report' (= ἀκόη, φήμη), a further noun *mereins* 'news, gospel' (= κήρυγμα), and

[4] The first member of Gmc. *Barzimeres* 'reputed for X' is entirely unclear, but there is no basis for Celtic pace Schönfeld (1911: 44). The validity of the spelling of *Suomarius* is not assured, and Celt. *Sumarius* 'very great' is likely (cf. Schmidt, 1957: 60 & 239).

[5] Against Schmidt (1957: 79) there is no basis for claiming that Gk. -μωρος must mean 'large, great' and be cognate with the Celtic adjective. The former may represent either *-*moh*$_1$*ro*- 'reputed for' or *-*moh*$_2$*ro*- 'large, great in': ἐγχεσί-μωρος, ἰό-μωρος, ὑλακό-μωρος 'famous for/great in spears, power, barking'. The *-měr* of Slavic personal names may well be borrowed from Germanic (Schmidt, 1957: 78–79), but see Wenzel (2021: 149–163) for arguments in terms of their diachronic and diatopic distribution for a native morpheme. In either case, they merely reinforce *-*meh*$_1$-*ro*- in the sense 'reputed (for)'.

also in compounds an adjective **merja-* in *waila-merei-* 'of good repute' (= εὔφημος) and a noun **merei-* in *waila-merei-* 'good repute' (= εὐφημία) and *waja-merei-* (= δυσφημία) 'ill repute', aptly glossed by Heidermanns (1993: 408) as 'guter Ruf' and 'schlechter Ruf', with a word for 'repute' based on a verbum dicendi.[6] The major point is the consistently neutral sense of all Gothic derivatives of **mēro-*, which show evidence only for a verbum dicendi 'report, proclaim, speak of'. Any amelioration to 'famous, illustrious' is limited to personal names, but since they unsurprisingly all have positive first members, 'reputed for' is equally possible. Contrary to all claims, there is no proof that such an amelioration ever took place in Gothic. No basis for a sense 'large, great' is found anywhere (see the open admission of Schmidt, 1957: 79[1]!).

2.3 West Germanic Appellatives

2.3.1 Old English

The evidence of all West Germanic languages unequivocally confirms the findings from Gothic. Amelioration has definitely begun in Old English and for some words has ousted the original neutral sense (*mǣrðu* is only 'fame, glory' versus Goth. *meriþa* and OHG *mārida*), but there is no doubt that it is an innovation. The oldest occurrence of the adjective *mǣre* is in Beowulf, where it is used equally of both Grendel and Beowulf: *Beo.* 6.102–103 *Grendel ... mǣre mearc-stapa* 'Grendel the notorious march-stalker', but *Beo.* 26.797 *mǣres þēodnes* 'of the illustrious prince' (et passim). The negative sense is also present elsewhere: *Mt.* 27.16 *Hæfdum ēnne gebundenne mǣrne monn se wǣs hāten Barabus* 'they had a prisoner, a notorious man who was called Barabbas' and Or. 3.8.1 *seō stōw gewearþ swīðe mǣre ... for Rōmāna bismere* 'the place became very notorious for the disgrace of the Romans'. Naturally, this did not preclude Aelfric using it to mean 'illustrious, celebrated'. The adjective still meant in Old English merely 'well-known, famous', whether the fame was good or bad (correct Heidermanns, 1993: 408 'berühmt, berüchtigt'). The

[6] The facts are available in Feist (1939) and Lehmann (1986).

verbs *mǣran* and *gemǣran* certainly mean 'celebrate' (Bosworth & Toller, 1898, s.vv.), but also still 'proclaim, report, spread word of': *PsTh* 70.14 *and þīn sōðfæst weorc … mǣreð* 'and will proclaim your true work' (pronuntiabit). The same mix of neutral and positive use is found with *mǣrsian* 'praise, glorify', but also simply 'make known, spread word of': *Mk.* 1.45 *mērsiga þæt word* 'make known that word' (diffamare sermonem); cf. *Mt.* 9.31 & 28.15. Likewise *mǣrsung* is 'praise, celebration', but also 'report, rumor': *Mt.* 9.26 *spranc mērsung … ðiūs* (fama haec) *in alle eorðo* 'this report/rumor went out into all the earth'. The original sense 'proclaim, make known' is still preserved in *mǣrsere* 'herald'.

2.3.2 Old High German and Beyond

There is widespread agreement among the handbooks regarding the Old High German reflexes and their subsequent history. We may begin with the foundational treatment of the *Deutsches Wörterbuch*, which focuses on the history of the neuter noun *māri* and feminine *mārī*, which are glossed as 'news, report, narrative' and 'rumor, news, repute (Ruf)'. The brothers Grimm underscore that the use is mostly of definite, concrete oral communication and that through Middle High German one can freely say: *gute*, *neue*, *falsche*, *böse mär(en) sagen*, *bringen*, *mittheilen* 'say, bring, communicate good, new, false, bad news/reports'. However, in the fifteenth to seventeenth centuries, *Mär* undergoes pejoration and mostly is used of a false narrative or report. By the seventeenth and eighteenth centuries, the word is obsolete in literary German, except for a brief revival of its original sense by the 'Hainbund' poets. The word does persist in dialect (presumably early nineteenth century) in the set phrase 'was ist der mer?' for 'what is the news, what is going on? (Grimm & Grimm, 1885: 12.1615–1617). A fictive sense obviously also adheres to the only reflex in Modern Standard German, the diminutive *Märchen* 'fable, fairy tale'.

This overall history of the noun has not precluded occasional ameliorative use of OHG *mārī* and far more such usage in the related OHG adjective *māri*, noun *mārida*, and verb *māren*. The Old High German adjective means in fact mostly 'famous, celebrated' (= Lat. *famosus*, *celeber*, etc.), but occasionally merely '(made) known'. The noun *mārida*, likewise, beside neutral 'Nachricht, Gerede' and negative 'Gerücht', can be used for 'Lobpreis, Ruhm', and the verb is attested as 'bekanntmachen, verbreiten', but also 'preisen, verherrlichen' (which in turn does not prevent the past participle from being used for 'verrufen, berüchtigt'): see Schützeichel (2004: 6.276–282) and Schmid (2015: 275–287).[7] The presentation in Splett (1993: 599) differs only in detail, and Lexer (1878: 2045–2047) affirms a similar range of meanings in Middle High German: adjective *mære* 'berühmt, bemächtig, herrlich', but neuter and feminine nouns *mære* 'nachricht, bericht, erzählung, gerücht', and verb *mæren* 'verkünden, bekannt/berühmt machen'.

2.3.3 Other West Germanic

MDutch *mare* had a positive sense 'fame' alongside neutral 'news, report' and negative 'rumor', but ModDutch *mare* means only the latter three, and OFris. *mêre* is cited only as 'news, tidings'. MLG *mêre*, likewise, is 'story, report' and 'rumor' (de Vries, 1971: 426; Franck, 1912: 413). In the Old Saxon *Hêliand*, the adjective *mâri* mostly means 'renowned, glorious', but sometimes merely 'known', and once is negative: Hel. 128.5402 *mâri meginthiof* 'notorious great thief'. Similarly, *mârian* is mostly 'proclaim, make known', but once 'praise (oneself)', while *mâriða* is 'news, proclamation', but once 'praiseworthy deed' (Heyne, 1883: 271–272).

2.3.4 North Germanic

In Old Norse, amelioration has been completed, and *mærr* means only 'famous, glorious, mighty' and the like. However, the runic inscription on the Thorsberg chape preserves the precious relic **niwajemariz** 'the not ill-reputed one', the second part of which is a word equation with Goth. **waja-mērei-* 'of ill repute' (Feist, 1939: 547; Lehmann, 1986: 252). We may, therefore, confidently assume that the sense was originally neutral as in Gothic 'repute'.

[7] Both works (and Splett, 1993: 599) also cite the negative use of neuter *māri* in the compound *māri-sagāri* 'rumor-monger'. Cf. the recreation cited by Grimm & Grimm: 'Märenträger'.

3 Summation

The combined evidence of Gothic and West Germanic is unequivocal: the base of Gmc. **mēro-* is a verbum dicendi: 'speak (of), make known, proclaim, narrate'. If one tries to begin with a sense 'magnify', whence 'praise', one must assume that there was a massive bleaching to the meanings above and then pejoration. Semantic bleaching is not unusual, but it must be motivated. I know of no published attempt to explain such a development in this case. Frankly, I doubt that anyone has ever tried. Based on an egregious case of slavish acceptance and mindless repetition of received opinion, manifest facts cited in every handbook have simply been ignored—because the equation of the Celtic and Germanic personal names was taken as fact, not as the mere hypothesis that it is. I do not wish to be sanctimonious. Without Yakubovich's root **meh$_2$-* 'grow (large)' and Hittite support for it, I would have followed everyone else. There was now reason for me to reexamine the long-held hypothesis and the Germanic facts, whose implications for the compound names I had ignored with others.

Once we give due respect to the latter, the long demonstrated meanings of the Germanic reflexes of **mēro-*, a plausible solution is immediately available. We have a Germanic root **mē-* reflecting a PIE root **meh$_1$-* with the senses attested in Germanic. The adjective **mēro-* meant 'spoken of, made known', hence 'known (for), reputed'. The widespread amelioration in all the Germanic languages except possibly Gothic (where it cannot be excluded) in not only the adjective, but also, to a lesser extent, the associated nouns and verbs is trivial. One need only cite the Paradebeispiel of Gk. φατός 'spoken, said' and 'famous' and the history of the loanword *fāma* in Latin and elsewhere. But fame can be positive or negative (and also easily changeable), and concomitant pejoration is also to be expected (cf. the full range of uses of Lat. *fāma*). Verbs of speech are quite prone to both: Lat. *acclāmāre* 'shout (at)' (with and without positive or negative associations) leads to Engl. 'acclaim' (since the seventeenth century in the sense 'praise, applaud'), but **ter-* 'say' (Lith. *tariù*, Hitt. *tar-*) becomes Luw. *tatariya-* 'to curse'.

A PIE root **meh*$_1$- 'speak' has been needed for more than a century. Previous etymologies for Hitt. *mēmi/a-* 'speak' have ranged from the preposterous (cognate with Skt. *mimāti* 'bellow, bleat') to the formally impossible (to the root of **men-* 'think'). A preform **mé-mn-V-* could lead only to Hitt. †*mēmmV-* (see the correct objection of Kloekhorst, 2008: 575). However, a **mé-moh*$_1$*i̯-ei*, **mé-mh*$_1$*-i̯-n̥-ti* leads regularly to the older plural *memianzi* with loss of laryngeal before yod (and to preconsonantal weak stem *memi-* < **mé-mih*$_1$-). Based on the present third singular *mē/emai* (always with short *-ai* in Old Hittite in more than 30 examples), the result of preconsonantal **mé-moh*$_1$*i-* (likely **mēmai-*) was altered to *mēma-* by analogy to the class of *tarna-* (with Kloekhorst, 2008: 145–147). We may add this to the list of unique Hittite and Germanic isoglosses: cf. *kuššan* 'wage, fee' and the Germanic family of Engl. 'hire' (Kloekhorst, 2008: 498 et al.).

References

Or. = Bosworth, J. (Ed.). (1859). *King Alfred's Anglo-Saxon version of the compendious history of the world by Orosius*. Longman, Brown, Green, and Longmans.

Bosworth, J., & Toller, C. N. (1898). *An Anglo-Saxon dictionary*. Clarendon Press.

de Vries, J. (1971). *Nederlands etymologisch woordenboek*. Brill.

Eichner, H. (1973). Die Etymologie von heth. *mehur*. *Münchener Studien zur Sprachwissenschaft, 31*, 53–107.

Feist, S. (1939). *Vergleichendes Wörterbuch der gotischen Sprache*[3]. Brill.

Franck, J. (1912). *Etymologisch woordenboek der nederlandsche taal*[2] (Ed. N. van Wijk). M. Nijhoff.

Grimm, J., & Grimm, W. (1885). *Deutsches Wörterbuch* (Band 12). S. Hirzel.

Heidermanns, F. (1993). *Etymologisches Wörterbuch der germanischen Primäradjektive*. De Gruyter.

Hel. = Heyne, M. (1883). *Hêliand. Mit ausführlichem Glossar herausgegeben*[3]. F. Schöningh.

Kloekhorst, A. (2008). *Etymological dictionary of the Hittite inherited lexicon*. Brill.

Lehmann, W. P. (1986). *A Gothic etymological dictionary*. Based on the third edition of *Vergleichendes Wörterbuch der gotischen Sprache* by Sigmund Feist. Brill.

Lexer, M. (1878). *Mittelhochdeutsches Handwörterbuch*. S. Hirzel.

Melchert, H. C. (forthcoming). Hittite UZU*mulaḫḫ(a)r(a)i-* 'flesh of the thigh, ham'. *Journal of cuneiform studies.*
Puhvel, J. (2004). *Hittite etymological dictionary vi, Words beginning with M.* Mouton de Gruyter.
Schmid, H. U. (2015). *Althochdeutsches Wörterbuch* (Band VI: M und N). Akademie-Verlag.
Schmidt, K. H. (1957). Die Komposition in gallischen Personennamen. *Zeitschrift für celtische Philologie, 26*, 33–301.
Schönfeld, M. (1911). *Wörterbuch der altgermanischen Personen- und Völkernamen.* Carl Winter.
Schützeichel, R. (2004). *Althochdeutscher und altsächsischer Glossenwortschatz.* Max Niemeyer.
Splett, J. (1993). *Althochdeutsches Wörterbuch. Analyse der Wortfamilienstrukturen des Althochdeutschen, zugleich Grundlegung einer zukünftigen Strukturgeschichte des deutschen Wortschatzes* (Band I, Teil 2). De Gruyter.
Vendryes, J. (1950/1951). Deux nouvelles inscriptions gallo-romaines. *Études celtiques, 5*, 237–247.
Weitenberg, J. J. S. (1979). Einige Bemerkungen zu den hethitischen Diphthong-Stämmen. In W. Meid & E. Neu (Eds.), *Hethitisch und Indogermanisch* (pp. 289–303). Institut für Sprachwissenschaft der Universität Innsbruck.
Wenzel, W. (2021). *Slawen zwischen Saale und Neiße. Namenkundliche Studien.* Barr.
Yakubovich, I. (2010). Indo-European **mā-* 'to grow'. *Индоевропейское языкознание и классическая филология, 14*, 478–492.

16

'Between uneducated and educated, or hot and cold, or bitter and sweet … there's a middle point': Varro and the Middle Accent

Philomen Probert

1 Evidence

The only extensive discussion of the 'middle accent', for either Greek or Latin, is the passage of a late antique grammatical grammarian ('Pseudo-Sergius') quoted under (1). The text quoted here is essentially Keil's (GL iv 529.1–532.28), but divided into thematic sections, each with an introduction and a translation. Between sections (h) and (i), as indicated, I omit a portion that does not mention the middle accent.

I am grateful for invitations to give talks related to this work at the University of Manchester, at the University of Warsaw, and in Paris at the invitation of Claire Le Feuvre (Sorbonne Université) and Daniel Petit (École Normale Supérieure de Paris); to the participants in those occasions, for discussion and feedback; and to Eleanor Dickey, for comments on a complete draft. I am honoured to offer this modest effort to Don Ringe, whose care for accuracy in scholarship has long been an inspiration. All inaccuracies are mine.

P. Probert (✉)
University of Oxford, Oxford, UK
e-mail: philomen.probert@wolfson.ox.ac.uk

J. F. Eska et al. (eds.), *The Method Works*,
https://doi.org/10.1007/978-3-031-48959-4_16

(1)

(a) The discussion begins with opinions on how many accents there were. Pseudo-Sergius warns that he will champion a view different from the one current in his day: he or his source will turn out to be an enthusiast for the 'middle' accent. But he first mentions a two-accent system ascribed to Athenodorus, then the ubiquitous three-accent system, before introducing the four-accent system ascribed to Tyrannio. The scholars mentioned at this point are Greeks discussing Greek, although Pseudo-Sergius will go on to move seamlessly between Greek authors' ideas on Greek and Varro's on Latin.

Today we understand the well-attested three-accent system reasonably well. The acute or 'high' accent was one falling on a short vowel, or considered to fall on the second mora of a long vowel or diphthong; the circumflex or 'turned around' accent was one considered to fall on the first mora of a long vowel or diphthong. Any vowel carrying neither acute nor circumflex—in our terms, any unaccented vowel—was considered to have a grave or 'low' accent. This chapter will not discuss the relationship between pitch-related terminology and the actual realisation of the accent at any period in Greek or Latin; for present purposes it suffices to say that pitch was at least a metaphor for accentual prominence. The three-accent system was taken over from descriptions of Greek to those of Latin, notwithstanding phonological differences between the languages (cf. Probert, 2019, pp. 187–244).

Pseudo-Sergius' discussion suggests that Athenodorus took the same view of the empirical facts of Greek as those operating with three accents, but saw no need to treat the circumflex as an independent unit of analysis: the acute and grave sufficed, with the circumflex being reducible to an acute followed by a grave on a single syllable.

quot ergo sint prosodiae, dicendum est. quae res eo maiore cum cura tractanda est, quod nostra ratio ab opinione iam inueterata et omnium ferme animis adfixa discrepat. Athenodorus duas esse prosodias putauit, unam inferiorem, alteram superiorem; flexam autem (nam ita nostra lingua περισπωμένην *uocauimus) nihil aliud esse quam has duas in una syllaba. Dionysius autem, Aristarchi discipulus, cognomento Thrax, domo Alexandrius, is qui Rhodi docuit,*	One ought then to say how many accents there are. This matter should be handled with all the more care because our own view differs from the one that is now time-honoured and pretty much fixed in everyone's minds. Athenodorus thought there were two accents, one lower and the other higher. For he thought the *flexa* (for this is what we call the circumflex in our language) was nothing other than these two in one syllable. But Dionysius the pupil of Aristarchus, nicknamed

lyricorum poetarum longe studiosissimus, tres tradidit, quibus nunc omnes utuntur, βαρεῖαν ὀξεῖαν περισπωμένην. *Tyrannion uero Amisenus, quem Lucullus Mithridatico bello captum Lucio Murenae concessit, a quo ille libertate simul et ciuitate donatus est, quattuor scribit esse prosodias,* βαρεῖαν, μέσην, ὀξεῖαν *et* περισπωμένην. *atqui memoriae proditum est hunc ante alios fuisse pronuntiatione potiorem, quod nequaquam assequi potuisset nisi tenore singularum uocum diligentissime perquisito.*

Thrax, an Alexandrian by abode, the one who taught at Rhodes, by far the most assiduous scholar of the lyric poets, handed down that there were three, which everybody now uses: grave, acute, and circumflex. But Tyrannio of Amisus, whom Lucullus granted to Lucius Murena after his capture in the Mithridatic war, and who was given freedom and at the same time citizenship by Murena, writes that there are four accents: grave, middle, acute, and circumflex. And it's been passed down that he was better in pronunciation than others—something he could in no way have achieved without carefully examining the accents of individual words.

(b) Varro followed Tyrannio, and argued on general grounds for the existence of a middle accent. (The implied subject of *affert* could be Varro or Tyrannio, but *quos ... commemorat* in section (e) suggests that Pseudo-Sergius' immediate source for the arguments in sections (b)–(d) is material that he took to derive from Varro.)

in eadem opinione et Varro fuit, qui in leges suas redigit accentus, ductus scientia et doctrina eius, qua omnibus a se propositis euidentissimas affert probationes, ut id quoque pro media prosodia facit dicendo ipsam naturam nihil facere totum, ubi non sit medium; ut enim inter rudem et eruditum, inter calidum et frigidum, amarum et dulcem, longum et breuem est quiddam medium, quod neutrum est, sic inter imam summamque uocem esse mediam, ibique quam quaerimus prosodiam.

Of the same opinion was Varro too, who reduces accents to their rules, guided by that man's (Tyrannio's) knowledge and teaching, by means of which he brings clear proof to all his doctrines, as he does for the middle accent too, saying that nature does nothing completely without there being a middle point: just as between an uneducated and an educated person, or hot and cold, or bitter and sweet, or long and short, there is a middle point which is neither the one nor the other, so between the lowest and the highest pitch there is a middle one—and there we have the accent we are looking for.

(c) Varro further argued that every kind of sound has a middle pitch between the extremes—although this can go unperceived, because it is the baseline against which higher and lower pitches stand out, and because the middle point of anything occupies too small a space.

neminem musicum esse, qui mediam uocem in cantu ignorauerit, nec quemquam potuisse dicere in sono chordarum aut bucinarum aut uoce cantantium μέσην *esse, si non in omni uocis natura esset medium; minimeque mirum ut in hanc multorum sensus non animaduertat, cum illa quae in cithara aut < > quia aliquando uberior est, saepe totum non sentiat meatum. praeterea minus reliquis notam, primum quod ea sit principium aliarum, ut* μέση *in musica est initium cantionis, et omnium rerum initia semper obscura sint; dein quod omne medium in angustis non uideatur, ut punctum in quamuis magno orbe, quod uocant* κέντρον.

(He said that) there was no musician who was unaware of the middle note in singing, and that nobody could have said that in the sound of strings or trumpets or the voice of singers there was a middle, unless there was a middle in every character of sound; and that it was hardly surprising that the perceptions of most people did not attend to this, seeing as that which in the cithara or ... because it is sometimes fuller, often it does not perceive the whole course. And besides, it is less well known than the others, first of all because it is the starting point of the others, just as in music the middle is the beginning of song, and the beginnings of all things are always indistinct; and secondly because every middle point goes unnoticed in its confined space, just like the point they call the κέντρον 'centre', in however large a circle.

(d) And further that the voice—*qua* body—must pass through a middle when passing from high to low, or *vice versa*. At the end of this section, Pseudo-Sergius rounds off his summary of arguments from Varro, adding that Varro produced many other arguments too.

nullum esse corpus, ubi non sit medium, et omnem uocem corpus esse; omnem igitur uocem medium habere. quod enim fuit deorsum prius in medium succedere, quam euolet sursum, et quod sursum est ante eodem uenire quam deorsum, quare utriusque compitum medium esse. et multa praeterea latius in eam rem disputata profert, quae nunc nobis longum est iterare.

(He said that) there was no body without a middle, and that every voice was a body; therefore, every voice had a middle. For what had been below went up to the middle before flying out above, and what is above comes to the same place before going below, whence the meeting point of both is the middle. And he brings forward many arguments besides to bear on this topic more extensively, which it would take a long time for us to repeat here.

(e) Varro's authorities for the middle accent. The presence of two Peripatetic philosophers, Theophrastus and Athenodorus, is of interest because a mention of the middle accent survives in Aristotle (see passage [2] below, and cf. Hanschke, 1914, pp. 113–114). (On the problem that the doctrine ascribed to Athenodorus here appears incompatible with that ascribed to an Athenodorus in section (a), see Fortenbaugh, 2005, p. 237.)

scire enim oportet rationis huius recens non esse commentum, sed omnium qui ante Varronem et Tyrannionem de prosodia aliquid reliquerunt plurimos et clarissimos quosque mediae huius fecisse mentionem, quos omnes sibi fuisse auctores Varro commemorat, grammaticos Glaucum Samium et Hermocraten Iasium; item philosophum Theophrastum peripateticum, cui diuina facundia nomen adsciuit, nec non eiusdem sectae Athenodorum, summi acuminis uirum, qui quandam prosodiam μονότονον *appellat, quae uidetur non alia esse quam media, licet diuerso uocabulo.*

For one must know that the invention of this doctrine is not recent, but among all those before Varro and Tyrannio who have left something behind on prosody, the majority and all the most distinguished have made mention of this middle. And Varro mentions that all these people are authorities for him: the grammarians Glaucus of Samos and Hermocrates of Iasos; and likewise the peripatetic philosopher Theophrastus, whose divine eloquence gave him his name; and also Athenodorus of the same school, a man of the utmost intelligence, who calls a certain accent μονότονος—and this appears to be none other than the middle, albeit under another name.

(f) Systems with more than four accents are said to be variants on the four-accent view, with the circumflex divided into various sub-types. Reflections on different authors' understandings of the circumflex accent follow. The view ascribed to Varro is not entirely clear (cf. Probert, 2019, p. 196[25]) but with *neque hoc facile fieri sine media* Pseudo-Sergius comes back to the middle accent (cf. Probert, 2019, p. 200), and tells us that for Varro the middle was 'generally an acute rather than a grave'. The claim *quod—inter se* hardly follows from what precedes, and Keil (GL iv 530–531) plausibly brackets it as an intrusion, perhaps from elsewhere in the text.

nec desunt qui prosodias plures esse quam quattuor putauerint, ut Glaucus Samius, a quo sex prosodiae sunt sub hisce nominibus, ἀνειμένη, μέση, ἐπιτεταμένη, κεκλασμένη, <ἀνακλωμένη>,[1] ἀντανακλωμένη. *sed hic quoque non dissentit a nobis. nam cuiuis ex ipsis nominibus intellectu procliue est tres primas esse simplices et non alias quam* βαρεῖαν, μέσην, ὀξεῖαν, *postremas autem tres duplices et quasi species unius flexae, quae est genere una. hanc enim flecti non uno modo omnes putauerunt: Eratosthenes ex parte priore acuta in grauem posteriorem, Theodorus autem aliquando etiam ex graui in acutiorem escendere, ceterum Varro in utramque partem moueri arbitratur, neque hoc facile fieri sine media, eamque acutam plerumque esse potius quam grauem {quod ea propior utramque est, quam illa superior et inferior inter se}.*

Nor are people lacking who have thought that there are more than four accents, like Glaucus of Samos, by whom six accents were posited under the following names: ἀνειμένη, μέση, ἐπιτεταμένη, κεκλασμένη, <ἀνακλωμένη>, ἀντανακλωμένη. But he too doesn't disagree with us: for anyone can easily understand from the names themselves that the first three are simple accents and none other than the grave, middle, and acute, while the last three are compound accents and variants (as it were) of one circumflex, which is a single one in type. For not everybody has thought that this inclined in the same way: Eratosthenes thought that it inclined from an acute first part to a grave second part, but Theodorus thought it sometimes also climbed up from a grave to an acuter part, and Varro thought that it moved in both directions, and that this couldn't easily happen without a middle, and that the middle was generally an acute rather than a grave {because it is closer to each than the higher and lower ones are to each other}.

(g) Three accents are in use in Pseudo-Sergius' day, with the middle subsumed under the grave. Keil (GL iv 531) brackets *tres prosodias—esse conplures* as an intrusion, in part because this material is incompatible with the claim *eamque acutam plerumque esse potius quam grauem* in section (f). However, the claims are compatible if Varro (to whom the point in (f) is attributed) generally considered the middle accent a species of acute, while those operating with three accents consider it a species of grave.

[1] The position of the lacuna and the supplement are Schoell's (1876, p. 81). For the final item of the list, I likewise follow Schoell (1876, p. 81) in printing ἀντανακλωμένη, after Wilmanns' (1864, p. 189) interpretation of the manuscript readings *antanaca homenehc* and *antanaca homenech*.

sed hoc <de> media prosodia satis, quo quis sciat esse quaerendam. ceterum qui hanc ignorant, quia sola nouerunt quae <in> scholis studuerunt, non sunt culpandi. sed nec magistros, qui tres solas demonstrant, erroris arguerim, si modo hoc docendi causa faciunt, cum ipsos quarta non lateat. tres prosodias in usu esse scire oportet et < >. media autem, quae inter duas quasi limes est, quod grauioris quam acutioris similior est, in inferioris potius quam superioris numerum relegatur. in hoc enim fere doctissimorum consensus est, acutam plus una in uerbo esse non posse, graues esse conplures.

But this is enough on the middle accent, so that anyone can know that it should be sought. But those who are unaware of this accent, because they only know the things they have learnt at school, should not be blamed. Nor would I accuse of error the teachers who only point out three accents—as long as they do this for didactic purposes while being aware of the fourth accent. One should know that three accents are in use, and that ... But the middle—which is essentially the boundary between the two—is relegated to the category of the lower rather than the higher (accent), because it is more like the grave than the acute. For on this point there is almost agreement among the most educated: that there cannot be more than one acute on a word, but there can be several graves.

(h) Names of the grave, acute, and middle.

prosodiam ibi esse dicimus, ubi aut sursum est aut deorsum. quae demissior est {quae} a pluribus βαρεῖα *appellatur Graece, Latine uero 'grauis', ideo quod deorsum est in sede scilicet ponderum grauiorum. at eam quae sursum est Glaucus* ἐπιτεταμένην, *item alius aliter, sed nemo adhuc 'leuem' uocauit, quamuis id erat graui contrarium; uerum ea nomen obtinet* ὀξεῖαν, *Latine 'acuta', ideo quod tenuis et omne acutum tenue. inter has est* μέση, *Latine 'media', quia limes est, per quem duae supra dictae ultro citroque commeant.*

We say that there is a 'prosody' where there is something above or below. The one which is below is generally called βαρεῖα in Greek and *grauis* ('heavy') in Latin, because it is below, that is in the place of heavier weights. As for the one which is above, Glaucus calls it ἐπιτεταμένη ('stretched') and others call it in other ways, but nobody has yet called it *leuis* ('light'), even though that would have been the opposite of *grauis*. But it has the name ὀξεῖα ('sharp'), and in Latin *acuta* ('sharp'), because it is slender and everything sharp is slender. Between these is the μέση, in Latin *media*, because it is the boundary through which the two above-mentioned accents pass back and forth.

[There follows discussion of names for the circumflex; of the acute as a briefer accent than the grave; and of the signs for acute, grave, and circumflex.]

(i) But Pseudo-Sergius can produce no sign for the middle.

mediae uero, cuius nunc usus non habetur, notam non ponimus, quia neque a maioribus accepimus neque fingere possumus.	But we do not lay out a sign for the middle, of which no use is made today, because we have not received one from our predecessors, nor can we invent one.

([Sergius], *In Donati Artem maiorem*, GL iv 529.1–532.28 ≈ Varro fr. 84 Goetz-Schoell ≈ Varro fr. 282 Funaioli ≈ Tyrannio fr. 59 Haas)

While Pseudo-Sergius mentions ample Greek precursors for Varro's concept of a middle accent, the main and (we shall see) only real precursor to survive in Greek is passage (2), from Aristotle's *Poetics*. Here a triad comprising ὀξύτης 'acuity', βαρύτης 'gravity', and τὸ μέσον 'the middle' makes a brief appearance in connection with speech sounds. The other speech sounds mentioned are ones that can create distinctive contrasts between one word and another, and in this context ὀξύτης, βαρύτης, and τὸ μέσον most plausibly refer to the distinct 'accents' a vowel or syllable might carry.

(2) στοιχεῖον μὲν οὖν ἐστιν φωνὴ ἀδιαίρετος, οὐ πᾶσα δὲ ἀλλ' ἐξ ἧς πέφυκε συνθετὴ γίγνεσθαι φωνή· καὶ γὰρ τῶν θηρίων εἰσὶν ἀδιαίρετοι φωναί, ὧν οὐδεμίαν λέγω στοιχεῖον. ταύτης δὲ μέρη τό τε φωνῆεν καὶ τὸ ἡμίφωνον καὶ ἄφωνον. ἔστιν δὲ ταῦτα φωνῆεν μὲν <τὸ> ἄνευ προσβολῆς ἔχον φωνὴν ἀκουστήν, ἡμίφωνον δὲ τὸ μετὰ προσβολῆς ἔχον φωνὴν ἀκουστήν, οἷον τὸ Σ καὶ τὸ Ρ, ἄφωνον δὲ τὸ μετὰ προσβολῆς καθ' αὑτὸ μὲν οὐδεμίαν ἔχον φωνήν, μετὰ δὲ τῶν ἐχόντων τινὰ φωνὴν γινόμενον ἀκουστόν, οἷον τὸ Γ καὶ τὸ Δ. ταῦτα δὲ διαφέρει σχήμασίν τε τοῦ στόματος καὶ τόποις καὶ δασύτητι καὶ ψιλότητι καὶ μήκει καὶ βραχύτητι ἔτι δὲ ὀξύτητι καὶ βαρύτητι καὶ τῷ μέσῳ· (Aristotle, *Poetics* 1456ᵇ22–33)

An element is an indivisible sound—not just any indivisible sound, but one which can give a compound sound. For the voices of some animals are indivisible, but I do not call any of them an 'element'. And the subdivisions of the element are the vowel, continuant, and stop. And as for these, a vowel is one that has an audible sound without contact, a continuant is one that has an audible sound with contact, like σ and ρ, and a stop is one that has contact and no audible sound by itself, but becomes audible together with those that have some sound, like γ and δ. And these vary in the shapes of the mouth and the places (where contact occurs), and in roughness and smoothness (i.e., aspiration and unaspiratedness), and length and shortness, and also in acuity, gravity, and the middle.

In a further passage of Aristotle which has been thought relevant (*Rhet.* 1403^{b}24–30) (see Ehrlich, 1912, p. 254), an apparently similar triad comprising ὀξεῖα 'high', βαρεῖα 'low', and μέση 'middle' (with φωνή 'voice' understood) appears in the context of a discussion of the tones of voice appropriate to each emotion in rhetoric. While the structural similarity between this triad and that of passage (2) may reveal an overarching characteristic of Aristotle's thought (cf. Hanschke, 1914, p. 113), the passage of the *Rhetoric* is not actually about word accents: the point is that orators need to judge when it is appropriate to speak in a high voice, when in a low voice, and when in a medium one.

At first sight, three passages from the Byzantine commentaries to the Τέχνη γραμματική attributed to Dionysius Thrax may appear more relevant:

(3) ἢ κατὰ περίκλασιν ἐν τῇ περισπωμένῃ] περίκλασις φωνῆς λέγεται ἡ ἐν τῷ αὐτῷ ἀνένεξις καὶ κατένεξις, μὴ ἐπιμενούσης τῆς φωνῆς ἐν τῇ ἀνατάσει, ἀλλὰ μετὰ τὸ ἀναταθῆναι καταφερομένης· ὅθεν καὶ τὸ σημεῖον τοῦ τόνου τούτου ἅμα ἄνεισι καὶ κάτεισι· καὶ παρὰ μὲν τοῖς γραμματικοῖς καλεῖται περισπωμένη, παρὰ δὲ τοῖς μουσικοῖς μέση. οὗτος οὖν ὁ τόνος δοκεῖ σύνθετος εἶναι, ὥσπερ καὶ τὸ σημεῖον ἐλέγχει συγκείμενον ἐξ ὀξείας καὶ βαρείας· (Sch. D. Thr. 23. 14–20 Hilgard)

'Or with a change of direction in the circumflex': the upwards and downwards motion on the same (vowel) is called a change of direction of the voice, with the voice not remaining at its height, but being brought down after being lifted up. Whence the sign of this accent also goes both up and down. And among the grammarians it is called περισπωμένη ('circumflex'), while among the musicians it is called μέση ('middle'). This accent appears to be a compound one, then—just as its sign proves, being composed of the acute and the grave.'

(4) ὁ μέσος τόνος παρὰ μὲν τοῖς μουσικοῖς ἐστιν ὁ μέσος ὢν ὑπάτης καὶ νήτης καὶ παρυπάτης καὶ παρανήτης. λέγεται δὲ ὁ μέσος τόνος καὶ συνηρημένος καὶ κοινός, ὅταν γὰρ τοῦ μὲν βαρέος τόνου εὑρηθῇ ὀξύτερος, τοῦ δὲ ὀξέος βαρύτερος. ὑπάτη μὲν οὖν ἡ παρὰ τελευτὴν τὸν βαρὺν τόνον ἔχουσα, ἤγουν ἡ παροξύτονος, παρυπάτη δὲ ἡ προπαροξύτονος. παρὰ δὲ τοῖς γραμματικοῖς μέσος τόνος ὁ περισπώμενος. <παρ>έχουσι δὲ τοῦτον ὁ βαρὺς τόνος καὶ <ὁ> ὀξὺς συναπτόμενοι ἀλλήλοις. διὸ καὶ συνεχῆ καὶ συνημμένον ἑκατέρου φαῖεν ἂν <αὐτὸν> οἱ σοφοί, ὥσπερ τινὰ κοινὸν ὅρον συναπτικὸν αὐτῶν ὄντα.' (Sch. D. Thr. 310. 12–20 Hilgard)

Among the musicians the middle τόνος (here 'pitch') is the one that is in the middle between the ὑπάτη and νήτη (i.e., the lowest and highest notes on a seven-note scale) and between the παρυπάτη and παρανήτη (i.e., the second-lowest and second-highest notes). And the middle τόνος is also called contracted or joint, since it is found to be higher than the low pitch and lower than the high pitch. The ὑπάτη is the one that has a low pitch next to the end, that is to say the paroxytone, and the παρυπάτη is the proparoxytone (?). And among the grammarians the middle τόνος (here 'accent') is the circumflex. And the grave and acute accents produce this one when conjoined with each other. For this reason the learned also call it continuous and conjoined out of each, as if there is some common boundary joining them.

(5) τόνοι μὲν οὖν εἰσι τρεῖς, ὀξύς, βαρύς, περισπώμενος.] τῆς προσῳδίας ὑποδιαιρέσεις εἰσὶ τέσσαρες. πάλιν ἕκαστον τῶν τεσσάρων ὑποδιαιρεῖται, οἱ μὲν τόνοι καὶ τὰ πάθη εἰς τρία, τὰ δὲ πνεύματα καὶ οἱ χρόνοι εἰς δύο. τόνος οὖν ἐστιν ἐπίτασις ἢ ἄνεσις ἢ μεσότης συλλαβῶν, εὐφωνίαν ἔχουσα. τὸ μὲν οὖν ἐπίτασις ἐτέθη ἐν τῷ ὁρισμῷ διὰ τὴν ὀξεῖαν, τὸ δὲ ἄνεσις διὰ τὴν βαρεῖαν, τὸ δὲ μεσότης διὰ τὴν περισπωμένην. καὶ ἔστι πάλιν ἡ μὲν ὀξεῖα ποιότης συλλαβῆς ἐπιτεταμένον ἔχουσα φθόγγον, ἡ δὲ βαρεῖα ποιότης συλλαβῆς ἀνειμένον ἔχουσα φθόγγον, ἡ δὲ περισπωμένη ποιότης συλλαβῆς συνημμένον ἢ κεκλασμένον ἔχουσα φθόγγον· εἶπε δὲ συνημμένον τὸν μετέχοντα καὶ ὀξείας καὶ βαρείας, κεκλασμένον δὲ τὸν ἀπὸ τοῦ ὀξέος ἐπὶ τὸ βαρὺ ῥέποντα. (Sch. D. Thr. 136.12–23 Hilgard)

> 'There are three accents: acute, grave, circumflex': There are four subdivisions of prosody. Each of the four is again subdivided—the accents and modifications into three subgroups (each), and the breathings and quantities into two (each). Τόνος ('pitch' or 'accent') is a tightening or slackening or in-between state of syllables with a harmonious sound. 'Tightening' has been included in the definition because of the acute, 'loosening' because of the grave, and 'in-between state' because of the circumflex. And the acute is a syllable quality with a taut sound, the grave a syllable quality with a slack sound, and the circumflex a syllable quality with a conjunct or deflected sound. And he called a sound partaking of both the acute and the grave 'conjunct', and one inclining from the acute to the grave 'deflected'.

Passages (3)–(5) have been taken to support an idea that the middle accent of at least some Greek authors was the circumflex under another name (see the next section),[2] because the grammarians' 'circumflex' is here equated or associated with the musicians' 'middle'. However, these passages involve attempts to map musical and grammatical τόνοι ('pitches' or 'accents') onto each other, and the 'middle' here belongs to music, not grammar. The musical middle pitch is mapped onto the grammarians' circumflex accent because like the latter, it can be treated as the third member of a three-member system whose other two members are called ὀξύς 'high' and βαρύς 'low'. We cannot infer anything from these passages about what was meant by any authors using the term 'middle (accent)' for a feature of speech.

With passages (3)–(5) taken out of consideration, the only surviving sources to explicitly mention the 'middle accent' are Pseudo-Sergius in passage (1), and Aristotle in (2).[3]

---

[2] See Sommer (1914, p. 96), Juret (1921, p. 73), Sommer & Pfister (1977, p. 81), and Luque Moreno (2006, p. 83).

[3] For completeness, two further passages of Latin authors, Quintilian, *Inst.* 1.5.22–23 and Aulus Gellius, *NA* 6.7.1–4, have been thought to mention the middle accent (Juret, 1921, pp. 73–74 and Scappaticcio, 2012, pp. 31–32, respectively), but in both places *media* means 'middle (syllable)', not 'middle (accent)'; cf. Probert (2019, pp. 129–130 & 203–204).

2 Modern Views

We may begin our survey of modern views with the most cautious. On one view, it is impossible to discern what was meant by the middle accent, in either Latin or Greek: there is too little evidence.[4] On a related view, the search for the middle accent can only be vain, because this accent never had more than a vague theoretical existence.[5] Although a partly different suggestion will be offered further on, both these views are worth serious consideration, given the exiguous evidence for the middle accent in Greek, the exceedingly general arguments for the necessity of a middle found in Pseudo-Sergius, the lack of specific examples, and Pseudo-Sergius' stated inability to produce any sign representing the middle accent.

Nevertheless, numerous attempts have been made to identify the middle accent of Aristotle and/or Tyrannio and/or Varro with a known or conjectured feature of the Greek or Latin language. For Aristotle, a suggestion already mentioned is that his middle accent is the circumflex under another name.[6] While the relevance of passages (3)–(5) for this question has already been rejected, it remains worth asking whether Aristotle's three-accent system with high, low, and middle accents should be equated with the later three-accent system.

The middle accent certainly cannot be the circumflex in the four-accent system of Tyrannio and Varro, where the middle and the circumflex coexist as distinct accents (see Ahlberg, 1905, p. 6; Leumann, 1977, p. 244; Fortenbaugh, 2005, p. 237), but it need not follow that Aristotle's middle was also distinct from the circumflex. It has been suggested that the four-accent system of Tyrannio and Varro was a meaningless construct resulting from a failure to understand the status of the middle

[4] See Lepschy (1962, p. 206); cf. Probert (2019, p. 7). On Aristotle, cf. already Steinthal (1890–1891, i 258).

[5] See Hanschke (1914, pp. 112–114), Bernardi Perini (2010, p. 13); cf. Usener (1892: esp., pp. 633–641) and Luque Moreno (2006, p. 72).

[6] See Laum (1928, pp. 8–10); cf. Sommer (1914, p. 96), Juret (1921, pp. 73–74), and Sommer & Pfister (1977, p. 81). For more bibliography, see Matthaios (2022, p. 22[21]).

accent in Aristotle, whatever this may have been;[7] this view, too, is worth serious consideration.

On the other hand, we must distinguish between the empirical facts of a language and the analysis these are given. Aristotle was plausibly aware of the phenomenon known to us as the Greek circumflex accent, but it does not follow that he treated it as an independent unit of analysis, nor that this is what he meant by τὸ μέσον: compare Athenodorus' two-accent system of passage (1), section (a) (cf. Weil & Benloew, 1855, p. 15; Fortenbaugh, 2005, p. 238; Matthaios, 2022, pp. 22–23). It is also at least noteworthy that elsewhere in the Aristotelian corpus, the words οὗ 'where' and οὐ 'not' are contrasted in terms of one being spoken ὀξύτερον 'on a higher pitch' and one βαρύτερον 'on a lower pitch', with no mention of a middle accent for οὗ.[8] Furthermore, the term τὸ μέσον would be somewhat surprising if a contour accent were intended, rather than something genuinely intermediate between accented and unaccented (Wackernagel, 1893, p. 11; Matthaios, 2022, p. 22).

A different suggestion is that the middle accent of Aristotle, Tyrannio, and the other Greek authors mentioned in passage (1), section (e), was the reduced accent of oxytone words when these were followed by a non-enclitic word with no intervening punctuation (a phenomenon reflected in our own practice of writing a grave rather than an acute accent mark under the relevant circumstances) (Ehrlich, 1912, pp. 253–254, followed by Haas, 1977, p. 171). This suggestion would accord better with some of Pseudo-Sergius' suggestions of an intermediate prominence between the grave (unaccentedness) and the acute, and with Aristotle's term τὸ μέσον, but there is no specific evidence that anybody thought middle accents appeared on final syllables in particular.

Varro's concept of a middle accent for Latin may or may not have corresponded closely to whatever Tyrannio understood as a middle accent for Greek. Further attempts to pinpoint a specific linguistic reality behind

---

[7] See Sommer (1914, pp. 95–96), Sommer & Pfister (1977, p. 81), and Luque Moreno (2006, pp. 72 & 84).

[8] Aristotle, *SE* 177^{b}35–178^{a}3; compare *SE* 166^{b}3–6, and cf. Ehrlich (1912, p. 254).

Varro's middle accent include the idea that this was the natural pitch of the voice, from which the voice deviated in an upward or downward direction (Della Corte, 1937, pp. 135–136², 1981, pp. 200–201); and that Varro's middle accent subsumed all the pitches between the lowest and highest, as the voice moves continuously in speaking (Camilli, 1949, p. 16; cf. Matthaios, 2022, p. 20).[9] Passage (1) might seem to suggest both of these ideas (see sections (c) and (d), respectively)—but the two ideas are not identical. Perhaps Varro intended both of them, or intended neither of them very seriously. The suggestion that the middle accent is the natural pitch of the voice is problematic, however, because the grave already conveys the absence of any special prominence.

Weil and Benloew (1855, pp. 13–16) offer a variant of the idea that Varro's middle accent was a transitional pitch, under which this transitional pitch had a syllable to itself on sufficiently long words, before and/or after the main accent (cf. Misteli, 1875, pp. 49–61). For instance, the word *pudicítia* might have had a middle pitch on the second and fourth syllables, as the voice moved from the unaccented first syllable up to the accented third syllable and then back down again. In support of this idea, Weil & Benloew adduce a quotation from Nigidius Figulus in Aulus Gellius, implying that Nigidius heard the vocative *Váleri̅* as having the highest accent on its first syllable, and then a stepwise descent (*in casu uocandi summo tonost prima, deinde gradatim descendunt*).[10] But Nigidius' perception of a step-wise descent does not prove that Varro would have analysed the second syllable of this form as carrying his 'middle accent'—even if we suppose that Varro would have made the same empirical observation as Nigidius involving a step-wise descent, which is far from certain.

Yet another suggestion is that Varro's Latin middle accent was a secondary accent, falling on certain syllables that did not carry the main

[9] As Andreas Willi reminds me, Allen (1987, p. 123) tentatively makes a similar suggestion for the Greek middle accent on the basis of Dionysius of Halicarnassus, *De compositione verborum* 11.17, where Allen sees an allusion to intermediate pitches in words of more than two syllables. I find Allen's interpretation of this passage unlikely, but even if this were accepted, it would be a further question whether these intermediate pitches corresponded to what anybody meant by the 'middle accent'.

[10] Aulus Gellius, *NA* 13.26.1/Nigidius Figulus fr. 35 Swoboda/Nigidius Figulus fr. 9 Funaioli.

word accent. But scholars who take Latin to have had a secondary accent take different views as to where this fell. For Stolz (1894, p. 99) and Ahlberg (1905, pp. 6–9), the middle accent continued the early Latin accent on the initial syllable of the word.[11] Differently, Corssen (1868–1870, ii 824–829) takes it to fall on the syllable of a compound or derivative that carried the accent of the corresponding simplex or base word (except that no accent fell on a syllable adjacent to the main word accent).[12] As comparanda, Corssen adduces German compounds such as *Wéchselbeziͯehungen* 'reciprocal relationships', with a secondary stress (here marked ˟) on the syllable of the second member where main stress falls in the corresponding simplex.[13]

For some compounds and derivatives, Corssen's system yields the same result as that of Stolz and Ahlberg, while for others the prediction is different, as the following examples illustrate:

(6)	simplex/underived form	compound/derivative (Stolz and Ahlberg's system)	compound/derivative (Corssen's system)
	uérsus 'turned'	*uĕrsi-péllis* 'skin-changer/werewolf'	*uĕrsi-péllis*
	dḗns, déntis 'tooth'	*dĕnti-frangíbulus* 'tooth-breaker'	*dĕnti-frangíbulus*
	géminus 'twin'	*gĕminitū́dō* 'difference between twins'	*gĕminitū́dō*
	supérbus 'proud'	*sŭperbi-loquéntia* 'proud talk'	*supĕrbi-loquéntia*
	incúruus 'crooked'	*ĭncurui-ceruîcus* 'with a crooked neck'	*incŭrui-ceruîcus*

(The location of the hypothetical secondary accent is marked ˟; the main word accent is marked ´, or ^ where the mainstream Latin grammatical tradition would have considered the accent a circumflex.)

[11] Ahlberg (1905, pp. 7–8) further specified that this middle accent only occurred on words whose initial syllable was non-adjacent to the syllable carrying the classical Latin accent, and suggested that Varro's middle accent was also conceived as falling on the main accented syllable of words pronounced with reduced prominence within the phrase.

[12] Similar views in Schoell (1876, pp. 44–49) and Kühner and Holzweissig (1912–1914, i 241–242); less clearly Sommer (1902, p. 108).

[13] The system Corssen envisages would have a secondary stress whose position is defined independently of that of the main accent, and belongs to a distinct (and prosodically downgraded) morphological domain such as a distinct compound member: in Garde's (2013, pp. 51–2) terms, an *accent secondaire* as opposed to an *écho d'accent*, or in Generative Phonology terms, a 'cyclic effect' (regardless of how this is implemented theoretically). For further typological parallels and further discussion of German compounds, see Garde (2013, pp. 75–82).

To sum up, the only explicit mentions of a 'middle' accent consist of passages (2) (Aristotle) and (1) (Pseudo-Sergius). Aristotle tells us too little in passage (2) to reveal what, if anything, he specifically had in mind, while the passionate display of arguments in passage (1) provides scant reason to accept or reject any of the suggestions just surveyed. But Schoell brings a further passage into the discussion in relation to Varro, and the next section will propose a modification to his proposal.

3 A Further Piece of Evidence

In support of the idea that Varro thought a word might have more than one accentual peak, Schoell (1876, p. 46) adduces a quotation of Varro by Aulus Gellius: *in priore uerbo graues prosodiae, quae fuerunt, manent, reliquae mutant* 'in the first word the accents which were grave remain, and the others change'.[14] Gellius' interest is in Varro's intransitive use of the active form *mutant*, but he leaves it for us to wonder what Varro might have been talking about. In Schoell's tentative interpretation, Varro had in mind compounds like *dextrouorsum* 'to the right', normally pronounced *dĕ̀xtrouórsum*, but with the possibility (on Schoell's suggestion) of *déxtrouŏ̀rsum*, with contrastive stress on the first member: 'to the *right*'.

The phrase *in priore uerbo* 'in the first word' would be better explained, however, if Varro was thinking of two simplex words being combined into a compound, should Corssen's suggestion for secondary stresses in Latin compounds be on the right lines: if, for instance, *supĕ̀rbiloquéntia* has a secondary accent on the second syllable, where *supérbus* has its main accent. If so, when a simplex word becomes the first member of a compound (and provided the second member is sufficiently long to retain the main accent) its grave accents (unaccented syllables) remain unchanged, while any other accents it may have are downgraded.[15]

[14] Aulus Gellius, *NA* 18.12.8 ≈ Varro fr. 85 Goetz-Schoell ≈ Varro fr. 45 Funaioli.

[15] For words 'changing their accents' when they combine to form a single word, cf. Donatus, *In Ter. Eu.* 255, on *intereā́locī* 'in the meantime' (here taken to be one word): *duae partes orationis cum coniunctae unam fecerint, mutant accentum* 'When two words joined together have made one, they change their accent.'

In principle, the downgrading of accents could take them all the way to unaccentedness rather than to a secondary accent. The two possibilities can be illustrated as follows:

(7) Possibility 1:
uérsus, péllis → *uĕͯrsipéllis*
supérbus, loquéntia → *supĕͯrbiloquéntia*

Possibility 2:
uérsus, péllis → *uersipéllis*
supérbus, loquéntia → *superbiloquéntia*

Under possibility 2, no middle accent need be involved. However, Varro's plural *reliquae* more naturally suggests that a first member might already have multiple non-grave accents before composition; this makes it likely that secondary accents were part of the system, and were conceptualised as something other than grave. While I do not have a complete theory as to the locations of secondary accents in Latin, suppose for the sake of argument (adapting a suggestion of Corssen's, 1868–1870, ii 828) that a form such as *cōnfidentis* 'trusting' (genitive singular present participle) had a secondary accent on *cōn-* (*cō̆ͯnfidéntis*), and was felt related to the *cōnfidenti-* of *cōnfidentiloquius* 'more confidently speaking'. If both the secondary and the primary accent of *cō̆ͯnfidéntis* were downgraded in composition, the result would be either *cōnfidĕ̄ntilóquius* or *cōnfidentilóquius*:

(8) Possibility 1:
cō̆ͯnfidéntis, lóquor → *cōnfidĕ̄ntilóquius*

Possibility 2:
cō̆ͯnfidéntis, lóquor → *cōnfidentilóquius*

Either way, the grave accents of the first member can be said to remain, while its other accents change: *in priore uerbo graues prosodiae, quae fuerunt, manent, reliquae mutant.* The details may or may not be correct for the form *cōnfidentiloquius*, but some comparable situation would make good sense of Gellius' quotation from Varro.

We can probably go further, however, and eliminate what we have been calling possibility 2. It is unlikely that if Latin had secondary stresses at all (as posited here, *exempli gratia*, for *cōͯnfidéntis*), it made no use of them in long and morphologically complex words such as *superbiloquéntia* or *cōnfidentilóquius*. Eliminating possibility 2 would leave possibility 1, under which both the primary accent and any secondary accent(s) on the first member of relevant compounds are downgraded just one notch in composition.

If the suggestion made here is correct, while the details of secondary accents in Latin would remain obscure, a compound such as *supĕͯrbiloquéntia* probably had a secondary stress on a non-initial syllable: the main accent of *supérbus*, downgraded one notch. If so, we gain a morsel of evidence against the idea that Latin secondary stress always fell on the word-initial syllable.

4 Conclusions

At this point, some tentative history of the middle accent concept can perhaps be drawn together. Aristotle mentions a middle accent (passage (2)), but, in what survives of his works he does not spell out what he means by it, and possibly he never did. We cannot even be sure that he had a clear concept in mind. Since he mentions high, middle, and low pitches in connection with stretches of utterance (*Rhet.* $1403^{b}24$–30), it is possible that he thought fairly mechanically of the same three pitch levels as the basic possibilities at the smaller domain of the syllable too. We simply do not know. Nevertheless, Aristotle's mention of a middle accent led subsequent Peripatetic philosophers and some others to pick up on the idea—but we cannot be sure any of them spelled out what was actually meant. In some form the idea was picked up by Tyrannio, although it is notable that the fragments of his work on Homeric prosody suggest he made no regular use of the concept.

Varro picked up on the idea and defended the notion of a middle accent with all sorts of philosophical arguments, which may or may not derive from Tyrannio. More than this, he possibly went *looking for* the middle accent in Latin (compare Pseudo-Sergius' *ibique quam quaerimus prosodiam*), and conceivably found it in some secondary stresses on compound words. Possibly he found other applications for the concept too, but we do not know.

References

Ahlberg, A. W. (1905). *Studia de accentu Latino*. Håkan Ohlsson.

Allen, W. S. (1987). *Vox Graeca. The pronunciation of Classical Greek*[3]. Cambridge University Press.

Bernardi Perini, G. (2010). *L'Accento latino*[5]. Pàtron.

Camilli, A. (1949). *Trattato di prosodia e metrica latina*. Sansoni.

Corssen, W. (1868–1870). *Über Aussprache, Vokalismus und Betonung der lateinischen Sprache*[2]. B. G. Teubner.

Della Corte, F. (1937). *La filologia latina dalle origini a Varrone*[1]. F. Casanova & c.

Della Corte, F. (1981). In Firenze (Ed.), *La filologia latina dalle origini a Varrone*[2]. La Nuova Italia Editrice.

Ehrlich, H. (1912). *Untersuchungen über die Natur der griechischen Betonung*. Weidmann.

Fortenbaugh, W. W. (2005). *Theophrastus of Eresus. Sources for his life, writings, thought and influence. Commentary volume 8. Sources on rhetoric and poetics (texts 666–713)*. Brill.

Garde, P. (2013). *L'accent*[2]. Lambert-Lucas.

GL = Keil, H., Hertz, M., & Mommsen, T. (eds). (1855–1880). *Grammatici Latini*. B. G. Teubner.

Haas, W. (1977). *Die Fragmente der Grammatiker Tyrannion und Diokles*. De Gruyter.

Hanschke, P. (1914). *De accentuum graecorum nominibus*. A. Marcus & E. Weber.

Juret, É. A. (1921). *Manuel de phonétique latine*. Hachette.

Kühner, R., & Holzweissig, F. (1912–1914). *Ausführliche Grammatik der lateinischen Sprache*[2]. Hahn.

Laum, B. (1928). *Das Alexandrinische Akzentuationssystem unter Zugrundelegung der theoretischen Lehren der Grammatiker und mit Heranziehung der praktischen Verwendung in den Papyri*. F. Schöningh.

Lepschy, G. C. (1962). Il problema dell'accento latino. Rassegna critica di studi sull'accento latino e sullo studio dell'accento. *Annali della Scuola Normale Superiore di Pisa: Lettere, storia e filosofia*, 2nd series, 31: 199–246.

Leumann, M. (1977). *Lateinische Grammatik i, Lateinische Laut- und Formenlehre*. C. H. Beck.

Luque Moreno, J. (2006). *Accentus (προσῳδία). El canto del lenguaje*. Editorial Universidad de Granada.

Matthaios, S. (2022). Den griechischen Akzenten auf der Spur. Der Varro-Traktat *De accentibus* und Eratosthenes' Zirkumflex-Definition. In T. Denecker, P. Desmet, L. Jooken, P. Lauwers, T. Van Hal, & R. Van Rooy

(Eds.), *The architecture of grammar. Studies in linguistic historiography in honor of Pierre Swiggers* (pp. 15–35). Peeters.
Misteli, F. (1875). *Ueber griechische Betonung: sprachvergleichend-philologische Abhandlungen i, Allgemeine Theorie der griechischen Betonung*. Ferdinand Schöningh.
Probert, P. (2019). *Latin grammarians on the Latin accent*. Oxford University Press.
Scappaticcio, M. C. (2012). *Accentus, distinctio, apex. L'accentazione grafica tra Grammatici Latini e papiri virgiliani*. Brepols.
Schoell, F. (1876). De accentu linguae latinae veterum grammaticorum testimonia. *Acta Societatis Philologae Lipsiensis, 6*, 1–231.
Sommer, F. (1902). *Handbuch der lateinischen Laut- und Formenlehre*[1]. Carl Winter.
Sommer, F. (1914). *Handbuch der lateinischen Laut- und Formenlehre*[2/3]. Carl Winter.
Sommer, F., & Pfister, R. (1977). *Handbuch der lateinischen Laut- und Formenlehre i, Einleitung und Lautlehre*[4]. Carl Winter.
Steinthal, H. (1890–1891). *Geschichte der Sprachwissenschaft bei den Griechen und Römern mit besonderer rücksicht auf die logik*[2]. Ferd. Dümmler.
Stolz, F. (1894). *Historische Grammatik der lateinischen Sprache*. B. G. Teubner.
Usener, H. (1892). Ein altes Lehrgebäude der Philologie. *Sitzungsberichte der philosophisch-philologischen und der historischen Classe der königlich Bayerischen Akademie der Wissenschaften zu München* 1892, 582–648.
Wackernagel, J. (1893). *Beiträge zur Lehre vom griechischen Akzent*. L. Reinhardt.
Weil, H., & Benloew, L. (1855). *Théorie générale de l'accentuation latine*. Ferd. Dümmler.
Wilmanns, A. (1864). *De M. Terenti Varronis libris grammaticis*. Weidmann.

17

Obscured figurae etymologicae and Word Origins. Two Examples Involving Gothic

Patrick Stiles

§1. The figura etymologica is a rhetorical device in which the slots of a grammatical construction are filled by cognate lexemes, as in Engl. *she sang a song* or *he told a tale*. As well as such cognate accusatives, which are perhaps the commonest type, other constructions occur, such as *a giver of gifts* or *a manly man*.[1] In examples such as these, it is not disputed that the elements are etymologically related.

This article suggests that similar, but not transparent, figures of speech can sometimes be used in reverse, as it were, to identify cognates that have not already been recognized. That is: the claim is made that they may be obscured figurae etymologicae. Gothic features in both examples.

The danger lies in confusing a figura phonetica with a figura etymologica. Though a distinction can clearly be made on theoretical grounds,

[1] More elaborate instances occur, such as Shakespeare's '*With eager feeding food doth choke the feeder*'.—*Richard II* II i,37. A specific type of figura etymologica is polyptoton, whereby a word is repeated in different cases or inflections.

P. Stiles (✉)
University College London, London, UK
e-mail: pvstiles@yahoo.ac.uk

J. F. Eska et al. (eds.), *The Method Works*,
https://doi.org/10.1007/978-3-031-48959-4_17

it is by no means easy in practice. And, more to the point, it would not have been always evident to more or less naive native language users. On the one hand, they may have unwittingly employed a fixed phrase that was an obscured inherited figura etymologica; on the other, they may have used unrelated material to create what seems to be one. An example of an obscured figura etymologica can be seen in the Rig-Vedic collocation *stokā́ ścotanti* 'drops drip' 3.21.2^{b}, where metathesis and palatalization have distanced the two forms (cf. de Saussure, 1889a; EWAI ii, 658–659 & 761). An instance of a specious figura etymologica might be *he kept a lock of her hair in a locket*, the implication being that the naming-motif of a locket comes from its possible use to preserve a lock of hair (not that it is lockable—and a French loanword).

We can start with a clear instance.

1 §2. PGmc. **huzdijan*.

§2.1. In the Gothic translation of the gospels (ed. Streitberg, 1998), the denominative weak class I verb *huzdjan* features in an undoubted figura etymologica with its base noun at Matthew 6.19–20 (mirroring one in the Greek original).

(1) *ni* ***huzdjaiþ*** *izwis huzda ana airþai … iþ* ***huzdjaiþ*** *izwis huzda in himina …*
μὴ θησαυρίζετε ὑμῖν θησαυροὺς ἐπὶ τῆς γῆς, … θησαυρίζετε δὲ ὑμῖν θησαυροὺς ἐν οὐρανῷ,
'Do not *store up* for yourselves treasures on earth, … But *store up* for yourselves treasures in heaven, …'

The only other example of the verb, at 2Cor 12.14, also means 'store up, gather riches':

(2) *ni auk skulun barna fadreinam* ***huzdjan,*** *ak fadreina barnam*
οὐ γὰρ ὀφείλει τὰ τέκνα τοῖς γονεῦσιν θησαυρίζειν, ἀλλὰ οἱ γονεῖς τοῖς τέκνοις.
'For the children ought not *to store up* for the parents, but the parents for the children'

§2.2.1. The Gothic translation of Matthew 6.19–20 is closely matched by the Old English North Mercian Rushworth 1 gloss to the gospels:

(3) *ne* ***hydeþ*** *eow hord in eorþe ...* ***hydeþ*** *eow þonne hord in heofunum*
nolite thesaurizate uobis thesauros in terra ... Tehsaurizate autem uobis tehsauros in caelo[2]

Apart from Goth. *iþ* and OE *þonne*, which each have no counterpart in the other version, the two renderings correspond word-for-word. This suggests not only that *hord hȳdan* might be an old collocation (especially in view of the synchronically aberrant meaning of the Old English verb here: 'store up' rather than usual 'conceal'[3]), but that the verbs in question are historically identical.[4] That is to say: OE *hȳdan*—like Goth. *huzd-jan*—descends from PGmc. **huzdijan*, a phonetically unexceptional derivation and one superior to the current etymology (see below §2.7.1). This would make the English phrase, too, originally a figura etymologica. Remarkably, it would also mean that the two passages consist entirely of cognates (in the same order), with the exclusions noted above and allowing for the variation of Goth. *ana* and OE *in*. It also means that the

[2] It must be borne in mind that the Old English is translating Latin, not Greek as is the Gothic version—although it makes little difference in practice, as the Latin words in question are adopted from the Greek.

[3] See DOE s.v. *hȳdan* sense a.ii. It may also be noted that *hȳdan* is not given by the DOE as one of the verbs with which *hord* regularly collocates (s.v. *hord* 1.b), although it does co-occur in *Elene* 1091 *hord under hrusan þæt gehyded gen, / duguðum dyrne, deogol bideð* 'treasure under ground that, still hidden, concealed from-the-retainers, remains secret'. But, judging by *Elene* 217–218 *hwær se wuldres beam, / halig under hrusan* ***hyded*** *wære* 'where the rood of glory, / the holy (thing) might be *hidden* under the earth', the set phrase is rather *(ge)hyded under hrusan*.

[4] Other Old English Bible versions do not correspond. The Northumbrian Lindisfarne Gospels gloss reads 19 *nællas gie gestrionaige iuh gestriono in eorðo* ... 20 *strionas gie soðlice iuh striona in heofnum*. The West Saxon gospels (Hatton MS) offer 19 *Nellen ge goldhordian eow on eorðan gold-hordas*, ... 20 *Gold-hordiað eow soðlice gold-hordes on heofenan*, featuring *hordian*, a later denominative creation from *hord*. All the quotations from Matthew in this note and (3) are from Skeat (1887, pp. 56–57; 248 for the Rushworth Latin).

However, that quintessential writer of Late West Saxon, Ælfric, when citing the gospel passage, echoes the West Saxon version in the heavenly part: *hórdiað eowerne goldhord on heofenum*, but offers a crucial difference in the earthly part: *Ne behyde ge eowerne goldhord on eorðan* (ed. Godden, 1979, p. 63). Although other instances in the Catholic Homilies clearly mean 'conceal', 'store, amass' seems more appropriate here. The version printed by Napier (1883, pp. 286–287), part of Homily LV, formerly attributed to Wulfstan, is effectively identical, which is hardly surprising as it is Ælfrician; see Napier (1883, p. viii) and Jost (1950, p. 261).

predominant Old English meaning ‘hide, conceal’ is a secondary development; see §2.7.1 with n. 12.

The proto-Germanic sequence *-*V̆zd-* has two recognized outcomes in West Germanic for which the respective conditioning factors are not clear (but may have been open versus closed syllable): *-*V̆rd-* and *-*V̄d-*. The first reflex is illustrated by the base-word of the verb of concern here: Goth. *huzd* ‘treasure’; ON *hodd*; OE *hord*, OS *hord*, OHG *hort*. Alternatively, Goth. *mizdō* ‘meed, reward’ corresponds to OE *meord* (essentially Anglian) beside *mēd*, OFris. *mēde*, OS *mēda*, OHG *mēta*, *mieta*.

A sentiment similar to that of Matthew 6.19–20 is expressed in the poem *The seafarer* 97–102, although the passage most closely resembles Psalm 48 (49), 6–11 & 16–17 (ed. Gordon, 1960):

(4) *Þeah-þe græf wille golde stregan*
broþor his geborenum, byrgan be deadum
maþmum mislicum, þæt hine mid wille,
ne mæg þære sawle þe biþ synna ful
gold to geoce for Godes egsan,
þonne he hit ær hydeð þenden he her leofað.

A rough and ready rendering:
‘Although he would strew the grave with gold, a brother for his sibling, bury/inter beside the dead one, with various treasures, that he (the survivor) wishes [to go] with him (the dead one), gold cannot [be] of help to the soul that is full of sin for fear of God, when he *stores* it *up* beforehand, while he lives here (on earth).[5]

Gordon (1960, p. 45) refers to hoarding in the notes to her edition; her Glossary, 62 renders *hȳdan* as ‘hide, hoard’. The glossary to *Eight OE poems*, which includes *The seafarer*, likewise gives the meanings ‘hide, hoard’ for the verb (Pope & Fulk, 2001, p. 192), which was the entry in earlier editions. I do not think the ‘hide’ option is the best for this passage.[6]

[5] I realize the text is problematic; Gordon (1960, p. 45) calls it ‘[p]robably the most disputed passage of the poem’. Heretically, I wonder whether it might not read better if the second and third lines were transposed? However, line three could be a delayed parallelism.

[6] The meanings in the DOE entry for *be-hȳdan* under 3b ‘stop up, block’ are easy to explain from ‘store up’, as in ‘accumulate’.

§2.2.2. Traces of the meaning 'store up' seem to linger in Middle English. Thus, from the Wycliffite Bible (manuscript Bodleian 959), Deuteronomy 32. 34:

(5) *Wheþer been not þese þyngys hud* [v.r. *hid*] *anuntys me & marked in my tresours.*
Vulgate Latin: Nonne haec condita sunt apud me, et signata in thesauris meis?
RSV: 'Is not this laid up in my store with me, and sealed in my treasuries?'

The following example from the version of the *Poema morale* in Lambeth Palace 487 l. 28 supports the idea of an old collocation, although the wording is slightly different:

(6) *Al to muchel ich habbe ispent, to litel ihud in horde.*
'I have spent all too much and (have) too little laid up in a storehouse.'

§2.3.1. There is one Old (East) Frisian token of the verb in the Fivelgoer manuscript in the text known as *Morth* 'Homicide' (ed. Buma & Ebel, 1972, p. 136 XI 5, with their translation):

(7) *Hwersa ma anna mon slaith a morth and ma hine het and helit dey ende nacht,*
'Wenn man einen Mann erschlägt und ihn Tag und Nacht verbirgt und versteckt,'

The form *het* is interpreted as the third singular present of a presumed weak verb class I *hēda**, glossed 'verbergen' by Hoffmann and Popkema (2008).[7] However, a Frisian weak verb of this shape could descend formally not only from PGmc. **huzdijan*, but also from PGmc. **hōdijan* 'care for; watch over' and, thus, be cognate with, among others, OE *hēdan* 'take charge of; care for; take notice of' (Mod. Engl. *heed*), OS *hōdian*, and OHG *huoten* 'behüten, bewachen, beobachten'.[8]

[7] Parallel texts occur only in the Emsigo manuscripts (ed. Buma & Ebel, 1967) and they lack the lexeme *hēda**: E1 VIII 36; E2 V 2; and E3 II 2.

[8] This is how van Helten took it in his *Zur Lexicologie des Altostfriesischen* (1907, p. 162 top + n. 3): 'Die 3. sg. praes. ind. zu *hēda* = as. *hōdian*, ahd. *huoten*. Wegen der bedeutung vgl. mnd. *behoeden* "verstecken"'. On the confusion of the two verbs, see §2.4.2.

However, the Old Frisian equivalent of this latter verb appears to have a different form: *hōda*, *hūda*—either with non-Frisian phonology and, therefore, a loan, or a class II by-form and, thus, lacking *i*-mutation.[9] In addition, the meanings diverge. As noted, the sole example of *hēda** is defined by Hoffmann and Popkema (2008) as 'verbergen' (as in the Buma and Ebel translation), but they give *hōda*, *hūda* such glosses as 'hüten, schützen, überwachen; bestätigen'. The formal and semantic divergence increases the likelihood that 3sg. Pres. *het* belongs to the HIDE verb.

§2.3.2. At any rate, a reflex of proto-Fris. **hȳdan* survives in the Modern Island North Frisian dialect of Föhr and Amrum: *hidjle* (*forhidjle*, *henhidjle*) 'hide' (*Fering-Öömrang Wurdenbuk* svv.), with the characteristic Island North Frisian phonological development of proto-Fris. **ȳ* seen also in *bridj* 'bride', *hidj* 'hide, skin'. By contrast, in the dialect of Sylt, *for-hüri* 'verstecken, verbergen' (Møller, 1916 s.v.) is adopted from MLG *vorhūden*; compare Sylt *Brir* 'bride', *Hid* - *Hir* 'hide, skin'.

§2.4.1. No verb comparable to those in the Gothic or Old English Bible versions is found in the section of the Old Saxon *Heliand* that corresponds to the Matthew 6.19–20 Bible passage, ll. 1642 & 1647. Instead, the text uses the 2pl. impv. *samnod* of *samnō*(*ia*)*n* 'gather, collect'. I cite the Munich manuscript.

(8) *than ne samnod gi hir sinc mikil   silobres ne goldes*   1642
an thesoro middilgard …

…

Lestead iuuua godon uuerc,   1646
samnod iu an himile   hord that mera,

However, do not gather great treasure of silver and gold in this world …
Perform good works, gather for yourself in heaven the greater store,

Nor is a cognate of Old English *hȳdan* attested anywhere else in Old Saxon.

[9] The alternative -*ū*-vocalism, which runs right through the word-family, is mirrored by the duality of *hōden* and *hūden* found in Middle Low German (see §2.4.2), arguing for the loanword interpretation.

§2.4.2. However, the verb *hide* is found in later stages of Low German and Dutch. The latter attests a verb MDut. *huden, huyden*, Mod. Dut. *huiden* (now only dialectal), with the basic meaning 'hide, conceal' (see the relevant dictionaries). This matches OE *hȳdan* from PGmc. **huzdijan*.

The *Middelnederlandsch Woordenboek* warns that *hu*(*y*)*den* is prone to confusion with the verb *hoeden, hueden* from PGmc. **hōdijan*, mentioned when discussing Old Frisian in §2.3.1. Indeed, it mentions that the Middle Low German dictionary of Schiller and Lübben (1875–1881) jumbles the two verbs: entries *hoden, huden* (II 278) *1. verstecken, verbergen. 2. Acht haben auf etwas, hüten: abs. Vieh hüten.—Refl. sich hüten* and *huden* = *hoden* (ii 326). But some confusion was obviously linguistically real (which has fuelled failures to distinguish them historically in the secondary literature). Some kind of rapprochement between the two would not be surprising, given the phonological and semantic similarity. A classic discussion of the two verbs in both languages is de Vries (1879, pp. 96–104).

§2.5. Graff (1834–1846) in his *Althochdeutscher Sprachschatz* iv 1030 cites a headword *gahurtjan*, but the example he gives is from a twelfth-century text, so Middle High German. The lexeme (*ge-*)*hürten* is glossed as follows in the *Mittelhochdeutsches Wörterbuch* (2006–) under the headword *horden*, auch *horten, hürten* '1. (etw.) (als Schatz) sammeln, anhäufen; 2. (etw.) (als Schatz) bewahren; 3. zunehmen, sich mehren, sich anhäufen'.

Graff's example is from a metrical version of Genesis, published by him (1826–1829, iii 100, but here cited after Dollmayr, 1932, pp. 123–124, ll. 4204–4211). It concerns Joseph and the years of plenty and famine in Egypt.

(9) *Ioseph nieni tuelite,*
ê er sini stadele giladite.
er saminet iz gnote
ze dere chunftigen nôte.
er wesse wole wiez irgienge,
so dere iare wurt ente,
daz er so uil ni ***gihurte****,*
so ers bidorfte.

Joseph did not delay before he stocked his barns. He gathered assiduously against the coming hardship. He knew well how it would go, when the years were at an end, that he will not have *laid up* so much (grain) as he had need of.

For some reason, this attestation is not cited by the Middle High German lexica, which are by no means exhaustive. But the following is:

Gedichte Heinrich des Teichners (ed. Niewöhner, 1953–1956, ii 87, poem 347 l. 70):

(10) *da von habent sew sich bedacht*
wuechern, ***hurten*** *tag und nacht,* (verb is the reading of MS B)

on that basis they decided
to seek profit, *accumulate* day and night

Heinrich der Teichner also uses the form *horden, horten*, as can be seen from the standard dictionaries.[10]

As the entry for *hürten* in the *Mittelhochdeutsches Wörterbuch* cited above illustrates, in the dictionaries, *hürten* is lumped together with the headword(s) *horden, horten* as a variant, but it clearly has a separate phonological history: there is no *a*-umlaut and the form must be relatively old to have undergone *i*-mutation. Because of its shape, the verb can hardly be derived recently from *hort*, but corresponds to Goth. *huzdjan*, with which the semantics fit. The fresh denominative *horden, horten* is a later creation, appearing only from Middle High German.[11]

§2.6. The only contenders for attestation of a North Germanic cognate are found in East Norse and are probably loans of the Middle Low German hybrid verb *hōden, hūden* (see §2.4.2), so have no independent value.

[10] A further supposed instance of *hürten* given in the *Mittelhochdeutsches Wörterbuch* seems to be incorrectly assigned and most probably belongs to the verb *hurten* (adopted from French) 1 intr. 'stoßend losrennen, (heran-) stürmen' 2 tr. 'etw./jmdn. (nieder-) stoßen' to give the definition of that verb in *Mittelhochdeutsches Wörterbuch*. It occurs in *Der Göttweiger Trojanerkrieg*, (ed. Koppitz, 1926) 14.613: *Fraisse dir an dinem schiltt / Hie laider ist gehürdett* and seems to mean: 'Be concerned for yourself about your shield, / Unfortunately, it has been knocked down (= damaged?)'.

[11] The situation is identical with the older form MHG *mürden* 'kill; strike' beside younger *morden*, both denominative to the noun *mord* (< PGmc. **murþaⁿ*) at different times.

Söderwall in his dictionary of medieval Swedish (1884–1918, p. 542b) gives the following citation under the entry '*hydda* (imperat. *hydda*), v. [*Mnt.* huden] *gömma*'. The example comes from a translation of the shorter version of the *Ars morienda* (wrongly) attributed to Jean Gerson, printed by Klemming (1881, p. 12 of the unnumbered pages):

(11) *y ihsi cristi helga döde beskerma ok hydda tik.*

Söderwall is using *gömma* in the sense 'preserve, protect' (not 'hide'), see the Swedish Academy's Dictionary (SAOB). So, the passage means 'in Jesus Christ's holy death protect and preserve yourself'. This would be consistent with the meanings for *hydda* v2, obsolete and dialectal given in SAOB, which starts at 1521: 'underhålla, vårda [maintain, preserve; look after]'. Both Söderwall and the SAOB give Middle Low German *huden* (*hoden*) as the etymology. The apparent absence of the lexeme from West Norse strengthens this interpretation. For the vowel shortening and consonant doubling in Swedish, see Noreen (1904, pp. 229–231 §297). An umlauted *ȳ* in the source word is presupposed.

§2.7.1. It appears from the foregoing that the original meaning of the denominative verb was something like 'make a store (of), store up, amass', while that of 'conceal' is a secondary development of the Ingvæonic languages (including Low German and Dutch).[12] It follows that the etymology needs a rethink. As Calvert Watkins observed: 'if you get the meaning wrong, the etymology will be wrong too' (1990, p. 299).

§2.7.2. At present, OE *hȳdan* and congeners are widely considered to descend directly from a PIE root √**keudʰ*-, with Gk. κεύθω 'I cover; hide, conceal' regularly cited as another reflex.[13] However, in addition to the semantic inadequacy, this connection has a number of formal drawbacks.

[12] Any verb meaning 'store something' has the connotation 'securely' and this can readily encompass 'store something in secret', which is well on the way to 'conceal, hide something'. Compare the meanings of Lat. *recondō*.

English shows an archaism in preserving the older meaning alongside 'conceal' (see §2.2).

[13] For example de Vries (1879, p. 96); Mnl. Wb. s.v. *huden*; Onions et al. (1966) s.v. *hide*[3]; Kluge and Seebold (2011) s.v. *Hort*; Hellquist (1939) s.v. *hydda* expresses doubt: 'osäker'.

- it is not a canonical Indo-European root shape[14]
- one would expect the reflex to show up in Germanic as a (primary) verb with an *e*-grade (class 2) present and a strong preterite, rather than with a zero-grade present and a weak preterite
- there seems to be no reason why it should have a *-ja*-present
- one has to assume a special ablaut innovation, lengthening of the zero-grade to **-ū-*, which is precisely best represented in class 2 strong verbs

An alternative suggestion (Szemerényi, 1980, p. 49) is that the verb is a Germanic denominative to the noun **hūđi-* ‘hide, skin’, assuming a basic meaning ‘cover’ (and sometimes assuming derivation from the same root √**keudh-*, which seems rather abstract, even though skin is a covering), but, apart from the formal problems, such semantics are not compatible with those of Goth. *huzdjan* and the newly established meaning for Germanic. The long vowel of **hūđi-* itself would also need explaining.

The idea that not only Goth. *huzdjan* and MHG *(ge-)hürten*, but also OE *hȳdan*, etc. are denominative to PGmc. *huzda*^{n},[15] as elaborated above, is clearly to be preferred to these proposals. Etymological identity of the verbs is suggested by comparison of the Gothic and Old English renderings of Matthew 6.19–20 (§§2.1–2.2.1). The phonological development has been dealt with at the end of §2.2.1. OE *hordian* (cf. n. 4) is a fresh denominative, while MHG *horten* is an independent denominative (cf. §2.5).

§2.7.3. However, we are not rid of the alleged Indo-European root √**keudʰ-* ‘hide’ so easily, because it is deemed to underlie the base noun PGmc. *huzda*^{n} itself: Goth. *huzd* N; ON *hodd* F (poetry only); OE *hord* M,N; OS *hord* N (*Heliand* only); OHG *hort* N.

We saw in §2.7.2 n. 14 that the Greek and Iranian verbs do not need this construct. So, what is left that √**keudʰ-* is meant to explain are

[14] LIV^2 358 s.r. √**keu̯dʰ-* comments in n 1: ‘Das gr. und besonders das iran. Material wäre gut mit **gʰeu̯dʰ-* vereinbar’; the (Middle) Iranian initial otherwise needs to be explained by contamination. LIV^2 wishes to keep OE *hȳdan* separate, following Szemerényi (1980).

[15] So far as I know, Siebs was the first to suggest such an origin for the English and Frisian verbs (1901, p. 1259), although his further comparanda were incorrect. Klein (1979, p. 441 with n. 89) endorses Siebs’ basic etymology. Neither mentions the Matthew 6.19–20 locus.

huzda- and possibly Lat. *custōs*.[16] The three-witness condition is not met and they are adjacent West-Indo-European dialects, and the words could have a quite different origin or not be related. Further, the phonological development required to obtain the Germanic form is dubious (see further Casaretto, 2004, p. 461).

Beyond all this, the semantics still do not match particularly well. PGmc *huzda*ⁿ means 'a store (laid up), a store of things; treasure', which casts doubt on the connection.[17] A store of things or even a treasure does not have to be concealed; one stores things in a barn quite openly, for example. But the idea of doing it securely is inherent (hence the barn); similarly, a valuable heirloom may be displayed, but guarded. A hidden thing does not have to be a store or a treasure (it might be a cosh). The idea that OE *hȳdan* and Ingvæonic correspondents meaning 'conceal' descend directly from the supposed root √**keudʱ-* seems to have influenced attempts to explain *huzda*ⁿ. In my view, the semantic development works better the other way. Starting from a noun 'a store (laid up), a store of things; treasure', a derived verb meaning 'store up' is easy to envisage (and is attested in Goth. *huzdjan*). A suggested trajectory for the development to the meaning 'conceal' is given in n. 12.[18]

2 3. Goth. *wilwan*.

§3.1. Gothic has a class 3 strong verb *wilwan* with the meaning 'seize, snatch; plunder',[19] which also occurs with the prefixes *dis-* and *fra-*. The principle parts attested are: *wilwan*, *-wilwiþ*; *-walw*;—; *wulwans*. It has

[16] Rix's explanation for *custōs* as **kudʱ-to-sd-* as 'beim Schatz sitzend' (LIV² 359) is perhaps more ingenious than convincing.

[17] The North Germanic noun *hydda* etc. (Söderwall, 1884–1918, i 542) usually glossed as 'hut' is sometimes thought to belong to the alleged 'conceal' family of words (e.g. Hellquist, 1939 s.vv. *hydda* and *hytta*). It is, nonetheless, conceivable that, like its cognate Germ. *Hütte*, it does belong with **huzda*ⁿ and **huzdijan* after all and originally meant something like 'storehouse' and referred to a relatively small outbuilding.

[18] Concerning **keudʱ-* in Germanic, Adams (1994) posits **daug-*, a metathesized *o*-grade variant **dʱeuk-* with Verner's Law, which seems unlikely after a full-grade root, but it could just as easily be **dʱeugʱ-*, metathesized from **gʱeu̯dʱ-* (cf. n. 14). On this base in Germanic, see also Dietz (2000) (without mention of Adams).

[19] The meaning is frequently given as 'rob, räuben', but this is inaccurate (see the examples below), and presumably stems from Streitberg's glossary (1998, ii 175).

no Germanic cognates (cf. Seebold, 1970, p. 554). Its use can be illustrated by the following examples:[20]

(12) John 6.15: *iþ Iēsus kunnands þatei munaidēdun usgaggan jah* ***wilwan*** *<ina> ei tawidēdeina ina du þiudana, afiddja aftra in fairguni is ains.*
ἰησοῦς οὖν γνοὺς ὅτι μέλλουσιν ἔρχεσθαι καὶ **ἁρπάζειν** αὐτὸν ἵνα ποιήσωσιν βασιλέα ἀνεχώρησεν πάλιν εἰς τὸ ὄρος αὐτὸς μόνος.
'But Jesus, perceiving that they would come out and *seize* him, so that they might make him a king, went off again to a mountain himself alone'.

(13) Mark 3.27: *ni manna mag kasa swinþis galeiþands in gard is* ***wilwan****, niba faurþis þana swinþan gabindiþ; jah <þan> þana gard is* ***diswilwai****.*
οὐδεὶς δύναται τὰ σκεύη τοῦ ἰσχυροῦ εἰσελθὼν εἰς τὴν οἰκίαν αὐτοῦ **διαρπάσαι** ἐὰν μὴ πρῶτον τὸν ἰσχυρὸν δήσῃ, καὶ τότε τὴν οἰκίαν αὐτοῦ **διαρπάσῃ**.
'A man cannot *seize* a strong man's goods, entering his house, except he beforehand binds the strong man; and then *he may plunder* his house'.

Based on this sole occurrence, *diswilwan* does not appear to differ much in meaning from the simplex verb; one can distinguish 'seize his goods' (*wilwan*) from 'he may plunder his house' (*diswilwai*), but this may be just the result of the need to find translation equivalents. The Greek verbs are the same.

(14) John 10.28: *jah ik libain aiweinōn giba im, jah ni fraqistnand aiw, jah ni* ***frawilwiþ*** *ƕashun þō us handau meinai.*
κἀγὼ δίδωμι αὐτοῖς ζωὴν αἰώνιον, καὶ οὐ μὴ ἀπόλωνται εἰς τὸν αἰῶνα, καὶ οὐχ **ἁρπάσει** τις αὐτὰ ἐκ τῆς χειρός μου.
'And I give them eternal life; and they shall not ever perish, neither shall anyone *snatch* them out of my hand.

(15) Luke 8.29 *untē anabaud ahmin þamma unhrainjin usgaggan af þamma mann; manag auk mēl* ***frawalw*** *ina, jah bundans was eisarnabandjōm jah fōtubandjōm fastaiþs was,*

[20] The total attestation is as follows: simplex Jh 6.15; Mk 3.27; Mt 7.15; *dis-* MK 3.27; *fra-* Jh 10.29, 28, 12; Mt 11.12; 1Thes 4.17; LK 8.29; 2Cor 12.2, 4.
The Greek words translated are: ἁρπάζειν, (*dis-*) δι-ἁρπάζειν, (*fra-*) also συν-ἁρπάζειν.

παρήγγειλεν γὰρ τῷ πνεύματι τῷ ἀκαθάρτῳ ἐξελθεῖν ἀπὸ τοῦ ἀνθρώπου. πολλοῖς γὰρ χρόνοις **συνηρπάκει** αὐτόν, καὶ ἐδεσμεύετο ἁλύσεσιν καὶ πέδαις φυλασσόμενος
'For he had commanded the unclean spirit to come out of the man. For many times it had *seized* him: and he was bound with chains and was held in fetters'.

(16) 2 Cor 12.2: *wait mannan in Xristau faur jēra fidwōrtaihun, ...* ***frawulwanana*** *þana swaleikana und þridjan himin*;
οἶδα ἄνθρωπον ἐν χριστῷ πρὸ ἐτῶν δεκατεσσάρων ... **ἁρπαγέντα** τὸν τοιοῦτον ἕως τρίτου οὐρανοῦ.
'I knew a man in Christ 14 years ago, ... such a one *snatched up* to the third heaven'.

§3.2. There are two associated nouns. One is an agent noun *wilwa* M *an*-stem (3×) ἅρπαξ 'extortioner, robber', Lk 18.11; 1Cor 5.10 & 11. The other is an abstract *wulwa** F *ō*-stem ἁρπαγμός; both the Greek and the Gothic words are hapaxes, occurring only at Philippians 2.6, and, as the meaning of the Greek term is not entirely clear—indeed, it is one of the most discussed words in the New Testament (cf. Martin, 2016)—neither is the Gothic.

(17) Philippians 2.6: *saei in gudaskaunein wisands ni* ***wulwa*** *rahnida wisan sik galeiko guda*,
—ὃς ἐν μορφῇ θεοῦ ὑπάρχων οὐχ **ἁρπαγμὸν** ἡγήσατο τὸ εἶναι ἴσα θεῷ,

I favour the following rendering, although I realize it might not reflect the way the Gothic translator understood the Greek:

> who, though existing in the form of God, did not regard equality with God as *something to be seized upon (as an advantage)*

These derivatives are based on the verb, cf. Casaretto (2004, pp. 96, 97, 101, 208–209, 587). If, as seems likely, they are relatively recent (that is of Proto-Germanic date at the oldest), they can tell us nothing about the earlier shape or semantics of the verb.

§3.3. On three occasions *wilwan* occurs with the word for 'wolf' *wulfs*.

(18) John 10.12: *iþ asneis jah saei nist hairdeis, þizei ni sind lamba swēsa, gasaihviþ wulf qimandan jah bileiþiþ þaim lambam jah þliuhiþ, jah sa wulfs* ***frawilwiþ*** *þō jah distahjiþ þō lamba.*
ὁ μισθωτὸς καὶ οὐκ ὢν ποιμήν, οὗ οὐκ ἔστιν τὰ πρόβατα ἴδια, θεωρεῖ τὸν λύκον ἐρχόμενον καὶ ἀφίησιν τὰ πρόβατα καὶ φεύγει—καὶ ὁ λύκος **ἁρπάζει** αὐτὰ καὶ σκορπίζει τὰ πρόβατα.
'But a hireling, and he who is not the shepherd, whose own the sheep are not, sees the wolf coming, and leaves the sheep, and flees: and the wolf *seizes* them, and scatters the sheep.'

(19) Matthew 7.15: *atsaihviþ swēþauh faura liugnapraufētum þaim izei qimand at izwis in wastjōm lambē, iþ innaþrō sind wulfōs* ***wilwandans.***
προσέχετε ἀπὸ τῶν ψευδοπροφητῶν, οἵτινες ἔρχονται πρὸς ὑμᾶς ἐν ἐνδύμασιν προβάτων, ἔσωθεν δέ εἰσιν λύκοι **ἅρπαγες**.
'But beware of false prophets, of those who come to you in the clothing of sheep, but inwardly they are *ravening* wolves.'

(20) Bologna Palimpsest 2^{v} 16–18 seems to allude to Matthew 7.15: *þaiei iddjēdun in wastjōm lambē· iþ innaþrō þa(n) s<i>nd wulfōs* ***wilwandans.***
'who go in the clothing of sheep, but inwardly are *ravening* wolves'

§3.4. In a one-page article, de Saussure (1889b) suggests that Goth. *wilwan* might continue the Indo-European root from which the word for 'wolf' is derived: 'C'est très probablement du verbe **welk₂ō* que la langue primitive avait tiré **w̥lk₂o-s* «le loup», qui pour l'Arien a toujours été synonyme de brigand.' He went on to say: 'La vague sentiment de cette parenté subsistait peut-être encore lorsque Ulfilas écrivait *wulfs frawilwiþ, wulfōs wilwandans* ...' If the surmise is correct, this would mean that these phrases are faded figurae etymologicae, as de Saussure seems to be hinting.

§3.5. As is well known, the *-f-* of *wulfs* derives from a proto-Indo-European voiceless labiovelar; this is also a possible source of the *-w-* in the family of *wilwan*. There, it would be the reflex of the voiced Verner's Law alternant and presupposes levelling of the past allomorph throughout the verbal paradigm. This is not unparalleled: Goth. *hvairban* 'turn, roam' (only present forms attested), beside OE *hweorfan* and OS preterite singular *hwarf*, plural *hwurbun*, has levelled the consonantism of the preterite plural and past participle. By contrast, Goth. *saiƕan saƕ sēƕun saiƕans* has generalized the consonantism of the present through the averbo, while a reflex of the voiced alternant occurs in the associated *siuns* 'sight'.

§3.6. Despite an impressive array of cognates,[21] the Indo-Anatolian proto-form of the word for 'wolf', **u̯ĺ̥kʷos*, is technically no more than a formal equation, not an etymology, in so far as it lacks an established source (the root or other form from which it is derived) and a naming-motif. De Saussure's proposal would go some way to supplying both.

Current attempts to motivate the 'wolf' word posit a substantivized adjective. The form **u̯ĺ̥kʷos* is somewhat aberrant in Indo-Anatolian terms, in that it shows an accented zero-grade. While this is not unparalleled (the word for 'bear' **h₂ŕ̥tk̂os* and the numeral '7' **septḿ̥* come to mind), one could posit a thematic adjective ***u̯l̥kʷós*, with (for the sake of argument) a presumed meaning 'marauding, rapacious'; substantivized as **u̯ĺ̥kʷos* 'the marauding, rapacious one', possibly a taboo designation. (Hence some of the deformations among the cognates? See n. 21.) A convenient parallel for a substantivized thematic adjective of this type with accented zero-grade is provided by OInd. *kŕ̥ṣṇa-* '(black) antelope' (RV+) from *kr̥ṣṇá-* 'black', which continues in this use.[22]

§3.7.1. The Vedic privative adjective *a-vr̥ká-* 'unharmful; unthreatening' looks as if it could be formed, instead of from the noun 'wolf', from just this projected adjective. However, negative compounds whose

[21] Toch. B *walkwe*; OInd. *vŕ̥ka-*, YAv. *vəhrka-* (Hoffmann & Forssman, 2004, p. 92 §58ca & 112 §83A1); Goth. *wulfs*; Lith. *vil̃kas*; OCSl *vlьkъ*. Metathesized forms occur in Gk. λύκος; Lat. *lupus* (if it is a descendant, it has rural consonantism); and possibly OIr. *luch-* (McCone, 1985, pp. 175–176). A further variant appears in OAlb. *ulk*; and possibly the Old Irish name-element *Olc-* (see §3.7.2 for the phonology).

[22] Balto-Slavic offers a neat parallel in the family of Lith. *liũtas* 'lion'. This is the substantivization of an adjective *liũtas* 'wild, predatory, ruthless' found in dialects, but obsolete in the standard language. The adjective, adopted from Slavic, is attested in Old Lithuanian in the phrase *liũtas lẽvas* 'ferocious lion' in the 1573 Wolfenbüttel Postil (8ʳ 26). (The noun *lẽvas* 'lion' is now obsolete.) The phrase is echoed by Old Belarusian *ljutŭ levŭ*, and the adjective is widespread in Slavic languages, e.g., Russ. лютый 'ferocious, fierce, cruel'. Lehrman (1987, p. 17), recalling storytelling in his childhood, remarks that the Russian adjective can be used substantially 'to refer to aggressive quadrupeds, such as "lion" ..., "wolf", "bear", and "lynx", and even a ferocious steed'.

second member is an adjective tend to be accented on the negative particle, which makes derivation from the noun perhaps more likely (although the accent could be the result of secondary association with *vŕ̥ka-* 'wolf'). Semantically, the existence of RV *á-vājin-** M 'a poor-quality horse' (3.53.23) makes it seem less likely that *a-vr̥ká-* is built to 'wolf' (its accent is another matter).

The Vedic noun *vr̥káti* M 'Verderber, Räuber' (to give Graßmann's (1873) definition) is something of a puzzle morphologically, with its masculine gender and apparent derivation from a nominal base rather than a verbal root. It is probably too large a stretch to assume that it is derived from de Saussure's verb, although the semantics would fit well. All in all, however, it cannot contribute anything decisive to the matter in hand.

Ved. *vr̥kátāt* F 'Verderben, Raubanschlag' is a type of formation that is overwhelmingly de-adjectival, which provides some evidence for an (earlier) adjective.

Ved. *vr̥kāyú* adj. 'böse gesinnt, mordlustig' could be based on either a noun or an adjective.

The Old Indic evidence is suggestive of an underlying adjective, but ultimately equivocal.

§3.7.2. Old Irish has an adjective *olc*, glossed 'evil, bad, wrong' by the eDIL, which could descend from a pre-form **u̯l̥k*^{w}*ós*, with a phonological development parallel to that seen in *olann* 'wool' < **ulanā* < *h_2*u̯l̥*h_1*néh*$_2$- 'wool' (see the discussion in McCone, 1985, pp. 174–175). Semantically, rather than being forced to posit a development from 'wolf' to 'evil' (see McCone's suggestion 1985, p. 174), one could see a direct reflex of the presumed Indo-Anatolian adjective 'harmful, dangerous; (?hostile)'—compare the Vedic meaning of *a-vr̥ká-* 'unharmful; unthreatening'.

A reflex of the noun 'wolf' itself could be preserved in the elements *Olc-* and *Luch-*, which appear in personal-names (cf. McCone, 1985, pp. 172–174 & 175–76; and cf. n. 21 here).

§3.7.3. Anatolian evidence has also been adduced in the discussion of the word for 'wolf'.

Hittite has a twice-attested neuter noun *walkuwa-* of uncertain meaning, but generally considered to have negative connotations.

(21) KBo 22.2 obv.

1. [MUNUS.LUGA]L ^{URU}*Ka-ni-iš* 30 DUMU^{MEŠ} 1^{EN} MU-*an-ti ḫa-a-aš-ta UM-MA ŠI=MA*
2. [*ki*]-*i=u̯a ku-it u̯a-al-ku-an ḫa-a-aš-ḫu-un*

'The Queen of Kaniš bore 30 sons in one year. She (spoke) thus: 'What kind of *u̯a-al-ku-an* did I give birth to?'

(22) KBo 3.40b+

15. … *ú-k=u-uš pu-nu-uš-ke-m*[*i ki-i=u̯a? k*]*u-it u̯a-al-ku-u̯a-an*
16. [ ]x[-*t*]*e?-ni UM-MA ŠU-NU=MA* ERÍN^{MEŠ} [*Ḫur-r*]*i*(?) *ut-ni-i̯a ú-ez-zi*

'I ask them: "What [kind of] *u̯a-al-ku-u̯a-an* do you (pl.) […]?". They answer: "The [Hurr]ian army comes to the country"' (cf. Soysal, 1987, pp. 177 & 181).

Walkuwa- is often taken to mean something like 'monstrosity'. The most natural immediate Anatolian pre-form would have the shape **walgwan-* with voiced velar. However, the shape does not fit the rules for lenition of a voiceless velar in Hittite (as it is not between two unaccented morae). The word could be a substantivized adjective, but the form cannot continue earlier ***u̯l̥k*^{w}*ó-* directly (which would have given ‹ulkuwa-›), although it could alternatively be a nominal derivative of the same root. If related to 'wolf', pre-forms **u̯elk*^{w}*o-* or **u̯olk*^{w}*o-* are phonologically possible. This material would adjust the semantics of the presumed adjective to something like 'monstrous' or 'ferocious', which is not far from 'harmful, dangerous'.

However, it seems to me that a meaning 'troop, multitude' vel sim. for *walkuwa-* would suit both contexts well, as suggested by Hoffner (1980, p. 290), comparing the Latin *o*-stem noun *volgus* (later *vulgus*) M or N 'crowd, multitude', although the equation is not entirely straightforward. The Hittite form could be an extended *u*-stem **u̯olgu-*, and this latter could underlie the Latin *o*-stem. If cognate, OInd. *várga-* M 'class, set, group, company, family, party, side', also points to an *o*-stem, however. If we accept Hoffner's analysis, then the word would have nothing to do with 'wolf' or such things.

Luwian has a noun *walwa/i-* (with secondary *i*-inflection) meaning 'lion, sphinx', which is explicable as a substantivization, semantically parallel to 'wolf', of the projected Indo-Anatolian adjective (Lehrman, 1987; Herbordt, 2005, pp. 294–295; Craig Melchert personal communication), but with an apparent dialectal development of the labiovelar. There is also a personal name *Walkwi*, presumably also meaning 'lion', with the expected labiovelar reflex. The naming motif would be 'the ferocious one' (cf. n. 22). This may or may not be related to the Hittite lexeme. The Luwian data would appear to offer better evidence for a form related to 'wolf'.

Lydian *walwe-** 'lion'offers independent evidence for this interpretation; see Dale (2015).

§3.7.4. The Greek abstract noun λύσσα '(martial) frenzy' (also 'rabies' in later texts) < **luk*^{w}*-i̯a* could derive from an adjective 'ferocious' rather than be an abstract based upon the noun λύκος 'wolf' (as argued by Risch, 1973, p. 137; Lincoln, 1975). However, the derivation from 'wolf' remains plausible.

§3.8. Thematic adjectives of the type under discussion are often derived from verbal roots, so the posited ***u̯l̥k*^{w}*ós* 'marauding, rapacious' or 'ferocious, dangerous' could belong to a root of the shape √***u̯elk*^{w}-. As we have seen, this could be continued formally in Goth. *wilwan*.

Semantically, if one focuses on the substantivized adjective, one is in the territory of 'evil, dangerous one'; if one goes down the verb path, then it is more like 'snatcher, marauder'. The two meanings could be reconciled by positing an earlier meaning for the verb 'be ferocious', which then developed as follows down into Gothic: → 'run amok' → 'act like a predator', via transitivization to 'maraud' to 'plunder; seize'. The meaning 'seize' can be neutral, as well as negative, in Gothic, see (14) & (16).

§3.9. Concerning a possible Indo-Anatolian source verb for Goth. *wilwan*, Alfred Bammesberger kindly draws my attention to the verb reflected in Lith. *vil̃kti* 'drag', present 1sg. *velkù*, OCSl. *vlěkǫ* 'drag, tug'. It is certainly a good formal match, as the Balto-Slavic velar is likely to reflect a labiovelar and it shows a thematic present. However, if, with (Schindler and) *LIV*^{2} 289–290 s.v. *h_2u̯elk-*, one associates YAv. **-vərəciṇta* (3pl. pres. inj.) 'dragged off' and the Greek noun αὖλαξ 'furrow ← *having been drawn', then this root meant 'drag (away)' from early on. One would then have to abandon the other line of inquiry that derives the noun 'wolf' from an adjective meaning 'harmful; monstrous'. The Gothic collocations would then be phrases that accidentally have the aspect of obscured figurae etymologicae.

Alternatively, if we wanted to derive 'wolf' from this verb at the Indo-Anatolian stage as 'the one that drags things away', we must reject an initial laryngeal and, hence, the Greek noun as a cognate.

However, there is a further option that reverts to the derivation of the noun 'wolf' from an adjective meaning 'harmful; monstrous'. If one excludes the Avestan and Greek forms, the Balto-Slavic material could then go back to the surmised early verb 'be ferocious' (§3.8) from which 'wolf' is derived via substantivization of an adjective. It would, thus, belong with the Germanic (i.e., Gothic) verb along the lines that I have sketched. It would have shared the semantic development at a presumed Germanic–Balto-Slavic stage all the way to a neutral sense 'seize/drag'. Alternatively, the Balto-Slavic family could have been adopted from Germanic. However, shorn of wider cognates, it becomes a root candidate rather than an established root.

§3.10. Goth. *wilwan* is widely taken to be related to Lat *volvere* 'roll, turn' < **u̯el-u̯-*, Gk. (ϝ)ειλύω 'roll up' and variants.[23] This would involve assuming that in Gothic the *w*-present-formant was generalized throughout all tense forms, creating a new root-shape.[24] However, even creative attempts to explain the semantics, utilizing such ideas as 'turning something over to someone else' or 'rolling something to oneself', hardly bring us to 'snatch' and 'take by force'. Indeed, in Greek and Latin the verb often depicts a submissive state, where someone is crouched or curled up or 'rolls over' before an aggressor or worse.

(23) *Iliad* 24.509–510, when Priam has come to ransom his son Hector's body from the Greek champion Akhilles:

τὼ δὲ μνησαμένω, ὃ μὲν Ἕκτορος ἀνδροφόνοιο
κλαῖ' ἁδινὰ προπάροιθε ποδῶν Ἀχιλῆος **ἐλυσθείς**,
'The pair of them remembering, the one was weeping copiously for man-slaying Hektor, *rolled up* (= crouched) before Akhilles' feet …'

[23] Thus Holthausen (1934, p. 125), Feist (1939, p. 564), Seebold (1970, p. 554), and Lehmann (1986, W–67); *LIV*² 675 sees Goth. *wilwan* as continuing a *-u*-present to √**u̯el-* 'turn'.

[24] It is possible that there had been a Germanic strong verb ***wilwan* with such a history, from which the Gothic weak verb *-walwjan** 'roll' was derived, as de Saussure (1889b) notes.

(24) *Æneid* 9.433:
volvitur *Euryalus leto*
'Euryalus *rolls over* in death'

One cannot but concur with de Saussure (1889b) that: 'le *wilwan* de nos textes, qui signifie *ravir, emporter de force* (ἁρπάζειν), n'a vraisemblablement rien de commun avec cette famille.'

§3.11. Isolated archaisms are always possible. Germanic offers a parallel for a proto-Indo-Anatolian primary verb attested solely in this branch in its original meaning—and at a later stage of a single dialect to boot: early ME *wesan** 'pasture, tend (livestock)':

(25) Life of St Margaret (ed. Mack, 1934, pp. 6 & 9–11):
he … seh … Margarete, as ha ***wes*** *7 wiste up o þe feld hire fost[er] modres schep*
'he … saw … Margaret … as she *tended* and guarded on the field her fostermother's sheep'

See Stiles (1985, 2004). *LIV*^{2} lists the root as 3. **u̯es-*, but lacks this crucial example.

At present, the data are insufficient to establish the case for a presumed proto-Indo-Anatolian root √***u̯elkʷ-* being the derivational basis of 'wolf'; nor does it seem possible to disprove it. However, the circumstantial evidence is strong. The formal and semantic aspects argue for continuing to report the idea in etymological discussions.[25]

References

Adams, D. Q. (1994). A Tocharo-Germanic correspondence. TochB *tuk-* 'be hidden' and OE *dēog* 'she concealed himself" [sic, for he—PVS]. *Zeitschrift für vergleichende Sprachforschung, 107*, 310–312.

[25] Producing this article would not have been possible without help generously given by a number of individuals, who do not thereby endorse its contents. I should like to thank: Alfred Bammesberger, Michele Bianconi, the editors of the Dictionary of Old English, Carla Falluomini, Anne Helene Feulner, Jay Jasanoff, Jarich Hoekstra, Ron Kim, Jesse Lundquist, Craig Melchert, Henrik Rosenkvist, Matteo Tarsi, Elizabeth Tucker, Anthony Yates, and the editors of this volume.

Buma, W. J., & Ebel, W. (Eds.). (1967). *Das Emsiger Recht.* Vandenhoeck & Ruprecht.
Buma, W. J., & Ebel, W. (Eds.). (1972). *Das Fivelgoer Recht.* Vandenhoeck & Ruprecht.
Casaretto, A. (2004). *Nominale Wortbildung der gotischen Sprache. Die Derivation der Substantiva.* Winter.
Dale, A. (2015). WALWET and KUKALIM. Lydian coin legends, dynastic succession and the chronology of Mermnad kings. *Kadmos, 54*, 151–166.
Dietz, K. (2000). Altenglisch *digol, digle*, 'verborgen', 'heimlich'. Etymologie und Geschichte einer Wortfamilie. *Sprachwissenschaft, 25*, 200–227.
DOE = *Dictionary of Old English.* 1986–. University of Toronto. https://doe.artsci.utoronto.ca
Dollmayr, V. (Ed.). (1932). *Die altdeutsche Genesis nach der Wiener Handschrift.* Max Niemeyer.
eDIL = *Electronic dictionary of the Irish language.* Elaborated from the Royal Irish Academy's *Dictionary of the Irish Language* based mainly on Old and Middle Irish materials 1913–1976. Available at https://dil.ie
EWAI = Mayrhofer, M. (1986–2001). *Etymologisches Wörterbuch des Altindoarischen.* Carl Winter.
Feist, S. (1939). *Vergleichendes Wörterbuch der gotischen Sprache*[3]. E. J. Brill.
Fering-ÖÖmrang Wurdenbuk. (2002). *Wörterbuch der friesischen Mundart von Föhr und Amrum*, herausgegeben von der Nordfriesischen Wörterbuchstelle der Christian-Albrecht-Universität Kiel. Wachholtz.
Godden, M. (Ed.). (1979). *Ælfric's Catholic homilies, the second series. Text.* Oxford University Press.
Gordon, I. L. (Ed.). (1960). *The seafarer.* Methuen.
Graff, E. G. (Ed.). (1826–1829). *Diutiska. Denkmäler deutscher Sprache und Literatur, aus alten Handschriften.* Cotta.
Graff, E. G. (Ed.). (1834–1846). *Althochdeutscher Sprachschatz oder Wörterbuch der althochdeutschen Sprache.* Nicolaische Buchhandlung.
Graßmann, H. (1873). *Wörterbuch zum Rig-Veda.* O. Harrassowitz.
Hellquist, E. (1939). *Svensk etymologisk ordbok. Ny upplaga.* C. W. K. Gleerup.
Helten, W. L. v. (1907). *Zur Lexicologie des Altostfriesischen.* J. Müller.
Herbordt, S. (2005). *Die Prinzen- und Beamtensiegel der hethitischen Grossreichszeit auf Tonbullen aus dem Nişantepe-Archiv in Hattusa.* von Zabern.
Hoffmann, K., & Forssman, B. (2004). *Avestische Laut- und Formenlehre*[2]. Institut für Sprachen und Literaturen der Universität.
Hoffner, H. A. Jr. (1980). Histories and historians of the ancient Near East. The Hittites'. *Orientalia, 49*, 283–332.

Hofmann, D., & Popkema, A. (2008). *Altfriesisches Handwörterbuch*. Winter.

Holthausen, F. (1934). *Gotisches etymologisches Wörterbuch mit Einschluss der Eigennamen und der gotischen Lehnwörter im Romanischen*. Carl Winter.

Jost, K. (1950). *Wulfstanstudien*. A. Francke.

KBo = *Keilschrifttexte aus Boghazköi*. (1916–).

Klein, T. (1979). Zum altniederländischen 'Leidener Willeram' und zu einigen westgermanischen Pronominalformen. *Zeitschrift für deutsche Philologie, 98*, 425–447.

Klemming, G. E. (Ed.). (1881). *(Ars moriendi) Gersons lärdom huru man skall dö. Tryckt i Upsala 1514 (facsimile)*. Det Kungliga Boktryckeriet.

Kluge, F., & Seebold, E. (2011). *Etymologisches Wörterbuch der deutschen Sprache*^{25}. De Gruyter.

Koppitz, A. (Ed.). (1926). *Der Göttweiger Trojanerkrieg*. Weidmann.

Lehmann, W. P. (1986). *A Gothic etymological dictionary*. E. J. Brill.

Lehrman, A. (1987). Anatolian cognates of the PIE word for 'wolf'. *Die Sprache, 33*, 13–18.

Lincoln, B. (1975). Homeric λύσσα: 'wolfish rage'. *Indogermanische Forschungen, 80*, 98–105.

LIV^{2} = Rix, H., & Kümmel, M. (2001). *Lexikon der indogermanischen Verben. Die Wurzeln und ihre Primärstammbildungen*^{2}. Reichert.

Mack, F. M. (Ed.). (1934). *Seinte Marherete, þe meiden ant martyr*. Oxford University Press.

Martin, M. W. (2016). ἁρπαγμός revisited. A philological reexamination of the New Testament's 'most difficult word'. *Journal of Biblical literature, 135*, 175–194.

McCone, K. (1985). Varia II. OIr. *Olc*, *Luch-* and IE _*wĺ̥k^{w}os,*lúk^{w}os_ 'wolf'. *Ériu, 36*, 171–176.

Mittelhochdeutsches Wörterbuch. (2006–). Mainzer Akademie der Wissenschaften und der Literatur und Akademie der Wissenschaften zu Göttingen.Stuttgart: Hirzel. A fuller version is available at https://www.mhdwb-online.de/

Mnl. Wb. = Verwijs, E., & Verdam, J. (Eds.). (1885–1929). *Middelnederlandsch woordenboek*. Martinus Nijhoff. https://ivdnt.org/woordenboeken/middelnederlandsch-woordenboek/.

Møller, B. P. (1916). *Söl'ring Uurterbok. Wörterbuch der Sylter Mundart*. Otto Meissner.

Napier, A. (Ed.). (1883). *Wulfstan. Sammlung der ihm zugeschriebenen Homilien nebst Untersuchungen über ihre Echtheit*. Weidmann.

Niewöhner, H. (Ed.). (1953–1956). *Die Gedichte Heinrich des Teichners.* Akademie-Verlag.
Noreen, A. (1904). *Altnordische Grammatik ii, Altschwedische Grammatik, mit Einschluss des Altgutnischen.* Max Niemeyer.
Onions, C. T., Friedrichsen, G. W. S., & Burchfield, R. W. (1966). *The Oxford dictionary of English etymology.* With the assistance of G. W. S. Friedrichsen and R. W. Burchfield. Clarendon Press.
Pope, J. C. (Ed.). (2001). *Eight Old English poems*[3], rev. Robert D. Fulk. W. W. Norton.
Risch, E. (1973). *Wortbildung der homerischen Sprache*[2]. Walter de Gruyter.
SAOB = *Svenska Akademiens ordbok.* (1898–2021). C. W. K. Gleerup. https://saob.se
Saussure, F. de. (1889a). Sanscrit *stōkā-s. Mémoires de la Société de Linguistique de Paris, 6,* 162 (Reprinted in *Recueil des publications scientifiques de Ferdinand de Saussure,* 419. Sonor / Lausanne: Payot / Heidelberg: Carl Winter).
Saussure, F. de. (1889b). Gotique *wilwan. Mémoires de la Société de Linguistique de Paris, 6,* 358 (Reprinted in 1922 in *Recueil des publications scientifiques de Ferdinand de Saussure,* 434. Sonor / Lausanne: Payot / Heidelberg: Carl Winter).
Schiller, K., & Lübben, A. (1875–1881). *Mittelniederdeutsches Wörterbuch.* J. Kühtmann.
Seebold, E. (1970). *Vergleichendes und etymologisches Wörterbuch der germanischen starken Verben.* Mouton.
Siebs, T. (1901). Geschichte der friesischen Sprache. In H. Paul (ed.), *Grundriss der germanischen Philologie*[2] (i 1152–1464). Karl J. Trübner.
Skeat, W. W. (Ed.). (1887). *The Gospel according to Saint Matthew in Anglo-Saxon, Northumbrian, and old Mercian versions.* Cambridge University Press.
Söderwall, K. F. (1884–1918). *Ordbok öfver Svenska Medeltids-Språket.* Berlingska Boktryckeri.
Soysal, O. (1987). KUB XXXI 4 + KBo III 41 und 40 (Die Puḫanu-Chronik). *Zum Thronstreit Ḫattušilis I'. Hethitica, 7,* 73–253.
Stiles, P. V. (1985). EME (AB) *wes.* A reflex of IE **wes-* 'to pasture, tend (livestock)'? *Zeitschrift für vergleichende Sprachforschung, 98,* 295–301.
Stiles, P. V. (2004). Consumer issues. Beowulf 3115a and Germanic 'bison'. In J. H. W. Penney (Ed.), *Perspectives on Indo-European. Studies in honour of Anna Morpurgo Davies* (pp. 461–473). Oxford University Press.
Streitberg, W. (Ed.). (1998). *Die Gotische Bibel*[7] (P. Scardigli, ed.). Winter.
Szemerényi, O. (1980). Iranica VI (Nos. 71–75)'. *Studia Iranica, 9,* 23–68.

Vries, M. d. (1879). Middelnederlandsche Verscheidenheden (Critiek en Verklaring). *Taalkundige bijdragen, 2*, 62–104.

Watkins, C. (1990). Etymologies, equations, and comparanda. Types and values, and criteria for judgment. In P. Baldi (Ed.), *Linguisitic change and reconstruction methodology* (pp. 289–303). Mouton de Gruyter.

18

South Oscan κλοπουστ (with an Appendix on [Osco-?]Lat. BVRVS)

Brent Vine

1 Introductory

1.1. South Oscan κλοπουστ is one of several 3sg. fut. perf. forms in a fragmentary law code from Roccagloriosa (ST Lu 62; ImagItal Buxentum 1), discovered in 1999 and first published in 2001 (Gualtieri & Poccetti, 2001). Given the dates of discovery and publication, the form is absent from Untermann (2000), as well as from the list of Sabellic perfect forms compiled by Piwowarczyk (2011: 117–123, explicitly based on Untermann).[1]

The text uses scriptio continua, whence an indeterminacy with the reading of the phrase in question. Like the rest of the text, the line containing this form (side A, line 7) is broken at both the left and right margins, and reads as follows:]σταυτιαfκλοπουστ[. This is interpreted

[1] The form is also not registered in EDLIL, for unclear reasons.

B. Vine (✉)
University of California, Los Angeles, USA
e-mail: vine@humnet.ucla.edu

J. F. Eska et al. (eds.), *The Method Works*,
https://doi.org/10.1007/978-3-031-48959-4_18

by Rix (ST) as]στ αυτ ιαf κλοπουστ[, whereas Crawford et al. (ImagItal) offer]στ αυτ ιαfκ [κ]λοπουστ[, with the annotation 'κ omitted on bronze'. In other words, directly preceding κλοπουστ (or [κ]λοπουστ) we would have the third person pronoun (acc. pl. fem.), either without (as ιαf, Rix) or with (as ιαfκ, Crawford et al.) the final deictic particle -κ; cf. Umb. **eaf**, *eaf* vs. Marruc. *iafc*. There is no clear consensus: thus [κ]λοπουστ is registered by Zair (2016: 204), evidently following ImagItal, while ιαf κλοπουστ is given by McDonald & Zair (2012: 36), as well as Dupraz (2009: 113).[2] For expository convenience we will operate with … ιαf κλοπουστ[, but there is no essential difference in what follows between κλοπουστ and [κ]λοπουστ.[3]

1.2. The interpretation of the form in context is generally agreed upon, as is its etymology: 's/he will have stolen these (fem. pl.)', with the Oscan verb a cognate of Gk. κλέπτω and Lat. *clepō* 'steal' (among other cognate material), based on PIE **klep*-.[4] While the suffix morphology is normal, with the standard Sabellic fut. perf. formant /-us-/ (plus 3sg. desinence),[5] there is an interesting anomaly in the root vocalism of this hitherto (as of 1999) unknown (and still largely unnoticed) Oscan perfect-system verb form: as noted by McDonald & Zair (2012: 36[3]), '[t]he combination of *o*-grade and non-reduplication in this verb … requires explanation.' This is the problem addressed in this paper. There are two previous solutions, both in my view problematic; following critiques of those proposals (in §§2, 3), I will offer (in §4) my own attempt at solution. (The Appendix following §4 expands on a point related to the proposal assessed in §3).

---

[2] Dupraz (2009: 113[34]) suggests that the singleton ⟨κ⟩ may do double duty for both ιαfκ and κλοπουστ, and this may be correct; gemination is licit in South Oscan orthography, but generally associated with palatalization (Zair, 2016: 112–125), which would not be a factor here.

[3] For further discussion of the problem, see Martzloff (2021a: 202). It will be convenient to reserve for treatment below a rather different interpretation of the sequence.

[4] In addition to ImagItal (ad loc.), see already Gualtieri & Poccetti (2001: 222) for the etymology, followed by McDonald & Zair (2012: 36).

[5] Orthographic ⟨ου⟩ for /ŭ/ is not problematic: in this text, '/u/ from any source is spelt ⟨ου⟩ in any position in the word' (Zair, 2016: 70, further 63–79 and 86 on /u/ in South Oscan orthography).

2 Previous Solution #1: Root Aorist Relic

2.1. McDonald & Zair (2012: 36[3]) offer (somewhat tentatively, as a 'possible answer') the following two-part solution. PIE **klep*-, they suggest, may have formed a root aorist, with zero-grade weak stem **kl̥p*-, which would develop regularly to pre-Osc. **kolp*-. This form **kolp*-, however, was then remodeled to **klop*- after the present stem **klep*- (as in Lat. *clepō* 'steal'). This is ingenious and difficult to rule out; yet objections can be raised, most of them already anticipated by McDonald & Zair.

2.2. As for the assumption of a root aorist with zero grade: they acknowledge (citing Meiser, 2003: 103–104, 162) that 'original root aorists normally preserve full- rather than zero-grade in the root in Italic.' They claim, however, that 'this is not always the case,' as in Lat. *strāvī* 'I strewed', as well as relic forms like Lat. *parēns* 'parent' and *cliēns* 'client'. But these examples are not probative. In general, all Latin perfects with secure basis in a PIE root aorist (Weiss, 2020: 437–438; Lat. *līquī* 'I left', *fūgī* 'I fled', etc.) show full-grade roots, except *fuī* (OLat. *fūī*) 'I was' (cf. Ved. *ábhūt*, Gk. ἔφῡ), to a root notorious for displaying zero grades in full-grade contexts (Jasanoff, 1997).[6] There is, likewise, no Sabellic evidence for perfect stems based on the zero-grade allomorph of old root aorists; superficially possible instances have alternative explanations.[7]

2.3. Specifically for Lat. *strāvī*: this form is neither a 'root aorist' as such nor a form likely to continue a root aorist directly (of the type Lat. *līquī* etc.), but rather a '*v*-perfect'. The sources of Latin '*v*-perfects' are varied, and admittedly include root aorists in some cases; but here, Lat. *strā*- (the basis for the perfect stem *strā-v*-) is more likely analogical after the verbal adjective *strātus* (itself likely an inherited form < PIE **str̥h₃-tó*-, whence also Gk. στρωτός).[8]

---

[6] On such 'zero-grade roots' generally, see Vine (2022).

[7] E.g., Osc. *dicust* 'will have said' (cf. root aorist in Ved. *ádiṣṭa* 'showed') likely results from dereduplication (so *LIV*[2] s.v. 1. **dei̯k̂*-, n. 3; Meiser, 2003: 104); cf. Umb. *dersicust*.

[8] For this analysis of *strātus*, see *LIV*[2] s.v. **sterh₃*-, n. 4, following Meiser, and see now Meiser (2003: 228).

As for Lat. *parēns* and *cliēns*: these are, to be sure, likely relics of aorist active participles.[9] But such forms have little probative value for the issue at hand. While the original inflection of *-*nt*- formations is a highly fraught problem, with amphikinetic patterning often assumed,[10] one may say that descriptively, purely verbal *-*nt*- formations (as opposed to Caland *-*nt*- formations) tend to display hysterokinetic features. In this sense, then, zero-grade root in the aorist active *participle* is virtually canonic,[11] with little bearing on an Italic (alleged) *finite* root aorist with zero grade root.

2.4. A more fundamental problem is that no other evidence supports the assumption of a root aorist for PIE **klep*-, which is generally reconstructed with an *s*-aorist, on the basis of Gk. ἔκλεψα and Lat. *clepsī* (as in *LIV*[2] s.v.; recently also Willi, 2018: 425[21]). McDonald & Zair offer the following rejoinder: 'The fact that Greek ἔκλεψα and Latin *clepsī* point to an *s*-aorist is not necessarily a problem, since these were productive in both languages (Oscan κλοπουστ would then be a relic).' This is possible in principle, but the situation is more complicated. As shown by Pike (2009), Lat. *clepō* also had a lengthened-grade perfect *clēpī*, attested in Pacuvius (*Hermiona* 185, ap. Nonius 20M = 30.15L), as well as Cicero (*Leg*. 2.22, in an archaic legal formulation). This may point to an acrostatic present **klḗp-ti* (which Pike supports via Tocharian material),[12] the imperfect of which was shunted into the Italic perfect system, as seems to have occurred in other cases (Weiss, 2020: 438–439, with references). Thus Osc. κλοπουστ, if interpreted as a root aorist relic, would not match *either one* of the two types of perfect formations for **klep*- that may have existed elsewhere in Italic.

2.5. Finally for this solution, one may also question the presumed remodeling of pre-Osc. **kolp*- to **klop*- after the present stem **klep*- (not

---

[9] So, e.gg., Meiser (2003: 46) and Weiss (2020: 464); and probably *trāns* 'across' (with its cognates) can be added to these (Vine, 2008: 20–21 with references).

[10] For discussion, see recently Lowe (2015: 311–314) and Willi (2018: 554 with n. 18).

[11] Cf. Ved. *diśánt*- beside *ádiṣṭa* (cited above, n. 7), *gmánt*- beside finite root aorist **gʷém-t* in *ágan* and Osc. **kúmbened**, Arm. *ekn* to **gʷem*- 'come', etc.

[12] For Lat. *clēpī*: cf. TB *klep*- 'touch, test' (3sg. mid. *klyepträ* < **klḗp-e/o*- or **klḗp-tor* after **klḗp-ti*) < *'lay hand to'; in addition to Pike (2009), see also Adams (1989, 2013: 182–183 [s.v. *kälp*-], 186 [s.v. *kälyp*-], 246 [s.v. *klep*- and *klepe**]).

actually attested in Oscan, but cf. Lat. *clepō*). As McDonald & Zair note, this root is also attested in Osc. **kulupu** 'thieves' (gen. pl.) (ST Cm 14; ImagItal Cumae 8; cf. also Murano, 2013: 113–128), following Rix (ST), who interprets the form as based on the zero grade of a root noun (cf. Gk. κλώψ 'thief', -κλεψ in βοῦκλεψ 'ox-thief', and Lat. *cleps* 'fur' [CGL v 349.51]). I return to this form later; but for the present, it suffices to note that while PIE **kl̥p-* did indeed regularly develop to Ital. **kolp-* (whence, with regular anaptyxis, O. **kulup-**), this **kolp-* —clearly based synchronically on a verbal idea 'steal'—did not undergo remodeling to **klop-*.

3 Previous Solution #2: Dereduplicated O-grade Perfect

3.1. As an alternative, McDonald & Zair cite the earlier (and entirely different) account of Osc. κλοπουστ by Dupraz (2009: 112–116), according to whom the form reflects a dereduplicated primary perfect stem, therefore with *o*-grade root (as is normal for the strong stem of PIE primary perfects). A brief digression, however, is in order here, to explain that Dupraz, in fact, adduces Osc. κλοπουστ in support of something else (the main subject of Dupraz, 2009), namely a form BVRVS, in a Latin inscription from North Oscan territory. This form is interpreted as (almost) the same type of form as Osc. κλοπουστ: i.e., a dereduplicated (and thematized) *o*-grade perfect participle. In my view, however, this interpretation of Lat. (or 'Osco-Lat.'?) BVRVS is highly uncertain, with the result that (despite Dupraz) Osc. κλοπουστ and BVRVS are not mutually supportive. Since, therefore, full discussion of the issues surrounding BVRVS—as interesting as they are—would take us too far afield, and to little purpose, that material is treated below in an Appendix. We can now assess the analysis of Osc. κλοπουστ as a dereduplicated primary perfect on its own terms.

3.2. It should first be pointed out that the semantics in question—'will have stolen—render Osc. κλοπουστ a poor candidate for an inherited stative perfect (as already noted by Dupraz himself [2009: 113–114]). Thus, if the form reflects a 'perfect', this is necessarily a post-PIE innovative *o*-grade perfect, similar (e.g.,) to Gk. κέκλοφα (Aristoph.+).[13] This leads, in turn, to a general question as to the status of reduplicated *o*-grade perfects in Italic, where, in fact, such forms may not exist at all. In Latin, zero grade of the root has most often been generalized, or else the root vocalism of the present stem is used (see, e.g., Weiss, 2020: 435). The situation in Sabellic is essentially the same (Buck, 1928: 170–171; Meiser, 2003: passim).[14]

3.3. But even if one grants an original reduplicated perfect **ke-klop-* (for some stage of early Italic), we must ask whether such a form could have undergone dereduplication. This seems unlikely, given constraints on dereduplication in Italic, both phonological and morphological. Apart from the unusable comparison with (alleged) Osco-Lat. BVRVS (see above and, in much greater detail, the Appendix), Dupraz (2009: 112) compares the (alleged) dereduplication in κλοπουστ with that seen in OLat. *vortī* (1sg. perf.) and Umb. **kuvurtus**(**t**), *couortus*(*t*) (3sg. fut. perf.), both to **u̯ert-* 'turn'; but this is not actually supportive. If OLat. *vort-* and Umb. *-uort-* stem from an inherited primary perfect, such a form would show, in PIE terms, sg. **u̯e-u̯ort-* and pl. **u̯e-u̯r̥t-*. As it happens, however, both **u̯e-u̯ort-* and **u̯e-u̯r̥t-* would develop in Italic to **u̯ou̯ort-* (Meiser, 2003: 162); thus the 'dereduplication' here is essentially haplological, under these restricted phonetic circumstances (which would not be available for **ke-klop-*). At the very least, one must say that an actual old *o*-grade (as opposed to a zero grade) is not assured in any case as the basis for the Italic (unreduplicated) **u̯ort-*. Moreover, for Umb. **kuvurt-**/*couort-*, the preverb is perhaps another factor in the dereduplication; cf. the Latin type *repperī* 'I found', *rettulī* 'I brought back' (with syncope < **repeperī*, **retetulī*; Weiss, 2020: 436); cf. Class. *tulī* (vs. earlier *tetulī*; Leumann, 1977: 587), and comparable examples are probable for

[13] Predictably, under these circumstances, *LIV*² registers no PIE perfect for **klep-*.

[14] A few forms deviate from these patterns in a more or less idiosyncratic way: thus, for example, Pael. *pperci* 'she asked' shows a Schwebeablauting neo-*e*-grade beside Umb. **pepurkurent** 'they will have asked', with regular zero grade (< **pe-pr̥k̂-*), to PIE **prek̂-*. (Some onomastic material may show the same innovation as Pael. *pperci*, as with Osc. **perkens**/**perkedne**[**ís**], **perkium**, on which see Zair [2021: 189, 191–192, 194–195].)

Sabellic.[15] This is registered as a final possibility for κλοπουστ by McDonald & Zair (2012: 36[3]): 'de-reduplication of κλοπουστ < **ke-klop-* may have been due to generalisation of a syncopated form found in compounds'. Indeed, Gualtieri & Poccetti (2001: 220–222) attempted to interpret the sequence]...αυτιαfκλοπουστ[(see §1 above) as] ... αυτι αfκλοπουστ[, with a compound verb αfκλοπουστ, rather than] ... αυτ ιαf κλοπουστ[, with a different form of the connective followed by a third person pronoun. This is technically possible, given the existence of Osc. αυτι/*auti* beside αυτ/**avt**; but it is not an attractive possibility. First, it would have the undesirable consequence of removing the direct object ιαf. Second, while an Oscan preverb **af-**/αf- may exist, it is found for the most part in a few very obscure items (**aflakus**, **aflukad**, **afstist**, αfλκειτ; see Untermann, 2000 s.vv.); thus, one should not have recourse to such a form lightly. Finally, Lat. *clepō* is entirely without preverb usage (and the same is true for Goth. *hlifan*); there is no serious support from Gk. ἀποκλέπτω 'steal away, run away with' (*hMerc.*+) or from OPr. *auklipts* 'concealed' and similar Baltic material (cf. Toporov, 1975: 149–150, s.v.). We may also mention, finally, the analogical type of dereduplication, based on related stems, as with Osc. *dicust* beside Umb. *dersicust* (cited above, n. 7): cf. Osc. **dadíkatted**, Lat. *dicāre*/*dēdicāre* (Buck, 1928: 171). But there is no analogical basis for dereduplicated κλοπουστ.

3.4. For the sake of completeness, one further claim by Dupraz must be addressed, which he applies to all three forms that he regards as continuing Italic *o*-grade perfects (i.e., Osco-Lat. BVRVS, Lat. *uort-*, and Osc. κλοπουστ). According to Dupraz, these forms display a significant correlation with thematic presents (cf. **gʷérH-e*/*o-*, **u̯ért-e*/*o-*, **klép-e*/*o-*), with the *o*-grade perfects actually *derived from* the *e*-grades in some sort of ablaut relationship (2009: 114, 116), a process that is nevertheless unexplained. But there is nothing attractive about such a correlation, and one must agree with the evaluation of this claim by McDonald & Zair (2012: 36[3]), who write that this correlation would operate 'for unclear reasons'.

[15] Cf. Buck (1928: 171) on Umb. *procanurent* 'they will have sung'; similarly Untermann (2000: 366): 'Pf.-Stamm **kan-* oder wahrscheinlicher **kekan-*'.

§3.5. There is, to my knowledge, only one other possible *o*-grade perfect in Sabellic, namely Osc. ϝουρουστ 's/he will have found'—attested, as it happens, in the same text as κλοπουστ (side A, line 10; see McDonald & Zair, 2012 in detail). The interpretation as an *o*-grade perfect (i.e., sg. **u̯e-u̯roh₁-* / pl. **u̯e-u̯r̥h₁-* > **u̯ou̯r-*) is, in fact, McDonald & Zair's second option (2012: 35); but (despite some problematic issues, about which there is no space to comment further here) their first option is in my view superior, involving a reduplicated aorist **u̯e-u̯r̥h₁-e/o-* (comparable to Gk. εὗρον and OIr. *-fúair* 'found').[16]

4 A New Approach. Osc. κλοπουστ as Denominative 'simple perfect'

4.1. In principle, a more satisfactory account of Osc. κλοπουστ would have a direct explanation for the root *o*-grade—in other words, an explanation that operates without the remodeling called for by the presumed (but questionable) basis in a root aorist, and without the dereduplication called for by background in a reduplicated primary *o*-grade perfect (which is itself a fragile construct for Italic). And in general, an *o*-grade verbal formation that cannot be aligned with primary *o*-grade verbal categories would be explicable in the simplest way via a nominal *o*-grade, as long as the verbal morphology is compatible with a denominative source. For example, an abstract **klop-éh₂* 'theft' (cf. Gk. κλοπή 'id.' [Aesch.+]) could produce an Italic denominative **klop-āi̯e/o-* 'engage in theft'; or a 'τομός form' **klop-ó-* 'thieving, thief' (cf. Gk. κλοπός 'thief' [*h.Merc.*+]) could likewise yield an Italic denominative **klop-āi̯e/o-* 'steal'.[17] A denominative background, moreover, is perfectly natural for 'steal': see, for example, Rix (1985: 208–209) on VOL (S)TATOD 'he shall steal' (< PIE *(*s*)*teh₂-i-* 'steal') in the Duenos Inscription (CIL i² 4), mainly replaced in the Classical language by the denominative *fūrārī* (based on the root noun *fūr* 'thief').

---

[16] Perhaps the root in question is not **u̯reh₁-* (as in *LIV*² and traditionally), but rather **u̯erh₁-* (so Willi, 2018: 77–78), which would exclude a perfect stem **u̯e-u̯roh₁-*.

[17] While 'τομός forms' are rare in Italic, they are securely documented: see Weiss (2020: 292; Lat. *procus* 'suitor', *coquus* 'cook'), and for additional data, see Nussbaum (2017: 238[26]).

For a denominative background to be convincing, there are two further considerations to be faced. First is that the nominal forms just mentioned (**klop-éh₂*, **klop-ó-*) do not happen to be attested in Italic (although they could well have existed). In the ideal case, however, the *o*-grade nominal basis could be aligned with material that *is* attested in Oscan. Secondly, there is a 'big if' mentioned above, i.e., 'as long as the verbal morphology is compatible with a denominative source'. Yet, at first glance, this does not seem to be the case: Oscan denominatives should have *t*(*t*)-perfects, and these are abundantly attested, as in forms like **prúfatted**/πρωfατεδ 'probavit', **seganatted** 'signavit', **duunated** 'donavit', **teremnattens** 'terminaverunt', αfααματεδ 'iussit', Pael. *coisatens* 'curaverunt', and others, including the future perfect, as in **tríbarakattuset** 'aedificaverint'. Why, then, do we not see a form like †κλοπατουστ?

I now address these two considerations in turn.

4.2. The attested nominal form related to 'steal' is the root noun Osc. **kulupu** 'thief' (gen. pl.), as already seen (§2.5). While this form itself goes back to a zero grade **kl̥p-*, its background could well have included *o*-grade **klop-*, in view of the following considerations. First of all, according to the classic demonstration by Schindler (1972), the absolutely original form of (T)ReC- root nouns involves *ó*/*é*-acrostatic inflection; thus **klóp-*, obl. **klép-*, with nom. sg. **klóp-s* or (with analogical lengthened grade) **klṓp-s* (cf. Gk. κλώψ). Rix took the zero grade of Osc. **kulupu** to be decompositional (2002: 427); cf. Ved. *-tr̥p-* as in (e.g.,) *paśu-tŕ̥p-* 'cattle-stealing' (RV VII.86.5c, agreeing with *tāyú-* 'thief'), under the assumption of an Indo-Iranian root **trap-*, a deformed version of **krap-* < PIE **klep-*. Whether or not this analysis of Ved. *-tr̥p-* is correct,[18] the zero grade in Osc. **kulupu** could, indeed, be decompositional. At the same time, however, *ó*/*é*-acrostatic root nouns often developed mobile inflection, with oblique-case zero grades (Schindler, 1972: 34–35). Thus, the Oscan root noun could, in principle, be based on a secondarily mobile form **klóp-*, obl. **kl̥p-´* of the root noun itself.[19] However that may be, one can point to a series of other replacement patterns (mainly post-PIE)

[18] Mayrhofer (EWAia i 635) is skeptical.

[19] My thanks to Tony Yates and Sasha Nikolaev for helpful discussion of this point. On the pattern of secondary (or 'emergent') mobility in the development of acrostatic formations, see recently Yates (2022).

for original *ó*/*é*-acrostatic root nouns, in addition to the patterns just described, including the following: generalization of *ō* (Gk. κλώψ, gen. κλωπός; Lat. *vōx*, gen. *vōcis* 'voice'); generalization of *ŏ* (Gk. [Hom.+] φλόξ, gen. φλογός 'flame'; κρόξ [Hsch.], acc. κρόκα [Hes. *Op.* 538] 'thread'); ablauting *ō*/*ŏ* (e.g., **u̯ōkʷ*-/**u̯ŏkʷ*-, cf. Lat. *vōx* vs. [denom.] *vŏcāre* 'call', Umb. *subocau*/*subocauu* 'I invoke' and *suboco* 'invocation').[20] Thus, the root noun continued in Osc. **kulupu** could imply the prior existence of an allomorph **klop*-, at some stage of Italic, on the basis of several possible scenarios; this **klop*- could then serve as the basis for a denominative verb **klop-āi̯e*/*o*- underlying Osc. κλοπουστ (though **klop-éh₂* and/or **klop-ó*- could also have existed; see §4.1): e.g., survival for a time of an original acrostatic root noun **klóp*-/**klép*-, with **kulupu** decompositional; or post-PIE generalized **klop*- (of the type φλόξ), with **kulupu** decompositional; or post-PIE ablauting **klōp*-/**klop*- (of the type Lat. *vōx*/*voc*-), with **kulupu** decompositional; or (perhaps in the simplest way) post-PIE ablauting **klop*-/**kl̥p*- (as replacement for the original acrostatic root noun), with **kulupu** based on the weak stem and the strong stem **klop*- as basis for denominative **klop-āi̯e*/*o*-.

4.3. It remains to address the apparent conundrum of how a denominative **klop-āi̯e*/*o*- could produce an Oscan perfect stem that lacks both the stem-vowel -*ā*- and the characteristic *t*(*t*)-perfect suffix. Yet precisely such denominative-based perfects—i.e., suffixless and with *ā*-truncation (or *ā*-suppression)—are well-documented for Sabellic. There are, in fact, several subtypes of suffixless perfects in Sabellic,[21] of which the most prominent is that of *ā*-verbs (including denominatives) with suppressed or truncated -*ā*- in the perfect and lacking the characteristic *ā*-verb perfect suffix, i.e., -*t*(*t*)- in Oscan and -*nki̯*- in Umbrian: e.g., Osc. *urust* 'he will have declared' (which surely belongs with Lat. *ōrāre* 'speak, plead', thus an *ā*-verb), not †*uratust* (cf. **tríbarakattuset**; §4.1); Umb. *portust* 'he will have brought' (for its *ā*-verb status, cf. 2/3sg. impv. **purtatu**/*portatu*

[20] For Lat. *vocāre*, Umb. *suboc*- as based on the weak stem of an ablauting root noun, see, for example, Untermann (2000: 707) and EDLIL 692.

[21] For a good discussion, see Dupraz (2016: 344–345) on 'Die "einfachen Perfekta" des Sabellischen', with earlier references (to which add García-Castillero, 2000: 228[219]).

and 3sg. pres. subj. *portaia*), not †*portan̉sust* (cf. a regular denominative perfect like Umb. *combifian̉sust* 'he will have communicated'). One set of forms is particularly prominent, namely suffixless /ops/- and /ōps/- perfects based on denominative **op*(*e*)*s-āi̯e*/*o-* 'make, build':[22] Osc. 3sg. perf. **úpsed** and **upsed**, 3pl. **u**(**u**)**psens**, ουπσενς, Vestin. *ośens*; SPic. **opsút** and [**o**]**psúq**.

There are many questions surrounding these suffixless Sabellic perfects with *ā*-truncation, including the origin of the formation, why it appears for the limited set of verbs in question, and the explanation for the long-vowel /ōps/- forms. None of this can be explored here, except to mention, first, the fundamental treatment by Rix (1993) and some more recent discussions (e.g., Piwowarczyk, 2011: 110–111; Fortson, 2017: 850; Willi, 2018: 453[86], 491[205]), especially the detailed account by Lipp (2021: 299–301, 308–318; in briefer compass 2022: 506). Further, Lipp's proposal that the formation has an analogical origin based in imperfects (rather than perfects) seems promising; and, in my view, he convincingly refutes Rix's conception of the /ōps/- forms (followed by *LIV*[2] s.v. 1. *h_3*ep-* with n. 3) according to which these are based on an inherited *s*-aorist. But the fundamental point for present purposes is the fact that this pattern is firmly established for Sabellic, authorizing the proposal offered here that Osc. κλοπουστ owes its *o*-grade to a denominative **klop-āi̯e*/*o-*, recovering the pattern seen in **ōr-āi̯e/o-* ~ Osc. *urust*, **por-*(*e*)*t-āi̯e*/*o-* ~ Umb. *portust*, and **op*(*e*)*s-āi̯e*/*o-* ~ Osc. **úpsed**. It can be mentioned, finally, that there is good typological support from Greek for 'denominative perfects', as explored in a fundamental treatment by Ringe (1984: 428–433) and more recently by Hackstein (2002: 166–167) in his analysis of the 'ad-hoc Denominativperfekt' in Hom. συνοχωκότε (*Il.* 2.218).

---

[22] Cf., for the *ā*-verb status, Osc. gerund **úpsannúm**, Umb. 3 sg. impv. *osatu*, Pael. 3 (sg. or pl.) impf. subj. *upsaseter*, among other Sabellic material, in addition to Lat. *operārī* 'work, take pains'. A particularly interesting—but problematic—form of this type is SPic. **ọpesạ**[ ]**úom**: for the difficulties concerning the reading, see recently Fortson (2017: 850) and especially Lipp (2021: 314 with further references), the latter with discussion of the possibility that the form (if it belongs with other **op*(*e*)*s-āi̯e*/*o-* material) may reflect a stage of the language with medial syncope *in statu nascendi*, a perspective developed for South Picene in Lipp (2021).

5 Appendix: (Osco-?)Latin BVRVS

The title of Dupraz (2009) refers to a 'North Oscan participle *burus*'. In reality, however, there is no such 'North Oscan' form; rather, there is a form BVRVS attested in a Latin inscription (CIL i[2] 3253, 1st c. BCE) from Superaequum, in North Oscan (more specifically Paelignian) territory. The published version of the text is as follows:

L . SELVS . C . F
HERCOLO
DONVM
DAT . BVRVS

A trivial correction (see Dupraz, 2009: 106 for details) concerns SELVS, an error (perhaps having arisen in the original reading of the damaged stone, which is now lost) for SEIVS, a well-attested gentilicium of an important family in the area; the text can thus be read as *L(ucius) . Seịus . C(ai) . f(ilius) | Hercolo | donum | dat . burus*. This simple formulaic dedicatory text is easily interpretable as 'Lucius Seius, son of Gaius, gives a gift to Hercules …', apart from the mysterious final word BVRVS.

The simplest explanation takes the form as a cognomen BVRVS, representing *Burrus* (Enn. *Ann.*+), the Latinized version of Gk. Πῦρρος 'Pyrrhus'.[23] This is the position taken by both Vetter and Buonocore (see Dupraz, 2009 for the references), and held also by Paolo Poccetti (p.c., 19 January 2022). To this, however, Dupraz reasonably queries (2009: 107) why a cognomen should be positioned at the end of the text. For Vetter: the cognomen of L. Seius would have been added later; but this is highly unusual (as Vetter himself admitted), and there is no other indication that this word belongs to a different period from the rest of the text. For Buonocore: this is not the cognomen of L. Seius, but rather the cognomen of someone else, whose nomen, gentilicium, and patronymic are all missing; but (as Dupraz pointedly objects) it is unclear why all this material is missing, with the cognomen placed at the end of the text. And if we are dealing with a single text referring

[23] On *Burrus* with /b/: cf. already Quintilian 1.14.15, and further Biville (1990: 283).

to more than one grammatical subject (i.e., L. Seius and a separate personage BVRVS), why is DAT singular?

The goal of Dupraz (2009), then, was to explore an alternative already suggested in CIL ad loc. ('an vox Osca?'), given the facts that (1) the inscription is in Paelignian (i.e., North Oscan) territory, (2) the archeological context probably involved worship of Hercules, and (3) the name of Hercules in the text (i.e., HERCOLO) actually shows an Oscan feature, namely *o*-stem inflection (vs. the Latin consonant stem *Herculēs*), cf. Osc. dat. sg. **hereklúí**, Vestin. *herclo*. More specifically: in terms of standard votive phraseology in Latin, *donum dat* is often followed by *libens* 'willing(ly)' or *libens merito* 'willing(ly) [and] deservedly' (with reference to the service rendered to the divinity and the expected divine favor), while the (roughly) corresponding Oscan phraseology involves a phrase *brateis datas* (gen. sg.), elliptical for **bratom* (neut.) *brateis datas* 'thanks for favor rendered'. Dupraz reasons, then, that the Latin inscriptional sequence DAT . BVRVS may somehow be equivalent to Osc. *brateis datas*; i.e., BVRVS could mean 'grateful(ly)', based on PIE *g^{w}*erH-* 'show approval, express agreement, etc.' (the source of Osc. *brat-* and Lat. *grāt-*, as well as Ved. *gr̥ṇā́ti* 'praise' and other material).[24] The specific morphological proposal is that BVRVS continues a (dereduplicated) perfect active participle *g^{w}*orH-u̯ōs* (with *o*-grade root), which was then thematized as *g^{w}*orH-u̯o-*, whence pre-Osc. **boru̯os* and then Osco-Lat. †*borus*. (I return below to the further development of †*borus* to *burus*.) For the thematized perfect active participle, Dupraz appositely compares Osc. nom. sg. *sipus* and Volsc. abl. sg. *sepu* 'knowing(ly)' < **sēp-u̯o-*, a thematized version of an original perfect active participle **sēp-u̯ōs* (for the root, cf. Lat. *sapiō* 'taste, understand').[25]

The 'vox Osca' idea as developed by Dupraz is intriguing and clever, and has recently been accepted by Martzloff (2021b: 352); but the morphology is very problematic, as Dupraz admits to some extent. PIE

[24] On Osc. **brateís**, *brateis*, *bratom*, etc. 'thanks, favor' = Lat. *grāt-* as in *grātēs* 'thanks', *grātia* 'favor, service, thanks' < *g^{w}*r̥*h_2*-t-* (cf. verbal adjective *grātus* 'pleasing, thankful, deserving thanks'), see Rix (2000). For a possible reflex of this material in an early British divine epithet, see recently Prósper & Medrano (2022: 15–16).

[25] More recently, Martzloff (2021b: 350–351) has argued that only Volsc. *sepu* reflects a thematized version, while Osc. *sipus* continues a bona fide (unthematized) perfect active participle.

$^*g^werH$- (not surprisingly, given its semantics) did not make a perfect in PIE;[26] thus a perfect to this root in Italic would be an innovation, which lacks support otherwise in Italic. Moreover, as we have seen (§3.2 above), actual *o*-grades are all but unattested for Italic primary perfects (as opposed to zero grades and occasional *e*-grades, or carry-overs from present-stem vocalism), and dereduplication in Italic is highly constrained (§3.3). There is also a phonological problem: the expected outcome of Dupraz's pre-Osc. **boru̯os* for Latin-alphabet Oscan (with Latinized desinence) would be †*borus*, not *burus*; to address this, Dupraz appeals to a pre-/r/ raising process documented for Umbrian, but this is problematic, as we will see below.

What, then, is the solution for the odd (or at least oddly positioned) form BVRVS in this text? Can the cognomen idea be salvaged? Poccetti, for one, thinks so—as he remarks (p.c.), '[t]he final collocation of the *cognomen* could emphasize the status of Roman citizen.' Still, it is tempting to consider a different morphological version of the 'vox Osca' approach involving PIE $^*g^werH$- and Dupraz's interesting idea of comparing DAT . BVRVS and Osc. *brateis datas.* I suggest that BVRVS could continue a 'τομός form' $^*g^worH$-*ó*-; such forms are typically agentive and often develop as adjectives—the sense here would thus be 'expressing agreement/approval/ thanks etc.', hence 'thankful(ly), grateful(ly)', precisely as appropriate for the context.

Several points can be added to this suggestion. First, although τομός forms are somewhat rare in Italic (as opposed to τόμος forms), they are attested with certainty (as already seen in §4.1). Second, it is interesting to observe that τομός forms to this root are actually attested in Vedic (no doubt independently): note, e.g., the dual dvandva *abhigarāpagarau* (KS XXXIV.5 (39.1)), reflecting *abhigara*- + *apagara*-, roughly 'one who praises' + 'one who blames'.[27] Finally, to return to the phonological

[26] Ved. *saṃjagā́ra* (YV) is a Neubildung (LIV^2 s.v. $^*g^werH$-).

[27] Similar contexts for *abhigara*- and *apagara*- include PB V.5.13 and XXV.15.3. Likewise, *abhigarā́* (dual) at MS I.9.1 (131: 11) refers to two priestly figures, and is also most easily compatible with agentive meaning. Some related material (such as Ved. [TS, AB, ŚB] *pratigará*- 'response') seems to involve action nouns (i.e., a 'τόμος form'); but both types of compounds with preverb (agentive *abhigará*-, action noun *pratigará*-) regularly show oxytone accentuation (AiG ii/2 §31a, pp. 98–99). Warm thanks to Stephanie Jamison for assistance in evaluating the Vedic material.

problem mentioned above: a τομός form PIE *g^worH-ó-s* should develop to pre-Osc. **boros*, whence **bors* (with regular final-syllable syncope) and then †*bor* (with absorption of *-*rs* and degemination of *-*rr*; see Meiser, 1986: 59–60, 154). However, the *o* > *u* raising process to which Dupraz appealed is, in fact, best attested not before /r/ (as Dupraz states, 2009: 110), but rather before the clusters /rn/, /rf/, and /rs/ (Meiser, 1986: 115–116); thus, here we would actually predict **bors* > †*bur*. At this point, an echt-Oscan (but fatally opaque, in a Latin context) †*bur* could have been trivially repaired as *burus* (with transparent nom. sg. masc. desinence, agreeing with *L. Seius*). Alternatively, *g^worH-ó-s* could have developed regularly to Osc. **bur** (in pre-spelling-reform orthography); and, as Martzloff plausibly suggests (2021b: 352–353), this version of the word (or a recollection of it) may be what underlies the spelling of the repaired BVRVS in the Latin context of the inscription.

In the final analysis, one cannot press the τομός-form suggestion too far, and perhaps the cognomen interpretation remains worth considering. But the salient point for present purposes is that a deredupulicated perfect participle with *o*-grade (based on a primary perfect) is a questionable source for Lat. (or Osco-Lat.?) BVRVS.[28]

References

Adams, D. Q. (1989). Tocharian *kälp-* 'obtain', B *klep-* 'stroke, investigate', B *kälyp-* 'steal' and PIE **klep-* '±lay hand to'. *Historische Sprachforschung, 102*, 241–244.

Adams, D. Q. (2013). *A dictionary of Tocharian B (revised and greatly enlarged)*. Rodopi.

[28] I am happy to have the opportunity to offer this modest contribution to Don Ringe, as a token of longstanding friendship and admiration, and in emulation—however imperfect—of his characteristic erudition and methodological rigor. Previous versions of this paper were presented at meetings of the Graduate Seminar of the UCLA Program in Indo-European Studies (January and May 2022) and at the 41st East Coast Indo-European Conference (June 2022, Harvard University). I am grateful to the audiences on those occasions, as well as to Olav Hackstein, for helpful comments and criticism, and I take full responsibility for errors of fact or interpretation that may, despite their best efforts, persist in this version.

AiG II.2 = Debrunner, A. (1954). *Jacob Wackernagel: Altindische Grammatik*, Band II, 2 (*Die Nominalsuffixe*). Vandenhoeck & Ruprecht.

Biville, F. (1990). *Les emprunts du latin au grec. Approche phonétique i, Introduction et consonantisme*. Peeters.

Buck, C. D. (1928). *A grammar of Oscan and Umbrian, with a collection of inscriptions and a glossary*[2]. Ginn & Company.

CGL = *Corpus glossariorum Latinorum*. (1888–1923). (G. Loewe & G. Goetz, Eds.). Teubner.

CIL i[2] = *Corpus inscriptionum Latinarum*. (1918–1986). Vol. i[2] Pars II, fasc. I–IV. Walter de Gruyter.

Dupraz, E. (2009). Das nord-oskische Partizip *burus* als Spur eines *o*-stufigen Perfektstammes im Italischen. In R. Lühr & S. Ziegler (Eds.), *Protolanguage and prehistory* (pp. 105–118). Dr. Ludwig Reichert.

Dupraz, E. (2016). Zu einigen Perfektbildungen im Sabellischen. *Indogermanische Forschungen, 121*, 333–363.

EDLIL = de Vaan, M. (2008). *Etymological dictionary of Latin and the other Italic languages*. Brill.

EWAia = Mayrhofer, M. (1986–2001). *Etymologisches Wörterbuch des Altindoarischen*. C. Winter.

Fortson, Benjamin W. IV. 2017. The dialectology of Italic. In *Handbook of comparative and historical Indo-European linguistics*, ed. Jared Klein, Brian Joseph, & Matthias Fritz, ii 831–858. Walter de Gruyter.

García-Castillero, C. (2000). *La formación del tema de presente primario osco-umbro*. Universidad del País Vasco, Servicio Editorial/Euskal Herriko Unibertsitatea, Argitalpen Zerbitzua.

Gualtieri, M., & Poccetti, P. (2001). Frammento di *tabula* bronzea con iscrizione osca dal pianoro centrale. In M. Gualtieri & H. Fracchia (Eds.), *Roccagloriosa II. L'oppidum lucano e il territorio* (pp. 187–295). Centre Jean Bérard.

Hackstein, O. (2002). *Die Sprachform der homerischen Epen*. Dr. Ludwig Reichert.

ImagItal = Crawford, M. H., Broadhead, W. M., Clackson, J. P. T., Santangelo, F., Thompson, S., & Watmough, M. (2011). *Imagines Italicae. A corpus of Italic inscriptions*. Institute of Classical Studies, University of London.

Jasanoff, J. (1997). Where does Skt *bhávati* come from? In D. Disterheft, M. Huld, & J. Greppin (Eds.), *Studies in honor of Jaan Puhvel i, Ancient languages and philology* (pp. 173–186). Institute for the Study of Man.

Leumann, M. (1977). *Lateinische Laut- und Formenlehre*. C. H. Beck.

Lipp, R. (2021). The medial syllable syncope in the South Picene inscriptions. In M. Tarsi (Ed.), *Studies in general and historical linguistics offered to Jón Axel*

Harðarson on the occasion of his 65th birthday (pp. 269–328). Institut für Sprachwissenschaft der Universität Innsbruck.

Lipp, R. (2022). Umbrian *FEFURE* as a relic form of the proto-Indo-European perfect. In EQO \ DUENOSIO, A. Calderini & R. Massarelli (Eds.), *Studi offerti a Luciano Agostiniani* (pp. 499–534). Linguistica ed epigrafia dell'Italia antica, Università degli Studi di Perugia.

LIV^2 = Rix, H., & Kümmel, M. (2001). *Lexikon der indogermanischen Verben. Die Wurzeln und ihre Primärstammbildungen*^{2}. Dr. Ludwig Reichert.

Lowe, J. J. (2015). *Participles in Rigvedic Sanskrit. The syntax and semantics of adjectival verb forms*. Oxford University Press.

Martzloff, V. (2021a). *Rythme, métrique et poétique dans l'Italie archaïque (vénète, sud-picénien, osque, falisque, latin). Mémoire inédit d'habilitation*. École Pratique des Hautes Études, Paris Sciences et Lettres.

Martzloff, V. (2021b). Vestiges du participe parfait en **-wos-*/*-us-* en latin et dans les langues sabelliques. In H. A. Fellner, M. Malzahn, & M. Peyrot (Eds.), *Luke wmer ra. Indo-European studies in honor of Georges-Jean Pinault* (pp. 348–360). Beech Stave Press.

McDonald, K., & Zair, N. (2012). Oscan ϝουρουστ and the Roccagloriosa law tablet. *Incontri linguistici, 35*, 31–45.

Meiser, G. (1986). *Lautgeschichte der umbrischen Sprache*. Institut für Sprachwissenschaft der Universität Innsbruck.

Meiser, G. (2003). *Veni Vidi Vici. Die Vorgeschichte des lateinischen Perfektsystems*. C. H. Beck.

Murano, F. (2013). *Le tabellae defixionum osche*. Fabrizio Serra.

Nussbaum, A. J. (2017). Agentive and other derivatives of "τόμος-type" nouns. In C. Le Feuvre, D. Petit, & G.-J. Pinault (Eds.), *Verbal adjectives and participles in Indo-European languages* (pp. 233–266). Hempen.

Pike, M. (2009). The Indo-European long-vowel preterite. New Latin evidence. In J. E. Rasmussen & T. Olander (Eds.), *Internal reconstruction in Indo-European. Methods, results, and problems* (pp. 205–212). Museum Tusculanum Press.

Piwowarczyk, D. R. (2011). Formations of the perfect in the Sabellic languages with the Italic and Indo-European background. *Studia Linguistica Universitatis Iagellonicae Cracoviensis, 128*, 103–126.

Prósper, B. M., & Medrano Duque, M. (2022). Ancient Gaulish and British divinities. Notes on the reconstruction of Celtic phonology and morphology. *Voprosy onomastiki, 19*, 9–47.

Ringe, D. A., Jr. (1984). *The perfect tenses in Greek inscriptions*. Ph.D. dissertation, Yale University.
Rix, H. (1985). Das letzte Wort der Duenos-Inschrift. *Münchener Studien zur Sprachwissenschaft, 46*, 193–220.
Rix, H. (1993). Osk. *úpsannam – uupsens* und Zugehöriges. In F. Heidermanns, H. Rix, & E. Seebold (Eds.), *Sprachen und Schriften des antiken Mittelmeerraums. Festschrift für Jürgen Untermann zum 65. Geburtstag* (pp. 329–348). Institut für Sprachwissenschaft der Universität Innsbruck.
Rix, H. (2000). Oskisch *brateis bratom*, lateinisch *grātēs*. In A. Hintze & E. Tichy (Eds.), *Anusantatyai. Festschrift für Johanna Narten zum 70. Geburtstag* (pp. 207–229). J. H. Röll.
Rix, H. (2002). Oskisch *niir kulupu*. In M. Fritz & S. Zeilfelder (Eds.), *Novalis Indogermanica. Festschrift für Günter Neumann zum 80. Geburtstag* (pp. 417–431). Leykam.
Schindler, J. (1972). L'apophonie des noms-racines indo-européens. *Bulletin de la Société de Linguistique de Paris, 67*, 31–38.
ST = Rix, H. (2000). *Sabellische Texte. Die Texte des Oskischen, Umbrischen und Südpikenischen*. C. Winter.
Toporov, V. N. 1975. *Prusskij jazyk. Slovar'*, A–D. Nauka.
Untermann, J. (2000). *Wörterbuch des Oskisch-Umbrischen*. C. Winter.
Vine, B. (2008). On the etymology of Latin *tranquillus* 'calm'. *International Journal of Diachronic Linguistics and Linguistic Reconstruction, 5*, 1–24.
Vine, B. (2022). Myc. *tu-wo*, Hom. θύος and the vocalism of *s*-stems in proto-Indo-European. In M. Kazansky, P. Kocharov, & A. Shatskov (Eds.), *Acta Linguistica Petropolitana* 18 = *Colloquia classica et indogermanica* vii, *Miscellanea in honorem Nikolai N. Kazansky* (pp. 444–462).
Weiss, M. (2020). *Outline of the historical and comparative grammar of Latin*[2]. Beech Stave Press.
Willi, A. (2018). *Origins of the Greek verb*. Cambridge University Press.
Yates, A. D. (2022). Emergent mobility in Indo-European **-r/n*-stems and its implications for the reconstruction of the neuter plural. In D. M. Goldstein, S. W. Jamison, & B. Vine (Eds.), *Proceedings of the 32nd Annual UCLA Indo-European Conference* (pp. 271–295). Buske.
Zair, N. (2016). *Oscan in the Greek alphabet*. Cambridge University Press.
Zair, N. (2021). Vowel epenthesis in Oscan. In S. Hisatsugi (Ed.), *Die italischen Sprachen. Neue linguistische und philologische Aspekte* (pp. 185–203). Baar.

Index[1]

A

Accent, 308
Acute, 308, 309, 311–317, 319
Amelioration, 301, 303, 304
Analogical extension, *see* Analogy
Analogy, 66–69, 109, 111
Aorist
  root aorist, 71, 75n25
  s-aorist, 72n16, 73
Aristotle, 311, 314, 315, 317–319, 322, 324
Ā-stems, 66, 67, 67n5, 67n6, 71
Asyndeton, 294

B

Baltic, 66n3, 69
Bible Gothic, *see* Gothic
Blocking, 144, 149–152, 163, 172, 173
Borrowing, 46, 47, 49, 51, 105
Burgundian, 24, 24n7, 26, 31, 35–39

C

Celtiberian, 4, 4n4, 5, 10, 13
Celtic, 68, 298–300, 300n4, 300n5, 304
Circumflex, 308, 309, 311, 312, 314–319, 321
Cisalpine Celtic, 4n4, 6, 15, 16
Classical Armenian, 279–295
Contact edge, 46, 47, 49, 56
Continental Celtic, 3–16

[1] Note: Page numbers followed by 'n' refer to notes.

J. F. Eska et al. (eds.), *The Method Works*,
https://doi.org/10.1007/978-3-031-48959-4

Cowgill Particle, 189–191
Crimean Gothic, 22, 25–31, 30n31, 33, 34, 36–39

D

Denominative, 101–107, 106n2, 110, 111
Determinative compound, 299, 300
Determiner phrase (DP), 197, 199–214
Devoicing, 27, 32, 34, 36
Dialect area, 7–9, 15
Dialect continuum, 3–16, 24, 37n45, 38, 39
Dialect landscape, 8
Distributed Morphology, 143, 144, 149, 161, 173, 182–184
Double marking, 108–110
Dravidian, 99, 100, 105, 106

E

East Germanic, 21–39
Elsewhere rule, 144, 149–153, 172
English
  away, 162–164
  full, 162
  utter, 162–164
  would rather, 153
Extraposition, 202, 205–210, 214

F

Fifth-pocket phenomena, 148–153
Figura etymologica, 327–329, 327n1
Finite verb, 291
Functional projection, 196, 198, 203, 204

G

Galatian, 6, 10, 11, 11n15, 16
Gellius, Aulus, 317n3, 320, 320n10, 322
Genesis, 218–220, 223, 227, 228, 230, 235
Germanic, 21–23, 25, 27, 28, 31n33, 32, 35, 37n45, 38, 39, 66, 68, 71, 72
Germanic-speaking, 38
Gk. κλέπτω, 352
God names, 90
Gospels, 279–295
Gothic, 22, 24n7, 25–32, 25n11, 31n32, 33n37, 34–39, 286, 287, 287n9, 291, 292, 294, 300–301, 303, 304, 327–346
  huzdjan, 328, 329, 334, 336, 337
  wilwan, 337–346, 345n23, 345n24
  wulfs, 339, 340, 341n21
Gradience, 161–172
Grave, 308, 309, 311–317, 319, 320, 322, 323
Greek, 66, 68, 69, 71, 73–76, 200–208, 281, 281n3, 283n5, 284n6, 285, 286, 291–294, 307, 308, 313, 314, 317–319, 320n9

H

Heptateuch, 217–235
Herrschersuffix, 82, 82n7, 83, 89, 91, 92
Heterochrony, 147–161, 174
Hispano-Celtic, *see* Celtiberian
Hittite, 342–344
  walkuwa, 342, 343

Hoffmann suffix, 80, 82n7, 93n23
Holtzmann's Law, 27, 29, 33
Homoplasy, 47, 48, 50, 54, 59
Hom. συνοχωκότε, 361

I

Iceberg phenomena, 143–174
Indo-Iranian, 66, 68–71, 74, 75
Inheritance, 148, 151, 152, 158, 160, 161, 163, 173
Internal inflection, 156–158, 160
ī-stems, 66, 68

K

Kurux, 99–111

L

Language acquisition, 242–244, 252, 254
Lat. *clepō*, 352–355, 357
Latin, 113–136, 195, 196, 210–214, 217, 220–235, 225n7, 226n9, 307, 308, 313, 317n3, 318–324, 321n11
  assimilation, 129
  l-backing, 128, 130–134
  rhotacism, 118–122, 126–129, 131
  s-loss, 127–129, 135
  syncope, 127–129, 129n16, 131
  vowel weakening, 134
Left periphery, 179–192
Lepontic, 6, 11, 13, 15, 16
Leveling, 237–255
Linguistic phylogeny, 45
Locality, 182–184

M

Malto, 99–111, 106n2
Middle accent, 307–324
Middle Dutch
  huden, 332–335, 332n9
  huyden, 333
Middle English, 237–255
  Open Syllable Lengthening (OSL) rule, 238, 239
  Trisyllabic Shortening (TSS) rule, 238, 239
Middle High German (MHG), 333, 334, 334n11, 336
  horten, 333, 334
Minimalist program, 143
Modern Dutch *huiden*, 333
Modern Island North Frisian dialect of Föhr and Amrum, 332
  hidjle, 332
Modern linguistic theories, 143–147
Monophthongization, 23, 23n6, 24, 29, 30, 33, 34, 38
Morphosyntactic lags, 156
Multi-state linguistic character evolution, 47

N

Nasal assimilation, 15
Nasal effacement, 10n12, 15
New High German
  adjectives äußerer, 162
  adverbs in *-maßen*, 155, 156, 158, 173
  gender assignment, 154
  predicative voll, 165–172
  predicative voller, 168
  weg, 162–164
  wollte, 153

Nominal inflection
dative singular, 13, 14
genitive plural, 13
Northwest Germanic, 22, 24, 25, 25n11, 30, 38, 39
Noun phrase, 195–214
Nuclear Celtic, 4

O

Old Church Slavic, 286, 287, 287n9, 291, 292, 294
Old English (OE), 217–235, 329–333, 329n2, 329n4, 335–337, 336n14, 340
hȳdan, 329, 329n3, 333, 335–337, 336n14
Old Irish, 208, 210, 211
absolute *vs.* conjunct, 181
conjunct particles, 184, 190
preverbs, 186, 190
verb complex, 184–185
Optative, 72–75, 72n17, 73n18, 73n20
Osc. **kulupu**, 355, 359, 360
(Osco-?)Latin bvrvs, 362–365
Ostrogothic, 29, 34, 34n40, 35, 38, 39
Overt trace, 206, 208

P

Palaic, 263, 264, 266, 268, 268n9, 274, 275
Participle, 281n4, 283, 283n5, 285–288, 291, 294, 294n10
Perfect
dereduplication, 358
Phylogenetic network, 45–60
Phylogeny, 21
Productivity in language acquisition and data poverty, 243, 244
Proto-Germanic (PGmc), 328–337, 334n11, 339
huzdijan, 328–337
Proto-Indo-European, 200, 204, 210–214
Pseudo-Sergius, 307–312, 314, 317–319, 322, 324

Q

Quartet-Based Topology Estimator (QBTE), 51–52, 54–58
Quartet-Tree-Calculator (QTC), 51, 52, 55–58

R

Resegmentation, 93
Romance adverbs in *-mente, -ment*, 157, 158, 173
Root-Network, 52–55, 59, 60
Rounding, 86, 87
Rule fragmentation, 156, 157, 163

S

Serial verb construction, 280, 280n1
Slavic, 69, 70, 74
South Oscan, 351–365
κλοπουστ, 351–365
Stang's Law, 65–76

Stranded rules, 153–173
Subgrouping, 22, 23, 28, 34, 35

T

Tolerance Principle (TP), 238, 241–249, 255
Transalpine Celtic, 4, 4n4, 6, 10, 11n15, 13, 15, 16
Transitivity
  transitive verbs, 106n2, 111
  transitivizing suffix, 102
Translation effects, 217–235
Tree-based phylogentic network, 46, 47, 49, 57
Tyrannio, 308, 309, 311, 314, 318, 319, 324

U

Ū-stems, 66, 69, 70

V

Vandalic, 24n7, 26, 31–35, 34n42, 37–39
Varro, 307–324
Varying slope, 8
Vedic, 69, 71, 74, 341, 342
  a-vṛká-, 341, 342
Verbal derivation, 100
Verbal inflection, 189
Verb movement, 179, 182
Verbum dicendi, 301, 304
Very Old Latin, *see* Latin
Vulgate, 286, 287n9, 294

W

Weak demonstratives, 199, 200, 204, 213, 214
West Germanic, 22–25, 28, 30, 30n31, 34, 36
Word order, 218n2